Fo.

Contents

Acknowledgements   viii

Introduction   1

1   Jane Austen's Byronic Heroes I: *Northanger Abbey* and
    Sense and Sensibility   30

2   Jane Austen's Byronic Heroes II: *Persuasion* and
    Pride and Prejudice   61

3   Elizabeth Gaskell's Byronic Heroes: *Wives and Daughters*
    and *North and South*   93

4   George Eliot's Byronic Heroes I: Early Works and Poetry   124

5   George Eliot's Byronic Heroes II: Later Works   153

Notes   183

Bibliography   230

Index   248

Acknowledgements

I am indebted to the staff and students in the Department of English Studies at Durham University. This book has benefited enormously from the support and generosity of Michael O'Neill, an exceptional scholar and inspirational mentor. Mark Sandy and Jenny Terry kindly read and commented on work-in-progress, and their friendship has been invaluable. I am also grateful to Simon J. James, Pamela Knights, Jacqueline Labbe, and Barbara Ravelhofer. Thanks go to Nicole Bush, for her research assistance with Chapters 3–5, and to Rebecca White, for her excellent work on the index. Thanks also to Karen Robson, Senior Archivist at the University of Southampton Library, and to Helen Scott, Subject Consultant at the Bodleian Libraries, University of Oxford. I owe a debt to Ben Doyle and his colleagues at Palgrave Macmillan for their patience with this project, and to the anonymous readers for their helpful comments and suggestions.

I am grateful to my parents, Jennifer and Edward Wootton, and my late grandparents, Betina and James Hill, for their unfailing good humour and unquestioning support. My sister, Victoria Dowd, and her husband, Kevin Dowd, have been a source of kindness and warmth, as have my niece and nephew, Delilah and James, who deserve special mention.

This book is dedicated to my husband, Toby Watson, the best man I have ever known.

Sections of Chapters 3 and 5 originally appeared as an essay, 'The Changing Faces of the Byronic Hero in *Middlemarch* and *North and South*', in *Romanticism*, 14:1 (2008), pp. 25–35, and are reproduced here by kind permission of the editor, Nicholas Roe. Sections of Chapter 2 originally appeared as an essay, 'The Byronic in Jane Austen's *Persuasion* and *Pride and Prejudice*', in *Modern Language Review*, 102:1 (2007), pp. 26–39, and are reproduced here by kind permission. The cover illustration reproduces NPG D1158, 'George Gordon Byron, 6th Baron Byron' by Henry Meyer; published by T. Cadell & W. Davies; after George Henry Harlow, stipple engraving, published 30 January 1816, © National Portrait Gallery, London.

Introduction

> ... my soul shall find
> A language in these tears!
> [...]
> His grave is thick with voices
>> (Elizabeth Barrett Browning, *Stanzas on the Death of*
>> *Lord Byron*, 1824)[1]

> His name is on the haunted shade,
>   His name is on the air;
> We walk the forest's twilight glade,
>   And only he is there.
> The ivy wandering o'er the wall,
> The fountain falling musical,
>   Proclaim him everywhere,
> The heart is full of him, and flings
> Itself on all surrounding things.
>> (Letitia Landon [L.E.L.], *The Portrait of Lord Byron at*
>> *Newstead Abbey*, 1840)[2]

I

The Byronic hero is everywhere. From the autonomous assassin in recent instalments of the James Bond franchise to the stylish vampires that proliferate in popular fiction and on screen, this figure has captured the imagination of generations of readers and viewers.[3] The first Byronic hero, and a blueprint for the rest, became an overnight sensation in March 1812, when Cantos I and II of Lord Byron's *Childe Harold's*

1

Pilgrimage were published and sold out within three days.[4] Successive poems showcasing a spiritually isolated superman secured the literary fame and longevity of this Romantic poet and the legendary figure that bears his name. The Byronic hero remains, some 200 years after Byron became a bestselling poet, 'an unprecedented cultural phenomenon'.[5] His presence persists, for instance, in the immensely successful *Twilight* and *Fifty Shades* series, fantasy romances that reinscribe our fascination with a damaged and damaging anti-hero – a seductive outsider who is superior in suffering, sinfulness, subversions, and perversions – as encountered by an inexperienced, yet curious, young woman.[6] That girlish innocence can triumph over manly experience through the redemptive power of love constitutes the staple ingredient in countless Regency romances and Mills and Boon novels. This gendered formula for fiction appears in the following 'tip sheet' for writing mass-market contemporary romance: 'The hero is 8 to 12 years older than the heroine. He is self-assured, masterful, hot-tempered, capable of violence, passion, and tenderness. He is often mysteriously moody. Heathcliff (*Wuthering Heights*) is a rougher version; Darcy (*Pride and Prejudice*) is a more refined one'.[7] The template is unmistakably Byronic, with the sardonic and self-depreciating humour of Byron's poetry edited out, and yet the Byronic hero has been dispersed to such a degree that he no longer needs to be named; he is, in fact, more readily identifiable through his notable nineteenth-century progeny.[8] The genealogy of this cultural archetype has become congested – over-crowded even – with the Brontës' heroes and Bram Stoker's Dracula more familiar today than Byron's protagonists. But the archetype is no less recognisably Byronic for that.

It is beyond the scope of this book to give a comprehensive commentary on the descendants and permutations of this ubiquitous figure from the early nineteenth century to the present day. Although critics have ventured to provide a chapter or chapters in the history of the Byronic hero, no single study can cover what Mario Praz posited, in *The Romantic Agony*, as 'the innumerable Fatal Men who came into existence on the pattern of the Byronic hero'.[9] That said, this book employs a broad interdisciplinary lens that extends from close readings of nineteenth-century poetry and prose to twentieth- and twenty-first century films and television series, whilst also remaining attentive to intertextual issues of gender and genre, creative medium, and cultural contexts. *Byronic Heroes in Nineteenth-Century Women's Writing and Screen Adaptation* considers authors for whom the reception of Byron's poetry and the cult of Byronism were pressing concerns; it also considers the reconfiguration of the Byronic in recent screen adaptations. Tracing Byronic legacies in the fiction of major nineteenth-century women writers – including Jane Austen, Elizabeth Gaskell, and George Eliot – and examining the resurgence of Byronic heroes in film and television versions of their work are the main subjects of this book. The rationale for the focus of this book, on women writers and on the specific women writers selected, is discussed in detail below. In short, it is my contention that the charged, unstable, and instructive dialogues between Austen, Gaskell, Eliot, and a Byronic inheritance have not received the sustained scholarly attention they deserve. A further factor in determining the focus of this book is the cultural legacy of these literary encounters, specifically in terms of screen adaptations, which has yet to be explored.

Byronic Heroes in Nineteenth-Century Women's Writing and Screen Adaptation charts a new chapter in the changing fortunes of the Byronic hero and his afterlives. This is the first book to examine the legacy of a Romantic icon through the work of nineteenth-century women writers and screen adaptations of their fiction. I hope to establish previously overlooked crosscurrents between Byron's poetry, his posthumous reputation, and prose writers – from Austen to Eliot – whose novels have inspired successive screen adaptations. As such, this book will offer a timely reassessment of Byron's reception and cultural reach during the nineteenth century and beyond, some two centuries after the publication of the first two cantos of *Childe Harold's Pilgrimage* in 1812. It will also offer fresh readings of seminal nineteenth-century works as well as a broader and more diverse context of literary dialogues and artistic afterlives in which to situate these writers. *Byronic Heroes in Nineteenth-Century Women's Writing and Screen Adaptation* departs from previous scholarship that regards the Byronic hero as a redundant, repressive, or static figure by arguing for indeterminacy and malleability as preconditions of his prolonged afterlife. The writers and adapters considered in this book are not recycling a stereotype or commenting on the cult of Byronism from the sidelines; they are renegotiating and renewing the Byronic by also engaging with the subtler shades, tones, and forms of Byron's poetry.

Questions that underpin the subsequent discussion include, but are not limited to, the following: what can the work of nineteenth-century women writers, many of whom professed an aversion to Byron, tell us about the appeal and function of the Byronic hero as a cultural phenomenon? Conversely, what does the treatment of Byron and Byronism by these women writers tell us about their attitude, often divided, towards a persistent male Romantic presence? How does Byron's poetry fare in women's prose of the period and with what effect on how we read both his and their work? In what ways does this incursion of poetry and 'poetic' protagonists into predominantly realist prose speak to the gendered dialogue over genre that extends from Austen's *Northanger Abbey* (1818) to Gaskell's *Wives and Daughters* (1866) and Eliot's verse dramas, *The Spanish Gypsy* (1868) and *Armgart* (1871)? What role does Byron's poetry and the figure of the Byronic hero play in the reconfiguration of literary masculinities in screen versions of Austen's, Gaskell's, and Eliot's fiction? And, finally, what features of Byron's poetry induce such generic hybridity and enable such mobility of meaning?

Another woman novelist who enters these debates, sometime after Austen, Gaskell, and Eliot, is Virginia Woolf. Woolf's modernist writings, although outside the remit of this book, extend the conflicted commentaries on Byron, the Byronic, and related issues of gender and genre beyond the nineteenth century. The Romantic poet and his legacy proved to be a disruptive presence in her work, wrong-footing misreaders in an early novel, *Night and Day* (1919), and informing the figure of the male misfit in *Jacob's Room* (1922) and the later *avant-garde* novel, *The Waves* (1931). Byron remains a literary touchstone for Woolf in her last novel, *Between the Acts* (1941), and her continuing dialogue with the poet is the subject of 'Byron and Mr Briggs', an unfinished draft introduction for what would become *The Common Reader* (1925). 'Byron and Mr Briggs' demonstrates how vital a source of inspiration Byron was, especially the poet's letters, for her thinking on reading, reception, and criticism. Woolf's appreciation of the 'prose' Byron is attuned to what is 'very changeable' in his writing even as she tries to 'To make a whole' out of his and her own discordant voices.[10] As such, Woolf gravitates towards the vigour and 'elastic shape' of *Don Juan*, a poem to which George Eliot also returned on a number of occasions. This masterpiece, Woolf rhapsodised, 'showed how flexible an instrument poetry might become' (*Essays of Virginia Woolf*, IV, p. 434). With *The Waves*, as it opens out into the hinterlands between poetry and prose, Woolf 'followed his example to put this tool to further use', capturing a lyricism that rises above the 'character' of Byron that Bernard adopts. It is the Byron that, for Woolf, might have been a novelist, which drew her to him in spite of what she considered to be the vulgar Byronic personality. Likewise, it is the Byron of narrative agility and robust ideas, the Byron who experimented with genre and form, which proved so adaptable to the women novelists that came before her.

II

Frances Wilson states that Byron and the myth surrounding his life and work 'hypnotised his own generation and dominated the next [...]. Byron lent his name to the scornful, despairing, and burdened hero of nineteenth-century literature'.[11] Wilson is rearticulating Peter L. Thorslev's earlier pronouncement that 'the most popular phenomenon of the English Romantic Movement and the figure with the most far-reaching consequences for nineteenth-century Western literature was the Byronic Hero'.[12] Thorslev's landmark study traces the genesis of the Byronic hero from prototypes in the eighteenth century, such as the Gothic villain, to earlier incarnations, such as Satan and Prometheus, arguing that 'all the elements of the Byronic Hero existed before him in the literature of the age. This hero is unique, in one sense, in the powerful fusion of these disparate elements into a single commanding image' (*Byronic Hero: Types and Prototypes*, p. 12). In other words, Byron's protagonists were forged out of pre-existing hero figures; he skilfully, and with no little poetic flair, selected the sympathetic, and alluring, aspects of the villain to combine with the heroic traits that appealed most to the readers of the age. The poet's unparalleled success was the result of a considered recalibration of the hero-villain as lover. And yet, according to Thorslev, the reign of the Byronic hero began to wane in the Victorian period and was ultimately eclipsed by the advent of modernism. The defamiliarising effects of the early twentieth century – modern warfare in particular – shifted an emphasis in literature from immense passions, pride, and self-possession to suffering and emasculation. For Thorslev, as for Praz, in his study *The Hero in Eclipse in Victorian Fiction*, the cult of the common man prevailed over the cult of the hero.[13]

There is much value in contextualising the hero historically and rooting models of masculinity within specific social and cultural changes. This book will be guided by such an approach when considering the figure of the Byronic hero over a time span of 200 years – more specifically, within the literature of the later Romantic period, the mid and high Victorian periods, and, latterly, screen adaptations inspired by that literature and produced in the late twentieth and early twenty-first centuries. It is, however, my contention that Thorslev was premature in pronouncing the death of the Byronic hero.[14] The Byronic categories he identified (which include the interrelated figures of the Child of Nature, the Gloomy Egoist, the Hero of Sensibility, the Man of Feeling, the Noble Outlaw etc.) ultimately prove limiting when thinking of modern manifestations of the phenomenon in which 'angst-ridden individuals try to free themselves from an overpowering and entrapping sense of self'.[15] In this book, I intend to move away from deterministic hero 'types' to consider the mutability as well as the persistence of Byronic heroes. Indeed, while I focus on the Byronic heroes that distinguish screen adaptations of nineteenth-century novels, this figure has also attained a certain kudos in contemporary fan fiction, popular music, cult movies, and television series. That 'Byronic heroes are still hot popular culture commodities' at the start of the twenty-first century is proof, for Atara Stein, that the Romantic period never ended.[16] Audiences today are as drawn to the romance of the outlaw as they were in the nineteenth century, vicariously experiencing a powerful autonomy before reaffirming a shared humanity. Although underlying cultural patterns and trends such as these are worthy of note and supply a useful backdrop for the subsequent discussion, my approach to the Byronic hero is governed by an attention to individual works of fiction and to the particularities of form, medium, and period. Close analysis of both poetry and prose, and the involved transactions between genre, affords insights into Romantic dialogues and legacies that a consideration of cultural and historical context alone is unable to achieve.

III

Criticism, with the exception of Stein and a few notable others, has tended to focus on the reception of Byron in the nineteenth century. Much of that criticism has centred on male writers. A Byronic presence has been discussed in the novels of Thomas Love Peacock, Charles Dickens, and Anthony Trollope, among others.[17] These authors were drawn to and deflated a gloomily romantic Byron. For Elfenbein, in his invaluable study *Byron and the Victorians*, the 'development away from a youthful, immature Byronic phrase to a sober, adult "Victorian" phase became one of the nineteenth-century's master narratives, the *Bildungsroman* of the Victorian author' (p. 89, original emphasis). Elfenbein's 'master narrative' of Romantic infatuation tempered by Victorian stoicism is told through the self-fashioning of male writers, including Carlyle and Tennyson, and the dandified exponents of the silver-fork novel, Edward Bulwer-Lytton and Benjamin Disraeli. Elfenbein devotes one chapter to a woman writer, Emily Brontë, whose position as a post-Romantic 'voice from the margins' exemplifies her anomalous status.[18] The marginalisation of women writers within a prevailing schema that the Victorians outgrew the Romantics, particularly Byron, is not confined to studies of British writers. Further afield, the impact of Byron and his heroes on Russian writers, such as Mikhail Lermontov and Alexander Pushkin, has been explored, and his transatlantic influence has been traced through writers such as Nathaniel Hawthorne, Herman Melville, and Edgar Allan Poe.[19] Scholars have identified many of the major (and indeed minor) voices in the construction of a Victorian Byron and detailed his substantial presence within European Romanticism. Studies have often excluded or minimised the importance of women writers, however. Significant chapters in the story of Byron's afterlives have been abridged or occluded.[20]

Research has begun to explore the interplay between women writers, Byron, and a Byronic inheritance, even if important questions remain unanswered. Recent scholarship has moved away from a discourse of incompatibility on the basis of gender to a reassessment of creative partnerings in the context of a wider project to reconnect male and female writers of the Romantic period.[21] A number of female Romantics have been considered in this regard: consummate Byronists, such as Felicia Hemans and Letitia Landon (L.E.L.), whose poems were often mistaken for those of Byron, and prose writers who penetrated and parodied the Byronic protagonist, such as Mary Shelley and Lady Caroline Lamb.[22] The 'strange feelings' of adulation and aversion articulated in Landon's 'Stanzas, Written beneath the Portrait of Lord Byron, painted by Mr. West', which appeared in the *Literary Souvenir* of 1827, can be seen as indicative of the antithetical struggle between women writers and a Byronic Romanticism.[23] And yet the uncertain reflections mediated through this portrait by William West recede when recalling the subject's elevation to the 'glorious' dead (l. 75). It is Byron's selfless sacrifice, dying in the Greek War of Independence, that deflects attention away from a charged ekphrastic response to West's portrait and refocuses attention on a deeper Byron residing beneath a stunning surface. It is Landon's renewed enthrallment with and return to the Byronic fold that launches her audacious plea for emancipation: 'Oh, England! to thy young and brave/ Is not this stirring call,/ To free the fallen from the chain,/ To break the tyrant's thrall' (ll. 79–82). For Landon, as for women writing later in the nineteenth century, Byron's heartfelt humanitarianism is communicated through a lament at once deeply affecting and politically charged.

What Caroline Franklin argues for Victorian female novelists – that 'the Romantic movement as a whole unleash[ed ...] creative energies and larger ambitions[, and] Byron in particular engaged them in transnational issues of political, racial and sexual freedom' – is pertinent to a

Victorian female poet whose roots were firmly in the Romantic period.[24] Byron served as a springboard for the political and proto-feminist tenor of Elizabeth Barrett Browning's poetry, which gained momentum and strength in her experimental 'novel-poem', *Aurora Leigh* (1856).[25] From the grave that Barrett Browning envisages as 'thick with voices' in her early poem of 1824, *Stanzas on the Death of Lord Byron*, women writers spanning the nineteenth century found a language of defiance and liberation in Byron, adding their respective voices to an energised song in sorrow that speaks with a revolutionary's zeal (l. 34). His 'startling chords', a conduit of freedom and feeling with 'sweet' and 'salt' aftertaste, appealed not only to the avowed acolyte, EBB, but to fellow female authors who troubled the boundaries between the Romantic and Victorian periods (*Stanzas on the Death of Lord Byron*, l. 27).[26]

Fellow Romantic Victorians, Charlotte and Emily Brontë, have long been considered Byronic heirs. These sisters ingrained the imprint of the Byronic hero into our collective cultural memory. The literary fate and fortunes of the Byronic hero became bound up with two novels published in 1847, *Jane Eyre* and *Wuthering Heights*. The heroes of these widely read works, Mr Rochester and Heathcliff, have become bywords for the Byronic. The women writers featured in this book engaged extensively and intensively with Byron's poetry and Byronism, but none come close to Charlotte and Emily Brontë in propagating the 'myth' of the Byronic hero and ensuring a widespread and durable dissemination. The impact of Byron on the Brontës' fiction has been well documented.[27] Still, although it would not be appropriate to consider their work (and the many adaptations of it) in a book that examines creatively divided responses to the cult of Byronism, their revisionist readings of Byron and his heroes should be noted if only in brief. The uncritical conflation of the Brontës with the Byronic, which has rendered their hero figures synonymous, denies the depth and nuance of a mutually illuminating literary relationship. It is the Brontës' investment in Byron and the profundity of Byron's influence on them that inhibits imitation.[28]

In her novel *The Tenant of Wildfell Hall* (1848), Anne Brontë strips away an initial thrill of Byronic glamour to reveal a corrupt and corrupting charm. Arthur Huntingdon outdoes the other spoilt and sordid examples of aristocratic men in Brontë's novel with his grasping and hollow libertinism. Anne's explicit realism and commitment to a moral 'truth' resists the lure of a dark Romanticism and demystifies the cynical cruelty of her sisters' Byronic heroes to devastating effect.[29] Yet neither Charlotte nor Emily could be said to condone hero-worship. Indeed, their male protagonists, more Byronic in many regards than Byron or his poetic creations, denigrate what they regard as a formulaic or 'feminised' Byronism that seeks to domesticate romantic passions. The 'coyly self-referential' regard for the Byronic hero that Stein detects in popular television series and comic books can be traced back to the Brontës as well as to their wryly self-critical precursor, Byron ('Byronic Heroes in Popular Culture', p. 8). When, in *Wuthering Heights*, Heathcliff sneers at his wife's 'fabulous notion of my character', he distances himself from her misapprehensions.[30] In *Jane Eyre*, Rochester laments the staleness of his story:

> 'I am a trite common-place sinner; hackneyed in all the poor petty dissipations with which the rich and worthless try to put on life. [...] I had not, it seems, the originality to chalk out a new road to shame and destruction, but trode the old track with stupid exactness not to deviate an inch from the beaten centre.'[31]

Both Isabella Linton and Blanche Ingram are quixotic readers conversant with Byronic 'types'. The former 'pictur[es] in [Heathcliff] a hero of romance' (p. 187), with horrifying consequences, while the latter 'doat[s] on Corsairs', and casts Rochester as a 'gallant gentleman-highwayman' and an 'Italian bandit' (pp. 200, 205). Where Blanche's fashionable and disingenuous flirtations fail to secure a wealthy husband – as she is outmanoeuvred by Rochester's more calculating dissimulations – Isabella's abusive marriage deflates her fiction-fuelled fantasies and forestalls a false impression of Heathcliff as a 'star-cross'd' husband. Rochester and Heathcliff re-ignite a myth of heroic romance as they contest the 'romantic' attribution they now personify. The irony that underscores this iconic status brings the Brontës even closer to exemplifying the Byronic, as they share the poet's 'ambivalence toward the very Romantic ideals his hero espouses'.[32] Although the Brontëan marriage of minds with the Byronic (however troubled) prevents their inclusion in this study, their respective rewritings of Byron's poetry and the Byronic persona direct the reader to the ways in which the poet probed and parodied his own incarnations of the dangerously destructive self. In other words, an authentic imaginative affinity with Byron compels critical engagement and necessitates a degree of critical distance.

The women writers dealt with in this book have not, in contrast to the Brontë sisters, featured prominently in the cultural history of Byronism. In fact, Jane Austen, Elizabeth Gaskell, and George Eliot are invariably cited as expressing anti-Byronic sentiments when they are cited at all.[33]

Austen's arch comment, 'I have read the Corsair, mended my petticoat, & have nothing else to do', in a letter dated 5 March 1814, suggests an unengaged reader of the latest Byron bestseller.[34] Some half a century later, in a letter dated 23 August 1869, Eliot's declaration, 'Byron and his poetry have become more and more repugnant to me of late years', makes for a stronger disavowal.[35] Although Gaskell was not outspoken about the poet in her letters, direct references to Byron in her short stories and novels do not readily speak of a high regard. The tone of these comments is often taken as a measure of the Byronic male's defects when seen from the perspective of the nineteenth-century female author. It should be remembered, however, as individual chapters will take up and examine in detail, that such flaws are often associated with the misreading of Byron. Shortcomings are not so much levelled at Byron's poetry, but at Byronism, a fashion for the 'theatrical' Byron that Matthew Arnold held responsible for a blunted appreciation of the poet and his work.[36] Allusions to Byron by Austen, Eliot, and Gaskell are often quoted out of context (as Arnold's considered estimate of Byron is invariably misrepresented), curtailing discussions of this poet's influence on their creative development as writers.[37] Michael O'Neill's comment, that 'Arnold's responses to Byron and the Romantics double and divide themselves', not only redirects our attention to Arnold's discerning regard for Byron; it is pertinent to the reception of Byron by the authors considered in this book.[38]

The alleged denigration of Byron by these women writers is interesting in itself. Austen read *The Corsair* (1814) shortly after publication, 'identifying herself as part of [a] community of readers' whose demand for Byron's poem sent it through multiple editions in a matter of weeks.[39] In her last complete novel, *Persuasion* (1818), Byron and Scott are hailed as the 'first-rate poets' of the age, registering the phenomenal impact of their respective writings and fame.[40] Austen's *Persuasion* is attuned to an audience for whom poetry was a common topic of conversation. The autumnal lyricism of her late prose is a tribute, a 'twilight-piece', to the Romantic poet and the popularity of Romantic poetry among the reading public from a prose writer who sought to defend the novel as a genre.[41] In similar ways, both Eliot and Gaskell read Byron's poetry over sustained periods and were drawn to the cultural commentaries on this unique literary figure. Byron was an early favourite with Eliot and she remained preoccupied with his Romantic individualism throughout her writing life. A central tenet of my argument, and a determining factor in the authors selected for discussion in this book, is that Austen, Eliot, and Gaskell are engaged in a 'double'

'One will represent me as a sort of sublime misanthrope, with moments of kind feeling. This, *par exemple*, is my favorite *rôle*. Another will portray me as a modern Don Juan; and a third [...] will, it is to be hoped, if only for opposition sake, represent me as an *amiable*, ill-used gentleman, "more sinned against than sinning." Now, if I know myself, I should say, that I have no character at all.'[51]

'Byron', the cause célèbre, was the product of a systematic evasion of self that projects a recurring pattern of potential selves. The confiding aside about 'myself' not only mocks the notion of knowing one's self, but also problematises the proximity between a stage-managed persona, or character, and a presiding self. The mythic vibration of masks that simultaneously conceal and reveal the contingency of performance is inextricably bound up with the rapid publication of 'blockbuster' poems, from *Childe Harold's Pilgrimage* (1812) through *The Corsair* (1814) and *Lara* (1814) to *Manfred* (1817) and *Cain* (1821), among others. Each of these works stages a protagonist who is suitably 'Byronic', consolidating previous market success, while remaining distinguishable from the others and coyly invoking, yet elusively distanced from, the poet.[52] Operating within this semblance of sameness is difference, an extension of the 'extreme *mobilité*' attributed to and fostered by Byron (Blessington, *Conversations of Lord Byron*, p. 110).

What Byron's successive narrative and dramatic works demonstrate is that there is not, and never has been, a standard Byronic hero. As Mary Shelley observed, in a letter of 16 November 1822, Byronic typecasting was subject to change: 'The "Eternal Scoffer" seems a favourite of yours. The Critics, as they used to make you a Childe Harold, Giaour, & Lara all in one, will now make a compound of Satan & Cæsar to form your prototype ...'.[53] Shelley is alert to a tendency towards the demonic in Byron's later writing – when transcribing his play, *The Deformed Transformed*, in the early 1820s – and she is sardonic about the tendency to conflate protagonists and then tally the template with the poet. It could be said that where Childe Harold and Manfred contemplate, the heroes of the Oriental Tales act. This distinction suffers from the reductive simplifications that Shelley disparages, however. The wandering exiles, Harold and Manfred, are as different as they are similar, and the impulsive aggression and anguish of Conrad and the Giaour is no less intense or affecting than the introspective gloom and isolation of their fellow Byronic heroes. Contrary states of passivity and assertiveness can be read as equally Byronic, with each hero acting out unsettled and unsettling phases of mood and temper within individual works. This theatre of the Byronic is populated by a cast of dramatic performances that are driven by restless energies and unappeased desires, which display and deflate the portentous 'pageant of his bleeding heart' paraded in exile, a two-fold acting out and ironic distancing that Arnold emulates in his poem 'Stanzas from the Grande Chartreuse' and in his essay on Byron.[54] Even the high priest of melancholia, Manfred, succumbs to moments of self-mockery – 'Oh! I but thus prolong'd my words,/ Boasting these idle attributes' – and his overblown solemnity is not always taken seriously by a poet whose métier was the mock-heroic.[55]

V

The most divided and divisive Byronic signifier relates to sexuality. Sex appeal and scandal were integral aspects of the contemporary 'craze' for Byron, a word that came to mean a 'trend' in response to the poet's popularity and press interest in him. The exploits of his Don Juan are as nothing when compared with his own reputation as a legendary lothario. High-profile lovers enhanced his '*rôle*' as seducer, and rumours of an incestuous affair with his half-sister and homosexual encounters abroad continued to court controversy throughout the later nineteenth century and beyond.[56] The 2003 BBC biopic of Byron, starring Jonny Lee Miller as the poet, did little to dispel this aspect of the myth.[57] On the plus side, the dialogue in this two-part dramatisation drew extensively on Byron's poems and letters, and the action focused on his circle of male friends and fellow writers as well as on the women who idolised him. The complicated nature of celebrity is also treated with acuity; the charismatic poet affects a pose to offset the social discomfort that only intensifies with the adulation he desires and detests. However, accentuating Byron's masculine bravado through physical pursuits and frequent sexual encounters serves to draw attention away from a detailed consideration of Byron as a writer, a failing common to films featuring Byron and to films of writers' lives in general. Miller's performance as the 'dissolute poet' would, according to the BBC's then controller of drama commissioning, 'explore what it meant to be a sex-god aristo'; highbrow 'costume' drama was marketed as lowbrow titillation.[58]

Similar criticisms could be levelled at the Byronic 'turns' in screen adaptations of the nineteenth-century novels examined in this book. Commenting on Rufus Sewell's portrayal of Will Ladislaw in the BBC series of *Middlemarch*, screened in 1994, Ian MacKillop and Alison Platt argue that 'there is not much more to Ladislaw than the drop-dead-gorgeousness of his appearance'.[59] A year later, Byromania, the contemporary rage for Byron and the Byronic, was reborn as Darcymania when Austen's hero became the pin-up of the BBC's phenomenally successful series of *Pride and Prejudice*, screened in 1995. So intensive was the interest in this Byronic Darcy that Colin Firth confessed to an exhaustion with the role: 'I'm so used to this word "Darcy" now that it's almost lost all meaning and resonance. I can't think of anything really to say about it'.[60] Despite his frustration at being typecast, the actor reprised his role as Darcy six years later – this time as the human rights barrister, Mark Darcy – for the film (2001) of Helen Fielding's metanarrative, *Bridget Jones's Diary* (1996), with a critic for the *Evening Standard* exclaiming, 'Colin Firth's love-god status rages on'.[61] The in-jokes between Firth and Darcy (Jane Austen's, Andrew Davies's, and Helen Fielding's) became even more involved in the sequel, *Bridget Jones: The Edge of Reason* (1999), which was made into a film in 2004. Nearly a decade after the BBC's *Pride and Prejudice* was first shown, repeated comparisons between Firth's iconic performance and Richard Armitage's portrayal of Mr Thornton in the BBC mini-series of *North and South* (2004) reaffirmed that this on-screen renaissance of the Byronic hero relied heavily on the visual impact of a male body.

Does this mean that Byron has become little more than a sex object or a badge for what Stein refers to as the 'bad boy syndrome' ('Byronic Heroes in Popular Culture', p. 3)? Has the byword subsumed the enigmatic open-endedness, rendering the Byronic hero 'everything by turns and nothing *at all*'? For Jean Hall, Byron is the 'great trickster', whose heroes feign 'profound innerness without actually possessing it'. Hall is by no means alone among critics, authors, and reviewers in mistaking Byron's 'glittering surface' for a lack of substance.[62] The 'glittering surface' of today's on-screen Byronic heroes owes much to the poet's meticulous maintenance of his personal appearance and his manicured image in portraits.[63] Looking, by both men and women, was central to Byronism as a cultural and commercial venture. That Byron's body was 'a seductive object of curiosity' subject to scrutiny and repeated reproduction does not necessarily diminish his cultural value or 'authenticity'.[64] In fact, Byron's sexualised self-display – what Diego Saglia refers to as his 'theatricalized masculinity' – resists a monolithic understanding of an objectifiable, 'one size fits all' production line of poetic protagonists. The women writers featured in this book move beyond Byron's exhilarating exterior to grapple with what Hall denies – the 'hidden' depths that reside beneath an appearance of heroic rigidity. Indeed, Letitia Landon's 1840 poem, *The Portrait of Lord Byron at Newstead Abbey*, rewrites the relationship between Byronic innerness and an outer façade. What lies beneath in Byron's mind are 'dangerous thoughts and things' – abstract fires and indistinguishable fears; by contrast, 'on the surface springs/ A prodigality of bloom,/ A thousand hues that might illume/ Even an angel's wings!' (ll. 59, 61–4). Women writers like L.E.L. look at Byron and to Byron for a reservoir of inspiration, 'The lavish wealth that lies/ Close to the surface', complicating preconceptions about art, artifice, and meaning, as well as spatially reconfiguring the expansive interiority, the 'visionary world', of the Romantic imagination (ll. 43–4, 110).

The complex interconnections between surface, subjectivity, and substance, which Landon reconfigures through poetic dialogue with her fellow Romantic poet, are prominent concerns in Byron's five-act tragedy, *Marino Faliero, Doge of Venice* (1821). The eponymous Doge meets our expectations of a Byronic hero. Marino Faliero is 'proud', 'fiery', and 'austere', with an 'ungovernable temper' from which only his wronged wife, Angiolina, is immune.[65] He is isolated by his singularity and by his status, elevated to a member of the ruling elite and yet estranged from them, a defender of the downtrodden working man who is oppressed by the regime he ostensibly governs. Faliero's precarious position as a soldier turned leader turned traitor, lastly occupying the role of reluctant outlaw, is counterbalanced by his distinguished record in battle, the injustice he has suffered, and his faith in freedom from social falsehoods (the Chief of the conspirators, Israel Bertuccio, values, above all, Faliero's 'liberal' mind: II. ii. l. 174). Rejecting the trappings of rank and refusing to recognise the authority of the Council of Ten does not represent a departure from earlier protagonists like Manfred, and neither does his contempt for pageantry, with the Doge bemoaning his part as a 'poor puppet' in the metadrama of Venetian politics (I. ii. l. 415). What distinguishes *Marino Faliero* from some of the poet's other works are the ways in which Byronic theatre reaches beyond issues of identity to issues of semantics. The dramatic form facilitates a word play that estranges the relationship between language and meaning, and renders the position of the protagonist untenable. For Faliero, the value of his title, 'Doge', previously held in esteem, has been 'degraded', reduced to a 'worthless by-word' (III. ii. l. 202; I. ii. l. 100).[66]

This late drama, completed in Ravenna and published in 1821, can be read as the poet's commentary on the fate of the Byronic hero as a term, a concept, and a cultural figure. What, Byron asks, has become of his own 'by-word', the Byronic, since its conception almost a decade before? The drama contemplates futurity by fostering a sense of the past, particularly through Angiolina, as she tries to salvage the nobility of her husband ('Him, who, whate'er he now is, *was* a hero': V. i. l. 453, original emphasis), while the Doge himself rejects the fatal formulations of the present: 'I deny nothing, defend nothing' (V. i. l. 295). This denial of purpose and intent is hard to square with a protagonist who looks to interpret 'misty letters' and clings to the adage that meaning transcends words (I. ii. ll. 54–5). In the same speech as he moves towards Manfred's defiant autonomy, he proclaims positively, if inscrutably, 'for true *words* are *things*' (V. i. l. 289, original emphasis). Words have substance when they are 'authentic'. But Byron does not rest with this consoling turnabout. As the realignment of word and meaning seems within reach, with a line that borders on platitude, another apparent misalignment or disconnect emerges; Faliero looks to posterity through the 'death-black veil' that will be drawn over his portrait in the Doge's Palace (V. i. l. 497). In a play that interrogates the efficacy of verbal communication, an erased image ensures longevity even as the form of a portrait nuances the poet's dramatisation of historical record and transmission.[67] It is the absent presence of the Doge's veiled portrait that, for Byron, 'struck forcibly upon my imagination' ('Preface', p. 408), and proves indefinably suggestive.

The closing scene is enlightening in this regard. Byron's telling shift in focus, from the interior viewpoint of Faliero's imminent execution to the viewpoint outside the Palace, is reflective of an expectant anxiety of audience. That the people in St Mark's Square cannot hear the Doge's incendiary dialogue emulates a Romantic poet's fear of failing to connect with his public. And yet, although his final words are pathetically 'inarticulate', the 'voice' itself, the sound of speech, 'Swells up like mutter'd thunder' (V. iv. ll. 12, 13). If *Marino Faliero* dramatises the reception of a once distinguished speaker and his posthumous reputation, then a literal interpretation of the Byronic becomes impossible. The citizens cannot decipher a 'sole sentence', and no single lyric carries to the crowd (V. iv. l. 14). The untruth that is proclaimed – 'Justice hath dealt upon the mighty Traitor!' (V. iv. l. 28) – is accompanied by the one true 'thing' in the play – the severed head that unambiguously transmits the sentence (and silence) of death and triggers the end of the play. If, however, the Byronic amounts to little more than a vague 'by-word' for Byron by 1821, with the cord of communion cut off at the root, then the effect, or wider resonance, of that Romantic imprecision 'Swells up' and speaks volumes. *Marino Faliero* orchestrates the demise of an aged Byronic hero whose disillusionment extends from politics to a 'language strange' that may be heard or misheard but rarely understood.[68] Yet those same indecipherable mutterings retain a potency that is capable of ascribing significance to a life, a death, and an afterlife.

VI

The term 'Byronic' is bandied around with a looseness of meaning that Faliero would decry. And yet the sexuality with which this 'by-word' has become perennially associated is embedded within the fabric of Byronism in evocative ways. Sex is not straightforward, and often not 'straight', when it comes to Byron and his afterlives in fiction and on film. It is testament to Byron's mercurial personality and the polymorphous Byronic heroes that evolved in his eclectic verse that he is both a lover noted for tender constancy and a libertine. Where the *British Critic* denounced *Don Juan* (1819–24) as 'a manual of profligacy' and the *Literary Gazette* described Canto VI as 'the gloating brutality of a wretched debauchee', passionate devotion to one woman attains the intensity of religion in the Oriental Tales ('for him earth held but her alone', *The Corsair*, I. l. 480).[69] Identifying the Byronic hero as a stronghold of voracious heterosexuality is only part of his gender profile, moreover. The Byronic can be encoded as both manly and effete, a superhuman overreacher and a coxcomb, apparent contradictions signalled by Thomas Carlyle when describing the poet as 'our English Sentimentalist and Power-man; the strongest of his kind in Europe; the wildest, the gloomiest, and it is to be hoped the last'.[70] In effect, the Byronic simultaneously epitomised diverging strands of masculinity in the nineteenth century, drawing attention to and challenging 'normative' gender roles.

That Byron's poetry and his protagonists play with rather than reinscribe prevailing attitudes towards gender has been at the forefront of criticism of the last two to three decades. Susan Wolfson has emphasised the homoerotic in *Don Juan* and Jonathan Gross has argued for a gay narrator in the same poem, for instance.[71] For Paul Cantor, it is homosexual rather than heterosexual tensions that drive the Oriental Tales, with the most intense and impassioned exchanges occurring between the hero and his adversary.[72] The heroines are often sidelined in a hypermasculine world of violence and war, an argument made persuasively by Jacqueline Labbe.[73] Both Cantor and Labbe transpose Eve Kosofsky Sedgwick's influential theory of triangulated desire in the nineteenth-century novel onto Romantic poetry to argue that Byron's heroes are more concerned with homoerotic combat than with heterosexual romance.[74] This approach is compelling when considering an Oriental Tale like *The Giaour* (1813), but perhaps not as convincing when considering the wider range of Byron's poetry, the varying views of women expressed throughout his writings and voiced by his protagonists, and the heroines whose functions exceed the 'bit' part played by Leila (who is drowned and dispatched).[75] That said, Cantor and Labbe usefully rethink the abiding fiction of a Mills and Boon Byron, with the latter noting a 'reliance on full frontal violence' in poetry that sidelines opposite-sex attraction (*Romantic Paradox*, p. 139). Commentaries that focus attention on the eroticised violence between men offer a valid counterpoint to Thorslev's view that 'Byron's heroes [...] are all lovers – for most of them it is the ruling passion in their lives – and they remain faithful, in true romantic fashion, until death' (*Byronic Hero: Types and Prototypes*, p. 149).

This persistent gender mutability and unstable, often volatile, sexual politics drew male and female writers to Byron. Victorian novelists like Edward Bulwer-Lytton and Benjamin Disraeli 'amassed symbolic capital by performing Byron's effeminacy', as Elfenbein has shown.[76] These men cultivated and ultimately cast off the sexually ambiguous role of the Byronic dandy in their public personae and in their silver-fork novels (*Pelham* [1828] and *Venetia* [1837] among them). Such initial investment in a passing vogue for the Romantic, affecting an outward show of 'being Byron', amounts to a reactionary Victorianism.[77] Where male writers, such as Bulwer-Lytton and Disraeli, sought in Byron a model of gender self-fashioning to secure literary success and enhance a political profile, women writers found a model of masculinity to refashion or reform. The poet and his legacy became a rite-of-passage for both male and female authors alike; and yet, 'for women writers', as Dorothy Mermin has argued, 'Byronism was not just a stage to be outgrown: it was a psychological impulsion to be cherished and an artistic problem they had to resolve' (*Godiva's Ride*, p. 11). Even though some women writers, such as Harriet Beecher Stowe, could not be said to 'cherish' Byron in later life, they were engaged with the 'artistic problem' that his poetry and posthumous reputation presented. By defending Lady Byron and denouncing Lord Byron, Stowe was attempting to recreate the literary strategy of submerging or expunging the Byronic in a biographical account.[78] This American writer positioned herself within a transatlantic community of nineteenth-century women writers who sought to destroy, disable, or domesticate the anti-hero as a defence against the degenerate aristocratic male.

Reports of Byron's debauched ancestors and his own marital dishar-
mony invite and belittle the pious female 'saviour' that became a recurring feature in popular modern romance novels. This figure attempts
to redeem the fallen hero through earnest endeavour and example, a
strategy popularised by *Jane Eyre* (and problematised by *The Tenant of
Wildfell Hall*). Rochester must pass through the literal fire of Thornfield
Hall and the purgatorial fire of losing Jane before he can secure the
heroine, 'the first Byronic hero ever to be so purified', as Winifred
Gérin noted ('Byron's Influence', p. 18). Taming or transforming the
Byronic hero reinforced women's assumed spiritual superiority during
the Victorian period and simultaneously functioned as a 'lightning-rod'
for their own misgivings about religion, particularly the thorny issue
of Calvinist predestination, as Franklin has argued.[79] Women writers
thereby retained their propriety *and* evoked an erotically subversive
voice in their work. As will become apparent throughout this book,
Byron's ambivalent sexuality and satirical scepticism, as well as his lyric
tones, formed 'a locus of positive creative attention' for the woman
writer (Newey, 'Rival Cultures', p. 68).

This 'oppositional conversation' – Wolfson's phrase for Felicia
Hemans's formative and fluctuating regard for Byron – characterises
nineteenth-century women writers' encounters with Byron and the
Byronic.[80] Eliot's response to the revelation of Byron's incestuous relationship with Augusta Leigh is instructive in this regard. By declaring
'He [Byron] seems to me the most *vulgar-minded* genius that ever produced a great effect in literature' (21 September 1869, original emphasis), Eliot reaffirms her outrage at his reported misdemeanours without
questioning the power, or at least the powerful 'effect', of his poetic
brilliance. Subtle distinctions between the poet and his personality,
Byron and 'Byron', contend with an admiration for his artistry. That
the Byronic hero became a model of profligacy upon which Victorian
heroes could be judged is accurate in so far as Felix Holt, the protagonist
of Eliot's novel of that name (published in 1866), is contrasted favourably against the Byronic Harold Transome: the Victorian visionary and
artisan signals a departure from a self-indulgent Romantic past. Yet Eliot
is careful to sidestep stereotypes and breaks down the barriers between
her new breed of hero and the anti-hero. Transome is, in alternate
measure, the 'phallocentric patriarch' that Malcolm Kelsall identifies as
a Byronic archetype, the 'huge *sulky Dandy*' that Carlyle derided, and a
reimagining of Byron's exotic 'hero', Sardanapalus.[81] In similar fashion,
Gaskell's portrait of the poet pretender, Osborne Hamley in *Wives and
Daughters*, draws on and complicates a parody of Byronic romance,

extending the critique of the sentimentalised anti-hero embedded in Byron's own poetry and in the work of the Brontës. When tackling the 'Byronist dilemma' of his sardonic style and sullied reputation, the woman writer 'might regret Byron, yet remain Byronic' (Wolfson, *Romantic Interactions*, p. 268).

The Byronic hero's embodiment of paradoxical personae – including, among others, the rake, the dandy, the devoted and diabolic lover – provided a unique opportunity for women writers to engage with and contest contemporary gender ideologies. As such, this book examines the conflicting pressures that the Byronic hero brought to bear on female authors in the wider context of nineteenth-century models of masculinity. Byron's poetry and his legacy offer a point of entry into contentious gender debates that relate specifically to changing standards of male behaviour within the context of renegotiated class boundaries. In Eliot's *Middlemarch*, Will Ladislaw's pseudo-Grand Tour reads more like the youthful foibles of a student's gap year than Byron's colourful adventures abroad or Rochester's 'useless, roving, lonely life', keeping mistresses and engaging in a duel, before returning to England and the prospect of personal reform in *Jane Eyre* (p. 349). Underwhelmed by this aristocratic finishing school, Ladislaw's experiences on the continent – exposing himself to the stimuli of exotic foods, drinks, and substances – are ill-matched to a Romantic vision of 'ruinous perfection' (*Manfred*, III. iv. l. 28). The Byronic pilgrim who worships a woman as an antiquity, an angel, or a saint, as Ladislaw regards Dorothea in Rome, can no longer be countenanced by following in the footsteps of upper-class pursuits that had become, by the time Eliot began writing *Middlemarch* in the late 1860s, more pedestrian than profound.

At the forefront of these Victorian concerns about a prescriptive and elitist male experience is the vexed question of what constitutes a gentleman and whether such a figure can survive the cultural and social upheaval of the age. From Elizabeth Bennet's branding judgements of the landed gentry in the early nineteenth century – rebuffing Darcy's first proposal with the cutting retort '... had you behaved in a more gentleman-like manner' (p. 186) – to Margaret Hale's declaration that the mid-Victorian industrialist falls short in her estimation, being 'not quite a gentleman; but that was hardly to be expected', the 'gentleman' was no longer predetermined by rank, inheritance, and European escapades alone.[82] Austen's reactions to Byron, amidst a broader engagement with Romantic writers, were instrumental in shaping the 'new gentleman' that emerges in her fiction. In *Persuasion*, Captain Wentworth's ascent in status and accumulation of wealth through his own endeavours is a significant precursor to the aspiring middle-class mill-owner in Gaskell's *North and South*. In the figure of Mr Thornton, the Romantic hero meets with the ambitions of the Victorian self-made man. The heroes in these novels, published nearly half a century apart, deconstruct preconceived ideas about male behaviour and class. The heroines, in turn, reconstruct masculinity not in but through an image of Byron and his fictional protagonists.

VII

The figure of the Byronic hero plays a pivotal part in gendered dialogues over social position in the fiction of nineteenth-century women writers, primarily due to an extremist edge that disturbs convention and denounces 'cant'. Social commentators and philosophers from across the political spectrum, including Matthew Arnold, Thomas Carlyle, Friedrich Engels, John Stuart Mill, and John Ruskin, recognised the revolutionary power of Byron's poetry, a lyric mode of dissent that spoke to a prevailing mood of disenchantment. While some of these writers were outspoken critics of Byronism, in so much as it promoted an image of the poet as a misanthropic poseur, they also praised an authentically heroic voice that sympathised with the subjugated and satirised social hypocrisy. For Eliot, who was eager to denounce the poet's profligacy (and the public discussion of it), Byron was best remembered as an upholder of liberty, as a defender of the Luddites, and a fighter in the Greek War of Independence. She writes, in an article published in the *Westminster Review* in October 1855, that his 'career was ennobled and purified towards its close by a high and sympathetic purpose, by honest and energetic efforts for his fellow-men'.[83] The pathos of his 'melancholy heroism', striving for freedom amidst a post-revolutionary malaise, sheds an airbrushed 'afterglow' over his final poems. Byron achieved a spiritual victory, for Eliot as for other writers in Britain and across Europe, when harnessing his talents for what he knew to be imperfect political ideals.[84] This portrait of a 'forlornly brave' poet, as Elizabeth Barrett Browning imagines Byron in 'A Vision of Poets' (l. 413), or the 'passionate and dauntless soldier of a forlorn hope', as Arnold has it in his essay on Byron (p. 403), is a central feature of Eliot's major works, *Felix Holt* and *Middlemarch* (broader issues of nationality and emancipation are also considered through a Byronic lens in her long poem, *The Spanish Gypsy*, and her last novel, *Daniel Deronda* [1876]). The figure of the fiery artist as respected social reformer comes to the fore in *Middlemarch* as the Romantic wanderer Will Ladislaw is recalibrated into a wider political life; angst and ambition are transmuted into the 'beneficent activity' of communal values and mutual support (p. 686).

The portrayal of Ladislaw as an 'ardent public man' (p. 686) in the BBC series of *Middlemarch*, screened in 1994, marks the rise of the Byronic hero in screen adaptations of the last two decades. Where Eliot's youthful pretender is a playfully ironic 'poetic dyad' of Shelley and Byron, Rufus Sewell's Ladislaw is a fully-fledged Byronic hero (Stabler, 'Romantic and Victorian Conversations', p. 232). In this version of *Middlemarch*, with screenplay by Andrew Davies, Mrs Cadwallader's wry surmise that Ladislaw may be 'A sort of Byronic hero – an amorous conspirator' is writ large in Sewell's compelling screen presence and political moment (p. 313). *Middlemarch* is the first of Davies's screenplays adapted from nineteenth-century novels by women writers that makes explicit and implicit reference to the Byronic hero. Augmented and added allusions to Byron and his poetry appear in *Wives and Daughters* (1999), *Northanger Abbey* (2007), and *Sense and Sensibility* (2008), among others. In the former, references to Felicia Hemans in Gaskell's novel are edited out in an extended scene where Byron's poem, 'I Would I Were a Careless Child', is read aloud and the poet taken up as a subject of discussion. In the latter, references to Cowper and Scott in Austen's novel are replaced by a recital of Byron's 'So, we'll go no more a roving'. Davies's preference for Byron – over Hemans, Cowper, Scott, and, in his adaptation of *Northanger Abbey*, Radcliffe – is pragmatic in presupposing his audience's familiarity with the notorious poet as opposed to his contemporaries. Byron functions as shorthand for sexual intrigue in screenplays that are anxious to 'enhance' the appeal of nineteenth-century heroes for a modern audience. The portrayal of a Byronic Darcy in the 1995 BBC adaptation of *Pride and Prejudice* drove home an overriding sense that, for Davies, 'The engine of the plot is Darcy's sexual desire for Elizabeth'.[85] The scriptwriter was similarly at pains to emphasise the 'fresh energy' of his 2008 adaptation of *Sense and Sensibility* (1811), with a darkly erotic subplot and male characters engaged in 'manly' physical exertions.[86]

This brings the argument about Byronic afterlives back to reinvestments in an 'intertextual archetype', Umberto Eco's term for a process of abstraction that Bertrand Russell predicted when passing sentence on Byron: '[t]he world insisted on simplifying him'.[87] Both approaches, in different ways, presuppose a 'reality' that is discernible, recoverable even, from the obfuscation of myth. Disentangling the man 'as he really was', in Russell's words, from the myth is not only counterintuitive when considering Byron and the Byronic; it also misses the meanings that arise out of, and generate a cultural legacy from, a close approximation between life and legend. That the Byronic hero should communicate brooding sexuality is predictable and yet not devoid of subtler significance. The ideological tension of promoting a Byronic 'machismo' in adaptations that also promote free-thinking female leads indicates a more complex on-screen configuration of desire than is often acknowledged. It is my contention that the Byronic hero speaks to contemporary fault-lines in masculinity, as adaptations occupy seemingly opposing territories of traditional and revisionary romance.

Channelling a Byronic dissonance, the provocative political friction discussed above, is not limited to Davies's screenplays. Captain Wentworth, in Nick Dear's *Persuasion*, and Colonel Brandon, in Emma Thompson's *Sense and Sensibility*, were conspicuously Byronic in films released in 1995 – the same year as Colin Firth's Darcy became a cultural phenomenon. Mr Knightley underwent a similar yet perhaps more surprising transformation in two screen versions of *Emma* (1815) released in 1996. The cumulative effect of this trend made it impossible to watch film and TV adaptations based on Austen's works, a Romantic novelist, without recalling the presence of Byron, a Romantic poet. Indeed, the uptight eroticism of these Byronic performances was a crucial component in the Austen revival of the late twentieth and early twenty-first centuries, securing screen time and commercial success. 'Byromania' not only resurfaced as 'Darcymania' – it ignited and fuelled 'Austenmania' also. This potent ingredient was consequently added to the on-screen remix of other nineteenth-century women writers. The influence of these Byronic Austen leads was still visible, nearly a decade later, in the depiction of Gaskell's Mr Thornton in the BBC mini-series of *North and South* (2004), which also drew on the subtext of political insurgency previously promoted through a Byronic Will Ladislaw in the BBC's *Middlemarch* (1994).

A primary concern of this book is to ascertain whether such a pronounced Byronic presence in screen adaptations of the last 20 years is evident, and in what form, in the novels themselves. Do adaptations augment or improvise a Byronic presence in screen versions of novels by nineteenth-century women writers and, if so, to what end? What effect does this raised Romantic profile have on our understanding of their work, the continued cultural impact of the Byronic hero, and the study of Romantic dialogues and legacies more generally? Moving beyond issues of 'fidelity' per se, what remains, if anything, of the involved intertextual relationships between nineteenth-century women novelists and this Romantic poet in the creative process of adaptation? Is the imprint of these charged textual encounters visible, and in what ways is it reimagined, as the Byronic hero is 'translated', in his most recent reincarnation, from page to screen? In contrast to a common assumption that art inspired by other works of art somehow diminishes or detracts from the donor, I am mindful of the various ways in which adaptation ' "talks back" even in the process of passing on the legacy', refocusing critical attention on the text and stimulating challenging conversations (Stoneman, 'Brontë Legacy', p. 6). Screen versions and spin-offs of nineteenth-century novels have substantially expanded the horizons of Romantic and Victorian afterlives, as I hope to demonstrate in this book. A focus on 'faithfulness', when considering any form of translation, diverts attention away from issues of interpretation and cultural transmission. Adaptations are as much in dialogue with each other and trends within the genre as they are with a given *urtext*, for example. Film and television versions of nineteenth-century novels, post-*Pride and Prejudice* (1995), were highly conscious of an adaptation that became a cultural touchstone, with Colin Firth's star turn as Darcy casting a long shadow over his own career and that of other actors in costume dramas.

VIII

Chapters 1 and 2 of this book focus on creative conversations between Austen and Byron within a wider context of Romantic dialogues. The first of these chapters seeks to demonstrate that Austen and Byron are connected, as contemporaries, through shared cultural stimuli and an engagement with changing models of masculinity in the early nineteenth century. Both authors inherit and interpret literary 'types', from the Regency rake to the Gothic villain, and seek to modify, albeit in different ways and to different ends, what constitutes 'manly' behaviour and appearance. In *Emma*, for instance, Austen looks forwards as well as backwards for her male characters, reconfiguring literary antecedents and making permeable the preconceived boundaries between the hero and the anti-hero. What I hope to demonstrate is that this practice of revision connects Austen's 'new gentleman' and Byron's hero-villain. Romantic anxieties over influence and originality underpin Austen's parodic novel, *Northanger Abbey*, where we are introduced to a heroine who must navigate between the truths and falsehoods of her over-crowded imagination. Catherine Morland is the first of many quixotic heroines discussed in this book, including *Sense and Sensibility*'s Marianne Dashwood, whose misreadings of romance are indicative of a prevailing pattern, a governing schema, of immersion in, followed by resistance and readjustment to, a Romantic sensibility. Austen recognises, in both *Northanger Abbey* and *Sense and Sensibility*, that Romantic topoi are unstable. That the 'more deeply interfused' Romanticism of Colonel Brandon displaces the flamboyant romantic attractions of Willoughby demonstrates a discomforting proximity between the hero and the anti-hero.[88] As such, this early Austen novel stages a double and divided Romanticism that develops out of, and is dependent on, destabilising and rehabilitating masculine 'types'. Screen adaptations of both *Northanger Abbey* and *Sense and Sensibility* are conversant with and extend these Romantic dialogues, promoting the presence of the Romantic hero and of Byron in particular.

Byron takes a leading role in Austen's literary dialogue with the Romantic poets in Chapter 2. *Persuasion*, Austen's last and most 'Romantic' novel, is permeated with the poetic 'richness of the present age' (p. 94). On the one hand, Byron's poetry, as well as Scott's, is read, and misread, to excess, with near-fatal consequences. On the other hand, Byron's poetry and Byronic preoccupations are integrated into the fabric of a novel that navigates the pains, pleasures, and regrets of romantic love, social and familial isolation, depression and deprivation, and the prospect of a sea-faring freedom. After establishing that Romanticism gathers momentum as a means of articulating existential anxieties in Austen's novel, this chapter will focus on the male protagonists of *Persuasion* and *Pride and Prejudice*, both of whom, I argue, constitute hybridised Byronic heroes. Captain Wentworth and Mr Darcy bear the Byronic hallmarks of pride, self-reliance, and resentment, among other characteristics, but it is their chameleonic uncertainty and capacity for change that demonstrates a greater debt to the Romantic poet. The erotic indeterminacy that captivates the heroine and the reader marks a significant departure in romantic literature with far-reaching implications for the figure of the hero in nineteenth-century novels and film versions based on these works. Where more recent adaptations of Austen novels, such as *Persuasion* (2007) and *Pride and Prejudice* (2005), rely on a subtle interplay of Romantic undercurrents, earlier adaptations of these novels, screened in 1995, demonstrate noticeably Byronic leanings. An issue that arises from this discussion is whether Wentworth and Darcy lose some of their subjectivity, their Byronic inscrutability, when codified as 'Byronic'. What, I ask, in the final part of the chapter, are the consequences of Colin Firth's phenomenally successful portrayal of a Byronic Darcy in the BBC adaptation of *Pride and Prejudice* for the reception of Austen's novel, for an appreciation of Austen as an early nineteenth-century woman writer, and for the fortunes of Austen adaptation more broadly?

Chapter 3 moves from a female Romantic writer's reception and reinvention of Byron and the Byronic to a female Victorian writer's treatment of the same subjects some half a century later. Elizabeth Gaskell's early work indicates a predictable pattern, in keeping with Austen and Eliot, of debunking Byronism as a genuine dialogue with Byron's poetry takes root. There are more allusions to Byron in Gaskell's last novel, *Wives and Daughters*, than elsewhere in her fiction, extending and intensifying an ongoing textual relationship with the Romantics. The dangers of a descent into a Romantic sensibility are drawn out in the characters of Mrs Hamley and her son, Osborne, whose pose as a tortured poet also masks a touching and tragic portrait of familial disaffection. Osborne Hamley, in many ways a more intriguing prospect than his 'rational' brother, Roger, complicates our understanding of masculine ideals throughout the novel. In the 1999 BBC mini-series, with screenplay by Andrew Davies, direct references to Byron foreground the attractions and distractions of the Romantic anti-hero, bringing into sharper focus the semantic strains and synergies between romance and realism in Gaskell's writing. The heroine, Molly Gibson, is caught between genres and must regulate a romantic predisposition to reside seamlessly within a broad canvas of realism. The fate of this reframed romantic outlook remains unclear, partly because the novel was not finished. Yet the screen adaptation embellishes an ending that shows Molly as a pioneer working alongside her husband in exotic climes – spirited femininity is now coupled with masculine scientific endeavour, the romantic cemented into a 'female-friendly' realism.

The second part of this chapter focuses on Gaskell's earlier novel, *North and South*. A defiant yet ambivalent attitude towards the acts of insurrection that prove so central to the novel is brought into sharp focus through an analysis of the epigraph taken from Byron's poem, *The Island; or, Christian and his Comrades* (1823). As the master of Marlborough Mills, Mr Thornton's abrasive dissonance reconfigures the received 'ideal' of the patrician hero into a stark portrait of the self-made man. Byronic tendencies to self-reliance and solipsism are scrutinised and arguably sublimated through the interlocking plotlines of social reform and romance. The Byronic hero's vaunted free will is fiercely guarded by the on-screen Thornton in a BBC adaptation, first shown in 2004, that grapples with Gaskell's portrayal of industrial relations and gender politics amidst a vividly realised northern cityscape.

The final chapters of this book, 4 and 5, focus on George Eliot's complex and enduring regard for Byron. Her outrage at renewed speculation over the poet's incestuous affair is often cited as indicative of a Victorian writer's rejection of a Romantic writer's moral turpitude. Eliot's response to 'The Separation' scandal has diverted attention away from the author's fixation with Byron.[89] Chapter 4 begins by examining Eliot's fascination with Byronic individualism in the context of aesthetic concerns over the common man. How, I ask, can we reconcile the lure of Byronic hubris with a larger literary project of everyday altruism? Eliot's fiction does not advocate anti-heroism, as has sometimes been posited by critics. On the contrary, her fiction formulates an alternative heroism that draws on as it deflects a Romantic inheritance. Byron's poetry, along with a range of writing from the period, informs and facilitates the figure of the Romantic artist-reformer that evolves over the course of Eliot's work. Eliot's 'inexhaustible dialogue with Byron's work' involves, as O'Neill persuasively argues in relation to Arnold, 'a dual response of recognition and redefinition' ('Byron and Arnold', p. 68). Where, for example, the first-person narrative of 'The Lifted Veil' (1859) exposes a myopic Victorian misreading of Romantic ideology, the verse drama, *Armgart*, tests the assumed ascendancy of Romantic interiority with competing voices and viewpoints (the latter is comparable, in this sense, with Byron's dramatic poem, *Manfred*). The form of Eliot's long dramatic poem, *The Spanish Gypsy*, enables an intense and intimate engagement with Byron's work. Different faces, or facets, of the Byronic hero (and, in Fedalma's case, the Byronic heroine) are refracted through characters who function as critical commentaries on isolation, exile, ethnicity, and doubt as both creatively enabling and disabling. Eliot's early fiction, this chapter argues, demonstrates a deep, if not always congenial, appreciation of Byron quite apart from the public profile of the 'debauched' poet.

Eliot extends her literary dialogue with Byron in the novels discussed in the last chapter. Esther Lyon, the heroine of *Felix Holt: The Radical*, is disabused of the exotic fantasy of Byronic romance through the figure of Harold Transome as she is drawn to the righteousness of the eponymous hero. Harold Transome amounts to more than a show of *faux* Romanticism, however, and Felix Holt betrays flaws more usually associated with the anti-hero, resuming the 'dual response of recognition and redefinition' noted in the previous paragraph. It is in Eliot's late major novels, *Middlemarch* and *Daniel Deronda*, that the Byronic hero comes of age and finally attains credibility in 'serious' Victorian literature. That this figure should be fated to flourish in the vast demographic of Eliot's novels may be surprising at first glance; but this would be to overlook Byron's tendency to dramatise politics and philosophy through his poetry, as Eliot does in her prose, and it would be to likewise overlook the humanist contours and hues of Byron's chameleon heroes. The reach of the Byronic, in *Daniel Deronda*, extends from the Princess Halm-Eberstein and Grandcourt, as equally unattractive portraits of contrasting Byronic extremes, through the thwarted Romantic potential of Gwendolen Harleth's stage-managed self, to Daniel Deronda himself. In the title character, creative uncertainty graduates into a mode of thinking and being that is capable of rendering spiritual idealism socially responsible. Deronda's pioneering, if indistinct, vision for the future is not a rejection but a reformulation of the Romantic. Both Daniel Deronda and Will Ladislaw herald a new breed of hero for whom an immense capacity for empathy becomes indivisible from reformist aspirations. In *Middlemarch*, the sensuous receptivity of the Romantic heir evolves into a heroism that values the communal and prizes the unexceptional without disowning his Romantic roots. In the BBC adaptation of *Middlemarch*, first screened in 1994, Ladislaw and his Byronic credentials are brought further into the foreground. Portraying Ladislaw as 'A sort of Byronic hero – an amorous conspirator' (p. 313) – synthesising political activism and sex appeal – leaves a lasting legacy for male protagonists in screen adaptations of the next decade and beyond.

1

Jane Austen's Byronic Heroes I: *Northanger Abbey* and *Sense and Sensibility*

I

Jane Austen and Lord Byron are strange bedfellows. Perhaps even more so than Elizabeth Gaskell and George Eliot, the focus of subsequent chapters, the inclusion of Austen in this book may seem misplaced. Yet, despite the seeming incompatibility of Austen and Byron, authors and critics have commented on this unlikely couple if only to emphasise differences in the scope and style of their work and in their respective life experiences. As Rachel Brownstein suggests,

> Austen and Byron, close contemporaries, beg to be talked about together, and frequently have been. They seem to embody and invite and thus reinforce familiar binary oppositions: male and female, free and constrained, celebrated and obscure, self-indulgent aristocrat and saving, respectable homebody; Romantic poet and domestic novelist, careless producer of endless versions and careful rewriter, oversexed and asexual, sinner and saint; a handsome creature we have many gorgeous portraits of and a sharp little face in a sketch.[1]

Fixing these 'binary oppositions' – which cast Austen as a prudish, parochial novelist to Byron's profligate poet – has served, according to Brownstein, to sustain their remarkable posthumous careers. The codification of their life and work has contributed to cultural and commercial success for both authors, at different times and for different reasons. An extraordinary proclivity for satire, a sceptical regard, or disregard, for 'perfection' (particularly in relation to romance), and a predilection for 'wandering with pedestrian Muses' could describe either author (*Don Juan*, I. viii).[2]

Nevertheless, it is invariably argued that Austen, as the author of 'stories about three or four families in a country village in England [...] who sewed up her plots so neatly and never wrote a scene without a woman in it', could have little interest in Byron, 'the author of verse romances about solitary, sullen wanderers in exotic, distant lands' ('Romanticism, A Romance', p. 175). What could Austen, and her composed detachment and finely-textured prose, have in common with Byron, and the intensely personal and rapid, almost dizzying, dynamism of his poetry? Such polarisations speak to cultural constructions of these authors and their afterlives, as well as to gendered assumptions about genre. Setting up any Romantic pairing as antithetical invariably belies the authors' respective range and value. And, in this instance, it has served to separate Austen and Byron in terms of scholarship. As I hope to demonstrate in this chapter and the next, stereotypes that separate Austen and Byron deflect attention away from the Romantic concordances and discords that connect their work.

Austen's position as a Romantic writer, in terms of style, ideology, and literary inheritance, has been the subject of much debate. Beth Lau has marshalled a convincing case for treating Austen as a 'true' Romantic: 'Such stark dichotomies between Austen and the male poets do not hold up, however, upon close examination of their works. In a number of ways her novels endorse individualism, chafe at ties to others, and express the angst of solitude and alienation'. While I have reservations about 'integrating Jane Austen within the Romantic movement and canon', in the sense of absorbing Austen within a pre-existing 'fold' of Romanticism (if such an exclusive grouping were now to be identifiable), it is important to acknowledge the common ground, in terms of affinities and anxieties, between Romantic writers.[3] It is equally important to acknowledge that Austen and Byron were reflecting, through their own distinctive literary style and approach, the changeful cultural milieu of the early nineteenth century. Stressing differences between specific authors or subdividing Romanticism by gender does not alter the overriding fact that both authors worked within a climate of revolution (and post-revolution) that extended to all aspects of political and literary life. Conversely, Austen's dialogues with her fellow Romantics, whether antagonistic or affable, go beyond a nebulous 'spirit of the age' or a set of shared motifs. Exploring the tensions between Austen and other Romantic writers is, in many ways, more important than detecting parallels.[4] Re-contextualising Austen among the Romantics reveals a shared if unstable creative nucleus that deepens, broadens, and complicates an understanding of her writing as well as the authors Austen is considered alongside. I argue, in what follows, that Austen remains distinctive as a Romantic writer in the subtlety, insight, and verve with which she encounters and interacts with her contemporaries.

An expanding and intensifying interest in Romantic dialogues and legacies has the capacity to guide scholarship beyond the ideological battlegrounds of gender and canonicity, offering a light at the end of a dark road for what Elizabeth Barrett Browning tellingly described, in *Aurora Leigh*, as 'these foot-catching robes of womanhood'.[5] The study of male and female writers as 'fellow' Romantics builds on much valuable work to recover forgotten or marginalised voices and contexts, shifting the focus from Romanticism, as a master narrative, to multiple romanticisms. It is now possible to refocus attention onto securing the foothold of women writers by embedding their cultural and literary exchanges with male writers, as well as with each other, firmly into the fabric of Romantic studies. This approach does not seek to collapse creative distance or expunge difference. On the contrary, this revisioned Romanticism encompasses the conflict between writers such as Austen and Byron, acknowledging that indebtedness and even admiration often involves dissension as well as harmony. Exploring Romantic engagements – and, indeed, disengagements – reorientates our perceptions and preconceptions of individual writers and their writing, the conversations between writers, and expands the parameters of what constitutes Romantic studies and the influences of Romanticism. This dynamic enterprise directs attention onto the communications and miscommunications between the Romantics and the generations of authors and artists that have inherited this tradition and its successive evolutions. A focus on Romantic partnerings opens up new horizons for what we understand by Romanticism and Post-Romanticism, and provides us with a powerful lens through which we can see how far, and in what ways, the impact of the Romantics and reconstructions of them extends.[6]

II

There is no evidence that Austen and Byron ever met. Had they met, it is difficult to envisage how they would have acted or what, if anything, they would have said. Perhaps their first meeting would have suffered from the same strained misunderstandings and snubs as the hero and heroine's in *Pride and Prejudice*, where 'he looked at her only to criticise' and she met his 'satirical eye' with impertinence.[7] The social gulf between Austen, the daughter of a rector, and the sixth Baron Byron also approximates that between Elizabeth Bennet and Mr Darcy. But, as with these fictional counterparts, encounters were possible if improbable.

Notwithstanding the largely separate social spheres they occupied, a few family connections can be traced between the two writers, leading Gaye King to argue that 'Byron was among those in an outer circle within Jane Austen's ken'. Byron also knew a number of Austen's neighbours in Hampshire, most notably Lord Portsmouth.[8] Austen might have encountered the poet had she accepted an invitation to meet Madame de Staël. Other near misses occurred when Austen saw Mrs Jordan in the Gothic play, *The Devil to Pay*, a performance that Byron praised when he saw it three nights later, and both saw Edmund Kean as Shylock in early March 1814. At a commemorative exhibition of Joshua Reynolds's paintings at the British Institution in 1813, Austen looked for portraits that resembled the protagonists of *Pride and Prejudice*, only to surmise that Darcy's delicacy of feeling would protect his wife's image from public display, while Byron, unperturbed by reservations over female modesty, sought out a portrait of Lady Melbourne, the mother-in-law of Lady Caroline Lamb and aunt of Annabella Milbanke, on or around the same date.[9] Where Austen's thoughts were preoccupied with imaginary romance and Byron's were fixed on real-life erotic intrigue, both writers were engaged in reading, or framing, character through art.

We know from Austen's letters and later fiction that she was familiar with at least some of Byron's poetry, whereas we do not know what Byron thought of Austen. We know that Byron read and begrudgingly enjoyed John Gibson Lockhart's 'Letter to Lord Byron', written under the pseudonym John Bull, in which characters from Austen's novels are appropriated to satirise the poet's female fans:

> Now, tell me, Mrs. Goddard, now tell me, Miss Price, now tell me, dear Harriet Smith, and dear, dear Mrs. Elton, do tell me, is not this just the very look, that one would have fancied for Childe Harold? Oh! what eyes and eyebrows! Oh! what a chin!—well, after all, who knows what may have happened. One can never know the truth of such stories. Perhaps her *Ladyship* was in the wrong after all.—I am sure if I had married such a man, I would have borne with all his little eccentricities—a man so evidently unhappy.—Poor Lord Byron! who can say how much he may have been to be pitied? I am sure I would; I bear with all Mr. E.'s eccentricities, and I am sure any woman of real sense would have done so to Lord Byron's: poor Lord Byron!—well, say what they will, I shall always pity him.[10]

Austen's irony, in her portrait of Mrs Elton's showy exclamations and shrewd husband-hunting, is here reconceived and directed onto those

who admire Byron, and would exonerate him of any guilt in the breakdown of his marriage, while knowing little of his poetry. The snatched
lines that are recalled, from the poem 'To Inez' in Canto I of *Childe
Harold's Pilgrimage*, are given as evidence in support of the critic's point
that Byron's misanthropy is popularist 'humbug'. As such, Lockhart's letter makes a formative connection between a woman novelist and a male
poet, the figure of the female misreader, and the deflation of Byronism,
an involved relationship that persists throughout the nineteenth century and will be examined in detail in this and in subsequent chapters.

Byron engaged with and was influenced by the women writers of
the era. It is probable that he would have been familiar with Austen's
Emma (1815) given that John Murray, his own publisher since 1812,
published the novel. Byron owned copies of *Sense and Sensibility* (1811)
and *Pride and Prejudice* (1813), most likely sent to him by Murray, which
were the talk of his social circle. Annabella Milbanke read *Pride and
Prejudice* before marrying Byron, rendering her solemn praise for the
novel and attraction to Mr Darcy somewhat ironic in retrospect: 'A
very superior work. [...] I really think it is the *most probable* fiction I
have ever read. [...] the interest is very strong, especially for Mr. Darcy'.
Her first encounter with Byron is dramatised through the lens of *Pride
and Prejudice* in the two-part BBC biopic of the poet's life, screened in
2003.[11] Byron churlishly refuses to dance with Annabella and retorts,
when informed that she is seeking a husband, 'Could she not find one
in Jane Austen?', an arch allusion aimed at an audience familiar with
recent period dramas. For Nick Dear, who also wrote the screenplay for
the 1995 film version of *Persuasion*, Byron was not only familiar with
Austen's work; his courtship replicates the pattern of initial rejection
and subsequent consternation in *Pride and Prejudice*, with Annabella puz-
zling over the 'unfathomable' poet even after they are married. Indeed,
the combative conversations between Annabella and Byron in Dear's
script are indebted to a romance of resistance reinscribed by the 1995
BBC adaptation of *Pride and Prejudice* and the Austen revival that followed. It is tempting to think that Byron discussed the author who had
so impressed his future wife, and that he discussed *Sense and Sensibility*
with Lady Bessborough, who was 'much amused by it'.[12] Although there
is 'little to support such literary wishful thinking', as Doucet Devin
Fischer concedes, this does not preclude eager supposition:

> One might hope to report concerning Byron and Jane Austen that
> he had told Lady Holland that he admired *Sense and Sensibility*; or
> that he had asked Lady Melbourne to save him from his incestuous

relationship with Augusta Leigh by finding him a wife like Elizabeth Bennet; or that he had wished out loud when Lady Caroline Lamb published her exposé of their romance that she were a little more like Fanny Price. It would be wonderful to discover among some scribbled notes on the drafts of *Don Juan* an admission that his send-up of Gothic conventions in Canto XVI owed something to *Northanger Abbey*. It would be even better to find that he ranked Austen with Sir Walter Scott, his favorite novelist. ('Byron and Austen: Romance and Reality', p. 71)

Better still would be the poet conversing directly with the novelist, as Byron is facetiously invited to 'tell Jane Austen, that is, if you dare,/ How much her novels are beloved down here' (p. 171), in W. H. Auden's 'Letter to Lord Byron' (1937).

In terms of Austen reading Byron's poetry, the comment in a letter to her sister, 'I have read the Corsair, mended my petticoat, & have nothing else to do' (5 March 1814), has understandably been read as dismissive or even, as Michael Williams suggests, evidence of an 'unengaged mind'.[13] In response to this line, John Halperin states 'So much for Byron' – despite noting the poet's influence elsewhere in his biography of Austen – and Brownstein detects a 'giggle' in Austen's flat remark.[14] Jane Stabler's observation that 'Austen's view of Byron is teasingly enigmatic' comes closer to acknowledging the difficulty of gauging her reaction to particular authors and to what Richard Cronin refers to as her 'habitual dryness'.[15] To see 'Austen's satire as a mark of disdain is fundamentally to misunderstand it', according to William Deresiewicz in his study *Jane Austen and the Romantic Poets*: 'For Austen, satire was the sincerest form of flattery'.[16] Satire is often an indicator of what Austen admired and found intellectually engaging. The work of Samuel Richardson, probably Austen's favourite novelist, was the subject of youthful pastiche – in the form of a very short five-act theatrical based on *The History of Sir Charles Grandison* – and gentle parody in her later fiction.[17] Although Catherine Morland's reading habits are suspect even before she succumbs to the sensationalism of Gothic shockers in *Northanger Abbey*, it is her enjoyment of *Sir Charles Grandison* – 'not like Udolpho at all; but yet I think it is very entertaining' – that distinguishes her as not only more widely read but somewhat more discerning than the shallow Isabella Thorpe.[18] As much as Austen is testing Richardson and deflating his solemn style, she is also paying homage by revisiting him.

Brownstein observes, in an essay comparing Austen's and Byron's juvenilia, that both writers 'developed their distinctive engaging styles in the process of imitating the works of other writers' ('Endless Imitation', p. 135). Their shared talent for parody and impersonation is channelled directly by Austen onto Byron. As well as reading a number of the Oriental Tales – *The Corsair* only a month after it was published – Austen copied out lines from a poem by Byron. In 'Jane Austen's Verses', David Gilson notes in an appendix that her version of the poem 'differ[s] considerably from Byron's original': the title is changed from 'Napoleon's Farewell' to 'Lines of Lord Byron, in the Character of Buonaparté', and other alterations are evident in the manuscript.[19] Austen was actively engaging with and adapting a Byron poem that she considered worth keeping in her own editorialised version. This situates Austen within a collective of women readers whose commonplace books invariably featured verses by Byron. For Austen, however, the activity was unusual as was her choice of poem. Austen selects a poem, 'Napoleon's Farewell', which contemplates the potent yet fallen stature of Napoleon when faced with exile for a second time over and above the love lyrics or extracts from a longer work that were among the more popular subjects for transcription.[20]

Rather than dispel the myth that had arisen of the great defeated Napoleon, the cumulative effect of Austen's alterations intensifies the heroics of war. Take, for example, lines 21–22 in the final stanza, which appear in Byron's poem as 'Yet, yet, I may baffle the hosts that surround us,/ And yet may thy heart leap awake to my voice', and in Austen's version as 'Once more I may vanquish the foes that surround us,/ Once more shall thy heart leap awake to my voice'.[21] Napoleon's hopes of a return to power are tentatively entertained by Byron's repeated use of 'yet', whereas Austen's use of 'Once more', carried over from line 18 of the original poem, becomes a rallying call to battle. In addition, the subterfuge of Byron's 'baffle' is replaced with the explicit 'vanquish', and 'hosts' become 'foes'. The incremental repetition of 'Once more' in lines 21–22 of Austen's version gains force and momentum from the resonant opening line of Henry V's famous speech in Shakespeare's play, 'Once more unto the breach, dear friends, once more', rendering her portrait of a persuasive and even patriotic Napoleon less ambiguous and more controversial than Byron's.[22] His poem was published anonymously in *The Examiner* on 30 July 1815, with a disclaimer by the editor, Leigh Hunt, to distance the magazine's, and to some extent the author's, opinion from that presented in the monologue. Byron's wary lament for Napoleon's fate and Romantic overreaching is not only endorsed by Austen; her sympathy is heightened, with Byron's melancholy 'gloom of my Glory' exchanged for 'bloom of my glory' in the opening line of

Austen's revised version, for instance. First, it is telling that Austen chose to re-author a poem by Byron even though her alterations – the occasional word, phrases in the final stanza, and matters of punctuation – do not amount to the 'creative "fan activity" ' that Corin Throsby sees as typical of the Romantic period.[23] Second, and perhaps more surprising, is that Austen should lessen rather than deepen Byronic scepticism over the fortunes of this illustrious anti-hero.

'Napoleon's Farewell' was published in *Poems 1816* after appearing in *The Examiner*. If Austen encountered Byron's poem in the former, she would have seen a group of poems 'From the French' in which Byron oscillates between condemning Napoleon – 'goaded by ambition's sting,/ The Hero sunk into the King' ('Ode from the French') – and praising his bravery (the voice of 'To Napoleon', for example, is that of a loyal Polish officer who celebrates 'My chief, my king, my friend', 'Idol of the soldier's soul').[24] It is well known that Byron regarded Napoleon as a foil for his own troubled and 'fated' personality; less immediately apparent, Napoleon can be seen as instrumental in the formulation of some of Austen's attitudes and ideas. Austen, somewhat facetiously, contemplated writing a history of Napoleon, partly due to the strong naval connections in her own family, but principally because she associated the lure of ambition and celebrity with his fate.[25] Darryl Jones argues that the fortuitous publication of *Persuasion* with *Northanger Abbey* in 1818, novels connected by political subtexts, 'effectively bookend not only Austen's mature writing career, but also the Napoleonic Wars which were obliquely to shape that career'.[26] More specifically, Deresiewicz traces the timescale of *Persuasion* to the period of Napoleon's first exile, stating that the novel 'takes place in the shadow of Napoleon's return— the shadow of Waterloo', accounts of which fascinated Austen.[27] The Napoleonic wars and the charismatically flawed leader, Napoleon, were as much of a creative spur for Austen as they were for Byron, a view brought into sharp focus by the former's transcription of and revisions to the latter's poem, 'Napoleon's Farewell'.

III

Austen was as prodigious a reader as Byron and her tastes were equally eclectic. Having proudly worked her way through her father's library, Austen would have been familiar with many of the literary sources that shaped the Byronic hero. *Pride and Prejudice*'s Wickham and *Sense and Sensibility*'s Willoughby look back to Samuel Richardson's Lovelace and Pierre Choderlos de Laclos's Valmont, archetypal eighteenth-century

seducers of the epistolary tradition who also inform Byron's protagonists and the Byronic personae, for example.[28] Both authors draw on
as well as rehabilitate the Regency rake for their respective anti-heroes,
with even Wickham amounting to more than a commonplace scoundrel. A related figure that looms large in Byron's poetry and underscores
a complex intertextual dialogue in Austen's *Northanger Abbey* is the
Gothic villain, as will be discussed in Part IV. Before analysing Austen's
first completed novel in this context, it is worth considering a broader
issue relating to the figure of the hero that connects these authors. It
is in large part their male characters and, in Byron's case, masculine
personas that have shaped the literary legacies of these authors and
ensure the continuing appeal of their work. Austen's heroes did not
have quite the commercial cachet of Byron's or leave such an immediate cultural imprint, and yet they 'survive as icons of masculinity [...]
emerging as heroic characters on the silver screen'.[29] The longevity of
Pride and Prejudice's Mr Darcy, *Emma*'s Mr Knightley, and *Persuasion*'s
Captain Wentworth is testament, as is the case with the Byronic hero,
to shrewd and inventive renegotiations of masculinity in the transition between the eighteenth and nineteenth centuries. Both authors
participate in and profit from the shifting terrain of gender politics
that revolutionised male behaviour and manners during the Romantic
period and beyond.

The male protagonists of Austen's and Byron's fiction may initially seem
to occupy opposite ends on the spectrum of early nineteenth-century
masculinity. Austen's gentleman looks back to an eighteenth-
century model characterised by Richardson. Yet her heroes move beyond
the exemplary 'man acting uniformly well', Sir Charles Grandison. The
moral 'perfection' of the patrician hero, the subject of satire in Austen's
'Plan of a Novel', gives way to an individualism that is even more
strenuously cultivated by the Byronic hero ('perfection is/ Insipid in this
naughty world of ours' announces the narrator of *Don Juan*, I. xviii).[30]
As Joseph Kestner contends, 'Austen initiates for the nineteenth century
the process of renegotiating masculinity itself'.[31] This is exemplified in
the character of Mr Darcy who, whilst retaining the honour advocated
by Richardson, must reflect on and revise inherited notions of the gentleman. His modified mode of address is evident in the two proposal
scenes where a sense of entitlement gives way to modest supplication.
Both Elizabeth Bennet and the reader chart the change in Darcy's
behaviour from his 'selfish disdain of the feelings of others' (p. 187), at
a local ball, to the warm welcome the heroine and her relatives receive
when they visit Pemberley.[32] This gentleman can no longer rely on an

innate sense of proper conduct passed on from his father. Darcy must concern himself with a wider community, outside of his 'comfort zone', if he is to retain respectability and secure his, as well as his future wife's, happiness. What becomes apparent in Austen's fiction – and, indeed, in the fiction of Gaskell and Eliot discussed in subsequent chapters – is the increasing value of 'character', an independent mind, and personal integrity in the hero's dealings with those around him irrespective of their social standing.[33]

The hero's acclimatisation to a civility that reconfirms his status as gentleman and landowner is the subject of Michael Kramp's *Disciplining Love: Austen and the Modern Man*, published in 2007. Kramp, building on the work of critics in the 1990s that examined how Austen 'remakes English manhood' in a nationalistic and cultural context, argues convincingly for her heroes to be read as a new breed of disciplined male assuming civic responsibilities in the aftermath of the French Revolution.[34] For Kramp, it is the 'ideal' maleness of characters like Darcy and Knightley, who subdue sexual desire for a wider social agenda, that accounts for the Austen revival of the 1990s. These heroes offer some form of resolution for a contemporary crisis in masculinity that gave rise to the late millennial men's movements in the US. Sarah Frantz similarly views Austen's fiction as engaging with the profound historical changes in Western conceptions of masculinity between the eighteenth and nineteenth centuries, arguing that the 'Great Masculine Renunciation', or 'the Great Divide', as reflected in fashion – where luxurious fabrics, bright colours, and embroidery were replaced with the more sober style of dark coat and white shirt – externally exhibits the tendency towards a male denial of emotional display. Whether through discipline (Kramp) or renunciation (Frantz), Darcy's mastery of his feelings bodes well not only for the prosperity of his personal relationships, but also for the secure management of his estate. Austen's hero successfully regulates the male energies and suppresses the volatile emotions that were central concerns within debates about masculinity in the early nineteenth century.

Problems can arise, however, when literature is considered within an overarching framework of this kind. In approaching Austen's novels as 'a collection of cultural documents' (*Disciplining Love*, p. 10), Kramp does not note, for instance, that it is the narrator's averted gaze that cools the warmth of Darcy's ardour, becalming 'a man violently in love', when he is accepted by Elizabeth (p. 354). It is the narrator's voice, inflected by the consciousness of a man now chastened by earlier extremes of temperament, which moderates masculinity here. Darcy offers, in the concluding chapters of the novel, an account of his emotional history from his upbringing to the 'dreadful bitterness of spirit' that followed his rejected proposal (p. 357). The hero, now assured that his feelings are reciprocated, speaks candidly of the intensity of sensation embedded within and occasionally rupturing his reserve, answering Elizabeth's charge, 'You might have talked to me more when you came to dinner', with 'A man who had felt less, might' (p. 369). Gender, in Austen's world, is a constantly contested site, mediated through the interplay between social and cultural contexts and the multilayered techniques of fiction.

Frantz equates Darcy's 'diffidence' with the 'grim, unfathomable male characters' in Byron's poetry, arguing that it is the inaccessibility of the hero's feelings in *Pride and Prejudice* that sparked the 'Darcymania' of 1995.[35] Austen's protagonist is predisposed to Byronic traits, as I will argue in the next chapter, but not necessarily for the reasons given here. Both Darcy and the Byronic hero internalise emotions, and yet Byron's protagonists do not foster the stoicism that Frantz seems to equate with them. The Byronic hero's inner life is turbulent with conflicted passions that cannot be contained; as the Witch of the Alps confirms of Manfred: 'I know thee for a man of many thoughts,/ And deeds of good and ill, extreme in both,/ Fatal and fated in thy sufferings' (*Manfred*, II. ii. ll. 34–6). Darcy most closely resembles his Romantic relation when he gives voice to his feelings as well as when he struggles to articulate the fervent life within, a complex relationship between private interiority and public disclosure that is touched on above. What is more, the Byronic 'look', and indeed the pains the poet took to convey the impression of a dishevelled appearance, is hardly commensurate with the new male wardrobe that Frantz sees as reflective of sober self-regulation.[36] Byron's Romantic image was carefully stage-managed, distancing him visually from the effeminacy of eighteenth-century fashions, while also providing the capsule wardrobe for the dandy's customised flamboyance. In particular, the white shirt, open at the neck, became synonymous with portraits of the poet, his Byronic protagonists, and their descendants. This Byronic attire, gradually loosening to reveal a more expressive underbelly, has captured the popular imagination in recent screen adaptations. It is not the abstinence that Frantz associates with Darcy (or Kramp's asexual Austen, 'cleansed of the messiness of sex and desire', p. 14) that female viewers of the BBC's 1995 adaptation of *Pride and Prejudice* responded to when, as Martine Voiret recalls, they 'would repeatedly play the scene of Darcy diving and emerging in his wet clothes, his opened white shirt sexily sticking to his dripping body'.[37] This screen Darcy, dishevelled and damp, re-embodied the intense sexual dynamic between restraint and release, configuring a fulcrum of desire, that fuels Austen's romance plots and is encapsulated in the Byronic hero. Innately sceptical of the restrictive gender stereotypes that she is often seen to uphold, Austen is adapted so frequently and so freely precisely because her work is attuned to the 'instability of masculinity' that Herbert Sussman equates with the rapid social changes of the late eighteenth and early nineteenth centuries.[38]

Darcy is regarded, by Kramp, as 'an exemplar of a vanishing type of man; he is a resplendent figure who is at once chivalric, rational, and romantic', a hero capable of encompassing the competing claims of masculinity in Austen's fiction (*Disciplining Love*, p. 12). I would also add that given the premium on individuality and interiority in his character, traits shared with the Byronic hero, Darcy emerges as a paradigm for the 'new gentleman' in Victorian fiction. Even so, Knightley improves on Darcy, for Kramp, as he most effectively illustrates the self-disciplined and disciplining Austen hero. He, like the Byronic hero, cannot wholly be understood within a late eighteenth-century cultural context, however, as I hope to demonstrate. Knightley, in contrast to Darcy, embodies 'that general good will and regard for all people which makes anyone have a care not to show in his carriage any contempt, disrespect, or neglect of them', that Locke associates with civility in *Some Thoughts Concerning Education* (1693).[39] His relationships with both men and women, extending beyond agreeable manners and undemonstrative acts of kindness to Mr Woodhouse, Miss Bates, and Harriet Smith, reinforce a strong sense of nationhood. For Kestner, 'Knightley IS England'; he is 'the first great character in nineteenth-century fiction constructed as masculine by the paradigm of St. George' ('Revolutionizing Masculinities', p. 150). Emma's acceptance of Knightley's suit, presented in 'plain, unaffected, gentleman-like English', secures her status as the heroine of the novel and serves to reaffirm the values of manly restraint and civic duty.[40]

It is Emma's recognition that Knightley has become her benchmark of an English gentleman that prompts her keenest moment of self-revelation. Harriet's affectionate admiration for Knightley, after his 'noble benevolence and generosity' towards her, leads Emma to reflect 'that there never had been a time when she did not consider Mr Knightley as infinitely the superior, or when his regard for her had not been infinitely the most dear' (pp. 397, 402). Knightley may lack the assumed address of the lover, admitting to a Darcyesque deficiency in expressing his feelings ('If I loved you less, I might be able to talk about it more. But you know what I am', p. 417), yet his masculine dignity remains intact. Mr Elton's seemingly impeccable manners, aimed at ingratiating himself with those he deems to be worthy of his attentions, shed a positive light on what is termed Knightley's 'unfinished gallantry' (p. 378). Frank Churchill's finessed 'gallantry' presents more of a challenge for Emma's affections and a threat to the stability of Highbury. While his effusiveness and desire to please echo Elton's overtures to Emma, Frank Churchill presents a more appealing prospect. Frank, as 'a *very* good looking young man', is made more attractive by his wit, taste, and an animated spirit that is sometimes wanting in Knightley (p. 202, original emphasis). In his self-possession and apparent ability to 'love without feeling', however, Frank Churchill is akin to the seducer Wickham in *Pride and Prejudice*; and, in his calculated double-dealing and want of integrity, in the 'system of hypocrisy and deceit, – espionage, and treachery' that Emma dramatically charges him with, he is the forerunner to *Persuasion's* William Elliot (pp. 344, 390). In addition, the long letter that Frank writes to Mrs Weston, and the effect it has on Emma, recalls Willoughby's audience with Elinor in the wake of her sister's illness in *Sense and Sensibility*. Yet, where Willoughby's confession lays bare the deflated façade of the romantic courtier, Frank's mode of address oscillates between a dangerous hyperbole and, what Willoughby cannot quite capture, 'the language of real feeling' (p. 269). Frank is a subtle yet significant revision of Austen's handsome, secretive game-players. The ambivalence of his character is highlighted as he acquiesces in Highbury's disapproval of him, in travelling to London for a haircut, when that is not his primary motivation for making the journey; he would rather be thought of as a coxcomb than reveal his true intentions towards Jane Fairfax.

This 'touch of anarchy in an organized world' is ultimately regulated.[41] Emma rejects the disingenuous Mr Elton and the flirtatious Frank Churchill, accepting instead a revived chivalry that considers the wider well-being of the community. However, it should be remembered that, while the reader echoes Mrs Weston's feelings of estrangement from Frank when she declares 'I thought I knew him' (p. 387), it is the anti-hero's energy and charm that unsettles Highbury long enough for the hero and heroine to entertain the desirability of their own union. Knightley's hostility towards Frank's 'unmanly' conduct throughout the novel disturbs his own equanimity and exposes his attachment to the heroine. In judging his perceived rival to be guilty of a dereliction of duty, Knightley reaffirms his own status as a gentleman.[42] Yet the force of feeling conveyed by the exclamation 'His letters disgust me', followed by a penetrating critique of his handwriting, leads Emma to believe that his view of Frank 'was unworthy the real liberality of mind which she was always used to acknowledge in him' (pp. 166, 168). Knightley's rebukes are startlingly hot-tempered, as he openly states: 'He is a disgrace to the name of man' (p. 414). His romantic declaration to Emma, 'in a tone of such sincere, decided, intelligible tenderness', is an example of monitored desire; and yet, at the same time, he makes little effort to suppress his outrage at Frank's irresponsible behaviour – 'Abominable scoundrel!' (pp. 417, 413). Knightley's uncharacteristic antipathy to Frank Churchill departs from and complicates an assumed portrait of 'the fully civilized man'.[43]

On the one hand, 'Mr Knightley represents a new ideal of gentle-manliness that incorporates elements of the chivalric ideal', as Michèle Cohen argues.[44] On the other hand, *Emma* contests the notion of a 'pattern' gentleman and contemporary standards of male behaviour. Knightley fails to master his volatile behaviour towards Frank Churchill and, on occasion, towards Emma too. He is cutting, brutal even, when remonstrating with the heroine at Box Hill. Albeit hard for the heroine to hear, it is this forcefulness that energises his character and renders him the antithesis of the effeminate Frank Churchill and the tediously sentimental Mr Woodhouse. The hero is in a notable state of confusion, as is the heroine, with regards to his own feelings about and attraction to her, moreover.[45] It is in these moments of self-doubt, the times when he vacillates or stumbles, that the hero is most compelling. Austen observes and disrupts the gendered certainties of Samuel Richardson, responding to as well as rewriting narratives of masculinity. As Claudia Johnson contends, '... far from embodying fixed or at the very least commonly shared notions of masculinity, there is nothing in Scott, Burney, More, Burke, Radcliffe, or Edgeworth remotely like him' (*Equivocal Beings*, p. 201). *Emma*'s Mr Knightley is therefore positioned at a crossroads; he is governed by nationalistic ideals of chivalry and yet he is atypical when compared with the leading men of the age. While it is Knightley who stands firm against the contrived gallantry and *politesse* of other suitors, it is also Knightley who puts forward the claims of Robert Martin, an educated local farmer, and challenges Emma's outmoded notions of the gentleman. Austen's most ostensibly conservative hero, in his civic defence of Hartfield as a stronghold of managed manhood, is able to adapt to and promote a more egalitarian model of masculinity. In Knightley, then, Austen offers a progressive male protagonist whose outlook is rooted in but not determined by tradition – a description that could equally apply to the Byronic hero.

IV

Austen and Byron inherited and reworked eighteenth-century ideals of manhood at a time when the figure of the hero was in flux.
Renegotiating gender is in the foreground of Austen's prose and Byron's
poetry, whether in a domestic or a dramatic setting, and both writers
made significant and lasting impressions on emerging models of masculinity in the nineteenth century. Both writers offer insightful commentaries on cultural trends and cut their respective literary teeth on
critical rewritings and parody. The figure of the Gothic villain is part of
this shared literary landscape; his lurid misdeeds are appropriated and
adapted to varying degrees in Byron's and Austen's fiction. Mario Praz,
in his landmark study *The Romantic Agony*, sees the Gothic novel as a
key stage in the transformation of Milton's antagonist, Satan, into the
Byronic hero. He goes as far as to say that Byron's rebels border on a
'slavish imitation' of Ann Radcliffe.[46] Byron's poetry undoubtedly demonstrates a debt to Radcliffe's best-selling Gothic romances, drawing on
the *chiaroscuro* of her villains for his poetry and the theatrical staging
of his poetic personae, yet Praz makes no effort to disentangle the man
from the myth. Byron himself is cast, to dramatic effect, as a flamboyant
Gothic villain whose life was a 'gloomy tragedy' and whose marriage
was a 'moral torture-chamber' (*Romantic Agony*, p. 76). Peter L. Thorslev,
in his influential study of the Byronic hero's origins and evolution,
readily identifies borrowings from Radcliffe's novels in Byron's most
popular poems. Byron's heroes were influenced by the many Gothic
melodramas he would have read when serving on the committee to
select plays for Drury Lane.[47] His familiarity with Gothic drama, and the
increasingly sympathetic portrayal of the Gothic villain on stage, can
be felt in *Childe Harold's Pilgrimage*, the Oriental Tales and, most notably, in *Manfred*. With Manfred, Byron moves his audience well beyond
the recognisable features of the remorseful Gothic villain to a dramatic
exploration of lyric suffering and melancholy sensibilities. Although the
existential angst of Byron's protagonist may seem to have little or no
place in Austen's world, both authors are concerned with the subjective
interiority behind Gothic exteriors.

Austen was, as David Nokes suggests, an 'avid connoisseur of Gothic
shockers' (p. 104), and visited the theatre to see, amongst other popular
plays of the period, a pantomime, *Don Juan; or, the Libertine Destroyed*
(based on Thomas Shadwell's play *The Libertine*). She wrote, in a letter of 15–16 September 1813, that her young relatives 'revelled last
night in Don Juan, whom we left in hell at half-past eleven.—We

had Scaramouch & a Ghost—and were delighted'. Although a note of personal reserve is added – her own 'delight was very tranquil' – she declares, striking a unpredictably Byronic chord, 'I must say that I have seen nobody on the stage who has been a more interesting Character than that compound of Cruelty & Lust'. Austen's comments on this burlesque are instructive; her penchant for the Gothic is both appreciative of macabre melodrama and alert to the genre's potential for parody and self-parody. The heroine of *Northanger Abbey*, Catherine Morland, is, like her author, a voracious reader of sensational fiction. But her delight in 'horrid' novels leads to a misreading of character and situations, and a misuse of language: a lamp is not just a lamp – it is a 'treacherous lamp' (p. 139).[48] Austen's critical take on 'the trash with which the press now groans' is reinforced through the connection made between Isabella Thorpe's familiarity with generic 'shockers' and her flirtatious conduct; it is also derided as a widely-held misconception, with heroines penned by 'sister author[s]' called upon to protect one another (pp. 23, 81). The target of Austen's famous 'defence of the novel' passage is not so much pulp fiction as the more general prejudice against novels and the gendering of genre.[49] The disdain of the male critic is lampooned in the character of John Thorpe whose sneer – 'Novels are all so full of nonsense and stuff' (p. 32) – is hypocritical (as he has recently read *The Monk*), ignorant (he does not know who has written *The Mysteries of Udolpho*), and indiscriminate (undeterred by this blunder, he quickly castigates 'that other stupid book', Fanny Burney's *Camilla*). Henry Tilney's condemnation of those who refrain from reading novels, as 'intolerably stupid' (p. 77), further exposes John Thorpe's hasty and ill-informed opinions. Singled out, albeit sardonically, as the 'hero' of the novel, Tilney admits to enjoying Radcliffe's fiction as much as women readers while also retaining a judicious superiority by correcting Catherine's 'loose' diction.[50] Tilney's 'pleasure in a *good* novel' (p. 77, added emphasis) achieves Austen's aim of disengaging the reader from a predictable response to popular fiction.

Henry Tilney's cautious regard for Catherine's reading habits is complicated further when she mistakes his father, General Tilney, for a Radcliffean Montoni. Although the hero's father may not be the stage villain that our heroine imagines, Austen allows that 'in suspecting General Tilney of either murdering or shutting up his wife, she [Catherine] had scarcely sinned against his character, or magnified his cruelty' (p. 183). What have previously been regarded as novelettish fears are partially vindicated when the heroine is unceremoniously turned out of the Abbey. The boundaries between unrestrained romanticism (misreading) and realism (reading aright) become blurred when, as Waldo S. Glock observes, 'General Tilney's cruel dismissal [...] is neither caused by nor related to her extravagant misconception of him'.[51] Catherine is neither the naïve heroine that the novel's opening satirises nor the anti-heroine of her deflated daydreams; the Abbey is neither the scene of 'barbarous proceedings' nor the English sanctuary that Henry defends (p. 138). Her now legitimate night terrors confirm a debt to Radcliffe's psychologised Gothic and her so-called 'explained' supernatural. The following description of Emily St. Aubert, the heroine of *The Mysteries of Udolpho* (1794), could equally describe Catherine at Northanger Abbey, as she tries to quell her fears, or the chastened Marianne Dashwood in *Sense and Sensibility*, as she reflects on her former conduct. Both Radcliffe and Austen explore the complex terrain of an unregulated romantic imagination (and the mental duress suffered in consequence), with Emily here torn between reason and irrationality, sense and sensibility:

> She shuddered at the recollection, which confirmed her fears, and determined not to meet him [Barnadine, the porter] on the terrace. Soon after, she was inclined to consider these suspicions as the extravagant exaggerations of a timid and harassed mind, and could not believe Montoni liable to such preposterous depravity as that of destroying, from one motive, his wife and her niece. She blamed herself for suffering her romantic imagination to carry her so far beyond the bounds of probability, and determined to endeavour to check its rapid flights, lest they should sometimes extend into madness.[52]

It is, however, the exercise of reason that leads the heroine into Barnadine's trap, as he incarcerates her in a torture chamber with a decomposing corpse and then attempts to have her abducted. As the heroine of *Udolpho* realises, 'All the horrid apprehensions, that had lately assailed her, returned at this instant with redoubled force, and no longer appeared like the exaggerations of a timid spirit, but seemed to have been sent to warn her of her fate' (p. 347). For Radcliffe's Emily, as for Austen's Catherine, it is terror that speaks a truth inconceivable to the rational mind. Exploring the subterranean recesses of the imagination, as facilitated through the reading of Gothic novels, proves crucial for Catherine's progress.

Similarly, the Gothic villain of *Northanger Abbey* draws on a darker psychology that characterises the more innovative works of the genre. As Emily looks upon Montoni, after he has foiled her would-be abductors, 'with a kind of half curious, half terrified look' (p. 351), so Catherine is distracted by a plausibly charismatic tyrant who, like Manfred in *The Castle of Otranto* (1764), might be prepared to take his son's place to secure the attentions of the heroine.[53] General Tilney presents an indeterminate tension between imitation and critique in *Northanger Abbey*, which culminates in the novel's wryly inconclusive closing remark: '... I leave it to be settled by whomsoever it may concern, whether the tendency of this work be altogether to recommend parental tyranny, or reward filial disobedience' (p. 187). Even this explicit narrative interjection does not fully capture the complexity of a novel that is so conscious of itself as fiction and the ways in which fiction constructs or reflects an illusion of reality.[54] Catherine's distress towards the end of the novel arises from a need to read reality imaginatively and *vice versa*, a predicament also encountered by Madeline in Keats's poem 'The Eve of St Agnes', as Beth Lau has observed.[55] Yet neither Catherine nor Madeline are simply duped by romance or awakened by its antithesis. Both heroines, alongside the reader, must adjust to a shifting and amorphous spectrum of vision and experience, the 'painful change' of an uncertain consciousness.[56] Austen, in common with Keats and Radcliffe, cultivates an implied reader of romance who can decode literary dialogues that assimilate, estrange, and debunk. This conflicted critique over the possibilities and pitfalls of the imagination, what Karl Kroeber refers to as 'constructive skepticism', establishes Austen as a Romantic writer engaging with the foremost aesthetic concerns of her day.[57]

V

Fantasy and fiction are prominent features of ITV's recent adaptation of *Northanger Abbey*, directed by Jon Jones and screened as part of a Jane Austen series in 2007.[58] As our heroine approaches the suitably Gothic home of the hero, Henry Tilney makes an arch allusion to its literary source: 'Why don't you imagine the worst thing you can and write your own Gothic romance about it. Northanger Abbey would make a very good title don't you think?' This adaptation, with screenplay by Andrew Davies, is conscious of itself as an Austen adaptation and of the Gothic novel as eminently adaptable. 'Appropriately enough for an adaptation of the most insistently intertextual of all Austen's novels', Lisa Hopkins argues, 'this is indeed a film that is both self-conscious in its own right, and also knowing it is coming after other films'.[59] An ironic sense of artistic licence pervades, as added scenes inspired by Gothic fiction and a *tableaux* based on Henry Fuseli's painting 'The Nightmare' (1782) dramatise the heroine's increasingly explicit fantasies of abduction and bondage. The adaptation is conversant with and creative in exploiting the salacious aspects of the genre while maintaining an Austenian regard for the absurd. Catherine's awakening desires lead her to conflate Henry, a clergyman, with the lustful Ambrosio of Matthew Lewis's *The Monk* (1796), for instance.[60]

The adaptation professes further literary credentials when, during a discussion of the 'horrid' novels (specifically *Udolpho*), references are made to Byron. Byron, in a number of screenplays by Andrew Davies, supplements or supplants allusions to other Romantic writers in the source novel, as will be examined later in this chapter and in succeeding chapters. It is assumed, perhaps, that a twenty-first century audience will be more familiar with Byron than with Radcliffe:

Catherine Morland:	'Is it really very horrid?'
Isabella Thorpe:	'You can't even imagine. But I wouldn't tell you for the world. Well, perhaps one instant to whet your appetite [she whispers in Catherine's ear].'
Catherine:	[startled] 'Can such things really happen?'
Isabella:	'Well, just think of Lord Byron.'
Catherine:	'I have heard that he is very wicked … but I don't know exactly what he's supposed to have done. [Isabella leans in to whisper again; Catherine is even more shocked]. Oh!'
Isabella:	'And, I have heard that he is here, in Bath. Shall we go to the Pump Room and see if we can see him? Perhaps your Mr Tilney will be there too.'
Catherine:	'He's not my Mr Tilney, Isabella. Indeed, you musn't say he is.'
Isabella:	'Isn't he? Well, there's a certain person who'll be very glad to hear that.'
Catherine:	'Who do you mean?'
Isabella:	'Never you mind.'

That Byron should be spoken of as though he were an antagonist in Radcliffe's Gothic novel is apt if anachronistic. *The Mysteries of Udolpho* was published in 1794 and Austen wrote the first draft of *Northanger Abbey* between 1798–99, under the working title *Susan*. By the time Austen's novel was published, in 1818 (or, more precisely, December 1817), Byron had been living in Italy for some time after the breakdown of his marriage to Annabella Milbanke. The grounds for separation remained the subject of overheated and outraged gossip, but he would not have been in Bath or likely to have visited the spa resort. Byron, here, makes fiction seem more 'real' and, conversely, life more sensational, as his scandalous reputation had become as lurid as any Gothic tale. His misdeeds – which, like the exquisite terrors of *Udolpho*, cannot be uttered openly – incite girlish excitement and prompt Isabella's coy remarks about Catherine's suitors. That Byron becomes a shorthand for sexual intrigue and impropriety is made clear in the following scene when Captain Tilney, who will seduce and then discard Isabella, is compared with the notorious poet.

Austen's dialogism in *Northanger Abbey* is channelled on screen through the hero.[61] Henry Tilney complicates Catherine's preconditioned polarisation of 'the real world' and 'the world of stories' by hinting that 'a kind of vampirism' has cursed the ancestral home. This Austenian Gothic, whereby the disturbed psyche supersedes more conventional horrors in both the novel and the adaptation, extends beyond *Northanger Abbey*. General Tilney, who we are told in the adaptation 'drain[ed] the life out of her [his wife] with his coldness and his cruelty', resurfaces in the figure of Sir Walter Elliot, the heroine's father in *Persuasion*. For Darryl Jones, Sir Walter, a 'harbinger of the death of aristocracy', can be read alongside the unnatural bloodsuckers of nineteenth-century fiction (*Jane Austen*, p. 169). These figurative vampires, or social parasites, connect Austen's fiction with the later Romantics and particularly Byron, the blueprint for the aristocratic vampire whose presence still resonates with audiences today. A scene from the start of the 2007 BBC adaptation of *Persuasion*, which will be considered at greater length in Chapter 2, depicts Sir Walter presiding over a ghastly dinner at Kellynch Hall before the family have to vacate the ancestral seat due to insolvency.[62] Furniture shrouded in white sheets, against dark wooden panelling, creates a suitably Gothic setting for Sir Walter and Elizabeth's ostentatious consumption and corrosive disdain for Anne. The greatest threat to the heroine, in both Austen's fiction and the Gothic novel, comes not from an inscrutable villain, but from the neglect and scheming of near relatives. Cruelty in *Persuasion*, as in *Northanger Abbey* (and *Udolpho*), is most biting when familial.

VI

Austen's interactions with Romantic ideals and anxieties, with depth and shadow, are no-where more evident than in another early work, *Sense and Sensibility*, drafted in the mid to late 1790s and published, after revision, in 1811. This novel, and recent adaptations of it, draw together and extend the issues, addressed above, of misreading, masculinity, and an embryonic Byronism that is brought to full term on screen. As Sarah Ailwood contends, 'In *Sense and Sensibility* Jane Austen embarks on the ambitious project of reforming contemporary literary masculinities', educating her characters and her audience to recognise 'their susceptibility to narrative bias, and [...] the generic assumptions about literary masculinities which they bring to the courtship novel'.[63] Marianne Dashwood is a romantic heroine who is well-versed in courtship rituals. She falls in love through the poetry of William Cowper and Walter Scott, a regard for the picturesque, and a rapturous refinement of feeling; and, she nearly dies from her conviction in a soul mate. Marianne's consuming passion for a male projection of her own tastes and desires – 'He must enter into all my feelings; the same books, the same music must charm us both' – and the consequent fever that takes hold when she is disillusioned of her ideal briefly foreshadow Cathy and Heathcliff's immolation in *Wuthering Heights*.[64] Although tragedy is averted in Austen's novel, the 'altered looks' of Marianne, as she appears to Colonel Brandon, with 'the hollow eye, the sickly skin, the posture of reclining weakness' (p. 289), comes close to the description of Emily Brontë's wasted heroine before she dies. Heathcliff can barely bring himself to look at the changed Cathy, with 'white cheek, and a bloodless lip, and scintillating eye', after her 'brain fever'.[65]

Marianne is no Cathy, and Willoughby no Heathcliff, but the darker side of Marianne's romantic fantasies, intuited by her sister when she enquires '... is not there something interesting to you in the flushed cheek, hollow eye, and quick pulse of a fever?' (p. 34), brings her into the company of Keats's knight-at-arms, Shelley's poet-figure in *Alastor*, and Byron's Manfred, among others. It is as though Astarte's simulacrum or the Arab maiden, whose 'voice was like the voice of his own soul',[66] has been conjured up, in male form, to satisfy the heroine's notion of a hero: 'He [Willoughby] was *exactly* formed to engage Marianne's heart' (p. 43, added emphasis). Handsome, animated, and spontaneous, Willoughby is predisposed to act out the role of lover that he readily adopts. Willoughby is 'in character', for Marianne, from their first encounter, when he 'rescues' her, playing a part taken from the pages of a heroic poem or romantic novel. Marianne then perpetuates the Romeo and Juliet solipsism to which she subscribes through her conviction that they have been cruelly driven apart by social forces after Willoughby leaves Devonshire. Marianne is disabused of these falsehoods when 'the hero of [her] favourite story' is unmasked, and her dream romance turns into a Romantic nightmare of deprivation and despair (p. 38). Like Keats's protagonist in 'La Belle Dame sans Merci', Austen's heroine is lulled into a romance plot where love is implied but never stated explicitly. For Marianne, as for the knight, the pain of recollected romance punctuates the dejection of arrested desire and betrayal.

An instrumental moment in how we regard Marianne's relationship with Willoughby occurs about halfway through the novel, when we are told that 'She felt the loss of Willoughby's character yet more heavily than she had felt the loss of his heart' (p. 179). More important than the love she grieves for is the shuddering realisation that reality is not synonymous with fictional romance; after his former behaviour is uncovered, Willoughby must marry for money and settled prospects. This romantic hero proves to be a hard-headed profiteer of women. Romance is found wanting on a deeper textual level, moreover. It is not so much the content as the language of Willoughby's impersonal letter to Marianne that 'proclaimed its writer to be deep in hardened villany' (p. 155). When Willoughby offers an account of his conduct to Elinor later in the novel, he subjects his own stylistic shortcomings to scrutiny:

> Every line [of Marianne's first letter to Willoughby], every word was— in the hackneyed metaphor which their dear writer, were she here, would forbid—a dagger to my heart. To know that Marianne was in town was—in the same language—a thunderbolt.—Thunderbolts and daggers!—what a reproof would she have given me!—her taste, her opinion—I believe they are better known to me than my own,— and I am sure they are dearer. (p. 276)

The 'language of love' is here exposed as empty melodrama. Faltering without Marianne's example to inspire him, Willoughby's recourse to 'hackneyed metaphor' reveals the sort of uninspired mind that the heroine has previously denounced: 'I detest jargon of every kind' (p. 85). And yet the language used by Willoughby recalls the rest of Marianne's speech, when she confesses: '... sometimes I have kept my feelings to myself, because I could find no language to describe them in but what was worn and *hackneyed* out of all sense and meaning' (added emphasis). Marianne, too, suffers from a Romantic anxiety about authenticity. Her paean to Norland, at the end of Chapter 5, while not as trite as Willoughby's platitudes, likewise suffers from mannered, and vaguely embarrassing, exclamations. Marianne's failure to recognise that the man she falls in love with is a cliché – the antithesis of what she holds him to be – speaks volumes about the implied author's views on the contemporaneous cult of sensibility and the figure of the 'romantic' hero.

Marianne is a misreader *par excellence*. She is unable to distinguish Romantic originality from imitation. Her near-fatal flaw, however, is not so much the 'abuses of language' (p. 98) that numerous characters are guilty of in Austen's novel, nor is it even the principles that govern, or fail to govern, her immoderate behaviour; it is, as Elinor identifies, that 'her opinions are *all* romantic' (p. 49, added emphasis). While it is made clear that Marianne is capable of the mental exertion and empathy needed to cultivate a nuanced sensibility, her romantic absolutism breeds an unhealthy self-absorption – 'She [Marianne] expected from other people the same opinions and feelings as her own, and she judged of their motives by the immediate effect of their actions on herself' (p. 170) – which leads her to slight the other suitors in the novel, Edward Ferrars and Colonel Brandon. Although the latter is contrasted against Willoughby throughout the novel – prudence as opposed to indulgence, integrity as opposed to dissimulation etc. – Brandon is not the antithesis of Marianne's first love interest. His often cited 'gravity and reserve' (p. 44) are not as appealing as his rival; and yet his credentials as a romantic hero are confirmed when he relates his lovelorn history. Brandon is afflicted by the melancholy temperament that Marianne affects and then succumbs to, and both descend into 'gloomy dejection' when brooding over sorrows in solitude (p. 179). Whereas Willoughby has only the hollow resemblance of a hero, Brandon is the genuine article – a man scarred by, and yet able to rally from, a tragic past. Brandon's sobering romantic grief enables him to identify with Marianne's broken heart and offer her the passionate constancy she craves.[67]

Edward Ferrars, who is also contrasted unfavourably against Willoughby in the early stages of the novel, is deemed to be a 'second Willoughby' by Marianne when his secret engagement to Lucy Steele comes to light (p. 220). Indeed, Elinor's initial reaction to Edward's concealment – 'Her resentment of such behaviour, her indignation at having been its dupe' (p. 117) – is not far removed from her fiery condemnation of Willoughby's inconstancy, although shorter-lived. The want of occupation that Edward cites as the reason for his youthful dalliance with Lucy concurs with Elinor's supposition that idleness led to Willoughby's seduction of Eliza. Elinor here seeks to rationalise romantic subterfuge by commenting critically on the models of masculinity available to, and endorsed by, the upper classes. There is integrity in Edward honouring his former obligation as well as dishonour to both Lucy and Elinor in his compromised position. Edward's struggle with this secret, his 'self-mortification', generates a comparison with another character in the novel (p. 88). His reserve and his melancholy strike what could be a Byronic note of accord with Brandon. Edward is even allowed 'the rapturous profession of the lover' – an Austenian touch of amused irreverence in the romantic resolution – which directly contradicts Marianne's earlier contention that 'there was [in Edward] a deficiency of all that a lover ought to look and say' (pp. 306, 76). Although Austen presents what appear to be three distinctive 'types' of maleness in *Sense and Sensibility*, these suitors, with their respective flaws and virtues, represent composite characters rather than simplified stereotypes.

It is Willoughby, the character most self-conscious of roles, who is afforded the most significant opportunity to subvert them. While he is all too aware that his former part of lover in the first 'act' of the novel has been recast into that of 'hard-hearted rascal', 'villain', 'scoundrel', and 'blackguard' (pp. 275–8), the recourse to stock characters exposes and challenges the reductive labels that are applied to his behaviour and actions. It is when Willoughby is most candid about his limiting social performances, finally 'forced to play the happy lover to another woman' (p. 277), that Elinor is most compassionate about his shortcomings. The heroine is so affected by what she takes to be his confession, during which he vacillates between self-derision and defensiveness, that her own language is permeated by his histrionics – 'cruel neglect', 'wanton cruelty', 'irreparable injury' – in a chapter framed by the Gothic touch of Elinor's 'look of horror at the sight of him' (pp. 273, 280, 269). It is Willoughby who triggers an uncharacteristic emotional confusion in the heroine. Elinor's carefully monitored equanimity remains 'too much oppressed by a croud [sic] of ideas', and her esteemed sense is tested: 'She felt that his influence over her mind was heightened by circumstances which ought not in reason to have weight' (p. 283). Her sympathetic response to 'poor Willoughby' (p. 284), a man she had come to regard as a serial womaniser, is one of the most intriguing aspects of the novel. Why is 'his influence over her mind' so great (p. 283)? Why does the impression he leaves on Elinor, and on the novel in general, have such a lasting effect? The most ready answer is that Elinor is drawn to a handsome man professing a 'still ardent love' that is stymied by social obligations and expectations, bringing her closer, in effect, to Marianne's earlier belief in Willoughby (p. 283). It could be argued, in addition, that the painful ambivalence Elinor negotiates as a result of her encounter with Willoughby fuels the 'spontaneous overflow of powerful feelings' in the dénouement when she is 'everything by turns but tranquil' on hearing that Edward is still unmarried (p. 308).[68]

In other words, Elinor develops an emotional maturity, a lyric intensity even, not through her own love interest, but through her proximity to another man and her pity at his predicament. The heroine's shift on the spectrum of romantic sensibility may not be as dramatic as her sister's but it is no less profound.

Elinor's increased empathy with Willoughby, while arguably heroic itself in some respects, is related to the recurring, and proto-Byronic, theme of social role-play in the novel. As Willoughby displays a greater dramatic range, with a theatrical repertoire that extends from lover and libertine to villain, so Elinor responds by attributing a greater 'depth' of character to him. It is through an appreciation of the pressures of his position as an eligible yet dependent bachelor that she comes to an understanding of the person circumscribed by personae, a Byronic coalescence of identities. In a novel where private happiness is often dictated by public appearances, Elinor, too, is adept at playing parts. She has mastered the artful 'post of civility which she had assigned herself', and is capable of 'telling lies when politeness required it' (pp. 135, 104). Austen makes clear that Elinor 'joyfully profited' from her discretion when she finally receives a proposal of marriage from Edward (p. 122). Her happiness is deserved, after shouldering the burden of familial responsibility, and yet the dim shadow of dissimulation descends. Mrs Jennings detects a slyness in Elinor which, although only half-serious, is echoed in Mrs Dashwood's recognition, towards the end of the novel, that 'she had erred in relying on Elinor's representation of herself [...]. She found that she had been misled by the careful, the considerate attention of her daughter' (p. 301). The mother has misread her daughter, as she does Willoughby, and a conflicted sense of admiration and estrangement ensues. It is Elinor's convincing 'representation of herself', divulging little beyond a customary reserve, that distances her from intimate family members and generates her 'pang for Willoughby' (p. 288), a fellow player on the social stage.

VII

Both recent screen adaptations of *Sense and Sensibility* re-orchestrate the dynamics of romance and role-play in Austen's novel. In the 1995 film version, with screenplay by Emma Thompson and directed by Ang Lee, Marianne's credentials as a romantic heroine are established from the opening scenes as she indulges in the melancholy melody of 'Weep You No More Sad Fountains'.[69] An even greater sense of irony accompanies the scene in which Greg Wise's Willoughby, astride his white horse, gallops through the rain to rescue Kate Winslet's Marianne. Where the scene in Austen's novel gestures towards the kind of generic device parodied in her 'Plan of a Novel' – '[he] took her up in his arms without farther delay [...] and quitted not his hold' (p. 37) – screen audiences tended to respond with awkward laughter to the filmic formula of a hero on his charger and a damsel in distress, as we are directed from Willoughby taking liberties with Marianne's ankle to her genuinely frightened sister, Margaret. Once Winslet's Marianne is safely deposited on the sofa at Barton Cottage, Wise's Willoughby 'moves smoothly', as Penny Gay argues, 'into the exaggeratedly polite behavior of the young courting gentleman'; his 'jejune theatrical gesture[s]', combined with his gallant good looks, reinforce the interpretation, outlined in Part VI above, of Willoughby as a charming pretender.[70]

It is the less gregarious male characters in *Sense and Sensibility* that undergo the most significant transformation on screen. According to Cheryl L. Nixon, viewers are treated to 'extra Edward and extra Brandon', in an effort to rectify what is perceived as underrepresentation in the original novel and to enhance their desirability with a modern audience, a comment that could as easily apply to Andrew Davies's screenplay for the 2008 television series of *Sense and Sensibility*.[71] Alan Rickman's performance as Colonel Brandon in the 1995 film version undoubtedly makes Austen's character a more attractive prospect for Kate Winslet's Marianne, especially when we see him galloping at speed to bring Mrs Dashwood to what may be her dying daughter. In his anguish at Marianne's illness, and his dashing yet dishevelled appearance, this Brandon is, as Gay asserts, 'transmogrified into the image of the romantic Byronic hero' (*'Sense and Sensibility* in a Postfeminist World', p. 98). The concern expressed by critics at Brandon's enhanced courtship profile is his consequent proximity to Willoughby. Marianne basically exchanges one romantic hero for another according to this interpretation. Yet it is not altogether accurate to state that Rickman's Brandon is 'remade as a character of sensibility', or that 'sensibility has won its battle', when behavioural 'types' rooted in emotional restraint or excess are eroded within both the novel and the adaptation (Nixon, 'Balancing the Courtship Hero', pp. 27, 41). Thompson amplifies what Marianne comes to realise; the experienced, benevolent gentleman is, in fact, more 'manly' than the unreliable rake.[72] It is to Thompson's credit, and in keeping with Austen's rehumanisation of the romantic hero, that Brandon's sense of civic responsibility, combined with emphatic feeling, emerges as a genuinely attractive prospect in the film of *Sense and Sensibility*.

Thompson should also be credited for the screen time devoted to reading verse aloud. Poetry offers as subtle a subtext for the involved inter-relationships between the characters in this film as it does in Austen's novel.[73] Thompson retains a reference to William Cowper, a firm favourite with Austen and with Marianne, despite his relative obscurity for a modern audience. The concluding stanza from his poem 'The Castaway' (1799) is recited by both Edward Ferrars and Marianne; the lines speak to the latter's penchant for romantic despair and prefigure her soon-to-be outcast state. Marianne's reading of Hartley Coleridge's 1833 sonnet VII, 'Is love a fancy, or a feeling? No,/ It is immortal as immaculate Truth', is another interesting intertext in the film, chosen to emphasise this character's commitment to steadfast love, even though the date means that Austen could not have known the poem. By contrast, Willoughby's recital of Shakespeare's sonnet 116, 'Let me not to the marriage of true minds/ Admit impediments', is more predictable. Willoughby's misreading of line 6, from a copy of pocket sonnets, offers an early indication of his untrustworthy conduct, as Arthur F. Marotti and Marcelle Freiman observe:

> The Dashwoods value fine recitation and appreciate poetry, while Willoughby's emotional inattentiveness is signified by his inability to recognise the line's missing stress when he substitutes 'storms' for the correct 'tempests' in the poem. The irony is enhanced by Willoughby's proffered gift of a miniature pocket volume of Shakespeare's Sonnets to Marianne, the tiny size of which unwittingly predicts his affection's ultimately minor stature.[74]

Colonel Brandon similarly woos Marianne with Renaissance poetry; but his tender reading of lines from Edmund Spenser's *The Faerie Queene* conveys a discerning intellect and a refined romantic understatement. Poetry is employed on screen to convey Mrs Dashwood's sentiment that 'his [Brandon's] disposition, I am well convinced, is *exactly* the very one to make your sister happy', and to voice the range of romantic temperaments in Austen's novel (p. 287, added emphasis).

Romantic intertexts are equally, if not more, instructive in the 2008 BBC series of *Sense and Sensibility*.[75] Andrew Davies's screenplay, as with his adaptation of *Northanger Abbey* (discussed in Part V), makes frequent reference to Romantic writers, generating a sense of the contemporary cultural climate in which Austen wrote and offering a revealing commentary on her main characters. Charity Wakefield's Marianne is confirmed, in the first episode, as 'very romantic', and she finds her poetry partner in Dominic Cooper's Willoughby (whose name even has a 'poetic ring' for the heroine). Their mutual passion is confirmed not through Shakespeare or Spenser, but through Byron. The arbiters of Romantic sensibility that are cited in Austen's novel, Cowper and Scott, are replaced on screen when Willoughby recites the opening stanza of 'So, we'll go no more a roving'.

Willoughby:	'... he [Pope] is too rational for me. More to be admired than loved.'
Marianne:	'That is just what I think.'
Willoughby:	'Do you know Lord Byron?'
Marianne:	'No ... I have heard of him.'

Willoughby:	'"So, we'll go no more a roving
	    So late into the night,
	Though the heart be still as loving,
	    And the moon be still as bright."[76]
	He is a true romantic.'

Marianne:	'That is just the sort of thing I like.'
Willoughby:	'And I.'

The Byron poem selected is predictable – it is one of his best-known lyric poems – and ambiguous. As it mourns the passing of romantic youth, the poem may speak to Willoughby's resolve to reform his conduct, on meeting Marianne, and yet it also predicts his later pragmatism. The reading of Byron in this scene signals both Willoughby as an archetypal seducer and his desire to take refuge from performing what Matthew Arnold referred to as Byron's 'theatrical personage'.[77] The poem proceeds,

> For the sword outwears its sheath,
>   And the soul wears out the breast,
> And the heart must pause to breathe,
>   And love itself have rest. (ll. 5–8)

It nonetheless becomes clear that Willoughby's flamboyant romanticism is as cynical as Marianne's raptures are naïve. Poetry designed to outwardly display and inwardly harmonise the couple's compatibility discloses the telling distance that will lead to their estrangement; that Marianne does not know Byron's poem indicates her romantic innocence in direct contrast to his experience.

Although the contrast between Dominic Cooper's Willoughby and David Morrissey's Brandon is incisive in this adaptation, their characters do not occupy opposing ends on a spectrum of Romantic masculinity. Rather, Brandon reveals another face of the Byronic hero. After hearing Willoughby's pretensions to the Byronic, with his recital of 'So, we'll go no more a roving', the first episode concludes with Brandon leaving Barton Cottage, a lone figure looking back longingly on what he is excluded from. Davies draws on Austen's revisionary reading of sensibility, as well as her individuated male characters, to distinguish between Byronic affectation and the authentically Byronic. As Marianne comes to recognise, Willoughby amounts to little more than a petulant playboy whose actions are secretive, whereas Brandon is a 'true' romantic. The main difference between the characterisation of Colonel Brandon in the 1995 and 2008 screen versions of *Sense and Sensibility* is that where Rickman's wounded Byronic despair is subdued for most of the film, Morrissey's Byronic brooding is heated. Morrissey's Brandon appears savage in a duel with Cooper's Willoughby, only just holding back from fatally wounding his rival, and he can barely contain his vitriol when relating the story of Willoughby as the seducer of his ward. Impulsive and intense, this Brandon 'saves' Marianne twice, catching her after she faints when snubbed by Willoughby in London and later carrying her back to Cleveland in a dramatic scene that borrows from the 1995 film. Although such acts afford his character more screen time, Morrissey's Brandon remains, to some extent, the 'mystery' man of Austen's novel, engaging the viewer's interest and intensifying his Byronic intrigue.[78] In an involved scene where Brandon offers a commentary on Marianne's piano playing, she remains puzzled as to whether he is being evasive or critical. Marianne does not know how to 'read' Brandon, a response shared by both *Pride and Prejudice*'s Elizabeth Bennet and *Persuasion*'s Anne Elliot with regard to their respective romantic partners, as will be discussed in the next chapter.

Davies's high romantic gloss, what Kate Harwood refers to as his 'fairydust', does not rely solely on the conventions and stereotypes that Austen takes pains to deconstruct.[79] Willoughby, in the 2008 adaptation, is framed as the 'libertine', from a racy opening sequence that reveals what we later understand to be his seduction and abandonment of Eliza. And yet Davies's trademark sexualisation of Austen's fiction does not confine Willoughby's character to a sentimental villain. Even Marianne is prepared to acknowledge the complex individual behind the façade of idealised or immoral manhood: 'I think he deceived himself as well. He wanted to believe in his own fine words, as I did'. Further depths of character are glimpsed when Willoughby's poetic repertoire extends to Wordsworth's 'Tintern Abbey', a poem that William

Deresiewicz argues laid hold of Austen's imagination. The lines spoken aloud suggest, as with the extract from Byron's poem 'So, we'll go no more a roving', a longing to appreciate and even love something beyond the immediate pleasures of self-gratification. This manifold sense of self, attuned to the pervasive spirit of nature, is also awake to the pathos of human suffering:

> For I have learned
> To look on Nature not as in the hour
> Of thoughtless youth, but hearing oftentimes
> The still, sad music of humanity,
> Nor harsh, nor grating, though of ample power
> To chasten and subdue. And I have felt
> A presence that disturbs me with the joy
> Of elevated thoughts, a sense sublime
> Of something far more deeply interfused,
> Whose dwelling is the light of setting suns,
> And the round ocean, and the living air,[80]

That these excitable lovers are affected by a 'solemn-thoughted idyl', as Elizabeth Barrett Browning would later describe Wordsworth's poetry, gestures towards the 'veined humanity' of *Sense and Sensibility*.[81] The most apparently self-absorbed characters in Austen's novel have the potential for 'chastening thoughtfulness'.

Something of a Wordsworthian spirit is discernible in Elinor's character too. This distinctive poetic timbre has the effect of enmeshing Elinor's sense of the romantic, which treasures the affectionate gift of a book of flowers given to her by Edward, with Willoughby's ostentatious and impractical gift of a horse named Queen Mab for Marianne. It is Hattie Morahan's Elinor who hides in the privacy of caves to give relief to her pent-up feelings and who experiences the greatest joy at the marriage proposal she receives. Indeed, Morahan's portrayal of Elinor in Davies's adaptation brings her character into close proximity with *Persuasion*'s Anne Elliot. The pervasive sense of a romantic subtext and of 'elevated thoughts', with Elinor's eyes fixed longingly on the prospect of the sea, strengthens the ruminative mood that characterises both heroines.

This evolving and enigmatic romanticism is reinforced through the use of setting in the 2008 BBC adaptation of *Sense and Sensibility*. Barton Cottage, battered by waves on the north Devon coast, acts as a barometer for its inhabitants. Marianne's exclamation at the prospect of her new home – 'Oh, mama, how romantic' – indicates a youthful exuberance that overlooks the exposed, inclement, and isolated position. Unseasoned sensibility cannot conceive of everyday inconvenience. Davies's commentary on the choice of location, 'this tiny little windswept cottage in the full force of the Atlantic gales', emblematises Marianne's precarious romantic spirit as she is buffeted by the unremitting sea of social pressures. Yet any division between romance and reality melts as the landscape is becalmed by a serene beauty. This remote cottage, itself synonymous with the Romantic, offers an architectural equivalent for Austen's novel, where sense and sensibility are housed together, 'etymological *relatives* rather than linguistic *strangers*'.[82] This does not mean that Austen or screen adaptations of her novels uncritically incorporate cultural trends. On the contrary, as Jocelyn Harris contends, 'the very origins of Jane Austen's creativity lie in her allusiveness, her confident, even cheerful intertextuality with other authors' ('Austen and the Burden of the [Male] Past', p. 88). Her regard for what would come to be known as Romanticism may be as fractious and as probing as it is 'cheerful', and yet her intertextual range reaches increasingly towards, and is bound up with, the aesthetic concerns and reputations of Romantic writers. As I have begun to explore in this chapter, and will address further in the next, Byron, and the Byronic hero in particular, emerges as a pivotal figure in these literary and filmic dialogues.

2
Jane Austen's Byronic Heroes II:
Persuasion and *Pride and Prejudice*

I

Persuasion (1818) is, like *Northanger Abbey* (1818) and *Sense and Sensibility* (1811) before it, concerned with misreading and masculinity. It is also, above Austen's other novels, conversant with the literary scene of the day. As Janet Todd and Antje Blank explain,

> In the years just prior to her death, then, Jane Austen showed herself more open to her immediate historical and literary moment than at any other period of her life. [...] But only in *Persuasion* does she interact profoundly with the major writers of her present moment, with the poets Byron, Southey, the later Crabbe and Scott, with the political prose of Helen Maria Williams, and with the latest novels of Scott, Burney, Hawkins and Edgeworth.[1]

Austen's dialogues with a groundswell of British Romantic writers are given further moment by the specific time frame of the novel. By setting the events of *Persuasion* from mid-1814 to early 1815, the debates about Byron and Scott that take place during the central episode in Lyme speak to the public appetite for 'heroic' poems. Austen recognised that her readership now came to her from Byron and Scott, as Marilyn Butler has noted, and she sought to establish herself as part of a like-minded reading community.[2] More specifically, Austen records, with something akin to nostalgia, a shift in cultural taste from Scott's poems to Byron's (it is the astounding success of Byron's Oriental Tales that is contemporary with the novel's setting; Scott had already turned his hand to prose with the publication of *Waverley* in 1814). Parts I and II of this chapter examine the literary context of Austen's most

recognisably 'Romantic' novel and its related screen adaptations, focus-
ing specifically on allusions to Byron, his poetry, and his protagonists.
Parts III and IV of this chapter consider *Pride and Prejudice*'s (1813) Mr
Darcy as an embryonic Romantic anti-hero. What I take to be the nas-
cent Byronic inflections in Austen's male protagonist are magnified on
screen to great popular acclaim. The Byronic Darcy that defined the
1995 BBC series of *Pride and Prejudice* was largely responsible for, and
remains a major presence in, an Austen revival that shows little sign of
abating.[3] This late twentieth-century incarnation of the Byronic hero
precipitated, in part, an on-screen bonanza of period dramas, many of
which were based on the novels of nineteenth-century women writers.

On the face of it, Byron's presence in *Persuasion* is anything but
positive. The references to his poetry are invariably cited as evidence of
Austen's disdain for all things Byronic. So strong seem Austen's objections to Byron's poetry, or more precisely the 'impassioned descriptions
of hopeless agony' that Captain Benwick takes solace in, that they
should come with a health warning.[4] The heroine, Anne Elliot, pre-
scribes, in the course of her conversations with Captain Benwick, 'a
larger allowance of prose [...] to rouse and fortify the mind'. The issue of
genre seems somewhat forced here, however; no specific prose texts are
named – in contrast to the best-selling romances of Byron and Scott –
and Anne's remedy 'takes on something of the character of minimum
daily requirements for moral nutrition', according to Susan Allen Ford.[5]
Austen is not being entirely straight-faced about her heroine's earnest
proposal or Benwick's ready acceptance of a reading list with curative
properties. Nevertheless, subsequent discussions about the relative merits
of Byron and Scott occur immediately before Louisa Musgrove's almost
fatal fall on the harbour wall at Lyme. So seamless are these events that
John Halperin views the accident as 'the fruit of excessive romanticism'.[6]
Certainly, Louisa's fall is the outcome of a wilful delight in sensation that
is correlated with Benwick's indulgence in Romantic poetry.

The accident functions as a symbolic punishment for Louisa's head-
strong high spirits, recalling Marianne's spontaneity, breakdown, and
subsequently subdued disposition in *Sense and Sensibility*. And yet
romantic feelings and language are probed rather than purged by this
incident. The manner with which Louisa's accident is reported, in
stylistic terms, veers between the declarative – 'There was no wound,
no blood, no visible bruise' – and hyperbole punctuated by exclamation marks (p. 102). The scene is alarming, to judge from Anne's quick
response, and also absurd, with Henrietta's swoon, Wentworth's 'bit-
terest agony', and Mary's 'hysterical agitations'. Austen's near-tragic

comedy is captured in the reaction of the locals who have gathered round '... to be useful if wanted, at any rate, to enjoy the sight of a dead young lady, nay, two dead young ladies, for it proved twice as fine as the first report' (p. 103). Patricia C. Brückmann reads this scene through the lens of Byron's poem, *The Corsair*, published (and read by Austen) in the same year as her novel is set (1814), arguing that while 'the scene has as much potential domestic tragedy as the Byron it echoes [...] a flicker of comedy hovers even over Byron'.[7] Austen is not reading against but with the Byronic grain when she combines the agitation of those involved with those who witness the event as bemused bystanders. Both Austen's prose and Byron's poetry invest in a subtly dualistic perspective of intimacy and critical detachment, oftentimes affecting humour and pathos from moments of personal crisis, a technique that Mikhail Bakhtin would later refer to as the 'double-accented, double-styled *hybrid construction*'.[8]

A more pressing concern with regards to intertextual relations in *Persuasion* emerges if we accept the standard verdict that Captain Benwick is a defective reader. If we misread Benwick as an uncomplicated critique of Byronic melancholy, how can we then account for Louisa's alliance with him – a man who woos his bride with the same literary diet of 'richness' and 'wretchedness' that supposedly infected the atmosphere at Lyme (p. 94)? Benwick's reading marks him out, not as an ignorant John Thorpe in *Northanger Abbey*, but as a 'clever man' (p. 172). Whereas the heroine of *Sanditon* – the unfinished novel Austen worked on after *Persuasion* – scoffs at Sir Edward Denham, the would-be hero, with his affected mannerisms and ostentatious misquotations, Benwick secures the good opinion and sympathy of Anne Elliot. It could be argued that with his investment in the emotional drama of the villain-hero and his 'looks of very gallant despair', Sir Edward is a 'silly' and 'un-intelligible' reprise of Benwick.[9] However, although he may over-indulge in sentimental novels, Sir Edward is notably schooled in eighteenth- rather than nineteenth-century fiction. Austen's most quixotic misreader is a seasoned seducer, 'quite in the line of the Lovelaces' (p. 328), bypassing the Byronic in revisiting Richardson's anti-hero.[10] In *Persuasion*, it is Benwick's idols, Byron and Scott, who are singled out as 'first-rate poets' (p. 94) in an admiring critique of contemporary literature that anticipates William Hazlitt's declaration, in *The Spirit of the Age* (1825), that 'Lord Byron and Sir Walter Scott are among writers now living the two, who would carry away a majority of suffrages as the greatest geniuses of the age'.[11] Those who do not care for poetry are considered to be, as Henry Tilney states in *Northanger Abbey*, 'intolerably stupid' (p. 77) (Anne's elder sister, Elizabeth, only reveals her ignorance by exclaiming, 'I really cannot be plaguing myself for ever with all the new poems', p. 202).[12] The Romantic poetry Benwick reads to Louisa assuages rather than heightens her nervous condition after the fall. And, before the accident, Benwick's 'melancholy air' shines a spotlight on the heroine's own despondency (p. 91). His apparently inconsolable gloom, cultivated through contemporary poetry, draws attention to a fellow sufferer whose Byronic torment will outlive his own. This kinship of distinctively Romantic feelings deepens and overtakes the exchanges about literary tastes and fandom.

Benwick and his union with Louisa remain topics of conversation beyond the episode in Lyme. As Lady Russell declares a 'curiosity to see the person who can give occasion to such directly opposite notions' (p. 124), so Benwick's relationship with Louisa prompts consternation. Captain Wentworth questions the compatibility of the couple, given Benwick's highbrow pastimes, and yet this second love sparks the debate that reunites the hero and heroine. Romantic sensibilities may precipitate Louisa's fall, but they also save her, aiding her recuperation and promoting the happy union of not one but two couples. The love that blossoms between Benwick and Louisa is learned through poetry and yet remains unschooled, 'a perfectly spontaneous, untaught feeling' (p. 172). Anne, likewise, 'learned romance as she grew older', which, we are told, is 'the natural sequel of an unnatural beginning' (p. 29). This Wordsworthian sense of an organic education checks the assumption that the Romantic poets are confined to a cameo role in *Persuasion*. Rather, the romances of Byron and Scott are instructive for Anne's, as well as our own, reading of romance. Austen, through Anne, rewrites the fortunes of her earlier female characters, such as Charlotte Lucas, who, at the age of twenty-seven (the same age as Anne), feels compelled to make a loveless match. 'But', as Nina Auerbach cautions, 'the point is not simply that Jane Austen has discarded an ethic of prudence and repression for an ethic of emotional release: she has shifted the axis of her created world'.[13]

What John Wiltshire refers to as *Persuasion*'s 'plaiting together of different strands of response' can be traced in a paragraph that prefaces the episode in Lyme.[14]

After securing accommodations, and ordering a dinner at one of the inns, the next thing to be done was unquestionably to walk directly down to the sea. They were come too late in the year for any amusement or variety which Lyme, as a public place, might offer; the rooms were shut up, the lodgers almost all gone, scarcely any family but of the residents left—and, as there is nothing to admire in the buildings themselves, the remarkable situation of the town, the principal street almost hurrying into the water, the walk to the Cobb, skirting round the pleasant little bay, which in the season is animated with bathing machines and company, the Cobb itself, its old wonders and new improvements, with the very beautiful line of cliffs stretching out to the east of the town, are what the stranger's eye will seek; and a very strange stranger it must be, who does not see charms in the immediate environs of Lyme, to make him wish to know it better. The scenes in its neighbourhood, Charmouth, with its high grounds and extensive sweeps of country, and still more its sweet retired bay, backed by dark cliffs, where fragments of low rock among the sands make it the happiest spot for watching the flow of the tide, for sitting in unwearied contemplation;—the woody varieties of the cheerful village of Up Lyme, and, above all, Pinny, with its green chasms between romantic rocks, where the scattered forest trees and orchards of luxuriant growth declare that many a generation must have passed away since the first partial falling of the cliff prepared the ground for such a state, where a scene so wonderful and so lovely is exhibited, as may more than equal any of the resembling scenes of the far-famed Isle of Wight: these places must be visited, and visited again, to make the worth of Lyme understood. (p. 89)

The passage begins with the quotidian concerns of accommodation and dinner, a hangover from the 'rationally considered' plans that prevail over the 'first heedless scheme' for the visit (p. 88). The long sentence that follows then takes the reader from a sense of peevish belatedness, in being at a seaside resort out-of-season, to a modest appreciation of the 'immediate environs of Lyme'. As the geographical compass broadens and diversifies, to take in the 'high grounds and extensive sweeps of country' around Charmouth, so too does the perspective; the sightseer's itinerary gives way to an intrepid and heady rush of pleasure, the climax of which is Pinny, 'with its green chasms between romantic rocks'.[15] The passage is more than a travel guide to Lyme and its surroundings; it is a guide for how to negotiate the events that will unfold in this location. Indeed, the concluding remark could be rewritten as: 'this passage must be read, and read again, to make the worth of Lyme understood'. It is as if Austen is saying that the traveller must be prepared for vexation – the lack of immediate enjoyment and the tedium of practical arrangements – to gain sight of sublime vistas. In other words, the passage offers a condensed history of Anne and Wentworth's relationship in which romance, as glimpsed momentarily by a picturesque view or in a Romantic poem, can be experienced and even exalted if the labyrinth of common life, of everyday obstacles, is successfully navigated.

Towards the end of the novel, the heroine's feelings of 'high-wrought love' are so intoxicating that 'It was almost enough to spread purification and perfume' through the streets of Bath (p. 181). The Romantic climax of *Persuasion* does not occur during the drama at Lyme, when a focus on 'the richness of the present age' demonstrates Austen's awareness of the cultural appeal of poetry (p. 94), but in an apartment at the White Hart Inn when, according to Keith G. Thomas, both the hero and the heroine alternately act the part of the Romantic poet. Wentworth composes a 'genuine love lyric' in response to Anne's elegiac ode on women's endurance; the hero's emotions are so ardent, however, that he is barely able to control his words or render them legible.[16] Seized by an 'irresistible governance', he conveys the agonising pitch of his feelings – 'You pierce my soul. I am half agony, half hope' – and confesses, 'I can hardly write' (pp. 226, 222).[17] In this way, Wentworth not only demonstrates 'an assimilation of Romantic lyrical ideology' ('Jane Austen and the Romantic Lyric', p. 895), as Thomas argues, but he also experiences the Romantic poet's frustration at the limits of expression. Anne's riotous emotions are similarly keen and she experiences the 'full sensation [of] overpowering happiness' (p. 223). In the cancelled chapters of *Persuasion*, the romantic resolution is despatched rapidly and incurs a sleepless night – the heroine must 'pay for the overplus of Bliss, by Headake & Fatigue'.[18] Although the declaration 'burst[s] forth in the fullness of exquisite feeling', a typical Austenian balance is reached, with a couple 'at once so rationally & so rapturously happy'. This moderation yields, in the final version, to ungovernable feelings, a 'joy, senseless joy!' (p. 158). The mutual pleasure of the hero and heroine is celebrated in the 1995 film version of *Persuasion*, directed by Roger Michell, when their 'spirits dancing in private rapture' (p. 225) are projected, publicly, through the street carnival that passes by as they kiss for the first time.[19]

Such 'overplus of Bliss' – offering something akin to a carnivalesque release – is not sustainable for Austen, as the adaptation also makes clear when the happy couple are once more left to their 'private rapture' after the performers leave the stage. Prior to this, Wentworth is tormented by his jealousy of William Elliot and Anne suffers from a restless anxiety throughout. It is the heroine's mixed emotions, with love and longing experienced as 'very painful agitation' (p. 75), that make the novel so intensely moving. Austen's exploration of an attachment, 'deep in the happiness of such misery, or the misery of such happiness, instantly' (p. 215), voices a Romantic preoccupation with the interrelatedness of love and loss that is explored as much, if not more so, through the heroine's mourning as through Benwick's aspirations to the Byronic and the repercussions of Louisa's fall. Fittingly, given the recurring theme of romantic bereavement in the Oriental Tales, the Giaour's entreaty to 'Give me the pleasure with the pain,/ So would I live and love again' (*The Giaour*, ll. 1119–20) reverberates in Anne's hazily oxymoronic feelings of '... pain, pleasure, a something between delight and misery' (p. 165).

This Romantic lyricism extends to the mood of the novel. *Persuasion* is infused with the bittersweet poignancy of autumn.[20] Although the heroine may be subject to a mild irony, as she teeters on the brink of literary cliché ('repeating to herself some few of the thousand poetical descriptions extant of autumn', p. 78), Austen is clear that Anne's sympathies have benefited from the cathartic release of verse. The heroine is resuscitated, brought back from the brink of emotional decline, by a poetry through which she can feel her formerly concealed sorrow. The passage anticipates a Keatsian sensibility, in 'that season of peculiar and inexhaustible influence on the mind of taste and tenderness' (p. 78), and in the experience of life as a vale of soul making.[21] In addition, the following lines from *The Giaour*, as the hero reflects gravely on the 'golden youth' of friendship gone astray (l. 1239), cast a long shadow in *Persuasion*:

> 'The wrack by passion left behind,
> A shrivell'd scroll, a scatter'd leaf,
> Sear'd by the autumn blast of grief!' (ll. 1254–6)

It would be difficult to reconcile the dramatic tone of these lines with the lingering pathos of *Persuasion*. Austen's novel nonetheless coincides with Byron's poem in terms of a tale impelled by pain and loss, as well as in the exploration of disturbing existential tensions. Indeed, for Darryl Jones, *Persuasion* concludes with a register of 'unadorned desire, a high Romanticism signalled by the novel's recurring intertextual preoccupation with Byron' (*Jane Austen*, pp. 186–7).

Slavery, in Byron's Oriental Tales, can be a literal state for both the hero and the heroine, with Gulnare exclaiming in frustration to the captive Conrad 'I felt—I feel—love dwells with—with the free./ I am a slave, a favour'd slave at best' (*The Corsair*, II. ll. 502–3), whereas Austen's female protagonists often internalise a metaphorical bondage.

The limits of Anne Elliot's existence are bound by duty (to a family she cannot respect), the restrictions of gender (that dictate a passive suffering), and the galling insensitivity of those around her. Her commentary on the relative spheres of the sexes resurfaces in the opening canto of *Don Juan*.

'We [women] certainly do not forget you [men], so soon as you forget us. It is, perhaps, our fate rather than our merit. We cannot help ourselves. We live at home, quiet, confined, and our feelings prey upon us. You are forced on exertion. You have always a profession, pursuits, business of some sort or other, to take you back into the world immediately, and continual occupation and change soon weaken impressions.' (p. 218)

'Man's love is of man's life a thing apart,
    'Tis woman's whole existence; man may range
The court, camp, church, the vessel, and the mart;
    Sword, gown, gain, glory, offer in exchange
Pride, fame, ambition, to fill up his heart,
    And few there are whom these cannot estrange;
Men have all these resources, we but one,
To love again, and be again undone.' (*Don Juan*, I. cxciv)

It is tempting to think that Austen's language and sentiment are given a Byronic inflection in verse. The first canto of *Don Juan* was completed in September 1818, some nine months after the publication of *Persuasion*, and it is possible that John Murray, the publisher they shared, sent the poet a copy of the novel (as he had with earlier Austen novels). Anne's lament that 'our feelings prey upon us', voiced in Donna Julia's complaint about the narrow circumference of 'woman's whole existence', establishes an accord between the plight of women and the interiority of Romantic poetry.[22] Above all, it is a narrative of intense emotional anguish, sometimes suppressed or masked, that defines both Anne Elliot and the Byronic hero.

The exploration of extreme psychic spaces generates one of the most telling connections between Austen's heroines and Byron's protagonists. Todd's comment about *Persuasion*, 'Through her [Anne's] years of depression and repression she had become, like Byron's passionate heroes, a connoisseur of pain, feeling it, stoking it, but hiding it inside', recalls the closing lines of Byron's poem, *The Prisoner of Chillon*.[23]

In quiet we had learn'd to dwell;
My very chains and I grew friends,
So much a long communion tends
To make us what we are:—even I
Regain'd my freedom with a sigh. (ll. 388–92)

Anne, like the persecuted prisoner, has become habituated to loss and privation. Indeed, the heroine's initial refusal of Wentworth suggests an assimilation of familial constraints, which results in a tortured solitude akin to what Byron describes as 'a living grave' (l. 114). As the 'heavy walls' of the inmate's captivity have become a reassuring 'hermitage' (ll. 377, 378), so Anne feels an ambivalent yearning for her home when removed to Uppercross and then to the alien environment of Bath. Kellynch Hall is both a sanctuary, a place of precarious security where the heroine can withdraw into herself, and a site of exile, where she endures a 'gnawing solicitude' among her closest relations (p. 213).[24] The isolation of Byron's prisoner is similarly made more acute by the separated presence of his brothers in the cell. As Auerbach contends, 'This continual tension between the security of a restricted world and its unrelenting imprisonment brings Austen into a special sort of agreement with her Romantic contemporaries'.[25]

A more explicit example of 'agreement' is evident between *Persuasion* and poems by Byron, cited in the novel, that celebrate the 'blue crystal' (*The Giaour*, l. 17) and 'purple diadem' of the sea (*The Bride of Abydos*, II. l. 356). In this respect, the allusion to 'Lord Byron's "dark blue seas"' on the Cobb in Lyme does not merely serve as an indication of Benwick's Byronic *idée fixe* (p. 101). The reference is taken, according to Gillian Beer, from Byron's exhilarating portrait of life on board a 'gallant frigate', as the hero travels through the Mediterranean in the second canto of *Childe Harold's Pilgrimage*.[26] 'The glorious main expanding o'er the bow' offers the prospect of renewal for the 'gloomy wanderer', Harold; and even the 'dullest sailer' is roused to activity, and valiant deeds, by this antidote to an otherwise stagnant existence (*CHP*, II. xvii, xvi). The allusion is, as Peter Robinson suggests, 'a perfectly polite and apt meeting point for Anne and Benwick' ('Captain Benwick's Reading', p. 166). A more involved literary conversation is also discernible. Austen's characters in Lyme provide an imagined audience for Byron's sailors – the lads and maids ashore who envy the sight of 'Long streams of light o'er dancing waves expand' (*CHP*, II. xxi) – as Anne and Henrietta, in silent rapture on the sands, likewise 'gloried in the sea [and] sympathized in the delight of the fresh-feeling breeze' (p. 95).

An alternative source for the allusion to 'dark blue seas' can be found in the opening of *The Corsair*, a poem that we know Austen read, and which makes the connection between seafaring and liberty even more emphatic:

> 'O'er the glad waters of the dark blue sea,
> Our thoughts as boundless, and our souls as free,
> Far as the breeze can bear, the billows foam,
> Survey our empire, and behold our home!
> These are our realms, no limits to their sway—
> Our flag the sceptre all who meet obey.
> Ours the wild life in tumult still to range
> From toil to rest, and joy in every change.' (I. ll. 1–8)

It is hard to imagine Austen's hero and heroine resorting to piracy, like Byron's wandering heroes, to ensure that there are 'no limits to their sway'. Yet, while Conrad's 'wild life' may not be entirely suited to Wentworth's future wife, the Navy offers freedom from the restrictions of a monotonous civilian life. Across *Persuasion*, *Childe Harold's Pilgrimage*, and the Oriental Tales, 'The breezy freshness of the deep beneath' serves as a rejuvenating refuge (*The Corsair*, I. l. 536): Anne, who 'gloried in being a sailor's wife' (p. 236), enjoys the informal manners of Navy families and the prospect of a varied existence, the 'joy in every change' that she has been denied; and Wentworth, 'who had nothing but himself to recommend him' (pp. 26–7), earns respect and status through his entrepreneurial endeavours, impressing Sir Walter with his 'personal claims' by the end of the novel (p. 232).[27] Scenes that present the Navy as a force for social and personal reform frame the 1995 film version of *Persuasion*. The opening sequence of Admiral Croft boarding his ship among the camaraderie of his men is interspersed with shots of debtors protesting outside Kellynch Hall. The closing scene shows Anne, taking her lead from the pioneering Mrs Croft, on board ship with Wentworth, a prosperous and happy future secured as a reward for her willingness to adapt to the new life offered by her husband's profession.[28]

Although this adaptation of *Persuasion* runs the risk of a rose-tinted re-visioning of the Navy (which overlooks the more unpalatable aspects of Wentworth's profession and possibly overstates the future he offers Anne), the fundamental point is that the sea, and occupations relating to the sea, offer new creative horizons for the writers of Romantic poetry and prose, and new prospects for their characters.[29] Anne and Wentworth not only seek diversion from what is described, in *The Bride of Abydos*, as 'inaction's sluggish yoke' (II. l. 338); the sea acts as a site of accumulated memories, shoring up 'the breast that inly bleeds' (*The Giaour*, l. 1155). The heroine is in danger of sinking beneath the waves of romantic regret. And yet constancy, in *Persuasion* as in the Oriental Tales, offers a redemptive lifeline. This resuscitated love is not only capable of writing a new plot – where romance ripens to fulfil the promise of a fleeting forerunner – it is also capable of resisting social pressure and forging new romantic modes of thinking and being. In addition to her brooding, the heroine's 'monastic' devotion to one man, judging all others unfavourably by comparison, is decidedly Byronic.[30] And, as becomes apparent at the end of the novel, 'eternal constancy' may not be the sole preserve of women (p. 181). When Wentworth confesses to the heroine that 'I have loved none but you. Unjust I may have been, weak and resentful I have been, but never inconstant' (p. 222), he champions Conrad's romantic fidelity.

> Yes, it was love—unchangeable—unchanged,
> Felt but for one from whom he never ranged; (*The Corsair*,
> I. ll. 287–8)

To see Wentworth as Byronic is, according to Mary Waldron, a misreading of his character that both the heroine and the reader 'must snap out of'.[31] Yet, notable characteristics mark him out as a contemporary of such heroes as Conrad and the Giaour. In addition to falling 'rapidly and deeply in love' with the heroine, Wentworth attracts and courts the attention of other women (p. 26). As Conrad proves irresistible to both his own forsaken wife and the wife of his enemy, so the handsome hero of *Persuasion* sparks a 'fever of admiration' that almost proves fatal to one of the Musgrove sisters, quite literally turning her head (p. 76).[32] A note of censure regarding Wentworth's flirtation is evident when we are told that 'He was only wrong in accepting the attentions—(for accepting must be the word) of two young women at once' (p. 76). It is his repentance and willingness to make reparation in the aftermath of Louisa's accident that absolves him of his former conduct. Mostly silent during the episode in Lyme, remaining mute like Conrad at crucial moments in *The Corsair*, the intensity of Wentworth's feelings are even more compelling than Louisa's lifeless form. 'Byronically distracted in manner and speech', as Brückmann argues, 'Wentworth looks fatally bound' ('Books, Readers, and Libraries', p. 15). Prior to these scenes, the narrative has reflected the heroine's sorrows, but her 'age of emotion' is more than matched by the hero's Byronic despair (p. 46).

Wentworth is praised, from the first description of his character, for being a 'remarkably fine young man, with a great deal of intelligence, spirit and brilliancy', qualities that distinguish his naval career (p. 26). As with nearly all Byron's protagonists, however, journeys overseas represent a bid for freedom, as discussed above, and a form of self-exile. Feeling ill-used and leaving the country after Anne's refusal lends some credence to Lady Russell's fears about his impetuous nature. Wentworth is described as 'dangerous' at both the beginning and the end of the novel, although the second reference checks Lady Russell's initial hasty judgement; his ardour and fearlessness are seen in a new light when used to assist the impoverished Mrs Smith in the penultimate paragraph of the novel (pp. 27, 233). In keeping with Byron's treatment of social pretension and vanity, Wentworth barely manages to conceal his contempt for Anne's family, flashing a 'dilating eye' reminiscent of the Giaour (*The Giaour*, l. 834). This aspect of the hero's behaviour anticipates, by half a century, Algernon Swinburne's applause for Byron's 'excellent contempt for things contemptible, and hatred of hateful men'.[33]

Yet these glimmers of the Byronic are tempered in Austen by an all-important civility. A notable example of Wentworth's civility occurs in Chapter 8 when we are reminded of the hero's 'bright eye, and curl of his handsome mouth', Byronic features that are quelled to sympathise with Mrs Musgrove over the death of her, by all accounts, worthless son (p. 63). Similar instances of kindness emerge when Wentworth releases Anne from her boisterous nephew and secures a place for her in the Crofts' carriage. While both acts suggest the assured presence and 'commanding art' of the Byronic hero (*The Corsair*, I. l. 177), these undemonstrative incidents also denote a thoughtful nature with a 'warm and amiable heart' (p. 84). A close reading of 'the little particulars of the circumstance', as practiced by Anne (and learned by Elizabeth Bennet in *Pride and Prejudice*), reveals the hero of *Persuasion* to be both a dynamic lover and a dependable partner (p. 74). As Margaret Wilson argues,

> When Frederick Wentworth re-enters Somersetshire, he displays the charms of the other man but he also demonstrates the solid qualities that denote a gentleman and an Austen hero.[34]

In other words, Wentworth is a kind of chameleon hero capable of blurring boundaries. His is, for Jason D. Solinger, 'a new yet necessarily familiar figure', a traditional portrait of valour in the vein of the man of commerce.[35] He is also a Romantic hero, a Georgian gentleman, and, as a Captain in the Navy, a prototype for the proud self-made man of Victorian fiction. This composite masculinity renders him arguably Austen's 'most perfect' hero and the closest, in her writing, to a hybridised Byronic hero.[36]

II

The most recent screen adaptations of *Persuasion* are telling in their contrasting treatment of Wentworth's Byronic affinities and the depiction of a broader Romantic context. Whereas the 1995 film version of *Persuasion* emphasises the Byronic, the 2007 ITV adaptation does not. This is perhaps unsurprising when we consider that Nick Dear, who also wrote the screenplay for the 2003 BBC biopic of Byron, wrote the screenplay for the 1995 film of *Persuasion*. Yet, although Simon Burke's 2007 screenplay omits Austen's references to Byron and other Romantic writers during the episode in Lyme, it is arguably engaged in a more involved dialogue with Romantic ideas and attitudes.[37] An early scene between Amanda Root's Anne Elliot and Susan Fleetwood's Lady Russell in the 1995 film of *Persuasion* foregrounds the Romantic poets. Lady Russell lends Anne a book of new poems, with the following dismissive comment: 'altogether, I care little for these Romantics'. That Lady Russell owns, circulates, and discusses a copy of Romantic poetry, during a conversation in which she fails to comprehend Anne's unresolved regret about rejecting Wentworth, generates an Austenian ambivalence about reading, or misreading, that reoccurs in Lyme. What is evident, when the action moves to this seaside resort, is that the heroine is familiar with popular verse and readily recites lines from Walter Scott's *The Lady of the Lake* (1810).

Anne Elliot is more guarded, however, when Captain Benwick recites the final stanza of Byron's poem 'Fare Thee Well', written on 17 March 1816, before the poet left England in the wake of his separation with Lady Byron.

> Fare thee well! thus disunited,
>   Torn from every nearer tie,
> Sear'd in heart, and lone, and blighted,
>   More than this I scarce can die. (ll. 57–60)

The controversy surrounding this poem, including George Cruikshank's vividly coloured satirical drawing in the *Champion*, pre-dates the timescale depicted in the novel yet coincides with the completion of the manuscript. Anne's caution, in the adaptation, that 'too much poetry may be unsafe', relates to the 'hopeless agony' (p. 94) which Benwick cultivates through a mnemonic recall of Byron's verse. Rather than advocating the propriety of prose, as in Austen's novel, Amanda Root's Anne questions the moral value of poetry occasioned by private pain and circulated publicly, fanning scandalous reports of Byron's misconduct and manipulating sympathies. That the camera pans from Anne and Benwick's literary debates to Louisa's fall establishes an even closer connection between Byron, or Benwick's Byronism, and feigned feelings that flaunt yet also withhold intimacy.

Benwick's suffering can be viewed as contrived or the expression of a deep-rooted pathology. When read through the register of 'Fare Thee Well' – in which Byron positions his speaker as the injured party, the accuser, and the architect of misery, with the reader as his confidante – dual responses can be entertained simultaneously. In response to Benwick's affected declaration, 'You have no conception of what I have lost', Anne's stark response, 'Yes, I have', is genuinely affecting. The discussion of Byron gives voice to the heroine's previously silent agony. The extended scenes between Anne and Benwick in this adaptation comment on the formulation of a Byronic persona that performs grief while also implying that poetry can offer meaningful consolation. Dear's adaptation, by invoking the 'disjunctive moment' of 'Fare Thee Well', draws out the subtle yet vital distinction that Austen makes between the public reception of Byron and the personal resonance of his poetry. Benwick is, as W. Paul Elledge states of Byron's poem, 'a portrait of indecision, taut with antithetical tensions', oscillating between painful remembrance and an exhibition of emotion, loyalty to the departed and longing for a renewal of love.[38] That poetry ceases to cloak or suspend heartfelt sorrow is even more pertinent to the relationship between the hero and the heroine. It is made clear in the adaptation, as it is in the novel, that a mutual regard for poetry ignites the romance between Benwick and Louisa, and also reanimates the romance between Anne and Wentworth.

Such conflicted dialogues and interactions over the Romantic poets, centring specifically on Byron, provide a conducive backdrop for Ciarán Hinds's portrayal of Captain Wentworth. Tom Hoberg praises Hinds's 'majestically sexy' take on what is the closest Austen comes to 'a quintessential romantic hero'.[39] His Byronic credentials come into view when, after Louisa's accident, he remains outside the Musgroves' house – a lone figure in the rain – where once he had danced and dined. But it is in Bath where Hinds's Wentworth emerges as a fully-fledged Byronic hero. The emotions that he struggles to communicate to Anne intensify to the point where he becomes almost unintelligible, as in the scene at the Concert Hall:

Anne:	'Oh Captain! Are you leaving already?'
Wentworth:	'Yes.'
Anne:	'But the music is good is it not?'
Wentworth:	'I neither know nor care.'
Anne:	'But will you not …?'
Wentworth:	[impatiently] 'What?'
Anne:	'This is too sudden.'
Wentworth:	'Is it?'
Anne:	'But what is the matter with you?'
Wentworth:	'Nothing, nothing at all.'
[William Elliot interrupts]	
Anne:	'But the next song is very beautiful. It is a very beautiful love song. Is that not worth your staying for?'
Wentworth:	'No. There is nothing worth my staying for.'

Whereas, in the novel, Wentworth is grave and abrupt in his misplaced jealousy of William Elliot, the veneer of polite conversation begins to crack here, with Wentworth's hostile challenge 'What?', and Anne's counter-challenge, 'But what is the matter with you?' In scenes like this, the adaptation disturbs a careful equilibrium that renders Wentworth, according to Serajul Islam Choudhury, 'Austen's masculine ideal'.[40] It is hard to imagine Hinds's Wentworth reconsidering the 'correctness' of Anne's initial refusal with anything like the 'cool deliberation' that Austen's hero is able to muster in the penultimate chapter of the novel (p. 231). It is even more unlikely that he would acknowledge his pride as a flaw and be open to reconciliation with Lady Russell. If anything, an inverse relationship is established with the novel in relation to Wentworth's Byronic anger and recklessness; what Austen takes pains to subdue through his penance after Louisa's accident is rekindled on screen. Such a premium on passion at the expense of civility makes for an uneasy ending and lessens the complexity of Austen's Wentworth as a revisionary, or 'hybrid', Byronic hero. The intelligent negotiation of Austen's reading of the Romantic poets elsewhere in the adaptation does not seem to extend much beyond Lyme.

Although the 2007 ITV adaptation of *Persuasion*, directed by Adrian Shergold, is less explicitly conversant with the novel's Romantic subtext, it is equally significant. Rupert Penry-Jones, as Wentworth, is able to still the occasional flicker of resentment within an overall impression of stern remoteness. Yet, while this male lead is not as genetically predisposed to the Byronic as the dark-haired Hinds, his character is often framed within a suggestive Romantic landscape. A visual trope of the lone figure lashed by the elements standing on the Cobb at Lyme – what I take to be an allusion to Caspar David Friedrich's 'Wanderer Above the Sea of Fog' (painted in the same year that *Persuasion* was published) – is repeated across several scenes: first, and most predictably, by Captain Benwick; then, more surprisingly, by William Elliot; and, finally, by Captain Harville and Wentworth, as the latter laments his foolish conduct with Louisa Musgrove and confesses to his feelings for Anne. An archetypal image of sublime Romantic solitude is employed here to connect Benwick's grand misery with Wentworth's enduring love. William Elliot's appearance as a mysterious figure on the breakwater complicates our understanding of this double Romanticism, gesturing towards the proximity, visually at least, between what constitutes a hero and an anti-hero in Austen's fiction. The interrelated masculine 'types' that every Austen heroine must successfully navigate are refracted, on screen, through Romantic iconography typically associated with the Byronic hero.

Elsewhere, Romantic estrangement and anguish underscore the adaptation, with the use of breathing camera animating the heroine's internal agitation. Where the warm if melancholy interiors of the 1995 film version offer some respite from an overall impression of 'rumpled realism',[41] the 2007 adaptation is unremittingly stark; a prevailing blue tint is only punctuated by 'the white glare of Bath' and the brighter glow of spring when Wentworth restores Kellynch Hall to Anne in the final scene (p. 32). The mournful chords of Beethoven's *Moonlight Sonata* (*Piano Sonata No. 14*), as played by Sally Hawkins's Anne to reflect that 'In music she had been always used to feel alone in the world' (p. 44), gives way at the close to birdsong. The shift from solitary, and sometimes majestic, reveries to the gentler effects of nature's chorus does not represent an ideological reconfiguration. Rather, it suggests the various sounds and sensations that constitute a Romantic sensibility and the various ways in which it is audible to, and plays on, an individual's temperament. The pathos and promise of renewal in this stylish adaptation comes close to Austen's subtle appreciation of Romantic seclusion and recuperation.

III

Captain Wentworth, a hero with discernibly Byronic attributes, looks forward to some of the aspiring middle-class male protagonists of Victorian fiction. Part III of this chapter will explore how Austen regards, and how the heroine negotiates, the Byronic attractions and distractions of the aristocratic male suitor in *Pride and Prejudice*. *Pride and Prejudice* was drafted in the late 1790s, along with *Sense and Sensibility*, and published in 1813, almost a year after the first two cantos of *Childe Harold's Pilgrimage* appeared and made Byron an overnight sensation. It is conceivable that Austen responded to the craze for all things Byronic when editing this novel. Yet despite what I consider to be the similarities between Mr Darcy and a number of Byron's protagonists, I am not arguing primarily for a direct influence. Perhaps more plausible is that Austen was responding to the same cultural stimuli that shaped Byron's heroes as well as to the broader social pressures on gender during this period, as discussed in Chapter 1. The remaining parts of this chapter are concerned with what Rachel Brownstein refers to as the 'near intersections' between Austen and Byron.[42] If we accept Doucet Devin Fischer's point that 'Not even the self-styled "grand Napoleon of the realms of rhyme" [...] could still Austen's voice, which offers a persistent, teasing corrective to the presumptions and patriarchal assumptions of Byronic heroes' ('Byron and Austen: Romance and Reality', p. 78), could Darcy therefore be read as an attempt to engage with and deflate this Romantic figure? Does the rehabilitation of the aristocratic hero in *Pride and Prejudice*, anticipating Charlotte Brontë's novel *Jane Eyre*, necessitate the suppression of Byronic traits? Alternatively, do vestiges of the Byronic hero remain in the latter stages of Austen's novel, and with what effect on the evolving romance between the male and female protagonists? Lastly, in what ways do modern adaptations engage with these intertextual gender politics? How is the figure of the Romantic hero rewritten for the screen and with what effect on Austen's reconfigurations of masculinity?

Pride and Prejudice's Mr Darcy struggles to maintain what D. W. Harding describes as 'the earlier ideal of narrowly reasoned control in emotional life'.[43] More than this, as I have established with regards to Wentworth, Darcy's character resonates with conflicted Romantic longing. It is the hero who reminds the heroine of the saying that poetry is 'the *food* of love', and he comes to experience a genuinely 'ardent love'.[44] Darcy's inability to regulate his desire is made apparent in the first proposal scene when he announces: 'In vain have I struggled. It will not do. My feelings will not be repressed. You must allow me to tell you how ardently I admire and love you' (p. 183). Elizabeth's response to the strength of his emotions, articulated in staccato sentences, is an astonishment 'beyond expression', which initially subdues her into an uncharacteristic silence. As G. M. Kooiman-Van Middendorp states, Austen 'allowed her hero to speak as neither the illustrious Grandison, nor any other gentleman of Darcy's standing would have done', which goes some way to explain Elizabeth's retort about his reprehensible conduct.[45] The hero's turbid interior beneath a rigid exterior both animates and alarms the heroine. Yet, her incredulity, both at his declared passion and the mode of declaration, is succeeded by a rising anger that is more than a match for his. The force of Darcy's unvarnished feelings is met by Elizabeth's disavowal of what she takes to be his shameless arrogance.

The socially awkward hero of *Pride and Prejudice* can be readily compared to the Romantic heroes of the Oriental Tales with their 'haughty gesture[s]': 'His [Conrad's] was the lofty port, the distant mien,/ That seems to shun the sight—and awes if seen' (*The Corsair*, I. ll. 570, 541–2). Darcy is deemed to be 'handsomer than Mr. Bingley', and the superior of his friend in many respects, yet 'his manners gave a disgust which turned the tide of his popularity; for he was discovered to be proud, to be above his company, and above being pleased' (p. 8). Although Austen raises a wry smile at the rapidity with which the 'tide' turns (a veiled reference perhaps to the fickleness of fame that Byron bemoaned), Darcy's faults immediately complicate a conventional portrait of the eighteenth-century patrician hero. As Byron's Manfred is found wanting – sometimes humorously so – when compared with the humble virtue of the Chamois Hunter, so Elizabeth, her family, and her neighbours are united in being 'disgusted with his [Darcy's] pride' (p. 74), a ubiquitous trait of the Byronic hero, which often prompts the battles in the Oriental Tales. The swift sentence against Darcy, in spite of his status and reported income, is telling. When Darcy famously slights Elizabeth, Mrs Bennet is repelled by his 'shocking rudeness' and proclaims, in her gauche manner, 'I quite detest the man' (p. 11). This impulsive if impolitic rejoinder echoes the sentiment of the wider community: 'The general prejudice against Mr. Darcy is so violent, that it would be the death of half the good people in Meryton, to attempt to place him in an amiable light' (p. 218). Local opinion, however, here both reflecting and reinforcing the heroine's ready acceptance of the hero's supposed 'inhumanity' (p. 77), is the subject of satire from the opening lines of the novel. Mrs Bennet overturns her earlier verdict as rapidly as she formed it, proclaiming Darcy to be 'a charming man!—so handsome! so tall!' on learning of her daughter's engagement to him, the quick succession of exclamation marks mirroring those used in her equally overstated condemnation of the hero (p. 367). Nonetheless, despite the amusing vagaries of personal and public opinion, Darcy commits the cardinal error, a particular danger for the aristocratic hero, of appearing to lack civility.

Austen, in *Pride and Prejudice*, takes the aristocratic hero out of his comfort zone and places him in unchartered social territory. The self-possessed protagonist, who, like Byron's Childe Harold, 'stood/ Among them, but not of them; in a shroud/ Of thoughts which were not their thoughts' (*CHP*, III. cxiii), is thrust unwittingly into a miscellaneous company. In this way, Austen tests some of the less inviting aspects of a character who is devoid of 'misanthropic hate', yet prefers not to mingle or converse with 'the throng' (I. lxxxiv). In his confessed snobbery – 'to care for none beyond my own family circle, to think meanly of all the rest of the world, to *wish* at least to think meanly of their sense and worth compared with my own' (p. 357, original emphasis) – Austen's hero epitomises Atara Stein's definition of the archetypal Byronic hero: '... he is an unattainable ideal, a hero who inspires awe but cannot be emulated. At the same time, he lacks social skills and an ability to relate to other people; [...] he can be arrogant, contemptuous of human beings, bad-tempered, overbearing, cold, ruthless, and emotionless'.[46] At the start of the novel, Darcy is the antithesis of the sociable gentleman who puts others at their ease; he is guilty of 'continually giving offence' (p. 14), particularly to the partnerless women at the local Assembly Room. Darcy's behaviour, at this point in the narrative, resembles contemporary reports of Byron standing aloof on the periphery of social gatherings and sneering at the dancing couples. The poet's occasional tone of aristocratic condescension is also caught in the hero's 'haughty composure' (p. 189). We are told, during Darcy's presumptuous first proposal, that 'he had no doubt of a favourable answer', and the heroine repeatedly expresses the belief that his attentions are intended to scare her into submission (p. 183). As Conrad's crew dare not question his decisions – 'all obey and few inquire his will' (*The Corsair*, I. l. 80) – so Mr Bennet capitulates to the hero's request for his daughter's hand in marriage because 'He is the kind of man, indeed, to whom I should never dare refuse any thing, which he condescended to ask' (p. 365). Even Bingley describes his friend as an 'aweful object', a pun that speaks to Darcy's impressive yet alarming appearance and the apprehensive admiration of those around him (p. 47). Above all, Elizabeth recognises the same 'will to power' that Jerome McGann detects in the Byronic hero: 'I do not know any body who seems more to enjoy the power of doing what he likes than Mr. Darcy' (p. 177).[47]

Darcy's desire to achieve autonomy, an aspiration common to Byron's heroes, is commendable in many respects. His refusal to join in with the Bingley sisters' insults and snubs, rendering him a detached outsider even among his closest friends, recalls Childe Harold's 'moral' credibility: 'I have not flatter'd its [the world's] rank breath, nor bow'd/ To its idolatries a patient knee,/ Nor coin'd my cheek to smiles, nor cried aloud/ In worship of an echo' (*CHP*, III. cxiii). Yet this 'real superiority of mind' (p. 54), prized by Austen's as well as Byron's hero, is often accompanied by, or perceived as, smug self-satisfaction. The heroine and the reader must wait until the end of the novel for the hero to critique his own conduct:

> As a child I was taught what was *right*, but I was not taught to correct my temper. I was given good principles, but left to follow them in pride and conceit. [...] I was spoilt by my parents, who though good themselves, (my father particularly, all that was benevolent and amiable,) allowed, encouraged, almost taught me to be selfish and overbearing ... (p. 357, original emphasis)

Darcy's birthright does not entail the 'noble mien' that he is assumed to possess at the very start of the novel (p. 7), nor does it inspire the 'sense of habitual native dignity' that Edmund Burke associated with a privileged descent.[48] His inheritance largely consists of defects, anticipating Thomas Babington Macaulay's comments on how Byron was spoilt by good fortune and rank: 'all this world, and all the glory of it, were at once offered to a young man to whom nature had given violent passions, and whom education had never taught to control them'.[49]

Darcy likewise betrays a bitterness of temper that lends credibility to Wickham's accusation of scandalous ill-usage. Elizabeth's suspicions over Darcy's implacable resentment seem to be confirmed by his unjust treatment of her sister, Jane, for which no adequate explanation is ever given.

> ... *he* [Darcy] was the cause, his pride and caprice were the cause of all that Jane had suffered, and still continued to suffer. He had ruined for a while every hope of happiness for the most affectionate,

generous heart in the world; and no one could say how lasting an evil he might have inflicted. (p. 180, original emphasis)

The contrast made between Darcy's 'pride and caprice' and Jane's 'affectionate, generous heart' is damning. Furthermore, the language employed here – 'suffer', 'ruined', 'inflicted', and 'evil' – has more in common with the Gothic villain, a figure considered in the previous chapter, than with the model of 'rational and manly freedom' advocated in Austen's later novel, *Emma*. The letter Darcy writes after his rejected proposal is similarly overwrought, especially when relating his dealings with Wickham: '... that I had, in *defiance* of various claims, in *defiance* of honour and humanity, *ruined* the immediate prosperity, and *blasted* the prospects of Mr. Wickham' (p. 190, added emphasis). It is unsurprising, given the theatrics relied on here, that critics such as Paul Giles detect a residual Gothic charge in *Pride and Prejudice*. As General Tilney remains something of an enigma in *Northanger Abbey*, indicated by the closing lines of the novel, so Darcy can be read as 'a haughty Derbyshire gentleman one moment and an enigmatic Gothic hero the next'.[50]

For the reader to accept Darcy as a partner for Elizabeth, Austen must rehumanise and reform the aristocratic hero. Where Byron's hero, Conrad, hopes in vain that Medora may still redeem him, Austen's heroine succeeds. As Darcy tells Elizabeth, 'What do I not owe you! You taught me a lesson, hard indeed at first, but most advantageous. By you, I was properly humbled' (p. 357). Darcy unlearns his pompous behaviour through his devotion to Elizabeth and what Paul Giles refers to as 'an orgy of teasing' ('Gothic Dialogue', p. 72). The hero is subjected to a pert playfulness, designed to deflate his solemn sense of superiority. Yet, although Darcy may be the recipient of many 'saucy speech[es]', he is outspoken about Elizabeth's defects and humbles the heroine in turn (p. 315). Darcy is not merely a malleable figure who can be understood 'wholly within the space of Elizabeth's psychology' (Wiltshire, *Recreating Jane Austen*, p. 121). The hero's flaws are not only 'remedied' by the heroine's impertinence, but by his own agency and exertions. Although Darcy may not engage in skirmishes, like the heroes of the Oriental Tales, his encounters with Wickham in London betray none of what is described elsewhere as his 'usual sedateness' (p. 240).

He had followed them purposely to town, he had taken on himself all the trouble and mortification attendant on such a research; [...] he was reduced to meet, frequently meet, reason with, persuade, and finally bribe, the man whom he always most wished to avoid. (p. 314)

Whereas Darcy's part in the separation of Bingley and Jane consists of concealment, this description reveals a move towards active engagement, and even confrontation, in his dealings with those around him. In other words, the detached Byronic hero is gradually integrated into a wider community.

Thus, the change in Darcy's behaviour is signalled. The chance meeting at Pemberley gives the hero an opportunity to impress the heroine with his kindness, and the success of his efforts is confirmed by the unbiased first impressions of Mr Gardiner: 'He is perfectly well behaved, polite, and unassuming' (p. 246). Immediately prior to the revelation of an improved Darcy, the housekeeper of Pemberley reminds us, and forces Elizabeth to acknowledge, that the hero is a 'very handsome gentleman' (p. 236). We are also introduced to a new aspect of his character. In marked contrast to Byron's Manfred, whose disregard for his social rank and responsibilities derives from a pained individualism, Darcy is reported to be a good master. Mrs Reynolds praises his 'generous-hearted' nature, casting previous views of his antisocial behaviour and unyielding temper in a more positive light, as she enthuses: '"He is the best landlord, and the best master," said she, "that ever lived"' (pp. 237, 238). In singling Darcy out from other young men of his age, who suffer from the 'upstart insolence' of an aspiring class, his long-standing distinction is preserved.[51] As if to reinforce this point, Wickham's earlier concession that Darcy is charitable and loyal now exposes the callow disloyalty of the steward's son and unwittingly adds weight to the housekeeper's portrait of patrician liberalism (echoed later when Elizabeth's aunt confirms that Darcy is acknowledged to be 'a liberal man [who] did much good among the poor', p. 253). Even his pride becomes subject to reappraisal, now seen as synonymous with dignity and duty, and is a source of gratification for both his housekeeper and the heroine. Austen bestowed on Darcy the feelings of 'Love, Pride & Delicacy' in a letter to her sister, significantly situating his supposed 'defect' among virtues, and demanded that her readers like the hero as much as they liked the heroine.[52]

According to Michèle Cohen, during the period Austen was writing, 'revived chivalry' emerged as a model for the 'new gentleman'.[53] Clearly, the second half of *Pride and Prejudice* acts as an antidote to the hero's improper behaviour in the first half of the novel. Yet, in line with the sceptical regard for 'gallantry' that emerges in both *Sense and Sensibility* (in relation to John Willoughby) and *Emma* (in relation to

Frank Churchill), Austen probes 'chivalry's plural meanings' in *Pride and Prejudice*. Darcy increasingly concerns himself with the reception of his conduct, and during the scenes in Derbyshire, he demonstrates 'perfect civility' with Elizabeth and her extended family (p. 240). It is whilst walking his grounds at Pemberley, proceeding towards a 'nobler fall of ground, or a finer reach of the woods' (p. 241), that the heroine is most pleased with the hero.

> They entered the woods, and bidding adieu to the river for a while, ascended some of the higher grounds; whence, in spots where the opening of the trees gave the eye power to wander, were many charming views of the valley, the opposite hills, with the long range of woods overspreading many, and occasionally part of the stream. (p. 242)

This picturesque vantage point 'forms Elizabeth's consciousness of her love for Darcy', according to H. Elisabeth Ellington.[54] The heroine comes to understand the hero not simply through the value of exteriors and what they signify (security and status in this instance), but what the presentation of his property signifies about his interior. This Romantic landscape is read as a reflection of the owner, modestly though advantageously improved, with a 'natural' yet managed 'rough coppice-wood' (p. 242). It is the heroine's estimate of his tasteful grounds, cultivated on the principles of gradual change and conservation, that leads her to appreciate, 'In essentials, [...] he is very much what he ever was' (p. 226). Yet, at the same time as the hero and heroine come to this mutual accord, both 'improved in civility', Mr Collins persists with his 'obsequious civility', and Caroline Bingley's resentment takes the form of 'sneering civility' (pp. 355, 372, 258). Civility, in its manifold guises, remains a source of irony even as it emerges as a mark of merit in Austen's novel. It is clear that Darcy must behave better, especially with those who are not his social equals, yet Austen is equally clear that the affectation of civility does not denote virtue. Manners may make the man, but they are the window dressing for solid qualities, revered 'essentials'.

Darcy presents for his author the same creative conundrum that Elizabeth Gaskell grapples with, nearly half a century after the publication of Austen's novel, when wondering how to make the industrialist hero of *North and South* (1855) 'large and strong and tender, and *yet a master*'.[55] Austen negotiates this 'dilemma of masculinity' (Cohen, '"Manners" Make the Man'), a defining characteristic of the nineteenth-century novel, by avoiding a straightforward trajectory from arrogant aristocrat to considerate suitor. Darcy retains, like Wentworth in *Persuasion*, a grave disposition with a contemptuous look to rival the Byronic hero's sneer. At the same time as Mrs Reynolds hails Darcy as the best of men – 'If I was to go through the world, I could not meet with a better' – he can still be found sunk in a typically Byronic 'meditation; his brow contracted, his air gloomy' (pp. 237, 266). Indeed, Wilson's observation that Wentworth can be seen as both the 'other' man and a gentleman need not be limited to *Persuasion*. Elizabeth does not simply acclimatise to the dull 'conservative' candidate; she is increasingly drawn towards a leading man who is desirable precisely because he blurs the boundaries between hero and anti-hero. The scene in which he happens upon Elizabeth after discovering the news of Lydia's elopement is revealing in terms of his conflicted character. The hero's initial response to the heroine's distress is expressed with 'more feeling than politeness', reminiscent of the explosive proposal scene, and yet here the forceful language of 'torment' and 'distress' is tempered by 'a tone of gentleness and commiseration' (pp. 264–6). Darcy appears to have achieved an emotional equilibrium, however precarious, 'which though it spoke compassion, spoke likewise restraint'. When Elizabeth accepts him, in Chapter 58 of the novel, his former effusions are now 'inexpressibly painful' to recollect (p. 356), giving an impression of heightened sensation by negating its utterance. 'In his ability to both veil and reveal', as Deborah Lutz states of Byron's Conrad, Darcy 'is both unreadable and signifying endlessly, [...] in a kind of seductive striptease of subjectivity'.[56]

The heroine's efforts to understand the hero generate momentum in both *Pride and Prejudice* and *Persuasion*. Even as Captain Wentworth's renewed affection for the heroine becomes clear, Anne Elliot still sees him as 'irresolute' (p. 179), and his erratic behaviour is often incomprehensible to her. Darcy remains equally difficult to decipher, with Elizabeth voicing her exhilarated exasperation at what she perceives to be his unpredictability – 'Teazing, teazing man!' (p. 327). As Byron describes Conrad as a 'mystery' (*The Corsair*, I. l. 173), an apt description for a protagonist who vacillates between tenderness and resentment, so Elizabeth and Anne remain puzzled by their prospective partners. Anne is in, according to Keith G. Thomas, a perpetual state of 'interpretive agitation prompted by the inscrutability of the object [i.e. Wentworth]' ('Jane Austen and the Romantic Lyric', p. 901). Darcy likewise excites a 'contrariety of emotion' (p. 197) in Elizabeth:

... she threw a retrospective glance over the whole of their acquaintance, so full of contradictions and varieties, sighed at the perverseness of those feelings which would now have promoted its continuance, and would formerly have rejoiced in its termination. (p. 267)

These recollected emotions capture a sense of Darcy as a Byronic hero to rival Lara: 'In him inexplicably mix'd appear'd/ Much to be loved and hated, sought and fear'd' (*Lara*, I. ll. 289–90). The passage also registers a significant shift from spontaneous response to careful deliberation. Where the 'style of his address' in the proposal scene is recalled with revulsion, his letter enables the measured study of 'every sentence', and shows Elizabeth to be a gifted close reader (p. 205). It is, in fact, through repeated readings of his letter that the heroine reinterprets the hero.[57] It is also through her own 'widely different' feelings about Darcy, ranging from indignation to compassion and respect, that Elizabeth comes not only to a sympathetic appreciation of the hero, but learns to reflect on her own psychological foibles. When relating the circumstances of Darcy's first proposal, Elizabeth subjects her previous prejudice to the relish of self-mockery and admits to the mental stimulation he affords her: 'It is such a spur to one's genius, such an opening for wit to have a dislike of that kind' (p. 217). Encroaching romantic feelings are depicted, in a manner that anticipates the mature sensitivity of Anne Elliot, as 'a flutter of spirits, in which it was difficult to determine whether pleasure or pain bore the greatest share' (p. 314). The heroine's emotional range now extends as far, if not farther, than the hero's, and previously held certainties give way to a brave new world of doubt and development.

The heroine's continuing confusion over the hero simultaneously enthrals and perturbs the reader. The commentary on Darcy's character in the concluding chapters of the novel implies disclosure. Yet, even after the account of his 'good principles' followed in 'pride and conceit' – with the 'heart-felt delight, diffused over his face' suggesting a correlation between inner feelings and outward appearance – Elizabeth subjects him to further scrutiny as she, in turn, is subjected to scrutiny by her sister and father (pp. 357, 354). The ending is punctuated by questions: Jane's first, '... but are you certain? [...] are you quite certain that you can be happy with him? [...] do you really love him quite well enough? Are you quite sure that you feel what you ought to do?' (p. 361); followed by her father's, '... what are you doing? Are you out of your senses, to be accepting this man? Have not you always hated him?' (p. 364). The reservations and consternation of Elizabeth's family compound her already 'agitated and confused' state (p. 360). In fact, the heroine's attempts to protect her future husband from uncongenial company 'took from the season of courtship much of its pleasure' (p. 372), and anticipates an uneasy path for the pair, socially at least, after they are married.[58]

It is this dampening or deferral of pleasure that makes Austen, as Emma Clery points out, 'the founder of the modern romance narrative'.[59] *Pride and Prejudice* is the prototype of the 'problem' romance that writers like Elizabeth Gaskell, George Eliot, and the Brontës inherited and remade. The unsettling yet eroticised suspense that sustains Austen's novel destabilises romantic expectations and offers new, if nettled, imaginative possibilities for the genre. Such ongoing consternation and narrative tension speaks, more broadly, to the Romantic aesthetics of Keats as well as Byron. The hero's opacity heightens the heroine's desire to interpret him, intensifying what Keats refers to as an 'irritable reaching after fact & reason', when uncertainty and 'half knowledge', indistinct insights, must suffice.[60] But it is Byron that is key to our understanding of *Pride and Prejudice* and its powerful hold on generations of readers. Austen's ambivalent response to Byron and the Byronic is choreographed, within the narrative, through the restless romance between Elizabeth and Darcy. The range of conflicted feelings that Darcy conveys takes on a more explicit political dimension in the Victorian Byronic heroes that will be addressed in subsequent chapters. Darcy ultimately challenges, in his partnership with a woman of lower social rank and his interactions with a widening, if selective, social circle, the hierarchies of class and gender that he initially seems to embody. And yet progressive ideas are couched, like Knightley and Emma's marriage, within a sense of reassuring stability. Framing a relatively radical vision within a conservative tradition is perhaps the most telling and fundamental affinity between Austen and Byron. Looking ahead, this process of cultural mediation, centred on the 'epistemological chasm' of the dissenting Byronic hero, is instructive when considering the presence and purpose of this Romantic poet in the work of women writers in the mid to late nineteenth century.

IV

'Austenmania' can be dated as specifically as the birth of 'Byromania' nearly two centuries before. Where the Romantic poet awoke to celebrity and, later, notoriety on 10 March 1812, with the publication of the first two cantos of *Childe Harold's Pilgrimage*, Austen became a celebrity not with the modest success of her novel *Pride and Prejudice*, published on 28 January 1813, but on 24 September 1995, with the screening of the first episode of the BBC's adaptation of *Pride and Prejudice*.[61]

Although Austen's appeal prior to this date should not be overlooked, the 'high' Janeites of the early twentieth century have been phased out by a new cult of fandom.[62] Austen has become a marketable name, a cultural fetish even, eclipsing her bestselling contemporaries, Byron and Scott. She was hailed as 'hot Hollywood property' after the BBC series triggered a plethora of Austen adaptations and reimaginings of her life and work (biopics in recent years include the BBC's *Miss Austen Regrets* [2008] and the film *Becoming Jane* [2007]).[63] In the wake of countless spin-offs, sequels, prequels, and mash-ups, *Newsweek* declared 'Jane-anything sells out'; 'Like BMW, Prada, and Martha Stewart, Austen is now a brand'.[64] When the BBC conducted 'The Big Read' in 2003, a survey to find the nation's favourite book, it is questionable whether *Pride and Prejudice* would have made it to second place had it not been for the success of this adaptation (re-energised in the collective cultural consciousness by the film version of *Bridget Jones's Diary*, released in 2001).[65] Austen's novel was rated above *To Kill a Mocking Bird*, *Nineteen Eighty-Four*, and even *Jane Eyre*, to be bettered only by Tolkien's trilogy, *The Lord of the Rings*, which benefited in the poll from the release of Peter Jackson's film versions, the first two instalments in 2001 and 2002, as well as from a dedicated fan base.

The television adaptation of *Pride and Prejudice,* screened over six episodes in autumn 1995, attracted viewing figures of 11 million. Sales of Austen's novel were boosted to 35,000 copies a week in England alone. It was Andrew Davies's decision to bring Darcy centre stage that turned this screen version into a cultural sensation and commercial success. New material in Davies's screenplay offered a visual narrative for his 'story' – including a twenty-minute sequence of flashbacks that dramatise the letter he writes to Elizabeth – and rooted Darcy's smouldering masculinity in action, in effect bringing him closer to the Byronic heroes of the Oriental Tales. Where Austen's Darcy is invariably reserved in the social scenes his character is largely limited to, Colin Firth's Darcy engages in 'manly' exertions from the outset. The adaptation begins with a prologue that is not in the novel, where Bingley and Darcy ride up to Netherfield as Jennifer Ehle's Elizabeth looks on before scampering down a slope. 'All three are attractive characters who exude a certain joie de vivre and sensuality. [...] We learn, for instance, that the handsome Bingley and Darcy are athletic young men, not dandies or fops', according to Ronnie Jo Sokol ('The Importance of Being Married', p. 95). Other added scenes include Darcy shooting, fencing, dancing, playing snooker, and, of course, swimming, when he emerges semi-clad from his pond at Pemberley.

Parallels can be drawn between what Cheryl L. Nixon refers to as Darcy's 'new physical vocabulary' in Davies's adaptation and Byron's impressive physical feats at swimming and boxing (masculine show-manship designed to counter what he saw as the physical deformity of his foot and to keep his weight in check).[66] A particular anecdote about Byron is pertinent to the ideological positioning of Darcy's body in the BBC mini-series. Byron's boatman, Maurice, recalled to Benjamin Disraeli a story about the inspiration for the famous storm in Canto III of *Childe Harold's Pilgrimage*: 'He told Lord Byron at first of the danger of such a night voyage, and the only answer which B. made was strip-ping quite naked and folding round him a great *robe de chambre*, so that in case of wreck he was ready prepared to swim immediately'. Diego Saglia's description of this moment, as 'a "heroic" body ready to plunge into the waters, a body that is suddenly and directly visible', captures the scintillated voyeurism of the audience when Elizabeth Bennet happens upon an unsuspecting and soaked Darcy in the grounds of Pemberley.[67] Austen's hero, in this screen version, makes good on Byron's promise of physical disclosure and assumes a mythic status. The enduring cultural reach of this scene was reaffirmed in 2008 when it was recreated as a homage in the fantasy adaptation, *Lost in Austen*, some thirteen years after the BBC series of *Pride and Prejudice* was televised.[68] More recently, in 2013, nearly two decades after the series was first screened, it was voted most memorable TV moment in a poll to celebrate the launch of a new channel devoted to drama. The installation of a twelve-foot high sculpture emerging out of The Serpentine Lake in Hyde Park (and subse-quently moved to the grounds of Lyme Park where the Pemberley scenes were filmed) re-embodied, in gigantic proportions, this Byronic Darcy. As the scene has become, in Colin Firth's words, 'part of the general canon of popular reference points […] immortalized', does this mean that Darcy is now circumscribed by a contemporary cultural frenzy where fame hangs on a celluloid image or a larger-than-life fibreglass figure (the modern-day equivalent of Byron's portraits perhaps)?[69]

The BBC serialisation of *Pride and Prejudice* sparked a resurgence of interest and investment in the screen adaptation, injecting renewed vig-our into what was a flagging genre. But did the revival of the costume drama come at the expense of Austen's hero turned pin-up? His iconic status, post-adaptation, was satirised in Posy Simmonds's cartoon for *The Guardian*'s 'Literary Life' series, when a bewildered Austen, thrust into the spotlight of celebrity, is questioned about the size of 'Colin Firth's lunch box'.[70] By fleshing out Darcy, and presenting him as, in Davies's words, 'a "natural" man as well as a "social" man', does the scrutinised body detract from, or even displace, the psychology of a character that Wiltshire regards as 'out of reach, an enigma, other'?[71] Does the BBC adaptation, and its success, illustrate only too well that the screen is, as Jean Domarchi puts it, 'above all *physical adventure* more than *interior adventure*'?[72] As these questions indicate, 'Darcymania' threatened to reach a point of semantic exhaustion comparable with 'Byromania'. Laura Thompson, writing for *The Daily Telegraph* in 2006, saw the 'Firth adaptation' as responsible for the repackaging of Austen as chick-lit, supermarket shelf romance, with *Pride and Prejudice* as 'a cultural touchstone, in a way that is almost completely meaningless. It symbolises art made accessible, literature as lifestyle choice'.[73] For Devoney Looser, also, '*Pride and Prejudice* has reached near ubiquity, having become a long-term "media event". [...] Austen serves as everyone's everything', rearticulating Henry James's aversion to her cultural amenability.[74]

Firth's Darcy certainly marks a departure from previous portrayals of Austen's hero. Laurence Olivier's Darcy, in the 1940 Hollywood film of *Pride and Prejudice*, was decidedly foppish.[75] In the 1980 BBC series, David Rintoul's Darcy was uptight, and his reproofs were cutting, in an adaptation that kept the claims of class and money to the fore.[76] 'Before the Firth treatment', as William Leith wrote in *The Observer*, 'Mr Darcy was seen as a dour, mildly unpleasant, if misunderstood character'.[77] It is worth considering what constitutes the so-called 'Firth treatment'. It is not, as Ellen Belton supposes, 'the 1990s' preoccupation with equality in romantic attachments' that excites us about this Austen adaptation.[78] 'Colin Firth's beefcake version of Darcy' was widely read, in post-heritage terms, as an antidote to the 'New Man' of the 1990s; 'He was in no way a feminized wimp', argues Virginia L. Blum.[79] Austen's novels cannot be readily adapted for the ideological purposes of post-feminist utopianism and neither are they amenable to a conservative cultural 'backlash', however.[80] Costume drama can offer regressive gender relations as fantasy, a 'reactionary escapism', even as the genre adjusts to, and seems to advance, progressive ideas, especially with regards to the representation of women and the relationship between the sexes.[81] Austen's Darcy – emerging out of and entering into early nineteenth-century debates about masculine behaviour – is poised between the 'traditional' and the 'modern', a composite of radical and conservative impulses. Drawing out the Byronic side of Austen's character in the BBC adaptation thereby intensifies a perennial pressure, with Darcy both dominating and liberating Elizabeth with his gaze, as he is also subject to the specularity of the viewer. As both a literary suitor with the 'ideal

C.V.'[82] and an antagonist, 'so cold and withdrawn that he could easily have been a villain',[83] Firth's Darcy became the most compelling romantic anti-hero for a generation (as Austen's portrait of the 'new gentleman' had been for her own and the next). It could be argued, therefore, that this Byronic Darcy, and the subsequent mythologising of the role, enhanced rather than diminished the enigmatic appeal of Austen's male lead. Firth's sense of detachment from the afterlife of his performance, regarding it as a 'hologram', recaptures an essence of the mystery and estrangement associated with this hero, as discussed in Part III of this chapter.[84]

In the 2005 film of *Pride and Prejudice*, directed by Joe Wright, Darcy's fixation with Elizabeth is neither as fierce nor as dominant as in the BBC adaptation, screened some ten years earlier.[85] In many ways, Matthew Macfadyen's portrayal of Darcy takes us back to a reserved male protagonist who is seen primarily from the heroine's viewpoint. As the film recentres Austen's story on Elizabeth, played by Keira Knightley, it is her initial impression of the hero that frames our perception of him: 'And the person with the quizzical brow? [...] He looks miserable, poor soul'. This Darcy is adversarial yet embarrassed in the first proposal scene; outbursts of anger are intermingled with painful shyness. He is as perplexing as he is perplexed by his own conflicted emotions, an impression reinforced by the mobility of the camera. For Deborah Moggach, the scriptwriter, Darcy is an outsider, 'bored, uncomfortable, restless, frustrated ...', who is only able to engage in meaningful conversation when removed from the confines of social expectation.[86] It is telling, in this respect, that both proposal scenes take place out-of-doors: the first in the driving rain at the Temple of Apollo at Stourhead, a torrent of feeling translated onto the body against an architectural backdrop that reinforces Darcy's latent identification with a classical heroic tradition; the second in fields at dawn with Darcy striding through the morning mists before the delicacy of touching fingers and foreheads confirm his physical and psychological connectedness with Elizabeth.[87] The hero framed by the golden haze of sunrise heralds the promise of renewal; and yet what might be interpreted as a visual indicator of fertility is here associated with subdued masculinity. Although Macfadyen's portrait of wounded sensitivity gestures towards a deeper and more nuanced understanding of Austen's Darcy, the memory of Firth's performance remains potent. For Cosmo Landesman, in a review of Wright's film for *The Sunday Times*, the ghost of Darcy past presides over what is, for him, in contrast with Davies's adaptation, a lacklustre, 'sexless Austen'.[88]

The success of Davies's *Pride and Prejudice* not only 'transformed the TV landscape', as claimed in a retrospective of the BBC series; it 'was so dominant, so universally adored, it has lingered in the public conscious- ness as a cinematic standard'.[89] Davies had already given Will Ladislaw a leading role in the BBC adaptation of *Middlemarch* (1994), magnifying his Byronic aspect in terms of appearance and temperament (as will be discussed in Chapter 5), but it was his screenplay for *Pride and Prejudice* that reignited 'Byromania' as 'Darcymania'. The impact and cross- pollination of Firth's Byronic Darcy can be felt, almost a decade later, in the 2004 BBC adaptation of Elizabeth Gaskell's *North and South* through the portrayal of the darkly erotic taskmaster, John Thornton (as will be discussed in the next chapter). Austen's 'new gentleman' and Gaskell's self-made man, separated by over forty years in terms of publication (not to mention social status and political leanings), are similarly defined on screen as Byronic. For Austen, this has the effect of rebrand- ing her as an early or proto-Victorian novelist.[90] Austen's male leads, as portrayed on screen, are conversant with the moody monomania of later Byronic heroes, such as Emily Brontë's Heathcliff, as well as with the afterlives of these figures in adaptations and artwork.[91] The 'long' nineteenth century is conveniently compressed in costume drama; and the Romantic hero, within this culturally congested context, becomes a shared shorthand for the sexily sardonic male protagonist.[92] If 'Austen's afterlives derive their life and livelihood from the new ways in which they are reread and restaged', as Clara Tuite contends, then Firth's Byronic Darcy constitutes a defining moment in this author's posthu- mous fortunes and in the fortunes of modern screen adaptations.[93]

In the novels examined in this and the previous chapter, Austen undertakes the interrelated project of rewriting Romanticism and reha- bilitating the figure of the Romantic hero. Andrew Davies's screenplay for the BBC draws on Austen's flawed and enigmatic protagonist, and recasts him as a quintessential Byronic hero. In Austen's *Pride and Prejudice*, Darcy's proximity to the Byronic and implicit Byronic traits are debated, derided, and desired; in Davies's *Pride and Prejudice*, Darcy's explicit debt to the Byronic is unambiguously desired. *Persuasion*'s Wentworth is, by turns, brave, irascible, and gentle, like the changeable protagonists in Byron's poetry. Portrayals of his character on screen similarly enhance a Byronic profile, sometimes at the expense of his indeterminate Romantic depths. In her last complete novel, Austen is in deliberate dialogue with both the past authors she revered and the present authors she had a sceptical regard for, differentiating between Byronism – as a cultural trend associated with extravagant posturing and exhibitionism – and a meaningful understanding of Byron's poetry that sheds light on the subtler emotional shadows cast by her central characters. In other words, she proves herself, and encourages others, to be a critically astute reader of both Byron's poetry and the Byronic persona. It is Austen and Byron who, however surprising the connection, provide us with the most influential and enduring Romantic male protagonists. These figures, taken from the poetry and prose of the period, are crossbred and synthesised, to great critical and commercial success, in film and television adaptations. The intertwined fates of Austen's and Byron's Romantic heroes, and the charged conversations out of which they were conceived, leave a lasting legacy for the Victorian women writers that this book will now consider.

3
Elizabeth Gaskell's Byronic Heroes: *Wives and Daughters* and *North and South*

I

The remaining chapters of this book move on from the reception of the Byronic hero in the Romantic fiction of Jane Austen, and adaptations of her work, to the reception of this figure in the Victorian fiction of Elizabeth Gaskell and George Eliot. The focus on these authors, and adaptations of their work, may be as surprising as the previous focus on Austen, and yet it is equally revealing. Establishing previously neglected connections between these authors and the legacy of the Byronic hero achieves a dual purpose. First, it opens their fiction to new lines of enquiry and new critical approaches, as well as situating their work within new literary contexts. For Gaskell and Eliot, the figure of the Byronic hero is central to the interrelated concerns of masculinity and Romanticism. Second, re-evaluating the relationship between these authors and the afterlives of this Romantic poet enables a reassessment of the extent and significance of Byron's influence, and the cultural reach of Byronism, in women's writing of the Victorian period. The Byronic hero presented a unique opportunity for Eliot and Gaskell to enter current debates about masculinity and the fate of the hero. This figure served both novelists as a means of surreptitiously transgressing gender conventions and of engaging with, if not endorsing, a Byronic voice of dissent, a position established more broadly in the introduction.[1] This chapter and the succeeding chapters will address the following questions: what is distinctive about Gaskell's and Eliot's treatment of this figure; what function/s does he perform; what does this tell us about their attitudes towards masculinity, and heroism in particular, when read in the context of a Romantic inheritance? Lastly, are these engagements and disengagements with the Byronic hero reflected, and to what effect, in modern screen adaptations of their work?

Both Elizabeth Gaskell and George Eliot sought, as Jane Austen had done before them, to redefine masculinity in their work. J. R. Watson claims that Gaskell answered Byron's famous call in *Don Juan*, 'I want a hero', by 'provid[ing] them in every story and every novel'.[2] From her earliest writings, including two tales – 'The Sexton's Hero' (1847) and 'The Heart of John Middleton' (1850) – which will be discussed shortly, Gaskell participated in narratives of heroism and engaged with broader issues of masculinity. Watson sees a preoccupation with heroism in *Sylvia's Lovers* (1863), particularly with the figure of the military hero, as indicating a debt to Thomas Carlyle. *On Heroes, Hero-Worship, and the Heroic in History*, given as lectures in 1840 and then published in 1841, had a significant impact on Gaskell, which is evident in the duty and courage demonstrated by her favoured male protagonists. The importance Gaskell accorded to Carlyle, as witnessed by the epigraph to *Mary Barton* (1848) and the store she set by his response to that novel, raises an immediate problem when considering the figure of the Byronic hero in Gaskell's fiction and subsequent screen adaptations of her work. Carlyle wrote his famous directive, 'Close thy *Byron*; open thy *Goethe*', in *Sartor Resartus* (1833–34), and objects to 'our general Byronism of taste' in *On Heroes*.[3] In the former, Carlyle sought to make space for himself as a writer by deriding the cult following of a privileged poet: '*Sartor* rewrote popular Byronic literature in order to redirect public taste toward the professional intellectual's voice', argues Andrew Elfenbein.[4] In the latter, Carlyle bemoans the 'sad state Hero-worship now lies in', and argues for writers such as Shakespeare and Dante to be considered the 'Saints of Poetry' (pp. 148, 113). Their superiority lies in their sincerity, their sympathy, the hope they offer, and the repentance they can affect; above all, as the 'blessed heaven-sent Bringer[s] of Light', they are 'Morally great' (pp. 146, 125). Such descriptions accord with what is often taken to be Carlyle's anti-Byronic stance. Yet, on closer inspection, the other qualities that are prized in *On Heroes* – including intensity, mystery, a power of vision ('The seeing eye!', p. 138), and, in particular, those 'suffering heroic hearts' – are not so far removed from the avowed nemesis (p. 143).

Carlyle's worship of genius in *On Heroes* is decidedly Romantic, as is his lifelong fascination with the 'disruptive energies' epitomised by a poet like Byron.[5] Carlyle's opinion of Byron – and, more specifically, the fad for Byronism – represents a heated response to the cultural and class politics of the day by a writer schooling himself and the reading public out of a dangerous devotion to this aristocratic forefather. He acknowledged Byron's literary power while also deriding a 'spasmodic Byronism, bellowing till its windpipe is cracked'.[6] Recent criticism on Carlyle's attitude towards Byron and Byronism is keen to stress parallels and contrasts, as Kristen Guest demonstrates: 'Carlyle's rejection of Byronism was prompted by his scorn for its self-absorption; yet, in describing his illness he generated a personal narrative of suffering that was Byronic in its excess'.[7] And Andrew Stauffer is concerned with instances of Carlyle's admiration for Byron: 'Like Shelley's Prometheus, Carlyle's representative must recall his curse, or at least grow beyond it, yet Carlyle celebrates the moment of anger in a Byronic manner, calling it a "Fire-baptism" that inaugurated Teufelsdröckh's "Spiritual New-birth"'.[8] Regarding Carlyle as a Romantic heir, in his simultaneous 'extension and rejection of Byronism' ('Dyspeptic Reactions', p. 157), provides a profitable and complex point of comparison for Gaskell's, as well as other women writers', ambivalent regard for the Byronic hero.

Despite her admiration for Carlyle, or perhaps because of it, Gaskell's hero figures are anything but derivative. The most innovative aspect of Gaskell's fiction, according to Joseph Kestner, is her ability to 'defamiliarize and individuate male prototypes'.[9] In *Mary Barton*, Gaskell depicts, in the character of John Barton, an 'exemplary manliness', which is marginalised and then driven to violence.[10] Victorian anxieties over the potential viciousness of the working classes are moderated by Gaskell's engagement with Chartist debates. Her sympathetic arbitration produced a portrait of what Lisa Surridge describes as 'the erosion of masculine power in the contemporary working-class family' ('Working-Class Masculinities', p. 332). With her later novel, *North and South* (1855), Gaskell broadens and deepens her exploration of manhood under siege by showing the conflicting male energies of the industrialist and his workers. Although middle-class men are shown to be attuned to and able to profit from the changing economic climate, they are also, in John Thornton's words, 'groping in new circumstances', disorientated by the losses and gains associated with their aspiring social status.[11] Catherine Barnes Stevenson sees *North and South* as extending the presentation of the so-called 'new man' in Charlotte Brontë's social novel *Shirley* (1849), and claims that, in both novels, Gaskell and Brontë 'wrote the masculine'.[12]

Contentious issues surrounding masculinity form an intrinsic part of the dialogue between gender politics and social change in both Gaskell's and Eliot's work. The potential for positive change in *North and South* is generated by connecting Margaret Hale and Mr Thornton's

erotically-charged and evolving relationship with the contemporary rel-
evance of the 'Condition of England' novel. Michiel Heyns comments
on 'the surprising boldness of Mrs Gaskell's exploration of conflict as an
element both of sexuality and of industrial relations, a conflict between
men and women as much as between "Masters and Men"'.[13] For Heyns,
this fusion of class and sexual relations makes clear the novel's underlying
preoccupation with power, as is demonstrated in the first proposal scene
where a discourse of war is employed. It is not only Thornton who vents
his anger and perceives Margaret as a challenge to be conquered; she also
demonstrates a quarrelsome disposition and an intractable will more
commonly associated with the Byronic hero. Like Elizabeth Bennet and
Mr Darcy before them, the exchanges between Margaret and Thornton
are combative and serve to enliven, and even electrify, the text. What
emerges from Gaskell's novel is that altercations between the hero and
the heroine, amidst the broader narrative strains of portraying a love
interest with a social agenda, need not be considered wholly negative.
Rather, the ongoing battles throughout the novel indicate that conflict is
beneficial to human relationships. As Gaskell wrote,

> I suppose we all *do* strengthen each other by clashing together, and
> earnestly talking our own thoughts and ideas. The very disturbance
> we thus are to each other rouses us up, and makes us more healthy.[14]

Gaskell's *North and South*, like Eliot's later novel *Middlemarch* (1871–72),
may advocate gradual growth, both psychologically and ideologically,
and yet the prospect of reform remains central to both novels through
a series of conflicts that are never fully resolved. In fact, Rosemarie
Bodenheimer sees *North and South* as Gaskell's most radical novel
'because it is so good at posing knotted issues and feelings that cannot
come formally to rest except in the depiction of ongoing process and
readjustment'.[15]

The Byronic hero, and Byron's poetry more broadly, plays an instrumental role in the vexed yet constructive questions that Gaskell put to
herself about 'reconcil[ing] all these warring members' (April 1850). His
ethos corresponds with hers in a number of important and illuminating ways. Byron was associated with liberty, rebellion, and revolution
throughout the nineteenth century, and writers such as Thomas Carlyle
and John Stuart Mill considered him seriously as a political poet in
the early Victorian period. Mill's progressive liberalism did not stretch
to Byron's 'transgressive eloquence', however, a poetics that spoke to,
instead of on behalf of, the masses.[16] Timothy J. Wandling suggests

that Gaskell's work accords with Mill's commitment to speaking for the masses – effecting change through private reflection rather than public uprising – and thereby acts as a counterpoint to Byron's verse. It is true that Gaskell attempted to voice the oppressed millworkers in her 'social' novels – 'to give some utterance to the agony which, from time to time, convulses this dumb people' (Preface to *Mary Barton*) – and yet such endeavours do not appear to be at odds with Byron's calls for freedom nor his appeal to a wide spectrum of readers.[17] Surely Gaskell's exposé of an exploited labour force shares something, if not in style or tone, with Byron's professed intent in *Don Juan*: 'I mean to show things really as they are,/ Not as they ought to be' (XII. xl). It could be argued, moreover, that the conflation of the political and the personal in Byron's poetry corresponds with the intersections between the public and the private in *North and South*. As the erotic invariably takes on a political edge in Byron's poetry, so Gaskell overlays public conflicts with the private concerns of romance. What Terence Hoagwood describes as Byron's 'disruptive dialectic' can be found in Gaskell's commitment to creative dissonance; both authors share a sceptical regard for conformist attitudes and beliefs, as well as a propensity to reside in doubt, however contentious or painful, over and above straightforward resolution.[18] Is Mill's perception of Byron as a radical rabble-rouser so far removed from Gaskell when we consider the controversy and hostile attacks that her 'fire brand' novels, namely *Mary Barton* and *Ruth*, met with on publication?[19] Crucially, for both Byron and Gaskell, despite their many and various differences, writing was a form of social redress through which they actively sought and entertained an audience.

II

Gaskell's response to Byron has received less critical attention than the other women writers considered in this book. Gossip about Byron, of the kind that Eliot objected to, was a popular topic in letters of the Holland family while Gaskell was growing up in Knutsford. Fanny Parkes (formerly Byerley), who established, along with her sisters, the school for young ladies that Gaskell attended for about five years, issued the customary warning against reading Byron in a conduct book that she published in 1825.[20] Some of Gaskell's early short stories could be read as equally anti-Byronic: in 'The Heart of John Middleton', for example, the protagonist, after being abused by his father, is misguidedly motivated by hatred and revenge, and gains pleasure from an eclectic literary diet that includes reading Byron's 'Narratives'.[21] An even earlier tale, 'The Sexton's Hero', advocates a Christian heroism of self-sacrifice, endurance, and pacifism. Gaskell's 'domestic' hero is far removed from the emotional excesses of the Victorian anti-hero, as Mariaconcetta Costantini argues:

> Compared with Emily Brontë's development of the Byronic hero, Gaskell's protagonist appears as a quite innovative figure, since his modest and faithful observance of the Gospel is totally devoid of the moral ambiguities that characterize Heathcliff's passionate behaviour.[22]

Gaskell's much vaunted 'commitment to verisimilitude' need not preclude Romantic concerns, however (Stone, *Romantic Impulse*, p. 11). Consider, for instance, the immediacy with which the narrator of 'The Sexton's Hero' recalls his former hatred for Gilbert Dawson, the love triangle that ensues, and the narrative frame that invites the reader to 'listen' and construct their own subjective version of the story. In fact, the following description of the narrator by Costantini could be describing one of Byron's heroes: 'a willing rejection of life and its lacerating passions. The same reference to his darkened sight, which is repeatedly stressed at the beginning of his tale, evokes images of death and voluntary isolation from people's society' (p. 79). Furthermore, what Costantini refers to as the difficulties, or the 'unresolved antithesis', of the story actually constitute part of its strength (p. 83). Seen simply as a realist tale with occasional lapses into the melodramatic and supernatural, 'The Sexton's Hero' is unremarkable. Conversely, what is, in my opinion, truly innovative about this tale is the recourse to romance within realism.

On balance, it may seem reasonable to assume (as initially appears to be the case with Eliot) that Gaskell equated Byron with little more than the profligacy he became synonymous with in the early Victorian period. Yet, shortly after she left school, her brother John praised some letters she had written to their father, 'particularly the one containing a criticism on Lord Byron's poetry'.[23] This was not Gaskell's only attempt at interpreting Byron. A particularly telling instance in Gaskell's literary relationship with this Romantic poet relates to a proposed series of works that were intended to imitate writers of the past depicting scenes of Victorian life. Gaskell read lots of Wordsworth, Coleridge, Dryden, Pope, and Crabbe for this purpose; and yet, significantly, she had finished 'all my *composition* of Ld Byron' before the project was eventually abandoned.[24] As Jenny Uglow reminds us, Gaskell read Byron's Romantic pirate tale *The Corsair* with enthusiasm, in marked contrast to

Austen's professed lack of interest.[25] If the epigraphs of her novels are an indication of her reading habits more generally, then Gaskell, like Eliot, read and quoted from Byron's poetry throughout her life. In her first full-length novel, *Mary Barton*, two chapters begin with quotations from *The Siege of Corinth* and *The Giaour* respectively, while other Romantic poets, such as Wordsworth, Coleridge, Keats, and Burns, also feature prominently. Likewise, Gaskell's later novel, *North and South*, teems with a range of Romantic writers, including Hemans, Barbauld, Southey, Landor, Coleridge, and Shelley, among others. And, once again, a quotation from Byron serves as an epigraph, which will be discussed in Part V of this chapter.

Byron even makes an appearance in *Cranford* (1851–53). Gaskell's portrait of a rural community in the mid-nineteenth century would seem to be the least likely place to encounter any mention of the poet. This series of stories constitute an affectionate satire on the relationships between women in a tight-knit community. A tone of pleasurable pathos pervades the work, commenting on both the delights and sadness of the commonplace, and the gradual, yet unstoppable, encroachment of modernity. Nonetheless, although the dominant mode in *Cranford* is undoubtedly realism, Miss Matty's renewed acquaintance with a former sweetheart, Mr Holbrook, affords a late flowering of romance and youthful flirtation. There is something mildly comical in the scene where Miss Matty flusters bashfully and then falls asleep as Mr Holbrook begins reading aloud Tennyson's poem about thwarted lovers, 'Locksley Hall'. Equally, Mr Holbrook seems out of place amongst the Cranford ladies with his eccentric, and somewhat exotic, talk of the Romantics: 'To be sure, he called Byron "my lord Bўrron", and pronounced the name of Goethe strictly in accordance with the English sound of the letters – "As Göethe says, 'Ye ever-verdant palaces',," &c'.[26] The intrusion of the Romantic is here the occasion for humour. However, Mr Holbrook is not merely an object of ridicule. The narrator is surprised by Holbrook's 'ever-increasing delight in the daily and yearly change of season and beauty', a delight that he expresses, without artifice, through poetry: 'He did this as naturally as if he were thinking aloud, that their true and beautiful words were the best expression he could find for what he was thinking or feeling' (p. 41). There is no hint of irony in the following description, which culminates in a quotation from Tennyson's poem 'The Gardener's Daughter':

> He walked before me, with a stooping gait, his hands clasped behind him; and, as some tree or cloud, or glimpse of distant upland

pastures, struck him, he quoted poetry to himself; saying it out loud in a grand sonorous voice, with just the emphasis that true feeling and appreciation give. We came upon an old cedar-tree, which stood at one end of the house;

'The cedar spreads his dark-green layers of shade.' (p. 44)

This 'natural' recourse to poetry flows easily within Gaskell's realist prose. Resistance to Holbrook's exuberant poeticising is apparent in Miss Matty's frequent references to Samuel Johnson, which not only introduce the spectre of her sister's stern rationalism, but also raise the fraught issue of what characters read (a subject of even greater concern in Gaskell's later novel, *Wives and Daughters*, as we shall see).[27] Despite Holbrook's impressively wide-ranging literary tastes, from Shakespeare and Herbert through the Romantics to Tennyson, he admits, tellingly, to an ignorance of Johnson. Yet, rather than being regarded as absurd, his eclectic tastes reflect Gaskell's own varied literary predilections, which include, according to Shirley Foster, a 'life-long love of poetry' (*Literary Life*, p. 15). The description of a room festooned with all manner of books, particularly poetry and 'wild weird tales', combines, seamlessly, a gentle mockery with indulgence.

The rest of the pretty sitting-room – looking into the orchard, and all covered over with dancing tree-shadows – was filled with books. They lay on the ground, they covered the walls, they strewed the table. He was evidently half ashamed and half proud of his extravagance in this respect. They were of all kinds, – poetry, and wild weird tales prevailing. He evidently chose his books in accordance with his own tastes, not because such and such were classical, or established favourites. (p. 42)

Gaskell evidently prefers Holbrook's eager if haphazard reading habits and lack of literary pretension to Miss Jenkyns's worthy yet stubborn conviction in the merits of a single author.

With his sudden death at the end of this chapter, Holbrook's re-entry into Cranford society represents a significant, yet all too brief, romantic interlude.[28] It is in Gaskell's last, unfinished novel that the ongoing dialogue between romance and realism takes centre stage. A strong romantic undercurrent is evident in the first few chapters of *Wives and Daughters* (1866), with allusions to fairy tales, Molly Gibson's childlike enjoyment of open spaces, and her disorientation and distress, which she describes in the dramatic terms of feeling 'like a lighted candle when they're putting the extinguisher on it'.[29] The novel is suitably full of references to Romantic literature by, among others, Hemans, Scott, Edgeworth, Barbauld, Coleridge, and, of course, Wordsworth.[30] Here, as elsewhere in Gaskell's fiction, a Wordsworthian presence is discernible in direct allusions to his poems and a more indirect voicing of his influence. Shortly after a reference to 'A Slumber Did My Spirit Seal' in Chapter 34, '...she was being carried on in earth's diurnal course, with rocks, and stones, and trees', appear the following lines: 'There, bathed in the almost level rays of the autumn sunlight, lay the landscape she had known and loved from childhood; as quiet, as full of low humming life as it had been at this hour for many generations'. This description of a tranquil pastoral, with the reassuring presence of a distant humanity and the restorative recollections of childhood, illustrates a Victorian reading of Wordsworth. Subsequent lines in Gaskell's novel depict a humble rural idyll, a domestic scene both registering and anticipating human activity, which evokes the opening lines of 'Tintern Abbey': 'the evening fires had just been made up in the cottages beyond, in preparation for the husband's homecoming, and were sending up soft curls of blue smoke into the still air' (pp. 372–3).[31]

Gaskell declared that 'my heart feels so full of him' when referring to Wordsworth (12 May 1836). For Bonnie Gerard, Wordsworth's poetry was instrumental in Gaskell's negotiations as a novelist between the ideals of the past and the present, the Romantic and the Victorian, the spiritual and the material; she even goes as far as to suggest that *North and South* 'can be read as a Victorian social novelist's reception of Wordsworth's Romantic neoplatonism', informed, in particular, by the recently published epic, *The Prelude*.[32] Donald D. Stone had previously outlined Gaskell's affinity with Wordsworth in his study, *The Romantic Impulse in Victorian Fiction* (1980). Here he argued that Victorian writers were divided between two opposing representatives of English Romanticism – Wordsworth and Byron – with Gaskell favouring the former's empathy and fortitude as opposed to, and also as a way of critiquing, the egotism that had become a byword for the Byronic. Demonstrating a debt to Wordsworth's poetry not only demarcates Gaskell's fiction as 'unByronic'; it also acts, according to Stone, as a 'literary conscience' (*Romantic Impulse*, p. 133). In this way, Wordsworth formed a kind of 'moral cloak' for Gaskell, a means of containing and even expunging outward signs of artistic ambition (p. 142). An identification of Wordsworth with didactic selflessness and Byron with self-indulgent wilfulness, which Gaskell either endorses or denies, is necessarily reductive, a point that Stone himself concedes: 'In truth, Byron and Wordsworth were alike altruistic and individualistic, humanitarian and narcissistic' (p. 136). As I have already touched upon and will return to later in this chapter, Gaskell does not shy away from the disruptive potential of Byronic rebellion. Where Stone regards *North and South* as a 'romantic lapse' for which the author spends the next decade trying to atone, I argue that a passionate and political individualism remains a prominent feature of her fiction (p. 160).

III

Byron is referred to and is the subject of commentary on more occasions in Gaskell's last novel, *Wives and Daughters*, than anywhere else in her fiction, suggesting an intensification of interest in the poet. The first instance involves Lord Cumnor misattributing a quotation from *Childe Harold's Pilgrimage* to Pope, which his wife corrects. The line, 'to make a Roman holiday' (IV. cxli), is, as Pam Morris suggests, 'comically inappropriate' in the context,[33] given that it relates to the Roman 'sport' of gladiatorial combat (the phrase is preceded by the word 'Butcher'd' in Byron's description of bloody barbarism), and prompts the following exchange:

> 'It's Byron, and it's nothing to do with the subject in hand. I'm surprised at your lordship's quoting Byron, – he was a very immoral poet.'
>
> 'I saw him take his oaths in the House of Lords,' said Lord Cumnor, apologetically.
>
> 'Well! The less said about him the better,' said Lady Cumnor. (p. 139)

Lady Cumnor is predictably scandalised by and dismissive of Lord Byron. Yet she also betrays a ready knowledge of his poetry and her husband admits to having seen the poet in person. The second reference to Byron's poetry in the novel is perhaps more telling than the first. At a dinner party organised for the express purpose of match-making, Mrs Kirkpatrick boasts that her daughter, Cynthia, can 'repeat the "Prisoner of Chillon" from beginning to end' (p. 267). Poetry is here learnt by rote to increase a young woman's value in the marriage market; reciting Byron's poetry is both a fashion statement and a cultural asset. As such, Mrs Kirkpatrick is piqued by having what she considers to be a sophisticated accomplishment mocked by her husband and then contradicted by Cynthia, who proclaims 'I've displaced the

Prisoner to make room for Johnnie Gilpin as my favourite poem'. This reference to William Cowper's popular comic ballad, *The Diverting History of John Gilpin* (1782), which predates Byron's success by some three decades, has been read as 'a substitution of healthy English humour for Romantic European-influenced melodrama' (Morris, p. 664). In *Wives and Daughters*, therefore, both of the direct allusions to Byron are sardonic and cautionary, aimed at illustrating the characters who misread or misuse his poetry. Lord Cumnor's gratification over his 'unusual aptitude at quotation' (p. 139) and Mrs Kirkpatrick's pride and affected poetic sensibilities are, to varying degrees, deflated and discredited through references to Byron.

Instances such as these have led Julia M. Wright to read Gaskell's novel as emphasising 'the importance of the maturing Molly as a symbol of the nation's progress from Romantic puberty to Victorian maturity'.[34] For Wright, the main characters in Gaskell's novel can be divided into two groups: the first is 'morally and medically pathologized: They have nervous bodies, superficial or flawed sentiments, and, through their egotism, cause most of the trouble of the novel. They all, moreover, favour the literature of the Romantic period, particularly romances and the poetry of Felicia Hemans, Samuel Taylor Coleridge, Byron, and William Wordsworth'. The second group have 'healthier bodies' and 'read "serious" literature, a category that, in Gaskell's novel, includes science, philosophy, agriculture, and specifically pre-Romantic literature' ('Growing Pains', p. 164). The most obvious example of the first group is Molly's stepmother. We are told that Mrs Kirkpatrick is a 'flimsy character', and her self-proclaimed sensitivities are a source of irony throughout the novel (p. 140). Her rose-coloured memories – of a previous marriage that indulged in an 'extravagance of feeling which misleads the judgment, and conducts into romance' (p. 637) – seem to be epitomised by her own name, Hyacinth, and the name given to her daughter. Mr Gibson's unfortunate comment, 'Cynthia seems to me such an out-of-the-way name, only fit for poetry, not for daily use' (p. 105), touches on the broader issue of genre, as is also highlighted by Wright in the quotations above.

In contrast to Mrs Kirkpatrick, Mrs Hamley's genuine passion for poetry establishes a firm maternal bond with Molly. At the start of the aptly-titled chapter 'Drifting into Danger', Molly's poetic proclivities are refracted through Gaskell's prose as the heroine, like one of Tennyson's doomed ladies, perceives herself to be in a ' "moated grange" [where] the booming buzz of the blue flies, in the great staircase window, seemed the loudest noise in-doors' (p. 83). Vibrant noises and delicious scents seep through Molly's Mariana-esque reverie as she 'lazily' copies out and memorises Osborne Hamley's poems. This vapid occupation, which becomes merely 'mechanical', connects the heroine with Cynthia's showy allurements and conveys a sense of foreboding. The invariably sharp lens of Gaskell's narrative viewpoint is filtered by the heroine's hazy impressions, with both Molly and the reader receiving the news of Osborne's disappointing degree result through a myopic dreamscape. Given their shared sensibility at this point in the narrative, it is almost as if Molly's romantic interlude precipitates Mrs Hamley's 'irrepressible half-hysterical fit of sobbing' on learning of her son's failings (p. 84). This passage not only indicates that Osborne falls short of his parents' expectations and that his poetry is something of a sham; it infuses the seemingly innocent distraction of reading and reciting poetry with a sense of the unreal, which consequently distorts or distracts from a focus on realist representation.

Osborne's poetry is found to be 'essentially imitative' and his refined sensibilities are described as '(pseudo) genius', the insertion of parenthesis heightening the ironic effect (pp. 259, 258). Even Osborne declares of his amateurish pastime: 'my day is past for purely ornamental work' (p. 326). This repudiation of the romantic in *Wives and Daughters* does not appear to be limited to the genre of poetry. While deeply immersed in Walter Scott's historical novel *The Bride of Lammermoor* (1819), Molly 'jumped as if she had been shot' when Squire Hamley requests her company (p. 71). An indulgence in diverting daydreams is depicted as isolating and even antisocial, an instance of the 'castle building' that Dorothy Mermin sees as characteristic of the woman reader in Victorian fiction.[35] We are told that Molly's 'little wavering maiden fancy dwelt on the unseen Osborne, who was now a troubadour, and now a knight, such as he wrote about in one of his own poems' (p. 147); and even after Molly has met Osborne, which necessitates a slight readjustment of these fanciful notions, she insists on seeing him as a hero akin to Ivanhoe. Molly, once again mirroring Mrs Hamley, cannot reconcile her idealised image of Osborne with what she discovers about him and the circumstances surrounding his secret marriage.

Molly is 'puzzled' – a term that, as we shall see, Margaret Hale uses when thinking about Mr Thornton in *North and South* – by the 'clever, brilliant, handsome son Osborne', who is distinguished and graceful, gloomy and overly-theatrical (pp. 233, 211). Mrs Kirkpatrick's pronouncement that Osborne 'is the perfect gentleman in appearance and manner' directs the reader to a romantic role-playing reminiscent of Willoughby in Austen's *Sense and Sensibility* (p. 182). Osborne is described as a 'popinjay' and a 'dilettante', the same charge that is levelled at Will Ladislaw in *Middlemarch*, with a 'point-device costume' that incenses his father for its vanity and 'girlishness' (pp. 257, 350, 252). Indeed, Thomas Babington Macaulay's description of young men infatuated with and keen to imitate Byron is uncannily similar to Gaskell's characterisation of aristocratic affectation and effeminacy: 'They bought pictures of him; they treasured up the smallest relics of him; they learned his poems by heart, and did their best to write like him, and to look like him. Many of them practised at the glass, in the hope of catching the curl of the upper lip, and the scowl of the brow, which appear in some of his portraits'.[36]

Mrs Hamley's final summation of her son, however, suggests that the showy cult of Byronism has seeped beneath the surface or that the Byronic surface has undiscovered depths: 'I've made such an idol of my beautiful Osborne; and he turns out to have feet of clay' (p. 194). The phrase, 'feet of clay', appears in Byron's poem 'Ode to Napoleon Buonaparte', which also includes the pertinent lines: 'Weigh'd in the balance, hero dust/ Is vile as vulgar clay'.[37] Byron's critical regard for his idol, Napoleon, which veered towards disillusionment on occasion, chimes with Mrs Hamley's wistful reflections on the idealisation of her son and his all too human inability to match up to those ideals. The following lines from Byron's poem could equally describe Osborne's unwitting part in his mother's death: 'Thine only gift hath been the grave/ To those that worshipp'd thee' (ii). Furthermore, Osborne's unnamed vices – as they are thought to be at this point in the narrative – as well as his unexplained sojourns from home, the questionable validity of his marriage, the performative aspects of his character, and his captivation with women all betoken authentic (as opposed to merely affected) Byronic traits.

Read in this way, Osborne's death is not only inevitable but also necessary for Molly to escape the Romantic and form a bond with Roger. Osborne performs a cautionary function in the novel; yet his significance reaches beyond the one-dimensional to a moving portrait of tragic romanticism. In Osborne, Gaskell personifies the graduation from 'being Byron' to a subtle Byronic sensibility, a transition that is discernible in many of the novels examined in this book. Osborne may cling to sad if farcical 'visions of poetical and romantic reconciliations' with his father (p. 332), yet he becomes increasingly aware of his own shortcomings and the grief that he has occasioned (Molly notes changes in him, both physical and psychological). In addition, although Osborne is often considered to be effeminate, as mentioned above, he is also at the centre of an ongoing debate about what constitutes 'manly' behaviour in the novel, developing a central theme in *North and South* (as will be discussed in the second half of this chapter). The young heir may not be the hero of Molly's, or even his own, literary imagination, but he seems content with his domestic life away from Hamley Hall and his choice of the unglamorous nursemaid, Aimée, as his wife. 'The account of their courtship and marriage', argues Jennifer Panek, 'elevates him [Osborne] further, for it rewrites the all too familiar story of a servant-girl seduced and abandoned by a wealthy young man'.[38] Gaskell comes close to, yet ultimately veers away from, a satire on poetic profligacy or an exposé of diseased Romanticism. Rather, as Osborne's range extends beyond that of a pretentious aesthete to a grieving son and loving husband and father, we are invited to reconsider our preconceptions of Byronic masculinities, especially in the light of Roger's misguided attraction to the local coquette, Cynthia.

There is merit in reading this novel ideologically, with battle lines drawn between romance and reason, poetry and prose, a Romantic and a Victorian sensibility. But Gaskell is also concerned with challenging prevailing ideologies and the fictions they create, as I have outlined with regards to Osborne and constructions of masculinity and heroism. *Wives and Daughters* is far too bound up with the vagaries of human behaviour, a hallmark of Byron's poetry also, to subscribe to a system-atic subdivision of characters, genres, and creeds. Molly can be a blunt voice of reason – 'That is all nonsense, papa' – yet, from the opening of the novel, we are given an impression of the heroine as 'wild and strange' (pp. 59, 22). Even Mrs Hamley is struck by the girl's 'impetuous romance', which generates a lasting connection in her mind between Molly and Osborne (p. 193). A Romantic sensibility is pointedly and poignantly present in moments of personal crisis. When, for example, the heroine hears the news of her father's impending marriage, 'It was as if the piece of solid ground on which she stood had broken from the shore, and she was drifting out to the infinite sea alone' (p. 111). On another occasion, she questions the Victorian virtue of self-sacrifice and becomes agitated at the prospect of a consequent loss of selfhood: 'Thinking more of others' happiness than of her own was very fine; but did it not mean giving up her very individuality, quenching all the warm love, the true desires, that made her herself?' (p. 134). A minor incident in the novel, when Molly excitedly proclaims that 'the dog-roses must be all out in flower', is indicative of her latent Romantic disposition more generally (p. 440). Osborne's earlier admission of ignorance as to when these flowers are in bloom – much to Cynthia's amazement, 'Not know, and you a poet?' – suggests that it is Molly, the heroine of the novel, who is the true inheritor of a Romantic tradition (p. 309).

It is towards the end of the novel that the heroine is at her most deeply Romantic (and most deeply unhappy). Molly sinks into a depression and her body, worn down by the constant demands of others, is afflicted by the same kind of 'feverish disturbance of health' that proves fatal to Mrs Hamley, Osborne, Mr Kirkpatrick, and the heroine's own mother (p. 586). Molly's only comfort, in the chapter 'The Storm Bursts', is in the landscape around her: a view of the Malvern hills, brilliantly coloured foliage, or the 'picturesque old cottages dotted here and there on the steep sandy banks' (p. 459).[39] The opening lines of this chapter are suggestive of Keats's 'To Autumn' and Austen's *Persuasion*, as Molly, like Anne Elliot, passes into a period of fretfulness, reflection, and longing:

> The autumn drifted away through all its seasons; the golden corn-harvest, the walks through the stubble fields, and rambles into hazel-copses in search of nuts; the stripping of the apple-orchards of their ruddy fruit, amid the joyous cries and shouts of watching children. (p. 457)

Gaskell's heroine reaffirms, as Austen's heroines had done before her, that a Romantic spirit (and poetic temperament) can be both a threat to the stability and standing of the female self and a source of considerable solace.

Other characters in the novel reveal a Romantic predisposition and are equally hard to pigeonhole. Squire Hamley, for instance, dismisses what he sees as 'silly fancy, and sentimental romance', yet Gaskell also portrays the 'romantic side of his nature' (pp. 57, 248). His passionate temper, which borders on a domestic tyranny over his sons, and his gloomy dejection after the death of his wife are more than a match for Osborne's melancholy. Mr Gibson, a man of science who takes a keen interest in Roger's research, is similarly given to unreasonable outbursts and confesses that he was 'once considered tolerably good-looking' and may even have been a great 'coxcomb' (p. 52). Gaskell's description of his 'dark penetrating eyes' and curling lip is part of a portrait of the doctor that anticipates Osborne's entry into the novel: 'His complexion was sallow, and his hair black; in those days, the decade after the conclusion of the great continental war, to be sallow and black-a-vised was of itself a distinction' (pp. 602, 38).[40] In addition, Mr Preston's imposing presence and romantic *idée fixe* suggest an anti-hero of sorts. Preston is 'pseudo-Byronic', according to Stone, and is only saved from being cast as a romantic villain by 'the helplessness of his possessive love for Cynthia' (*Romantic Impulse*, pp. 168, 167). When commenting on Preston's character, Gaskell makes the point that 'there were more lights in which he was to be viewed', opening up the prospect of alternative perspectives, a narrative strategy that is developed further when describing Cynthia: 'this constant brilliancy [...] was not the sunshiny rest of a placid lake, it was rather the glitter of the pieces of a broken mirror, which confuses and bewilders' (pp. 273, 345). Rather than remaining equanimously rational or romantic, Gaskell's characters resist conformity. Stereotypes are self-consciously invoked, such as when Cynthia refers to herself as 'the heroine of a mystery', yet she evades expectations and remains largely impervious to those around her (p. 519).

Such chameleonic uncertainty is not restricted to characterisation. Stylistically, Gaskell is anything but intent on purging Romantic influence from her novel. There is, as Morris suggests, a 'poetic movement of the prose' in *Wives and Daughters*, a ballad-like evocation of the seasons and, indeed, of everyday life (p. xvii). Consider, for example, Molly's initial reactions to her room at Hamley Hall:

> First of all, she went to the window to see what was to be seen. A flower-garden right below; a meadow of ripe grass just beyond, changing colour in long sweeps, as the soft wind blew over it. [...] The deliciousness of the early summer silence was only broken by the song of the birds, and nearer hum of bees. Listening to these sounds, which enhanced the exquisite sense of stillness, and puzzling out objects obscured by distance or shadow, Molly forgot herself... (p. 63)

Molly's reverie is not, on this occasion, a negative experience. This passage illustrates an appreciation of both the ornamental garden in the foreground and the rural landscape beyond. Molly is attuned to the hues and modulations of the grasses along with the sounds that becalm the scene. As well as capturing a moment of Wordsworthian quietude, Gaskell is also channelling Keats. Allusions to 'To Autumn' are here inflected with 'Ode to a Nightingale'. When Molly stands at her 'Charmed magic casement', she is both enraptured and disturbed by the sound of birdsong, the murmur of insects, and 'shadows numberless'.[41] Her heightened, almost intoxicating, sensory awareness leads to, as with the speaker of Keats's ode, perplexity and disorientation. Successive modifying transitions between near and far, light and dark, sound and silence culminate in a blurring of conscious and unconscious states: 'Do I wake or sleep?' ('Ode to a Nightingale', l. 80). These Romantic interludes may be interrupted, or even checked, by Roger, but they are persistently present throughout the novel. Gaskell's stylistic hybridity weaves together subtly different registers: a trite and mannered romantic sensibility that runs alongside and is superseded by a Romanticism that is 'far more deeply interfused' in both the outer landscape and the inner terrain of the imagination ('Tintern Abbey', l. 97). As Stone suggests, 'It is the realistic-minded characters, Roger Hamley, Dr. Gibson, and Molly, who embody the tendency in Victorian life and literature to invest everyday life with a new form of romanticism' (*Romantic Impulse*, p. 167).

IV

In the words of Andrew Davies, who wrote the screenplay for the BBC's 1999 adaptation of *Wives and Daughters*, 'we determined to go for the Romantic interpretation'.[42] Some of Molly's no-nonsense attitude is retained in this screen version, but a passionate fervour, bordering on emotional recklessness at times, emerges more strongly (particularly in such exclamations as 'I might as well never have lived' and 'I shall never be happy again', p. 135). The scene in which an agitated Mr Gibson asks Mrs Kirkpatrick to be his wife, against the backdrop of a dramatic storm, anticipates the penultimate scene in which Molly, rather than satisfying herself with a brief glimpse of the departing Roger (as in the novel), defies caution and convention by chasing after him in torrential rain.[43] The tension of Roger's proposal, a scene that Gaskell never got as far as writing, is heightened rather than diminished by the physical distance he maintains (due to the threat of Molly contracting scarlet fever from Hamley Hall). The final, added scene in Africa, where Roger assists a thoroughly modern Molly to view the exotic landscape before her, recalls – presumably unintentionally – Mrs Kirkpatrick's remark on observing Roger's vigil in front of their house: 'Really it is quite romantic' (p. 645).

Gaskell's concern with reading, and the importance of what you read, is apparent in the adaptation as the first shot of the grown-up Molly shows her 'lost' in a book. Later, Osborne makes a flamboyant entrance when he finishes some lines of poetry that Molly is reading aloud to Mrs Hamley (quoted below). Instead of a poem by Felicia Hemans, the writer named in corresponding scenes in the novel, the poem is by Byron.[44] Published in *Hours of Idleness* (1807), 'I Would I Were a Careless Child' concerns a disillusioned speaker reflecting on his younger, carefree self:

> Though pleasure stirs the maddening soul,
>   The heart—the heart—is lonely still.
> [...]
> Fain would I fly the haunts of men—
>   I seek to shun, not hate mankind;
> My breast requires the sullen glen,
>   Whose gloom may suit a darken'd mind.
> Oh! that to me the wings were given
>   Which bear the turtle to her nest!
> Then would I cleave the vault of heaven,
>   To flee away, and be at rest. (ll. 31–2, 49–56)

It is not only Osborne's dress and demeanour that mark him out as a direct descendant of Byron in this scene. These lines, from stanzas four and seven of 'I Would I Were a Careless Child', speak to Osborne's separation from his family and serve to prefigure his early death.

The conversation that ensues draws out further comparisons between Byron and Osborne. Molly finds her new acquaintance harder to read than the literature she immerses herself in, with Osborne being charming and narcissistic by turns. The final line of the exchange below, taken from the adaptation, conveys a certain cynicism, yet is said with a boyish naivety and intensity, conflicting characteristics that Byron juxtaposes to great effect in his poem, 'I Would I Were a Careless Child'.

Osborne: 'So, Miss Gibson, you're fond of Byron are you?'
Molly: 'Yes, and Mrs Hamley showed me some of your poems too.'
Osborne: 'Oh did she! And what did you think of them?'
Molly: 'I thought they were very beautiful.'
Osborne: 'Did you really?'
Molly: [looking puzzled] 'Yes, of course, or I wouldn't have said so.'
Osborne: 'Not like the rest of the world then. Good, I like that.'

Following the arrival of Squire Hamley and Roger, the conversation over Byron turns to the issue of fiction and non-fiction, poetry and prose, which serves to illustrate a central tension between the conflicting yet complementary characters of the two brothers:

Roger: [picking up and flicking through the pages of the book that Molly was reading from, mistakenly thinking it to be the one he has lent to her] 'Well, how are you getting on with Huber's book? Ah, Byron.'

Molly: 'Well, I am reading about the bees as well.'

Roger: 'But Byron's more congenial?'

Osborne: [wryly] 'There's no contest.'

It is clear that, for Andrew Davies, Osborne is the hero of *Wives and Daughters*: 'Tom Hollander's intense, deeply felt performance [as Osborne] was one of the best things in the production for me' ('Adapting *Wives and Daughters*', pp. 3–4). The BBC adaptation dwells on Osborne's feelings of estrangement at Hamley Hall. Following the death of Mrs Hamley, for example, the Squire and Roger walk passed a distraught Osborne, leaving him alone as they enter the family home. Shortly afterwards, Squire Hamley questions his son about gambling and womanising, accusations which Osborne denies as he goes on to declare: 'I'm only a cause of irritation to you ... and home is no longer home to me, but a place where I am to be controlled and scolded as if I were a child'. Certain scenes in the adaptation are staged to dramatise Osborne's Byronic traits. The lines read aloud from 'I Would I Were a Careless Child' establish a telling affinity between Byron and Osborne, as discussed above, but rather than the latter seeking gloom to 'suit a darken'd mind', he seeks out lively company. This Victorian Byronic hero, perhaps more akin to a Don Juan than a Manfred or a Conrad, is sociable and only occasionally sullen. In the later stages of the adaptation, Osborne's pale and diminished physical appearance betokens a mental torment as well as a fatal illness, yet this is not merely symptomatic of a Romantic affliction; his pain derives from family discord, grief, and long periods of time spent away from his wife and child. As Davies comments, 'the best thing we did was to include some scenes not in the book, showing Osborne with his young wife – there were hardly any lines in them, but there was no doubt about the passion, tenderness and maturity of their love for each other' (p. 4). The added scenes reveal a loving and devoted husband. Osborne can be considered truly 'poetic' when, fearing that his health may be failing, he speaks emotionally of his wife: 'She's the dearest, gentlest creature. The best thing in my life'. Intensifying Osborne's Byronic inheritance does not result in a series of romantic set pieces or in stereotyping Gaskell's complex character. On the contrary, Tom Hollander portrays a warm, sensitive, and deeply conflicted individual who has borne the pressure of competing expectations from his mother and father at the same time as becoming a husband and a father.

V

Although there may not be as many direct references to Byron in Gaskell's *North and South*, his influence is more widely diffused and, arguably, more significant than in *Wives and Daughters*. A quotation from Byron's poetry in *North and South*, three lines of *The Island; or, Christian and his Comrades* (1823), provides an epigraph for the final chapter of the first volume, titled 'Frederick':

> Revenge may have her own:
> Roused discipline aloud proclaims their cause,
> And injured navies urge their broken laws.[45]

Such epigraphs indicate, as Jeffrey. E. Jackson suggests, the extent to which Gaskell drew on different literary voices and genres, especially 'poets from earlier in the nineteenth century, including Lord Byron, Samuel Taylor Coleridge, Joanna Baillie and Felicia Dorothea Hemans'.[46] The lines quoted above from Byron's poem about HMS *Bounty* would appear, at first glance, to support the heroine's brother, Frederick's, act of mutiny and, by inference, the action taken by the workers in the strike scene: the masters, whether ship captain or mill owner, have 'broken' their duty of care and the men who are 'injured' seek redress. However, Byron's use of the word 'discipline', which has 'broken' in both the naval mutiny and the factory strike, raises the ethical problems of duty and conscience that also relate, in *North and South*, to Boucher's dealings with the Union and his subsequent suicide as well as to Margaret's dishonesty after the accidental death of Leonards. The tangled complexity of Byron's lines highlights and reinforces a number of competing claims in Gaskell's novel, as I will now demonstrate.

The quotation selected by Gaskell is the first instance in Byron's poem when the claims of the mutineers are considered. *The Island*, like *North and South*, ostensibly calls for liberty – with Acting Lieutenant Fletcher Christian proclaiming before his death, 'For me, my lot is what I sought; to be,/ In life or death, the fearless and the free' – and yet the rebels are not portrayed in a particularly advantageous light (III. ll. 163–4). Rather, it is the mutineers who are described as the 'foe', whereas those loyal to Captain Bligh, the 'gallant chief', are described, with affecting alliteration, as 'the faithful few' (I. ll. 51, 17, 125). The mutineers, whose drunken 'reign of rage and fear' reduces the 'proud vessel' to a 'moral wreck', are, in turn, hunted down and slaughtered at the end of the poem (I. ll. 54, 128). There is no gallantry in the mutineers' deaths, as their corpses become food for scavengers, and we are told unequivocally that 'Their life was shame, their epitaph was guilt' (IV. l. 270). Deborah Denenholz Morse argues that Gaskell's fictional mutiny on the *Orion*, which includes reports of the Captain's excessive cruelty, is based on the violent mutiny that broke out on HMS *Hermione* – when the mutineers brutally killed the officers and were subsequently hanged or sent into exile – as opposed to the more famous *Bounty* mutiny. Morse does not note the epigraph to Byron's poem about the *Bounty*, which complicates the historical connection to the *Hermione*, but her point that Gaskell differentiates between Frederick's involvement in the insurgency and Margaret's selfless and nonviolent resistance during the strike scene is apposite.[47] Margaret's dissenting fervour is counterbalanced by a commitment to the wider community: 'Loyalty and obedience to wisdom and justice are fine; but it is still finer to defy arbitrary power, unjustly and cruelly used—not on behalf of ourselves, but on behalf of others more helpless' (p. 109).

Our continuing fascination with Frederick does not derive from a protest about personal ill-usage; his culpability in the mutiny and the fate of his fellow mutineers remains unsettled in the novel. Our fascination derives from a broader association with the literary pirate. The great age of the pirate tale began in the nineteenth century when, according to Grace Moore, 'Representations of the pirate shifted from the dangerous, uncouth cutthroats like the notorious Blackbeard, to the brooding Romanticism of Byron's corsair'.[48] A literary sensation, selling over 10,000 copies on the day it was published, *The Corsair* refashioned the figure of the pirate within the mould of the brooding Byronic lover, 'a morally ambiguous personality to be admired but never understood', as Mel Campbell argues.[49] Fletcher Christian, the leader of the mutiny in *The Island*, is likewise a hybridised anti-hero capable of evoking pathos. His choices result, like the Romantic pirate Conrad, in a 'life misspent'; yet he is also singled out for his courage and is crippled with remorse (unlike Gaskell's Frederick) immediately after the mutiny: 'His feverish lips thus broke their gloomy spell,/ 'Tis that! 'tis that! I am in hell! in hell!' (IV. l. 351; I. ll. 163–4). Christian, as tortured mutineer, is sympathetically elevated above the masses, indicating a class bias that can also be seen in Conrad's disdain for his crew – 'With these he mingles not but to command;/ Few are his words, but keen his eye and hand./ Ne'er seasons he with mirth their jovial mess' (*The Corsair*, I. ll. 63–5) – lines that resonate, initially at least, with the depiction of masters and men in *North and South*. Gaskell's strikers, like Byron's mutineers in *The Island*, are represented as a ravenous, and most likely immoral, mob. By contrast, the master can be seen as a man apart, before coming to the table with his workers in a symbolical act of communal dining that Byron's pirate-hero shuns:

> Stern, and aloof a little from the rest,
> Stood Christian, with his arms across his chest.
> The ruddy, reckless, dauntless hue once spread
> Along his cheek was livid now as lead; (*The Island*, III. ll. 85–8)

Gaskell's epigraph, read in the context of Byron's poem, suggests anything but a straightforward treatment of insurgency in *North and South*. A process of 'argument and counterargument', whereby poetry and prose comment on and complicate each other, yields additional textual synergies.[50] Toobonai, the setting for Byron's poem, is depicted as an 'infant world', a paradise where man enjoys 'liberty to roam': yet such a sanctuary, free from naval authority, is constantly under threat from the outside world and constitutes, in large part, an idealised illusion (II. ll. 127, 248). As Margaret Hale's nostalgic and narrow view of her former home is undermined by her return visit to Helstone, so the islanders' halcyon days are clouded by inertia and troubled by thoughts of mortality. Torquil is, like Fletcher Christian, rebellious, intense, and tormented; nurtured on romantic legends, he is 'tempest-born', and the only companions for his 'craggy solitudes' are 'pensive moods' (II. ll. 168, 172, 171). His search for pleasure, like Manfred's before him, has only produced pain and cultivated disillusionment. Torquil's affinity with and love for his wife, Neuha, calms his fractious temperament; and yet he fears, like Gaskell's hero in *North and South*, that his passion for a woman will 'unman' him. This intertext invites a comparison between Gaskell's Thornton and Byron's Torquil, and forges a connection between Margaret and Neuha as both attempt to 'rescue' the hero. By introducing a dialectic that is both complementary and revisionary, whilst also commenting on Margaret's instinctive courage and challenges to prevailing gender codes, Gaskell's allusion to Byron's poem generates a semantic space on 'the dangerous edge of things' (Jackson, 'Epigraphs in *North and South*', p. 69).

VI

John Thornton, the master of Marlborough Mills, is, like Byron's heroes, abrupt, proud, and gloomy. Margaret Hale, the heroine of Gaskell's novel, likens her impressions of the hero to tasting an olive for the first time; he is for her, as Byron was for Elizabeth Barrett Browning, 'salt as life' ('A Vision of Poets', l. 413). Thornton concedes, like the hero of *Pride and Prejudice* before him, that 'I have not the elements for popularity' (p. 431). We are informed, in addition, that 'Mr. Thornton had no general benevolence,—no universal philanthropy' (p. 214). Yet this unequivocal statement is followed by a description of his 'feminine shopping' trip for fruit. Mrs Hale, touched by the humility with which this offering is presented, criticises Margaret's prejudice against this man. Thornton's 'unusual intellect' also draws out Mr Hale's innermost thoughts; the hero's eloquence, combined with the force of his argument, temporarily eclipses the workers' grievances in the former minister's mind (p. 167). The following lines by Byron, on Conrad's magnetic rule, chime with Thornton's skills of persuasion and his conviction that 'despotism is the best kind of government' (p. 120):

> The power of Thought—the magic of the Mind!
> Link'd with success, assumed and kept with skill,
> That moulds another's weakness to its will;
> Wields with their hands, but, still to these unknown,
> Makes even their mightiest deeds appear his own.
> Such hath it been—shall be—beneath the sun
> The many still must labour for the one! (*The Corsair*, I. ll. 182–8)

Gaskell was eager to address charges of class bias in *Mary Barton*, but she retracts nothing of her earlier social polemic. In *North and South*, Thornton's 'sound economical principles' preclude humanitarian concerns and he confesses to being an autocrat (p. 152). Indeed, it is his dominant energy that generates the most problematic, and noticeably Byronic, aspect of the novel.

Like all Byronic heroes, for whom 'Time hath not yet the features fix'd,/ But brighter traits with evil mix'd' (*The Giaour*, ll. 861–2), John Thornton is a 'puzzle', Gaskell's term for a character she intended to make 'large and strong and tender, and *yet a master*' (27 October 1854, original emphasis). Barnes Stevenson raises a number of insightful questions on this point:

> In a real sense, Gaskell here confronts the conflicting discourses of masculinity in her society: how can her character be 'a master', an 'entrepreneurial man', and also be a 'developed' human being? How can a novelist create consistency between inconsistent ideologies? ('Romance and the Self-Made Man', p. 14)

Similar concerns are voiced, in the novel, by Higgins as he describes Thornton's fractured subjectivity:

> 'To tell the truth,' said he, 'he fairly bamboozles me. He's two chaps. One chap I knowed of old as were measter all o'er. T'other chap hasn't an ounce of measter's flesh about him. How them two chaps is bound up in one body, is a craddy for me to find out.' (p. 339)[51]

Higgins is baffled by a man who he has previously portrayed as 'a tyrant, an' an oud bull-dog' now taking an interest in the education of his adopted children (p. 326). For Mr Bell, Thornton is 'about as brusque and curt a fellow as he had ever met with'; yet, when Thornton has lost all prospect of financial success or gaining Margaret's affections, we are reminded that 'he was as calm and gentle to the women in his home as ever' (this despite the fact that Mrs Thornton often finds her son's moods hard to read, pp. 332, 421). Pondering the hero's character, to which a significant proportion of the narrative is devoted, becomes a principal diversion for Margaret. The author's concerns over the reconciliation of warring members in *North and South*, as quoted in Part I, are reflected in the heroine's attempts to negotiate her widely conflicting responses to Thornton: 'How reconcile those eyes, that voice, with the hard-reasoning, dry, merciless way in which he laid down axioms of trade, and serenely followed them out to their full consequences? The discord jarred upon her inexpressibly'; and she openly tells him, 'I am trying to reconcile your admiration of despotism with your respect for other men's independence of character' (pp. 153, 124).

Margaret's perception of Thornton alters drastically over the course of the novel. But her desire to define and understand him does not diminish. In fact, as Margaret comes to respect Thornton, her preoccupation with 'solving' his subjectivity develops into a fixation: 'it seemed to her as if all subjects tended towards Mr. Thornton' (p. 329). The fluctuations and gradual changes in Thornton's behaviour only serve to intensify both the heroine's and the reader's consternation. Thornton's longing for Margaret renders him even more unpredictable; 'uneasy and cross', he desires to fall at her feet one minute, then strike her the next (p. 336). Despite concerted efforts to reconcile Thornton's character, he remains a repository of conflicting impulses. This 'epistemological chasm', encountered previously in *Pride and Prejudice*'s Mr Darcy, effectively represents the author's struggles with *North and South* and is indicative of her struggles with a Romantic inheritance more broadly.[52] Thornton functions as an embodiment of the ideological indeterminacy that exemplifies this novel and he is equally symptomatic of a Victorian writer's response to Byron and his reputation. A Byronic instability informs Thornton's 'stubbornly open presentation of character' (Bodenheimer, 'Permanent State of Change', p. 301), and is central to Gaskell's challenging depiction of masculinity as well as what might be regarded as the most innovative aspect of her novel, 'a romance plot inextricably implicated in and complicated by the politics of industrial relations and the clash of views between masters and workers and north and south'.[53]

The resonant tensions between social concerns and romance in the novel are immediately apparent in the scene where Thornton first appears in the 2004 BBC adaptation of *North and South*.[54] Upon entering the mill – where Gaskell never directly takes us in the novel – Margaret, played by Daniela Denby-Ashe, is bewildered by an intense working environment in which the air is thick with the effluvia of cotton. The scene is visually arresting; at once a winter wonderland and, as the heroine's cough reminds us, a cause of high mortality rates amongst the workers.[55] Margaret first sees the dark, imposing figure of the master through this confetti-like snow, which conflates, in a single image, both the social agenda and the romance plot of the novel. The unnatural calm generated by the rhythm of the machines is shattered by Thornton, played by Richard Armitage, as he shouts at a worker and beats him savagely even after he has fallen to the ground. When the worker begs to keep his job, so he can feed his children, Thornton continues to kick him and shouts after his victim, 'Aye, crawl away on your belly'. As a witness to this vicious attack, Margaret's intervention, which acts as an effective precursor to the strike scene, is met by a fierce, and gendered, invective when he barks 'Get that woman out of here'.[56]

Margaret Harris describes this scene as 'shocking to watch [...]. It would be easy to say, as some did, that the addition is gratuitous and needlessly violent'.[57] I would argue that this scene is not merely shocking; it is ideologically contentious, as the middle-class master now exhibits the brutal behaviour that the Victorians more readily associated with the working-class man.[58] We are told that Thornton 'quivered with rage' when he is confronted by the workers in Gaskell's strike scene, and yet his internal conflict is not actualised externally (p. 180). The depiction of the angry mob in *North and South* has been read as a displacement of the sexual, and potentially violent, threat that Thornton poses to the heroine – reminiscent of Margaret Oliphant's contemporary assessment of Gaskell's hero as a 'love-making monster' ('fierce', 'churlish', and 'ill-natured') – but it should be remembered that it is the master who is the intended victim of the workers' violence.[59] Crucially, what is described as Thornton's 'savage' manner towards Margaret when she rejects his proposal of marriage does not materialise in the strike scene when it is Boucher who is suspected of savagery (p. 196). The hero's volatility, which is narrowly contained in Gaskell's novel, is vented as soon as he appears on screen.

The questions Gaskell raises about class sympathies and criminality, individual actions and group mentality, among others, intersect with an ongoing dialogue in both the novel and the adaptation over the fate of an increasingly contentious figure: the gentleman. As Margaret wonders whether the master of a mill can ever meet her high ideals – declaring him 'not quite a gentleman' (p. 64) in the novel and accusing him of 'ungentlemanly' conduct in the adaptation – Thornton takes issue with what he considers to be an out-dated and superficial concept. Thornton formulates a revised measure of 'manly' conduct that accords more closely with his entrepreneurism and ethic of hard work.[60] Margaret ultimately endorses this steward of industry when, in the penultimate chapter, she admires Thornton's 'sense of inherent dignity and manly strength' (p. 429). The key word here is 'inherent'. Thornton's manners do not display the gentility that had traditionally conveyed an aristocratic status; they rather demonstrate an innate sense of worth. As such, Thornton's northern manliness emerges as a preferable alternative to the appearance of southern gallantry. And Margaret gravitates towards the values of an aspiring middle-class nobility in this economic environment.

In this respect, *North and South* marks a significant watershed in the rapidly changing constructions of masculinity in the mid-nineteenth century. In 'Thornton's middle-class, philistine Darcy', Gaskell is no longer grappling with *Pride and Prejudice*'s landed gentry or *Jane Eyre*'s aristocratic throwback.[61] Margaret Hale must negotiate and attempt to rehabilitate a new mould of meritocratic masculinity in the form of the self-made man. Stone sees the industrialist and the Byronic hero as sharing a common heritage. Both figures are indebted to a 'revolutionary spirit that liberated the individual', which chimes with the mood of reform in *North and South*; yet they also thrive – given the new premium on the individual – on self-sufficiency, an 'unimpeded force of will' (*Romantic Impulse*, pp. 9, 157). Thornton is, when Margaret first encounters him in the novel, a man who prides himself on assertiveness and autonomy, both hallmarks of the Byronic hero and, as Joseph Campbell posits in *The Hero with a Thousand Faces*, distinguishing features of the modern hero more generally.[62] However, as Austen's Darcy must be reintegrated into a wider society by the woman he loves, so Gaskell places her self-determining male protagonist at the centre of a romance plot where he can be guided, as is Margaret over her preconceived ideas about the gentleman, to re-evaluate his principles and re-learn humanitarian compassion. That the novel unsettles gendered patterns of behaviour eases our acceptance of Thornton as a reformed anti-hero, a warrior-leader who controls and redirects his middle-class masculine energies from the sole purpose of the cash nexus to the support of working-class men.

Mr Hale dismisses Thornton's credentials as a leading man – 'I don't set him up for a hero, or anything of that kind' – an impression reinforced by Margaret when she acknowledges that he is a 'very remarkable man', yet admits to not liking him (p. 88). Nonetheless, Nils Clausson detects, particularly in the language used during the strike scene, the presence of 'the dark and dangerous Byronic hero, a descendant of Ann Radcliffe's Gothic villains'.[63] Although Thornton's absence of guilt is notably un-Byronic, his drive has been determined by a past shame – what he regards as the weakness of his father's imprudent speculations, subsequent disgrace, and suicide. Furthermore, his imposing physical presence, with dark hair, low brow, curled lip, and pale, marble features, recalls the widely reproduced portraits of Byron and illustrations of his protagonists. Even more notable are the 'flaming eyes' (p. 313) and penetrating stare that call to mind descriptions of the awe-inspiring 'evil eye' in the Oriental Tales.[64] Thornton's defiance and steadfast resolve, which goads the desperate workers in the strike scene, also recalls Conrad's ability to say '"Do this!"—'tis done:/ [...] all obey and few inquire his will' (*The Corsair*, I. ll. 77, 80).

As might be expected, it is the intensity of Thornton's passion for Margaret that not only confirms, but also reconstructs this Byronic inheritance. The hero's desire is conveyed in visceral terms: he experiences painful physical symptoms as every nerve in his body thrills at the prospect of the heroine. Thornton's 'strange wild passionate way' (p. 197) closely coincides with the fevered veins and 'bursting heart' of the Byronic hero (*The Giaour*, l. 1107). What is more, Gaskell depicts the hero and heroine's relationship in pointedly sadomasochistic terms. Thornton's need to declare his love, 'I am a man. I claim the right of expressing my feelings', imposes 'invisible chains' on the recipient, and he is described as wilfully inflicting pain upon himself: 'He lashed himself into an agony of fierce jealousy' (pp. 195, 238, 310). The close-ness between love and hate, pleasure and pain is a prominent feature of the Oriental Tales. In *The Corsair*, for instance, Gulnare's exclama-tion, '*this* love—*that* hatred', equates her love for the Romantic outlaw with the bondage and oppression he has liberated her from (III. l. 351, original emphasis). Equally, Gaskell's erotic description of Thornton's 'Charybdis of passion', a 'stinging pleasure' that he attempts to crush, is a variant on the motif of the serpent coiled within the protagonist's chest that recurs throughout Byron's poetry (pp. 270, 239).[65] This '*positive* bodily pain', which reveals the hero's subversive longing for violent penetration, demonstrates not only the depths of his psycho-logical complexity, but also illuminates Gaskell's subtle revisions of her Romantic predecessor (p. 207, added emphasis).

VII

Where Gaskell presents a Northern man, rough around the edges, the BBC's glaring, brooding Thornton often has more in common with the 'peevish hectic' that passes along Conrad's cheek than with the original character (*The Corsair*, II. l. 109). The initial portrait of Thornton as a hard taskmaster in the television series is re-emphasised at the end of the first episode when we are taken back into the mill. Once again, the focus is on his dark profile, but now there is no suggestion of romance in either the work or the mill owner. Viewed through the perspective of Margaret's voice-over – 'I believe I've seen hell and it's white, snow white' – Thornton resembles a devil presiding over his satanic mill.[66] As a consequence of accentuating Thornton's explosive temper and tough exterior, any glimpse of his 'inexpressible gentleness' is omitted until later in the adaptation (p. 82). Gaskell, by contrast, is careful to coun-terbalance her hero's flaws with telling instances such as Thornton seek-ing forgiveness for his 'uncouth ways', his tearfulness before Margaret and then his mother, and his continued friendship with a woman who has rejected him. Thornton's integrity never wavers, even when he is faced with bankruptcy. Through him, Gaskell shows the reader a respectable man who suffers, alongside his men, from the vicissitudes of trade. Thornton's nobler actions not only offset his previous behaviour towards Margaret, and thereby enable us to accept him as a hero suit-able for our heroine, they also sustain the resolutely open-ended depic-tion of his character throughout the novel.

For the on-screen heroine, who has regarded Thornton with a mix-ture of disapproval and awe rather than attraction, the final scene poses even more of a problem than in Gaskell's novel. 'The closing scene', according to Harris, 'is Welch's most radical and most disconcerting change' ('Taking Bearings', p. 78). The rewritten ending of the BBC's *North and South* evoked strongly polarised reactions between those who thought it was moving – 'the perfect ending for this perfect story' – and those who thought it was 'the biggest anti-climax ever': 'The ending was perfect – for a soap opera'. One of the main objections to the final scene was the un-Victorian conduct and appearance of the hero and heroine. Yet I would argue that targeting apparent anachronisms side-steps the more important issue of what happens to Gaskell's precarious gender politics in this ending. The neck of Thornton's heavily starched shirt is loosened – a sign of physical release as well as a visual allusion to the trademark open-necked shirt of the Byronic hero. However, despite the softening of his features and the exchange of his sneer for a smile, Thornton refuses to engage with Margaret's business proposal, exacerbating the unease that Oliphant identified in the novel's ending: 'when [...] Margaret becomes an heiress, it is somewhat hard to see her delivered over to the impoverished Manchester man, who is as ready to devour her as ever was an ogre in a fairy tale' ('Modern Novelists', p. 560). The exquisitely ambivalent 'gentle violence' that transfers to Margaret in the closing lines of the novel (and indicates a continuing power struggle after marriage) is retained by the on-screen Thornton as he holds her face protectively in his hands (p. 436). What the adaptation controversially exposed as the hero's tendency to violence in the added mill scene has been sublimated and repackaged as a sexually alluring paternalism.[67]

I do not want to suggest, however, that Richard Armitage's portrayal of Thornton, or indeed the adaptation, is an example of what Umberto Eco refers to as an 'intertextual archetype', a term to denote a simplification of the source.[68] Armitage's performance was well-received and he won the accolade of Best Actor in a BBC Drama for 2004 (with 53 per cent of the vote). Within hours of the first episode of *North and South* being screened, eager fans had crashed the message board of the programme's website, and the BBC was forced to shut it down. A recurring theme of the messages posted was the inevitable comparison between this adaptation and the BBC's 1995 adaptation of *Pride and Prejudice*.[69] The connections made between Richard Armitage's Thornton and Colin Firth's Darcy often involved the pressing issue of their smouldering good looks – 'Richard Armitage is perfectly cast as the brooding but charismatic Thornton and Mr. Darcy is about to face some competition in the hearts of the ladies of the nation' – yet some messages also identified a 'wonderfully complex similarity' between the on-screen portrayals of Austen's and Gaskell's heroes.[70] The processes of change and growth in *North and South* are manifest in the metamorphosis Armitage's Thornton undergoes throughout the series. The actor stated that he tried to explore the contradictions in Thornton's character, which goes some way to explain the praise he received for the 'strength', 'vulnerability', 'despair', 'hope', 'joy', and 'desire' of his performance in the final episode.[71] However, while Armitage's Thornton emerges as a romantic hero to rival and even surpass Firth's Byronic Darcy in Episode 4, viewers bemoaned the absence of 'traditional' romance in the first three episodes. This portrayal of Thornton heightens the tensions in Gaskell's novel between north and south, the gentleman and the self-made man, genteel poverty and new money, which, in effect, renders the prospect of romance amongst such opposition and discord even more unlikely and renders the decision to opt for a conventional ending all the more disappointing.

It is easy to overlook what adaptations can bring to the afterlife of a literary text, however. Even though he may not achieve his full potential as a chameleonic anti-hero until the final episode of the BBC's miniseries, Armitage's Thornton serves to draw attention to the loaded issues of oppression and liberty that underpin much of Gaskell's, and indeed Byron's, work. Armitage's Thornton, like Rufus Sewell's portrayal of Will Ladislaw in the BBC's 1994 adaptation of *Middlemarch*, embodies the fervour that is at the heart of Gaskell's and Byron's radical debates about authority and power. 'It is the transgressive and confronting Gaskell that viewers encounter in Sandy Welch's script and Brian Percival's direction of the 2004 BBC-TV version of *North and South*', argues Harris ('Taking Bearings', p. 65). What Gaskell presents as Thornton's increasingly progressive outlook in the novel, as he assumes the mantle of a Carlylean 'Captain of Industry' capable of leading the working classes, is emphasised in the BBC adaptation as he strikes out among the masters to improve the working conditions in his mill.[72] Postings on the BBC website commented on the 'politicisation' of the adaptation. Along similar lines, critics of both the BBC adaptations of *North and South* and *Middlemarch*, despite being screened a decade apart, detected a New Labour agenda.[73] With regards to the former, this political bias is to be found 'lurking within the tale of Thornton's and Higgins's enlightened approach to industrial relations'.[74] Such responses touch on contested issues surrounding post-heritage drama and relate to the political friction between personal and public interrelations that energise Gaskell's novel and Byron's poetry. Armitage's portrayal of Thornton not only crystallises the ideological preoccupations of both authors; it demonstrates, more broadly, that a Byronic dissonance can be intensified and integrated into a Victorian social agenda through intertextual engagement and adaptation. This process of creative cross-pollination, expanding across fiction and film, and centring on the Byronic hero, gains further moment in the following chapters.

4
George Eliot's Byronic Heroes I: Early Works and Poetry

I

George Eliot, like Austen and Gaskell before her, was equally engaged with the reformulation of Romanticism and models of masculinity. For U. C. Knoepflmacher, Eliot's 'fiction offers what is probably the richest and most variegated cast of male characters created by any woman novelist'.[1] The fleshing out or dissolving of masculine stereotypes is a distinctive feature of Eliot's fiction, with the title characters in works such as *Adam Bede* (1859), *Silas Marner* (1861), *Felix Holt: The Radical* (1866) and *Daniel Deronda* (1876) remaining in the foreground. *Adam Bede*, Eliot's first novel, explores conventional as well as emerging models of masculinity through the theme of work, the interrelated issue of class, and the family.[2] The charming yet feckless aristocratic seducer, Captain Arthur Donnithorne, is found wanting when compared with the integrity of the carpenter, Adam Bede. *Middlemarch* (1871–72) is populated by, among many others, the mutable shades of Will Ladislaw's artistic sensibilities and Casaubon's pitiful frailties. In her last novel, *Daniel Deronda*, the title character's delicacy of feeling and Mordecai's spirit of self-sacrifice provide the counterpoint to Grandcourt's hard, yet meticulously studied, masculinity. Both *Daniel Deronda* and *Middlemarch* will be discussed in detail in the next chapter.

Eliot shares with Austen and Gaskell the ability to create a variegated spectrum of male characters that are 'subjected to a relentless process of transformation' (Knoepflmacher, 'Unveiling Men', p. 141). Her inclusion in this book may seem as, if not more, surprising than Gaskell's, given her outspoken aversion to Byron and distrust of the figure of the hero more generally. In *Adam Bede*, Eliot states that 'There are few prophets in the world; few sublimely beautiful women; few heroes. I can't afford

124

to give all my love and reverence to such rarities: I want a great deal of those feelings for my everyday fellow-men'; and continues, 'Neither are picturesque lazzaroni or romantic criminals half so frequent as your common labourer [...]. It is more needful that I should have a fibre of sympathy connecting me with that vulgar citizen [...], than with the handsomest rascal in red scarf and green feathers'.[3] For all the author's protestations that there are 'few heroes' in the world, her fiction features a good number of them. Eliot moves away from and complicates stock characters, such as the 'picturesque lazzaroni or romantic criminals'; and yet her Adam Bede, Felix Holt, Tertius Lydgate, Will Ladislaw, and Daniel Deronda are hardly 'everyday fellow-men' removed from Romantic influence. The 'relentless process of transformation' that Eliot's male characters are subjected to is partly precipitated by the Byronic hero and a Byronic ethos, as this chapter and the next will seek to demonstrate. Both chapters consider the extent to which Byron's poetry and his protagonists inform an alternative heroism in Eliot's writings. This chapter examines the function and fate of the Byronic across a wide range of literary forms and styles, including Eliot's shorter fiction, such as 'The Lifted Veil' (1859), the long dramatic poem, *The Spanish Gypsy* (1868), and the verse drama *Armgart* (1871). How, this chapter seeks to address, can the lure of Byronic hubris be reconciled with or incorporated into Eliot's aesthetic concerns over the common man and everyday altruism?

There is certainly more of Wordsworth's democratic human empathy, his Michael and Simon Lee, than of Byron's individualism in Eliot's commitment to the commonplace, to the 'Low and rustic life' at the heart of Wordsworth's pastoral vision.[4] The extent to which Eliot 'assimilated' Wordsworth's work is stressed by Donald D. Stone: 'The similarity between George Eliot's and Wordsworth's themes, choice of subject matter, and artistic aims is so striking that it is misleading to speak of the relationship between these writers as strictly a matter of "influence"'.[5] The epigraph for Eliot's first novel, *Adam Bede*, is taken from *The Excursion* (1814). The story of Ellen to which it alludes – a woman who becomes pregnant, is abandoned by her lover, and is buried with her dead baby – offers a sympathetic frame through which to read the story of Hetty Sorrel. Moreover, the emphasis on 'Clear images before your gladdened eyes/ Of nature's unambitious underwood,/ And flowers that prosper in the shade' is diffused throughout the novel – not only in relation to the landscape, but in the course of human interactions (Book VI, ll. 652–4; *Adam Bede*, p. 1). The following narrative digression on Dutch paintings in Eliot's novel might be compared with one of Wordsworth's famous 'spots of time':

I turn, without shrinking, from cloud-borne angels, from prophets, sibyls, and heroic warriors, to an old woman bending over her flower-pot, or eating her solitary dinner, while the noonday light, softened perhaps by a screen of leaves, falls on her mob-cap, and just touches the rim of her spinning-wheel, and her stone jug, and all those cheap common things which are the precious necessaries of life to her. (p. 195)

> Then, reascending the bare common, saw
> A naked pool that lay beneath the hills,
> The beacon on its summit, and, more near,
> A girl, who bore a pitcher on her head,
> And seemed with difficult steps to force her way
> Against the blowing wind. It was, in truth,
> An ordinary sight; but I should need
> Colours and words that are unknown to man,
> To paint the visionary dreariness
> Which, while I looked all round for my lost guide,
> Invested moorland waste, and naked pool,
> The beacon crowning the lone eminence,
> The female and her garments vexed and tossed
> By the strong wind.[6]

Eliot's prose defends Wordsworth's poetic illumination of the ordinary yet affecting 'incidents and situations from common life' (Preface to *Lyrical Ballads*, p. 596). What at first might be perceived as negative in the passages above – 'cheap common things' in the former and 'dreariness' in the latter[7] – are impressed upon the imagination. They are 'precious', unique in their ubiquity, and indicate a deep accord between two writers who sought to separate their work from previous or prevailing traditions.

However, while Eliot may be 'Wordsworth's ideal reader', as Stephen Gill asserts, her characters are often misreaders, a failing that, as we shall see, connects her treatment of Romantic poetry with that of Austen and Gaskell (*Wordsworth and the Victorians*, p. 147). Arthur Donnithorne, the redeemable rake of *Adam Bede*, dismisses the recently published *Lyrical Ballads* as 'twaddling stuff', for instance (pp. 72–3). Donnithorne's preference for what he describes as Coleridge's 'strange, striking thing ['The Rime of the Ancient Mariner']' over Wordsworth's poems (including the pertinent textual backdrop of 'The Thorn') is an early indicator of his impulsive conduct. Wordsworth, here, acts as an interpretative prompt, inviting the implied reader to adopt a more informed and judicious view than her character. This divided response complicates the 'literalness of Eliot's transposition of Wordsworthian themes' that Margaret Homans sees as indicative of her ambivalent regard for the Romantic forebear.[8] Clearly, Eliot is no straightforward Wordsworthian devotee, as she also demonstrates his limitations through characters such as Maggie Tulliver and Mary Garth. And yet this Victorian novelist was, in Gill's words, 'the most eloquent mediator of the humanist vision inherent in all of Wordsworth' (*Wordsworth and the Victorians*, p. 167).

Eliot's Reverend Amos Barton, from *Scenes of Clerical Life* (1858), can be considered an example of a Wordsworthian 'anti-character' (whereby a sense of identity is evoked through subtle effacements and displacements). Described in terms of what he is not, Amos Barton is effectively distanced from false expectations of the heroic that set the 'ideal' above the 'real':

> ... a man whose virtues were *not* heroic, and who had *no un*detected crime within his breast; who had *not* the slightest mystery hanging about him, but was palpably and *un*mistakably commonplace; who was *not* even in love, but had had that complaint favourably many years ago. "An utterly *un*interesting character!" I think I hear a lady reader exclaim—Mrs Farthingale, for example, who prefers the ideal in fiction; to whom tragedy means ermine tippets, adultery, and murder; and comedy, the adventures of some personage who is quite a "character."[9]

Amos Barton is the antithesis of the Byronic hero. He is formulated as an antidote to the theatrical inscrutability of a Manfred, although the quip about love as a 'complaint' has a flavour of Byron's *Don Juan*. 'Here is', as Eliot summarises in 'Worldliness and Other-Worldliness: The Poet Young', 'no railing at the earth's "melancholy map," [...] no vague rant about human misery and human virtue, but that close and vivid presentation of particular sorrows and privations, of particular deeds and misdeeds, which is the direct road to the emotions'.[10] Such a strenuous commitment to the benign and unexceptional caused Mario Praz to assert: 'Disillusioned observation of life as it really was, led to the eclipse of the hero and the disclosure of man's swarming interior world, made up of disparate and contradictory things'.[11] Praz's conclusion is understandable if conflicted. The latter part of the statement suggests a Romantic introspection that challenges or complicates the realist assertion that precedes it. The hero figure, with his 'swarming interior world, made up of disparate and contradictory things', is a central and ever-present source of consternation in Eliot's fiction. For her, as for Gaskell, the heroic can be found in the most unexpected places and in the imperfections of forgotten deeds. Even the heroes that are remembered by history retain a prominent position if only as a relief for those 'unvisited tombs'.[12]

Middlemarch has often been read as an anti-heroic novel. The community depicted by Eliot does not tolerate exceptional beings or deeds, and the narrative is resistant to the claims of a pioneering protagonist. Eliot praised Thomas Carlyle for inspiring men's souls with courage rather than 'teach[ing] men how to use sword and musket'.[13] Both writers shared a distaste for the 'falsehood' of Byronism, the cult of personality that grew up around the poet with its affected agitations and 'brawling theatrical insincere character'.[14] Yet, despite an admiration for Carlyle's 'great and beautiful human nature', Eliot was wary of a rhetoric that could convince us of 'the very opposite of what we think'. *Middlemarch* was written under the influence of Carlyle, as Eliot argued everything of her generation necessarily must be. It is also a novel alert to the 'dangerous paradoxes' that she detected in Carlyle (and similarly led Gaskell to sidestep allegiance with the revered social commentator). Carlyle struggled with, as discussed in Chapter 3, 'the rebellious and self-mocking Byronic aspect of his own nature', venerating as well as castigating a poet who he considered had the potential to be the English Goethe.[15] On the one hand, Lydgate is, in many ways, a model of the cerebral Carlylean hero-reformer, whose radical, and even romantic, views on medical reform are hampered by local politics and his own retrograde ideas of femininity.[16] Eliot exposes the failings of the intellectual overreacher, a figure with close ties to the Romantic artist, and consigns him to a premature death. On the other hand, Lydgate's tragic underachievement does not preclude the hero-reformer from emerging, in revised form, elsewhere in the novel.

Middlemarch's Will Ladislaw is perhaps no one's 'ideal' hero, with Henry James famously dismissing him as an 'eminent failure' and F. R. Leavis affirming that he only exists as a vehicle for Eliot's intentions.[17] Despite attempts to 'look again at that much abused young man', most notably by Gordon S. Haight ('Eliot's "eminent failure"', p. 24), Ladislaw is still regarded as one of those 'strange semi-heroes', whose questionable masculinity renders him unfit to partner the heroine.[18] But what objectors often miss is that this dilettantish drifter is capable of residing in a 'mixed' economy of being; he is an impulsive idealist who is also conscious of the limitations imposed by reality.[19] Ladislaw insists that the cause for political reform should not wait to 'find immaculate men to work with' (p. 384). His eloquent fervour and intensity may be 'beyond the limits of Middlemarch perception', but he is not indifferent to his audience, as he draws together talent and pragmatism in a manner that Lydgate is ultimately incapable of (p. 379). Dorothea's absorption within Ladislaw's 'arden[cy]' (p. 686), when combined with a sense of expediency and his 'lightness' of character, generates much of the pathos of the Finale. And yet this portrait comes close to Eliot's realist compromise of the hero: 'Their insight is blended with mere opinion; [...] obstinacy or self-assertion will often interfuse itself with their grandest impulses; and their very deeds of self-sacrifice are sometimes only the rebound of a passionate egoism'.[20] 'Real' heroes, as Eliot outlined in her early work 'Janet's Repentance', come to 'deep spiritual truths' through a somewhat romantic process of suffering, 'long wrestling with their own sins and their own sorrows'. She may be sceptical of an 'ideal' hero, whether Carlylean or Byronic, but the residue left by the latter is reflected in her recourse to words such as 'obstinacy', 'self-assertion', 'passionate egoism', 'sins', and 'sorrows'. Eliot draws on as she deflects a Romantic inheritance, with Byron driving and shaping her own heroic pursuit of 'deep spiritual truths', as we shall see in this chapter.

II

Eliot declared, in a letter of 23 August 1869, that 'Byron and his poetry have become more and more repugnant to me of late years'; and a month later writes: 'He seems to me the most *vulgar-minded* genius that ever produced a great effect in literature'.[21] These statements, more vehement than Austen's sardonic aside about *The Corsair*, have often been cited as evidence of Eliot's rejection of Byron. Eliot's language comes close to Carlyle's strenuous anti-Byronic sentiment in a letter to Macvey Napier, editor of the *Edinburgh Review*, dated 28 April 1832: 'In my mind, Byron has been sinking at an accelerated rate, for the last ten years, and has now reached a very low level [...]. I love him not; I *owe* him nothing; only pity, and forgiveness: he taught me nothing that I had not again to forget'.[22] The context of Eliot's remarks is often overlooked, however. Eliot is responding to a renewed interest in Byron's alleged affair with his half-sister, Augusta Leigh, following the publication of Harriet Beecher Stowe's essay, 'The True Story of Lady Byron's Life', in the *Atlantic Monthly* of September 1869, and the subsequent appearance of a book-length version, *Lady Byron Vindicated*, in 1870.[23] Eliot's extensive correspondence on 'The Separation' scandal – what Oliver Wendell Holmes called the 'Byron whirlwind' – clearly demonstrates that she was more indignant about the public discussion of incest than by Byron's involvement, the subject touching a nerve, perhaps, as she was writing the sonnet sequence, 'Brother and Sister', in the same year as the transatlantic Stowe controversy.[24] Years later, Eliot makes the connection explicit:

> I made a poem, in the form of eleven sonnets after the Shakspeare [sic] type, on the childhood of a brother and sister—little descriptive bits on the mutual influences in their small lives. This was always one of my best loved subjects. And I was proportionately enraged about that execrable discussion raised in relation to Byron. The deliberate insistance [sic] on the subject was a worse crime against Society than the imputed fact. (21 April 1873)

Eliot remains agitated by the subject when, in a letter of 15 May 1877, she exclaims to Sara Hennell – 'No! I do not agree with you about Mrs. Stowe and the Byron case. [...] In my judgment the course she took was socially injurious' – and cautions that the story 'may even *possibly* be false' (original emphasis).[25] In any event, even after Byron is denounced in the letter of 23 August 1869, quoted above, Eliot quickly relents: 'After all Byron remains deeply pitiable, like all of us sinners'. Eliot seems able to 'hate the sins [and] love the sinner', like Anne Brontë's heroine in *The Tenant of Wildfell Hall* (1848), before her disastrous marriage to a debauched, manipulative, and shallow rendering of the Byronic hero.[26]

Eliot's letters reveal that she was reading and quoting from Byron's poetry before, during, and after the impassioned censure of 1869. In fact, her frequent references to *Childe Harold's Pilgrimage* and *Don Juan*, among other poems, demonstrate an ongoing, if vacillating, fascination with the poet.[27] Erratic progress on *Middlemarch*, discussed in a letter of 19 February 1869, elicits a reference to 'the blue rushing of the arrowy Rhone' from Canto III of *Childe Harold's Pilgrimage*, for example (lxxi). Eliot was much preoccupied with Byron in the early 1850s, a period that coincided with her growing relationship with George Henry Lewes, and pre-dated Stowe's revelations by nearly 20 years. She asks, in particular, for 'my Shakespeare, Goethe, *Byron* and Wordsworth' to be sent on to her in a letter dated 5 May 1852 (added emphasis), and quotes from the 'Dedication' to *Don Juan*, inviting Charles Bray to 'explain his explanation', two months later (14 July 1852).[28] Eliot is full of Byron, once more, when she elopes with Lewes to Germany in 1854. When in Weimar, Eliot and her acquaintances consider one of the opera singers at the theatre to be 'something like Byron', and a scenic voyage to Mainz 'seemed to me really to deserve Byron's praise'.[29]

Eliot's familiarity with Byron emerges well before her relationship with Lewes, dating back to an adolescence spent reading Byron, Scott, and, as previously noted, Wordsworth.[30] Alicia Carroll argues that 'Her [Eliot's] enjoyment of him [Byron] is clear. He is irresistible, read and re-read. But', she adds, 'the pleasure is a guilty one'.[31] Byron becomes a byword for freedom, an ally in Eliot's 'personal rebellion or private war of independence'. Yet this prospect, for a young woman with a talent for writing, was both 'terrifying and exhilarating'. Eliot's avid reading habits were a source of concern for the author. Eliot fears, as she does for Maggie Tulliver in *The Mill on the Floss*, the dangers of unregulated fantasy:

> I am I confess not an impartial member of a jury in this case for I owe the culprits a grudge for injuries inflicted on myself. I shall carry to my grave the mental diseases with which they have contaminated me. When I was quite a little child I could not be satisfied with the things around me; I was constantly living in a world of my own creation, and was quite contented to have no companions that I might be left to my own musings and imagine scenes in which I was chief actress. Conceive what a character novels would give to these Utopias. I was early supplied with them by those who kindly sought to gratify my appetite for reading and of course I made use of the materials they supplied for building my castles in the air. (16 March 1839)

This portrait of insular girlish daydreaming fuelled by fiction is not unique to Eliot. Fanny Kemble, a noted nineteenth-century actress and writer, recalled 'quivering with excitement' as she took a volume of Byron's poetry to bed with her at boarding school, later renouncing the poet, as reading his verse 'always affected me like an evil potion taken into my blood'.[32] Kemble and Eliot sought to sanitise the mind and disinfect the body of pernicious moral pollutants. What is noteworthy about Eliot's famous disavowal, and renders it as complex as the fictional warnings issued by Austen and Gaskell (as discussed in previous chapters), are the exceptions Eliot makes in the same letter. The poems of Byron and Scott remain 'standard works whose contents are matter of constant reference' – the same authors who are deemed to be 'dangerous', on the face of it, in *Persuasion* and *Wives and Daughters*. Given Eliot's identification of the imagination as an 'enemy', it is tempting to ask, as does Jenny Uglow, 'how do they escape?'[33]

Eliot was only 19 years old when she wrote this 'singularly priggish letter'. And yet it is clear that Byron and Scott are singled out for their unquestionable worth. It could be argued that their worth is in what they epitomise, i.e. the antithesis of Eliot's realist empathy. Maggie Tulliver starts to question whether the sensations she derives from her immersion in 'all Scott's novels and all Byron's poems' (p. 298), sought out as an antidote to daily life, correspond with the dulled dissatisfaction and confusion she feels at human behaviour. Her uncontrollable impulses are responsible for inner turmoil and tragedy; yet Eliot is wary of suppressing such Romantic longing and waywardness. Maggie's interest in 'sages and poets', over 'saints and martyrs', mirrors her author's (p. 298). As I hope to demonstrate in this chapter and the next, Eliot's early inclinations are not the passing whims of a precocious teenager to be corrected by virtuous instruction. A discriminating interest in Byron is not exorcised but evolves in meaningful and instructive ways for reading Eliot's fiction and her regard for the Romantics. Byron is subjected to sustained criticism and serves as a testing ground for Eliot's creative concerns. Yet, as has already been established in previous chapters, the poet's hold over the nineteenth-century woman writer's imagination is not readily regulated or rejected.

III

Eliot's apparent disapproval of Byron, despite her continued engagement with his poetry and reputation, is often seen as part of the author's more general rejection of egotism. As K. M. Newton argues, in his study of George Eliot as a Romantic humanist, 'It is clearly one of the major philosophical concerns of George Eliot's fiction to face this problem [of the ego]. [...] The Byronic egoist is, I think, of particular importance'.[34] For Eliot, egotism can accompany artistic genius, but it is more often than not associated with narrow self-interest and sycophancy. An illustration of this can be found in Eliot's satirical short story, 'Brother Jacob', written in 1860 and published in 1864.[35] David Faux, under the assumed name Edward Freely, sets up a confectionary business in the fictional market town of Grimworth, where his 'Sultanic self-indulgence' (pp. 68, 76), a façade of jaded glamour, gradually inveigles its way into and corrupts the community. This 'infection' spreads through the character of Mrs Steene, the vet's wife, who is the first to replace home baking with Faux's expensive shop-bought goods (p. 65). Mrs Steene is more open to temptation because 'she had been rather over-educated for her station in life' and 'knew by heart many passages in "Lalla Rookh", the "Corsair", and the "Siege of Corinth" ' (p. 64). Not only has Mrs Steene's ability to recite Byron and Thomas Moore resulted in the neglect of her domestic duties, it has led to marital dissatisfaction as Mr Steene was 'not in the least like a nobleman turned Corsair out of pure scorn for his race, or like a renegade with a turban and crescent, unless it were in the irritability of his temper. And scorn is such a very different thing in top-boots!'. As Mrs Steene's expectations of a real-life Oriental romance are deflated, so Mr Faux is unmasked as a sham – a plain and unglamorous 'rascal' (p. 85) – and the housewives of Grimworth resume their culinary efforts. Yet, even with the reaffirmation of traditionally gendered pursuits, what 'Brother Jacob' demonstrates is, as Helen Small suggests, the 'comic acceptance that egotism and deception are the way of the world'.[36] It is hoped that Mrs Steene is reconciled to her domestic lot, but she only 'thought *less* of bulbuls and renegades' (p. 87, added emphasis). In other words, the source of 'infection' – the lure of exotic abandonment – survives even if the epidemic of Byronism is contained.

A number of problems present themselves with this approach to Romantic presences in Eliot's fiction. Mrs Steene's interest in Byron is driven by the trend for Oriental romances and literary pirates. It is her weakness for such fads, like purchasing Mr Faux's wares, that is subject to a disapproving irony. Byron functions here, as he does with Mrs Kirkpatrick in Gaskell's *Wives and Daughters* (1866), to expose the undiscerning reader and superficial follower of fashion rather than to provide a literary judgement. Eliot does not read Byron in the banal manner of a Mrs Steene. In a letter of 28 May 1840, for example, Eliot turns to the poet in an attempt to discipline her own tendency to self-absorption: 'Byron in his *Childe Harold* (which I have just begun the second time) checks reflections on individual and personal sorrows by reminding himself of the revolutions and woes beneath which the shores of the Mediterranean have groaned'. Byron, in this instance, offers solace and a safeguard against what Eliot herself judges to be an 'almost unpardonably egotistical letter'. That Eliot should look to Byron for moral fibre borders on the ironic, but it also demonstrates a finely tuned appreciation of his poetic strengths and resilience. Some 15 years later, she defends Byron in her attack on Dr Cumming's 'Evangelical Teaching':

Who that has a spark of generous feeling, that rejoices in the presence of good in a fellow-being, has not dwelt with pleasure on the thought that Lord Byron's unhappy career was ennobled and purified towards its close by a high and sympathetic purpose, by honest and energetic efforts for his fellow-men? Who has not read with deep emotion those last pathetic lines, beautiful as the afterglow of sunset, in which love and resignation are mingled with something of a melancholy heroism? Who has not lingered with compassion over the dying scene at Missolonghi—the sufferer's inability to make his farewell messages of love intelligible, and the last long hours of silent pain?[37]

Byron is here a poet of affecting verse, noble feelings, and selfless acts, the antithesis of the '*vulgar-minded* genius' that would be tainted by the Stowe scandal. His poetry pulsates with a 'generous feeling' that, at the last, strives for the common good of mankind, echoing Elizabeth Barrett Browning's earlier lament for the poet of liberty in *Stanzas on the Death of Lord Byron* (1824): 'That generous heart where genius thrill'd divine,/ Hath spent its last most glorious throb for thee—/ Then sank amid the storm that made thy children free!' (ll. 16–18).[38] The pathos of what Eliot refers to as his 'melancholy heroism', combined with 'a high and sympathetic purpose' – namely Byron's involvement in the Greek War of Independence – comes very close to the figure of the Romantic artist-reformer that assumes prominence in Eliot's fiction.

Eliot's dialogues with Byron complicate what both Newton and Stone view as the separation of Eliot's Romantic inheritance into the 'egotistical', related to Byron, and the 'organicist', related to Wordsworth.[39] It is a mistake to demarcate Eliot's Romantic allegiances so categorically. The ego, scorned if unchecked in Eliot's fiction, is seen as an unavoidable and perhaps even necessary part of life. Eliot's 'real' heroes, in 'Janet's Repentance', combine 'self-sacrifice' with 'passionate egoism' – altruism and egoism are converse, yet interdependent, impulses. As Eliot makes clear in her portrait of the Reverend Mr Tryan, it is this balance, or acceptance of flaws, that is truly heroic: 'he pushes manfully on, with fluctuating faith and courage, with a sensitive failing body' (*Scenes of Clerical Life*, p. 229). For Eliot, manliness resists prescribed patterns of behaviour (even Carlylean ones), and is open to change and doubt. A significant question therefore arises: does Eliot's formulation of a realist masculinity – with an insistence on human fallibility, the pains of mortality, and an accompanying agnosticism – necessarily rule out Romantic influence and Byron's presence in particular? The following discussion will re-evaluate Eliot's treatment of Byron, and what has traditionally been thought of as her hostility to Byronic egotism, across a number of her early prose works and poetry before moving on, in the final chapter, to a detailed study of her later fiction. This chapter and the next will also situate Eliot's literary relationship with Byron in a broader context of Romantic legacies.

IV

In 'The Lifted Veil', the companion piece to 'Brother Jacob' (and Eliot's only other self-contained short story), aesthetic and psychological concerns are presented from the perspective of the central protagonist and narrator, Latimer. Often seen as an aberration in her oeuvre, with its first-person fixation on scientific experimentation and psychic phenomena, 'The Lifted Veil', written and published anonymously in 1859, provides an early insight into Eliot's regard for a range of Romantic writers and reveals a profound yet critical indebtedness that informs her later work. The tale begins with Latimer's announcement of his impending death and culminates in that anticipated moment after a sensational scene of revivification. 'The Lifted Veil' marks a significant moment in the genesis of the romantic pseudo-artist from the Gothic tales of the Romantic period to the Gothic of the *fin-de-siècle*, anticipating such works as Oscar Wilde's *The Picture of Dorian Gray* (1891). Looking backwards as well as forwards, the parallels with Mary Shelley's *Frankenstein* (1818) are numerous, and include a formative friendship in Geneva that leads to penetrating the 'secret' sciences. Latimer's later wanderings and apocalyptic presentiments also recall *The Last Man* (1826) and Percy Shelley's 'Ozymandias' (1818). The title of the tale is most likely borrowed from Percy Shelley's sonnet, 'Lift not the painted veil', or 'The pale, the cold, and the moony smile', and directs the reader, more broadly, to the Romantic resonance of the veil image.[40] As well as the Shelleys, Wordsworth is, once more, in the foreground of Eliot's fiction. The scene of Latimer in a boat, gazing at the sky as successive mountain tops come into view, is an unmistakeable allusion to the famous rowboat passage in Book I of *The Prelude*.

Latimer is, in his youth at least, a disciple of Wordsworth. He regards his vision of Prague as a 'spontaneous creation' (p. 10), echoing the famous pronouncement in the Preface to the *Lyrical Ballads* that 'all good poetry is the spontaneous overflow of powerful feelings' (p. 598). And his attempt to recreate the experience follows a process of 'tranquil restoration'.[41] Latimer states, 'I concentrated my thoughts on Venice; I stimulated my imagination with poetic memories, and strove to feel myself present in Venice, as I had felt myself present in Prague' (p. 10). However, instead of the 'fructifying virtue' that Latimer hopes to harness, his efforts remain prosaic.[42] A sense of exaltation before the 'awful loveliness' of the Alps will, he anticipates, confirm his Romantic credentials as a Wordsworth or a Shelley. Yet, crucially, he has, or feels he has, 'the poet's sensibility without his voice' (p. 7). 'His sensitivity is a diseased condition', as Frederick Burwick argues, 'and it lacks all capacity to express itself'.[43]

The limitations of Latimer's acute sensitivities are not solely confined to expression. Eliot's tale traces a narrowing of vision, 'the curse of insight', to a deadening dimness that only reveals glimpses of an inner narcissism (p. 42).[44] The failed attempt to visualise Venice demonstrates not the active mental expansion or mature reflection advocated by Wordsworth, but a ponderous passivity bereft of intellectual ambition. Where Wordsworth acknowledges that there must be something 'altogether slavish and mechanical' about the process of composition, Latimer falls into the 'idleness and unmanly despair' that the poet is cautioned to ward against (Preface, p. 604). The 'fragile, nervous, ineffectual self' that Latimer regards as a precondition of the creative spirit is far removed from Wordsworth's 'man speaking to men: a man, it is true, endued with more lively sensibility, more enthusiasm and tenderness, who has a greater knowledge of human nature, and a more comprehensive soul, than are supposed to be common among mankind' (p. 14; Preface, p. 603). In seeking reflections of self in those around him, Latimer inverts the underlying ideology, 'the extension and intensification of our sympathetic nature', that drew Eliot to Wordsworth.[45] Absent in Latimer's tale is a sense of struggle in adversity, of benign empathy with and curiosity about the human condition, and the pleasure, combined with grandeur, that accompanies poetic feeling for Wordsworth.[46]

Other Romantic poets, besides Wordsworth and Shelley, populate the landscape of Latimer's thwarted artistic ambitions. When Latimer enquires whether Novalis, the German Romantic poet, felt 'his inspiration intensified under the progress of consumption',[47] the Victorian perception of Keats's tubercular genius is surely brought to mind, as is the suggestion of a 'vale of Soul-making' in the following: 'There is no short cut, no patent tram-road, to wisdom: after all the centuries of invention, the soul's path lies through the thorny wilderness which must be still trodden in solitude, with bleeding feet, with sobs for help, as it was trodden by them of old time' (pp. 10, 21). The principle that suffering can forge a human imprint is Keatsian. Yet the absence of salvation in Latimer's worldview at this point in the narrative, a precursor to his declaration of a demonic atheism – 'there is no religion possible, no worship, but a worship of devils' (p. 36) – reverts to the Old Testament vale of tears (Psalms 84:6) that Keats is attempting to counter in his famous letter.[48]

The parallels between Keats's 'camelion Poet' and Latimer's psychological intuitions assume an even greater importance in Eliot's tale (27 October 1818). Latimer epitomises, in many respects, the paradoxically 'unpoetical' nature of the Keatsian poet, 'continually in for—and filling some other Body', when he states: 'This was the obtrusion on my mind of the mental process going forward in first one person, and then another, with whom I happened to be in contact' (p. 13). Latimer, like Keats, is anxious about his 'acuteness of vision', and feels persecuted as 'the identity of every one in the room begins to press upon me [so] that, I am in a very little time an[ni]hilated' (27 October 1818). However, where Keats's chameleon poet takes 'relish of the dark side of things', it has an equal 'taste for the bright one'; dark or bright, essentially, 'It does no harm', which cannot be said of Latimer's dealings with his wife and her maid. Latimer experiences no delight, no sense of purpose, or even Keatsian 'gusto', only a benumbing irritation at the common thoughts of common people. Eliot depicts, through Latimer, an altogether darker chameleonic existence. His sinister vision, more accustomed to inhabit the 'foul' than the 'fair', views Keats's poetic empathy, reductively, through the lens of scientific exactitude: '[Souls] were seen as if thrust asunder by a microscopic vision, that showed all the intermediate frivolities, all the suppressed egoism, all the struggling chaos of puerilities, meanness, vague capricious memories, and indolent make-shift thoughts, from which human words and deeds emerge like leaflets covering a fermenting heap' (p. 14). Subjecting a Keatsian aesthetic to such scrutiny exposes the invasive and parasitic myopia of 'mind' sciences. Latimer describes a metaphorical dissection of the human psyche in which the organisms, or 'leaflets', he studies barely conceal the stagnating 'heap' of decomposition beneath. His tunnel vision detects and draws out the substructure of his own brain: an execrable wasteland. Latimer's medical precision constitutes a profanity, as he 'Unweave[s] a rainbow' of Romantic humanism.[49]

A further poet is added to this heady Romantic mix. The only direct reference to Byron in the story is a misquotation from *Manfred*. His reference is more broadly pervasive, however, and a parallel can be traced back to some of Eliot's first published writing (which originally appeared in the Coventry *Herald and Observer* between December 1846 and February 1847, and was later reprinted as *Poetry and Prose from the Notebook of an Eccentric*).[50] Eliot's introduction to the fictional artist, Macarthy, details the relationship between 'his highly-charged mind and the negatively electrified souls around him' (p. 15). Subsequent articles, purportedly by Macarthy, trace Romantic subjects that include the 'purity and simplicity' of the child (p. 20). The Wordsworthian overtones of Macarthy's visions anticipate Latimer's in 'The Lifted Veil'. And yet the description of Macarthy's 'sympathy with mankind [as] that of a being of analogous, rather than identical race' rearticulates Manfred's declaration: 'though I wore the form,/ I had no sympathy with breathing flesh,/ Nor midst the creatures of clay that girded me/ Was there but one—but of her anon' (*Poetry and Prose*, p. 16; *Manfred*, II. ii. ll. 56–9). Macarthy's 'ideal', not unlike Manfred's Astarte, was 'a beautiful shadow which was ever floating before him' (p. 15). But it is the combination of characteristics – 'misanthropist' *and* 'humourist' – that renders Macarthy such a telling portrait of Byron (p. 15). Eliot's account of Macarthy's writings indicates a careful reader of Byron's style and range. The articles themselves, on miscellaneous subjects from 'How to Avoid Disappointment' to 'Hints on Snubbing', demonstrate a readiness to adopt a sardonic Byronic posturing albeit under the guise of an imaginary, and deceased, artist.

> I have found the results of profound thought and widely extended research–productions, some of which have been carefully meditated, others apparently thrown off with the rapidity of inspiration; but in all of them there is a strange mixture of wisdom and whimsicality, of sublime conception and stinging caricature, of deep melancholy and wild merriment. (p. 17)

'The Lifted Veil', Carroll Viera argues, is 'undeniably an attempt at a fictional rendition of an aesthetic formulated over more than a decade' ('Eliot's Early Aesthetic', p. 752). Latimer's desperation, his recollection of former wounds, and his desire to meet a dramatically predicted end make him the direct descendant of Eliot's preternaturally perceptive poet Macarthy. The tale concludes with Latimer's death and a vision of unalleviated affliction. As Byron's Manfred describes himself as cursed in his opening speech, so Latimer's 'gift' is viewed cynically: 'I am cursed with an exceptional mental character, I shall not much longer groan under the wearisome burthen of this earthly existence' (p. 3). Latimer's 'exceptional' abilities render him, like a Byronic hero, singular, strange, and scarred. His sense of sorrowful superiority strikes a particular chord with Byron's Manfred. What Latimer describes as 'a fatal solitude of soul in the society of one's fellow-men' (p. 7), an alienating distinction experienced as exile, is expressed by Byron's anti-hero in the following terms:

> These were my pastimes, and to be alone;
> For if the beings, of whom I was one,—

> Hating to be so,—cross'd me in my path,
> I felt myself degraded back to them,
> And was all clay again. (II. ii. ll. 75–9)

Manfred's Shakespearean eloquence may elude Latimer, but his predilection for pain – as it is subjected to an intense, and staged, scrutiny – recalls Byron's protagonist. The following passage from 'The Lifted Veil' could be a summary of Byron's dramatic poem:

> My self-consciousness was heightened to that pitch of intensity in which our own emotions take the form of a drama which urges itself imperatively on our contemplation, and we begin to weep, less under the sense of our suffering than at the thought of it. I felt a sort of pitying anguish over the pathos of my own lot: the lot of a being finely organised for pain, but with hardly any fibres that responded to pleasure—to whom the idea of future evil robbed the present of its joy, and for whom the idea of future good did not still the uneasiness of a present yearning or a present dread. I went dumbly through that stage of the poet's suffering, in which he feels the delicious pang of utterance, and makes an image of his sorrows. (p. 24)

Latimer's description of Bertha as 'my oasis of mystery in the dreary desert of knowledge' forms a further parallel with Byron's poem (p. 18). As enigmatic for Latimer as Astarte is for Manfred (and Macarthy's 'beautiful shadow'), Bertha offers an initial respite of uncertainty in an exhaustively known world. However, instead of fulfilling her promise of negatively capable possibilities, Bertha turns into an implacable siren, closer to Keats's Lamia or Coleridge's Geraldine than to Manfred's fleeting spirit. Descriptions of Bertha 'look[ing] like a cruel immortal, finding her spiritual feast in the agonies of a dying race' (p. 41), anticipate Walter Pater's famous passage on Leonardo da Vinci's 'La Gioconda' in *Studies in the History of the Renaissance* (1873). Similarly, Latimer's response to what he takes to be a portrait of Lucrezia Borgia by Giorgione, and the after-effects it produces, of 'a strange poisoned sensation, as if I had long been inhaling a fatal odour' (p. 19), are reminiscent of Shelley's poem 'On the Medusa of Leonardo da Vinci in the Florentine Gallery' (1819), with its 'agonies of anguish and of death' and the 'thrilling vapour of the air'.[51] Latimer's horrifying 'revelation' about Bertha is triggered by a painting of an infamous woman, and that impression is fixed by the weight of his allusions to other notorious *femme fatales* (Bertha is also depicted as the 'dying Cleopatra' in his vision, for example, pp. 19, 34). Latimer compares Bertha to a 'Water-Nixie', with her pale green dress, blond curls, and 'fatal eye[s]', because his 'mind was full of German lyrics' (pp. 11, 12). It is the narrator's artistic projections, coupled with his 'compromised masculinity', that confine Bertha to, as Uglow suggests, 'a spectre of Romantic myth deadly to men'.[52] Bertha herself dislikes Latimer's 'pet literature' and scorns his overblown courtship rhetoric, 'dying with love and jealousy for her sake' (pp. 15, 16). Latimer paints an intricate self-portrait of Romantic sensibilities, constructing a Faustian persona that 'makes an image of his sorrows' (p. 24), but his pretensions are hollow and, for Bertha, hateful.

In 'The Lifted Veil', Eliot dramatises some of her most serious misgivings about Romantic aesthetics through a figure with aspirations that are constrained by an agonised subjectivity. This bleak prospect does not exclude Eliot's regard for Wordsworth. The 'community of feeling' that Latimer initially experiences in his friendship with Charles Meunier culminates in a macabre, not to mention merciless, scientific experiment; an early hunger for 'human deeds and human emotions' becomes 'merely a diseased activity of the imagination' (pp. 8, 6, 13). Rather than sharing an affinity with Wordsworthian values, Latimer's 'morbidly sensitive nature perpetually craving sympathy and support' (p. 15) is closer in spirit to the 'morbid, poetic soul' of Tennyson's *Maud* (1855).[53] Eliot was critical of the monodrama, declaring in the *Westminster Review* that 'We have in "Maud" scarcely more than a residuum of Alfred Tennyson'. But she concedes that it is 'undeniably strong in expression', with metrical lines that, like a 'vitriol madness', 'eat themselves with phosphoric eagerness into our memory, in spite of our will'.[54] In passing sentence on Tennyson's poem, Eliot comes close to summarising the short story she would write just four years later: '... its tone is throughout morbid; it opens to us the self revelations of a morbid mind, and what it presents as the cure for this mental disease is itself only a morbid conception of human relations'. In *Maud* and 'The Lifted Veil', youthful Romantic visions give way to a pathologised Victorian consciousness. As the fractured form of Tennyson's monodrama directs attention to – as it constructs – the speaker's distracted psyche, so the retrospective narration of Eliot's short story generates an interpretative distance to guard against the reader's immersion in the speaker's enclosed interiority and exhaustive self-analysis.

Do the allusions to poets in 'The Lifted Veil' amount to a challenge, or possible exorcism, of a Romantic inheritance that the Victorian author found both exhilarating and potentially damaging? Possibly so, if the narrator expresses Eliot's reservations about Romanticism. That a suspected Romantic sensibility may conceal a psychological disorder recalls Eliot's concerns, in the letter of 16 March 1839 quoted above, that an unsuitable literary diet has contaminated her with 'mental diseases'. The frequent references to a diseased, or infected, mind throughout the tale problematise a conflation of author and narrator, however. Latimer's suspected insanity ruptures the anticipated bond between the first-person narrator and the audience of the story, an effect that Tennyson was eager to stress when extricating *Maud*, as a literary work, from his speaker's hereditary insanity: 'The things which seem like faults belong not so much to the poem as to the character of the hero'.[55] Eliot unmasks, through her narrator's so-called 'superadded consciousness' (pp. 13, 18), the poverty of a Romantic aesthetic stripped of the sublime. Latimer proves to be unsuited to the grand poetic persona he adopts. In other words, it is not the Romantic 'speculation' on the creative process that is criticised, but the 'character' contemplating it.[56] If Latimer is an interpreter, as James Decker argues, then his role in Eliot's tale is to misinterpret, to mentally mutilate, Romantic literature.[57]

In the title's allusion to Shelley's sonnet, 'Lift not the painted veil', Latimer can be seen as the audacious 'one who had lifted it', and inhabits a shadow land peopled by the 'unheeding many'.[58] He aspires to be the 'exemplary' poet that Shelley came to represent for the Victorians. Yet he is far removed from a Shelleyan spirit searching for love and truth.[59] The tone of Shelley's sonnet, bordering on the sardonic, and the definite opening assertion serve as an implicit critique of Latimer's experiment; more sinister depths of hatred and revenge are revealed when 'the dark veil had completely fallen' (p. 41). 'The secret things of the grave' is the subject of an earlier Shelley poem, 'The pale, the cold, and the moony smile', where life is viewed as a pallid hinterland before the prospect of an insensate and 'unending' afterlife.[60] Where 'The Lifted Veil' can be read as an exposé of the nihilistic quests in these poems – 'The pale, the cold, and the moony smile' was originally part of the 'Graveyard Poems' in *The Esdaile Notebook* and was subsequently published in the *Alastor* volume of 1816 – this overlooks Shelley's sceptical regard of those, like Latimer, for whom courage fails: 'And the coming of death is a fearful blow/ To a brain unencompassed with nerves of steel' (ll. 15–16).[61] That the final stanza of Shelley's poem, 'The pale, the cold, and the moony smile', opens with probing questions – 'Who telleth a tale of unspeaking death?/ Who lifteth the veil of what is to come?' (ll. 25–6) – anticipates the sceptical voice of Eliot's implied author. Shelley's poems do not corroborate Latimer's desolate worldview. Rather, their shifting moods and tone unsettle a self-absorbed portrait of existential angst. Shelley's presence in 'The Lifted Veil' directs us to a subtle by-play wherein a discerning reader, one that appreciates the illuminating instability of Romantic poetry, critically detaches from Latimer's flat misconception of the artist. Allusions to the Romantic poets in Eliot's story cultivate a 'double consciousness' that suspends disbelief at the sensational aspects of the story and simultaneously scorns the wretchedly near-sighted speaker.

V

The presence of the Romantic poets is most conflicted in Eliot's shorter fiction and most pressing in her poetry. Eliot's most serious and sustained engagement with the Byronic can be found in her experimental verse play *The Spanish Gypsy,* where, as Stone points out, a 'romantic sensibility [is] celebrated in operatic manner'.[62] Don Silva, a Spanish knight, is an unabashed portrait of the Byronic hero: scornful, fierce, proud, and yet tender with the woman upon whom all his affections are bestowed. From the first, accounts of Don Silva affirm a Byronic status. His smile, a 'sudden opening flower/ On dark deep waters', recalls Conrad's contrasting moods in *The Corsair*: 'The lip's least curl, the lightest paleness thrown/ Along the govern'd aspect, speak alone/ Of deeper passions' (I. ll. 231–33).[63] Before Father Isidor brands the protagonist as a Cain, forming an intertextual reference with Byron's poetic drama, it is the primacy of Don Silva's will, the 'miracle-working will', that marks him out as a direct descendant of the Byronic hero (p. 321).[64] In *The Spanish Gypsy*, Eliot indulges in a Byronic romanticism where even the performing monkey, Annibal, is 'misanthropic' and aspires to a liminal existence ' 'Twixt "is" and "is not" ' (p. 332).

Such fervent romanticism is not without an attendant restraint for Eliot. Silva's chivalric enshrining of love may fill a spiritual vacuum, but his conscience cannot be absolved by this 'poet's strain' (p. 226). The hero's devotion to Fedalma does not affect his salvation and we witness him inwardly build 'a Hell in Heavens despite'.[65] The Prior's 'nets', which Silva sees as narrowing his life to one of duty and obedience, return as 'nets of guilt' when the Zíncali triumph over the countrymen that he has forsaken (pp. 344, 426). The hero's hollow betrayal, his 'hellish sacrament' (p. 428), is reinforced by the stylistic 'nets', or 'subtle cords', of enjambed lines when Father Isidor is brought before the victors for execution. The blank verse beats out the rhythmic 'throngs' and 'rush' of regret:

> Silva had but rebelled – he was not free;
> And all the subtle cords that bound his soul

> Were tightened by the strain of one rash leap
> Made in defiance. He accused no more,
> But dumbly shrank before accusing throngs
> Of thoughts, the impetuous recurrent rush
> Of all his past-created, unchanged self. (p. 429)

Eliot is clear that a Byronic autonomy, what Silva terms 'A heart without a livery – naked manhood' (p. 334), is not only disadvantageous, for both the individual and the community, but also futile.[66] The immediate concerns of *The Spanish Gypsy* may be the romance of knights, maidens, and battles, yet it is the claims of ancestry that are ultimately reinforced. Silva's allegiance to and veneration of love cannot evade the past; it is the 'long-shared pains/ Of far-off generations' that form and determine his identity (p. 410). Deprived of the camaraderie of his men and the 'close-linked fellowship' with his forefathers, Silva's feelings of isolation (as he is cursed by both his old and newly-adopted kinsmen) turn to rage and dejection when he compounds the dereliction of his duty by murdering Fedalma's father. Eliot depicts, through Silva's Byronic despair, 'the alienation of the modern consciousness from its past heritage' (Newton, *Romantic Humanist*, p. 36).

The poem ends with a suitably Byronic exile, 'cast down/ A blackened branch upon the desolate ground/ Where once I kindled ruin' (p. 449). Yet Eliot extends the possibility of redemption to her wandering hero. Whereas Byron's Manfred leaves himself with no option but self-oblivion, the departure from life's stage, Silva shuns suicide to salvage his honour. The individual's struggle with loyalty and love is played out within a wider context, moreover. Issues of race and religion are not merely an exotic backdrop and catalyst for the action, as they can be in Byron's Oriental Tales; here, they are pressing concerns that foreshadow Eliot's treatment of Judaism in *Daniel Deronda*. The fortunes of an outcast, nomadic tribe may be most vividly conceived in the characters of Zarca and his daughter, but Silva's Byronic inflections are also coloured by politics and religion. Eliot, like Gaskell before her, tests the Byronic hero by placing his inner turmoil and defiance in a situation of social crisis. In so doing, Newton argues, Silva's deficiencies are exposed:

> The individual was therefore not justified in creating his own personal values by an act of will. He was inextricably a part of mankind and could never achieve complete cultural transcendence. The ego itself was in a large degree a cultural product. It was an illusion, then, to believe that the egoist could completely separate himself from his fellow-men and feel totally self-sufficient.[67]

Eliot's various portraits of Silva – from his fractured self, with a 'soul [...] locked 'twixt two opposing crimes' (p. 437), to the grey-haired pilgrim of the final pages – lend weight to Newton's argument, as does the moment when Fedalma concedes to her former lover: 'We rebelled –/ The larger life subdued us' (p. 451).

However, to read *The Spanish Gypsy* as an opposition to Byronic egotism risks simplifying Eliot's characterisation and literary politics. The charge of doubleness that is levelled at the poem's hero for his divided loyalties cannot account for the complexities of a 'nature multitudinously mixed' and a face that 'flashed anathemas' (pp. 324, 261). Below is a fuller description of Silva's mercurial, 'many-blended consciousness' (p. 322):

> A nature half-transformed, with qualities
> That oft betrayed each other, elements
> Not blent but struggling, breeding strange effects,
> Passing the reckoning of his friends or foes.
> Haughty and generous, grave and passionate;
> With tidal moments of devoutest awe,
> Sinking anon to farthest ebb of doubt;
> Deliberating ever, till the sting
> Of a recurrent ardour made him rush
> Right against reasons that himself had drilled
> And marshalled painfully. (p. 252)

Silva's over-active, and unfixed, consciousness seems to lack resolve, an apparent flaw that is identified by Sephardo, the hero's former tutor, when he describes Silva as 'o'er-endowed with opposites/ Making a self alternate, where each hour/ Was critic of the last, each mood too strong/ For tolerance of its fellow in close yoke' (p. 343). The sense of a 'self alternate', or a 'nature half-transformed', is reflected in the use of half-lines; and the effect of 'elements/ Not blent but struggling' arises out of the syntactic complexity of blank verse. What Silva himself describes as his 'Certain uncertainty' (p. 343) is not a truly negatively capable state, despite the propensity to Keatsian doubt, as his indecision derives from a series of painfully contending perspectives rather than an ability to entertain multiple possibilities simultaneously. Silva is closer, in this sense, to Manfred's 'awful chaos', an inscrutable nature pessimistically described by the Abbot as 'contending without end or order' (*Manfred*, III. i. ll. 164, 166). Sephardo nevertheless makes the point that Silva's contrary behaviour is all too human; the hero epitomises the 'waywardness of mortal men' (p. 343). Therefore, the irreconcilable nature that separates Silva from his fellow man is also his strongest connection to them, an unwelcome reminder, as for all Byronic heroes, of his mortality.

The priority accorded to the communal in *The Spanish Gypsy*, as elsewhere in Eliot's fiction, is reinforced in the form of the verse drama. Silva may be the most readily identifiable Byronic hero in the text, but another character is arguably more formidable. It is Zarca, the leader of the Zíncali and Fedalma's father, who is portrayed as a 'Titan' and declares: 'The greatest gift the hero leaves his race/ Is to have been a hero' (pp. 434, 313). The scenes between Silva and Zarca stage a debate over the aspirations and fate of the Byronic hero. As the two men engage in a Sedgwickean struggle for supremacy over Fedalma, Silva is 'Locked motionless by forces opposite:/ His frustrate hopes still battled with despair;/ His will was prisoner to the double grasp/ Of rage and hesitancy', whereas Zarca 'stood/ Present and silent and unchangeable' (p. 399).[68] Zarca's reconciliation with his daughter heralds a light that contrasts with his former darkness, a tenderness to temper his hardness, yet he remains steadfast in his devotion to a social cause. Zarca is not primarily concerned with the inward reflections of his own soul, as Byronic heroes invariably are, but with the 'soul of multitudes' (p. 382). This viewpoint is illustrated in the following quotation, where a Byronic temperament is bridled, forcibly, for the greater good of his people:

> His eyes, his mouth, his nostril, all inspired
> With scorn that mastered utterance of scorn,
> With power to check all rage until it turned
> To ordered force, unleashed on chosen prey (p. 236)

Zarca's Carlylean sense of purpose and control is not presented without reservation, however. When Fedalma first sees Zarca in the plaza she fears that his is one of the 'long-imprisoned souls' in purgatory, as he transfixes her with his forbidding stare: 'His deep-knit brow,/ Inflated nostril, scornful lip compressed,/ Seem a dark hieroglyph of coming fate/ Written before her' (pp. 268, 250). Zarca's Byronic features are mixed with a sphinx-like 'glittering eye' and a 'strange power of speech' that compels and disturbs.[69] The knowledge he imparts to his daughter leaves her 'forlorn', both 'sadder' and 'wiser' like Coleridge's hapless wedding guest in 'The Rime of the Ancient Mariner' (ll. 623–4). At her father's behest, Fedalma sacrifices her own romantic fulfilment for a moral crusade. His unwavering will demands absolute loyalty from his subjects, including a daughter who will be scarred by this 'life-long wound' (p. 388). Both Zarca and Fedalma work towards a greater good, at immense cost to the latter's happiness, and yet the former's motivations are not completely altruistic; he is driven by a personal pride that is not too dissimilar to Silva's. What, if anything, separates Silva's autonomy from Zarca's Byronic declaration that 'I am no priest, and keep no consciences:/ I keep my own place and my own command' (p. 427)? Zarca here evokes Manfred's defiant tone when he denies the spirits his soul:

> *Thou* didst not tempt me, and thou couldst not tempt me;
> I have not been thy dupe, nor am thy prey—
> But was my own destroyer, and will be
> My own hereafter. (III. iv. ll. 137–40, original emphasis)

The broader limitations of Zarca's character are felt when he, like the Prior before him, scorns the poet's art: 'All further words are idle elegies/ Unfitting times of action' (p. 400). Prizing firmness of purpose at the expense of reflecting what Juan, the wandering poet, terms 'The momentary rainbow on the spray' (p. 374) is another form of short-sighted egoism. It is Silva's temperament that comes closest to the minstrel's art when Juan's 'babbling rills/ Of wit and song' are captured in the 'babbling currents' of the hero's thoughts (pp. 212, 342). It is Silva, not Zarca, who survives to begin his search for salvation; and it is Silva, not Zarca, who has the ability to grow and develop as a character. Ultimately, the many-sided Byronic hero vanquishes the single-minded Carlylean hero. The poetry of *The Spanish Gypsy*, through which the 'old epic voices ring again' (p. 205), functions as a critique of Zarca's prosaic resolve and complements Silva's effervescent lyricism.

The Spanish Gypsy dramatises a dialogue between contrasting aspects of the Byronic. Eliot's understanding of the various guises of the Byronic hero, his human failings and his existential complexities, is indicated by Sephardo's sage proto-modernism:

> So, I must grasp my morsels: truth is oft
> Scattered in fragments round a stately pile
> Built half of error; (p. 348)

The Byronic hero does not pursue *a* 'truth', and is often disabused of such a quest, as he draws back from and exposes the flaws of a unifying purpose or certainty. But he is part of the pattern, however scattered or discordant, that makes up Eliot's differentiated humanity (the seeds of which were planted in *Scenes of Clerical Life* and come to fruition in *Middlemarch* and *Daniel Deronda*). Eliot's Byronic hero, presented in the empathetic medium of poetry, may fall short of a 'high-souled man' who can 'move the masses', the prophet-poet envisaged by Elizabeth Barrett Browning in *Aurora Leigh* (1856).[70] Eliot, whose reputation is based first and foremost on her prose, is, as Romney Leigh is forced to learn, poet 'enough to understand/ That life develops from within'. The 'poet's individualism' – synonymous, for Eliot, with Byron – is necessary 'To work your universal'. Silva's individualism, in *The Spanish Gypsy*, may not effect the social and political change that Eliot looks towards, but he is a catalyst for, or conduit to, the 'universal'. His actions, his relationships with both men and women, and his poetic sensibilities are a precondition for the pioneer.

Eliot's staging of the relative merits and limitations of the Byronic condition is not confined to male protagonists. Rather than functioning as a facilitator for the power struggles between Silva and Zarca, Fedalma emerges as a principal character who may be the Spanish gypsy of the title. She is not the submissive recipient of Silva's affections, nor does she readily submit to her father. Fedalma refuses to be enslaved by another's Byronic will and derives the strength from her father's crusade to become a leader of men. It is Fedalma who undergoes the most significant transformation in the poem – from Silva's 'dark queen' to a selfless pioneer, from an 'infidel' suspected of bewitching the lovelorn knight to, as her father envisages, 'a goddess, sanctifying oaths,/ Enforcing right, and ruling consciences' (pp. 278, 397). If the Carlylean hero is to be found in *The Spanish Gypsy*, as Newton contends, it is in the moment when Fedalma stifles her grief at the personal loss of both her father and her lover to guide 'Her children through the wilds' (p. 439). Fedalma transcends the socially circumscribed limitations of her gender, without losing the singular strength of her womanhood, and adopts the role of prophet that Zarca strives for and Silva shuns. And yet she is not immune to the Byronic pain that consumes Silva. The 'dizzying flames of his [Silva's] own rage' are echoed, shortly after, in Fedalma's thrilling 'fire of rage divine/ And battling energy' (pp. 433, 435). Where Silva's pain distracts and perplexes, Fedalma's galvanises her cause.

Fedalma's is not a 'feminized Byronism' in which the politics of romance are incorporated into private affections.[71] Indeed, Fedalma must renounce the intimate pleasures of hearth and home to make possible the ethical enterprise of a homeland. Family, in *The Spanish Gypsy*, extends beyond the parameters of the domestic sphere to assume national importance. As such, Eliot's heroine heralds a radical refashioning of the

Byronic that prefigures, and in some senses surpasses, the conscience-stricken hero of her last novel, *Daniel Deronda*. Fedalma is a Byronic heroine with a difference. The genesis of her character from love interest to pioneer renders her unconventional by Victorian standards; and yet her ambitions are authored by men and sanctioned by sacrifice. Gender nonconformity in this instance is not punished but permitted by the patriarchy. Fedalma's spirited rebellion is not deemed to be socially or personally destructive, as it is for other nonconformist Byronic heroines in nineteenth-century literature, such as Catherine Earnshaw in Emily Brontë's *Wuthering Heights* (1847) or Eustacia Vye in Thomas Hardy's *The Return of the Native* (1878).[72] Rather than a threat that must be silenced or sidelined, she takes centre stage as the spokeswoman for her community. A rare balance between an outward-facing Carlylean altruism and an inward Byronic angst is struck in *The Spanish Gypsy* when Fedalma declares 'now I know I am an aged sorrow –/ My people's sorrow' (p. 311), a sentiment reiterated in the following:

> Firmly then she rose,
> And met her people's eyes with kindred gaze,
> Dark-flashing, fired by effort strenuous
> Trampling on pain. (p. 436)

VI

The Byronic heroine is a prominent, and often overlooked, feature of some of the novels examined in this book. In Eliot's early fiction, *The Mill on the Floss* centres on Maggie Tulliver's trials with her own wilfulness, vehement emotions, and sense of estrangement. Her response to Dorlcote Mill, 'a dim delicious awe as at the presence of an uncontrollable force', marks out this 'dark-eyed, demonstrative, rebellious girl' as a Romantic heroine with Byronic tendencies (pp. 32, 37). In Eliot's later fiction, *Daniel Deronda* in particular, recurring issues of Byronic egotism are closely associated with female characters.[73] Where Gwendolen Harleth is based on a real-life descendant of Byron, who was seen gambling by Eliot, the prototype for the Princess Halm-Eberstein can be found in the verse drama, *Armgart*, written by Eliot in 1870 and published the year after. The protagonist, Armgart, is a Romantic artist-figure, a successful female version of what Latimer, in 'The Lifted Veil', aspires and yet fails to be.[74] The reader is introduced to the female lead after her virtuoso performance in Gluck's opera *Orfeo ed Euridice*.

> She has found
> This night the region where her rapture breathes –
> Pouring her passion on the air made live
> With human heart-throbs. (p. 118)

Eliot's Armgart recalls another female tour de force in Charlotte Brontë's *Villette* (1853). For Vashti, based on the French actress Eliza Rachel Félix (known simply to her Victorian audience as Rachel), 'what hurts becomes immediately embodied'.[75] Likewise, for Armgart, pain is a recurring state and vital for sustaining her Romantic 'ideal' of 'sublimer dread': '... that fresh strength which anguish gives the soul,/ The inspiration of revolt, ere rage/ Slackens to faltering' (pp. 127, 139). Armgart, reprising Vashti's defiance and 'inordinate will' (*Villette*, p. 325), performs vocal 'revenges'; she is electrified by a rage that, when silenced, turns in on itself (p. 117). The loss of her celebrated voice, imagined as a premature burial, plunges Armgart into an unremitting anguish at the prospect of her own mortality and mediocrity. The melodrama of these hellish torments – comparable to the supposedly 'immortal nature' of Manfred's gothic sufferings (II. iv. l. 54) – denote a Byronic heroine whose consequence, like *The Spanish Gypsy*'s Fedalma, extends beyond a cross-dressing Byronism.

Lucien Jenkins argues that '"Armgart" can usefully be considered George Eliot's reply to Byron' (*Collected Poems*, p. 4). The many references to Armgart's pre-eminence recall the self-proclaimed 'affluence of [Manfred's] soul'; and her 'Caesar's ambition' (p. 116) suggests a similarly nostalgic reverence for the 'sceptred sovereigns' of Ancient Rome (*Manfred*, II. ii. l. 141; III. iv. l. 39). Such parallels assume a political dimension as supremacy is attained at the expense of what Manfred refers to as the 'brutes of burthen'. As Byron's anti-hero proclaims to the Chamois Hunter, 'I am not of thine order', in the manner of a Hamlet to his Horatio, so Armgart values her singing for 'lift[ing] me apart/ From the crowd chiselled like me, sister forms,/ But empty of divineness' (*Manfred*, II. i. ll. 36, 38; *Armgart*, p. 140). Armgart's despair in the final scene is not merely over the loss of her voice, but the consequent loss of her pre-eminence. Eliot's heroine, like Don Silva in *The Spanish Gypsy*, is not offered the dramatic exit of suicide, however. She must suffer the humiliation of anonymity, to 'drudge among the crowd' and wear 'the placid mask/ Of women's misery' (pp. 144, 145). It is another woman, the self-abnegating Walpurga, who offers the most searing critique of her cousin's artistic will, what she denounces as Armgart's 'monstrous Self' (p. 148). Towards the end of the poem, Armgart is forced to recognise her disdainful and even autocratic treatment of Walpurga: 'I wearied you it seems; took all your help/ As cushioned nobles use a weary serf,/ Not looking at his face' (p. 146). Armgart's greatest offence, for Walpurga, is that her defiant calls for liberty, on the basis of her artistic talent, preclude equality.[76]

> Where is the rebel's right for you alone?
> Noble rebellion lifts a common load;
> But what is he who flings his own load off
> And leaves his fellows toiling? Rebel's right?
> Say rather, the deserter's. Oh, you smiled
> From your clear height on all the million lots
> Which yet you brand as abject. (p. 146)

Walpurga's hostility is only voiced after Armgart has lost her own. Given Walpurga's earlier homage to the woman who 'fills my life that would lie empty else,/ And lifts my nought to value by her side', a bewildered Armgart observes towards the end of the poem that 'You humoured all my wishes till to-day,/ When fate has blighted me' (pp. 116, 147). Furthermore, Armgart may be Eliot's critique of a female Byron divorced from domestic affection, but the heroine is ultimately vindicated in her rejection of Graf Dornberg and the intellectual debates she marshals to evade his gendered vision of relations between the sexes. In light of the Graf's chilling comment, 'Too much ambition has unwomaned her;/ But only for a while', Armgart's adoption of a Byronic defiance can be considered reasonable (p. 117). Who would welcome the common plight of womanhood if it is nothing more than, as the heroine proclaims, 'a dog's life' (p. 143)? These observations do not negate Walpurga's accusation of elitism; they rather rationalise Armgart's attitude. The Byronic heroine's egotism is chastened at the end of the poem, when she accepts a hidden life of teaching music to the masses in Walpurga's hometown. But the stark grief and stifled note of assertion in the line – 'I will bury my dead joy' (p. 151) – concludes the poem on a note of resignation rather than affirmation. As Nancy Henry observes, 'the passion and anger of the main character's speeches suggest that such renunciation was far from an unambiguous good to Eliot'.[77]

What facilitates these conflicting viewpoints is form. '"Armgart" is a verse drama, which, like the libretto of an opera, is inherently polyphonous. It refuses the domination of a single voice', as Louise Hudd states ('The Politics of a Feminist Poetics', p. 79). In other words, the relativity of *Armgart* resists and challenges the dominant claims of the *prima donna*. Leo, for instance, oscillates between praising Armgart's brilliance and scorning her flamboyance, fanning and checking her ego simultaneously. The *dramatis personae* of *Manfred*, Byron's 'little *Hamlet*', play an equally important function, akin to the sub-plot of a Shakespearean tragedy.[78] The spotlight never shifts from Byron's protagonist, and yet Manfred's inner contemplations are subject to scrutiny in this theatrical arena. The rapid questions and answers exchanged between the Abbot and Manfred in the final act, ranging from the profoundly philosophical to the comically absurd, compel the protagonist to reflect on his self-imposed exile and extemporise histories of past misdemeanours. The Byronic hero, in *Manfred*, is formed and reformed through internal and external acts of interpretation.

Wider social issues are also brought to the fore by characters like the Chamois Hunter and the Abbot. They, as well as Manfred's dependants, Herman and Manuel, serve as a critical commentary on, and a device for deflating the melodrama of, the main protagonist (Walpurga and Leo similarly serve the function of a social conscience in *Armgart*). What Eliot's *Armgart* shares with Byron's *Manfred* is the situating of the Romantic individual within a contested space of veneration and vilification, thereby constructing and deconstructing the illusion of what Susan Brown refers to as a 'mental theatre', a 'unified self that transcends a largely irrelevant world' ('Determined Heroines', p. 105).[79] Both authors dramatise the magnetic pull and deficiencies of a self-regarding Romantic subjectivity. Seen in this light, Eliot is not reacting *against* the spirit of Romanticism. She is appropriating the proto-postmodernism of Byron's metaphysical drama, and the ambivalence with which he regards his anti-heroes, to 'stage' her own divided ideas about gender, art, and interiority. The 'polyphonous' verse drama is, as Byron and Eliot demonstrate, ideally suited to acting out all sides of the polygonal Byronic hero and heroine.

Form is an essential factor in determining the fortunes of the Romantic hero-artist in Eliot's early work. From the claustrophobic short story, 'The Lifted Veil', to the verse drama *Armgart*, Eliot probes the flaws of this figure, as she interrogates the propensity to misread or misconstrue the Byronic. Eliot comes closest to emulating Byron in the conducive medium of *The Spanish Gypsy*. But even here her use of blank verse bridles against Byron's quicksilver lyricism and her dramatic 'cast' fragments as it fosters Byronic strengths and shortcomings. Byronic individualism drives the narrative of, and provides the aesthetic and ideological framework for, *The Spanish Gypsy*; but it is also diffused within the vast scope of this experimental poem. Eliot draws on Byron's sceptical regard for his own protagonists to question and reconfigure heroic 'ideals' across an innovative spectrum of literary genres. The next chapter examines the fate of the Byronic hero in Eliot's later work, and traces the author's increasingly complex dialogues with Byronism and a broader Romantic inheritance in a series of seminal Victorian novels: *Felix Holt: The Radical* (1866), *Middlemarch* (1871–72), and *Daniel Deronda* (1876). This final chapter will conclude with an analysis of Byronic afterlives in the BBC's screen adaptation of *Middlemarch* (1994).

5
George Eliot's Byronic Heroes II: Later Works

I

Edward Dramin, in his article 'Romanticism in the Late Novels of George Eliot', argues that 'Eliot's ambivalence toward Romanticism in her late novels differs from the typical Victorian response in its intensity and complexity: finding more reasons for criticizing the Romantics than do other Victorians, she also finds more ways in which the Romantics are appealing'.[1] The 'intensity and complexity' of Eliot's divided response to Romanticism is best illustrated, for Dramin, in her last novel: '*Daniel Deronda* presents Eliot's [...] fullest examination of Byron. The growth of Eliot's fiction from *Felix Holt* to *Daniel Deronda* shows the evolution of her view of Byron from bemused disdain to a broader, more ambivalent image which acknowledges the complexity and attractive dimensions of his creations and of Byron himself' ('Romanticism in the Late Novels', p. 292). Put another way, Eliot's preoccupation with Byron's poetry and his reputation, not to mention his compelling politics, becomes more pressing in, and elemental to, her work. The persistent and intriguing presence of Byron in *Daniel Deronda* (1876) will be examined in Part II of this chapter. It is necessary, however, to pause over Dramin's comment about Eliot's earlier novel, given the number of direct references to Byron, and specifically the Byronic hero, in *Felix Holt: The Radical* (1866). The 'bemused disdain' that Dramin detects in Eliot's treatment of Byron accords with the established reading of *Felix Holt* as a novel of reform in which fanciful notions of romance are rejected in favour of level-headed realism. This chapter will begin by re-examining the fate and fortunes of the Romantic poet in this novel.

Esther's penchant for Byron is revealed during her first encounter with the novel's hero, Felix, when he accidently knocks over her frilly satin work-basket to reveal a hidden volume of Byron's poems. At Esther's professed admiration for the poet, Felix denounces Byron as a 'misanthropic debauchee', whose heroes 'are the most paltry puppets that were ever pulled by the strings of lust and pride'.[2] Felix's assault on the Byronic may lack 'the brake of George Eliot's usual irony', as Barbara Hardy suggests, yet his condemnation of Byron is not altogether without wit when he describes the poet's heroes as 'gentleman of unspeakable woes, who employ a hairdresser, and look seriously at themselves in the glass' (p. 71).[3] The charge of conceited dandyism that is levelled at the Byronic heroes Esther derives guilty pleasure from serves as a parody of Byromania – the fashion for posing as Byron and committing his poetry to memory – and as a means of puncturing what Felix refers to as the heroine's 'fine-ladyism' (p. 71). This spoof of Esther's clichéd reading habits accords with a number of novels published in the Victorian period that feature 'women comically falling all over Byron', including Arthur Clough's *Amours de Voyage* (1849), Anthony Trollope's *The Last Chronicle of Barset* (1867) and *The Eustace Diamonds* (1873), and Samuel Butler's *The Way of All Flesh* (1903).[4]

Eliot's gendered Byronism in this scene does not serve a straightforward admonitory function, however. Felix's ready references to Manfred, Childe Harold, and the heroes of the Oriental Tales constitute a telling, if unintentional, reflection of a broader cultural trend. The observation, made by the Reverend Rufus Lyon, that '[Byron's] books embodied the faith and ritual of many young ladies and gentlemen' (p. 69), is not only reinforced by Esther's and Felix's familiarity with the poet; it renders the latter's contempt for this 'alternative' religion somewhat narrow. As Denise Tischler Millstein points out, '[*Felix Holt*] seems largely to denounce Byron, although it can be seen as simultaneously questioning the value of his works and demonstrating the depths of his mythic importance'.[5] The poem that Esther has been reading before being disturbed by Felix is illuminating when seen from this perspective. On the one hand, 'The Dream' (1816), as it depicts the agonies of doomed relationships, reminds us of Eliot's censorious reaction to public interest in the poet's scandalous separation (discussed in Part II of Chapter 4). Felix's accusatory question, moreover – 'do you stuff your *memory* with Byron, Miss Lyon?' (p. 69, added emphasis) – implies the mechanical recall of Byron's poetry that Mrs Steene, in Eliot's earlier story 'Brother Jacob' (1864), indulges in and Mrs Kirkpatrick parades on behalf of her disapproving daughter in Elizabeth Gaskell's *Wives and Daughters* (1866). Esther is equated with the commonplace bad habits, and possibly loose morals, of the voracious Victorian reader of Byronic romance.

The reference to 'memory' during this scene, on the other hand, suggests a deeper resonance when read in the context of Byron's poem,
'The Dream'.[6] The opening line, 'Our life is two-fold: Sleep hath its own
world' (l. 1), reinforces the division between dream and reality that Eliot
appears to advocate in *Felix Holt*. Yet Byron is suggesting that both states
co-exist simultaneously and come to form our sense of being: 'They
[dreams] do divide our being; they become/ A portion of ourselves ...'
(ll. 9–10). 'The Dream' destabilises a schismatic separation of romance
and reality, as a 'wide realm of wild reality' partners the imagination in
Byron's sleep world (l. 4). Through the alliterative mirroring and asso-
nance of the line, one 'portion' of the mind permeates another, opening
our perceptive faculties to new stimuli. It is the bewildering sensations of the subconscious – 'they [dreams] have power—/ The tyranny
of pleasure and of pain' (ll. 13–14) – that precipitate Esther's decision
to renounce day-dreaming, as if, by an act of will, she can expunge the
longings that are ignited by Byronic romance. Esther is provoked by
and then drawn to Felix's chastening dominance; a frisson is generated
by the hero's desire to 'come and scold her [Esther] every day' (p. 72).[7]
It is, after all, an impulse, or unspoken sexual charge, that ultimately
locks Esther and Felix in an embrace which she cannot subsequently
recollect.

The divided yet symbiotic self in Byron's poem also speaks to Eliot's
conception of Felix's character. In this early scene with the heroine,
the hero's oratory skills are shown alongside his propensity for tactless
pedagogy. In other words, the discussion of Byron draws out this hero's
flaws as well as his virtues. The difference of opinion over this Romantic
poet generates a consternation that Felix himself is then subjected to:
Esther's father, the Reverend Lyon, is animated by yet also apprehensive
at Felix's intense behaviour and language; and Esther objects to Felix's
rudeness yet is disappointed to discover that he is nothing 'finer' than
a working man. This 'sporting with paradox' (p. 264), in the Reverend
Lyon's words, is nowhere more apparent than in the strike scene, where
the strength of Felix's personality is met by the rioters. Felix's principles
raise him above Eliot's depiction of the 'mob', and yet his passionate
sympathies are roused by the 'mass of wild chaotic desires and impulses
around him' (p. 316). It is during this episode of social unrest that
Felix's impregnable will, a recognisably Byronic trait, comes to the
fore. In fact, despite their political differences, the Reverend Lyon's
description of Felix's 'too confident self-reliance', during and after the
riot, brings to mind Gaskell's self-made man, Mr Thornton, in *North
and South* (1855), a figure with similar traces of Byronic influence, as

discussed in Chapter 3 (p. 350). I am not trying to argue that Felix Holt is an unwitting, or closet, Byronic hero. The latter evidently acts as a foil for the former. What is clear, however, is that allusions to Byron, both explicit and implicit, draw out the tensions and 'self-contradiction' that are discernible in Felix (p. 257). He may be a Carlylean critic of society, as well as an austere lecturer of Esther's caprices, and yet 'Eliot invests him with a romantic magnetic power every time he opens his mouth or even looks at others'.[8] Through Byron, then, Eliot not only interrogates reading habits and cultural trends; she also probes the compelling aspects of her radically divisive hero.

Byronic paradox is not limited to Felix. The other male protagonist of the novel can be seen to typify what Felix calls a 'Byronic-bilious style' (p. 257). A counterpoint to the 'peculiar-looking' Felix, a 'shaggy-headed, large-eyed, strong-limbed person' (pp. 68, 60), Harold Transome is, as his name suggests, handsome and charming. The portrait of the prodigal son hanging in the sitting-room of Transome Court bears all the hallmarks of the Byronic hero: 'a beardless but masculine face, with rich brown hair hanging low on the forehead, and undulating beside each cheek down to the loose white cravat' (p. 14). His dandified appearance and taste for finery, cultivated in the East, give rise to scepticism in some quarters – 'He has become a regular beast among those Mahometans' (p. 97) – and enhances his allure with others, much as Byron's travels divided the opinion of readers. For Esther, whose only experience of the exotic is through literature, Harold is a romantic hero from the Oriental Tales and the silver-fork novels of the 1820s and 30s; he occupies 'that brighter and more luxurious life on which her imagination dwelt' (p. 195). What Esther learns, however, is that Harold's experiences in Smyrna, then a centre of the Ottoman Empire, are quite apart from her 'atta-of-rose fascinations' (p. 262).[9] Her growing interest in Felix casts her 'favourite Byronic heroes' in an unfavourable light, 'like last night's decorations seen in the sober dawn' (p. 228), a shift in perception comparable to what her contemporary, Molly Gibson, experiences in Gaskell's *Wives and Daughters*. When Harold confesses that his son's mother was a slave, Esther refutes any claims of him being a tragic hero. Their sparring over his romantic credentials is good-natured and 'knowing' – Harold fears that Esther is in danger of becoming a 'ballad heroine' to a 'lowly lover' (p. 417) – but the heroine has already concluded that married life at Transome Court would be one of 'middling delights, overhung with the languorous haziness of motiveless ease, where poetry was only literature, and the fine ideas had to be taken down from the shelves of the library when her husband's back was turned' (p. 426). What she mistook for a hero of romance turns out to be the least poetic man in the novel.

It is important to note that Harold Transome's behaviour and manners, carefully executed, appear *'as if* he had been a legendary hero' (p. 341, added emphasis). In fact, given his imperialist activities overseas, Harold proves, in many ways, to be a 'false Childe Harold', as Alicia Carroll explains:

> Peeling the layers away from the multi-layered character of Harold Transome reveals that his Byronic 'Oriental' trappings are mere affectation. He is a bastardization of Byron, not the book of poems which Esther is reading against Felix's advice but merely its cover. Here Eliot seems deliberately to be challenging Felix Holt's moral perception of Byron, differentiating between the genuine article and its usurpation. ('Giaour's Campaign', p. 246)

Eliot is at pains, here as elsewhere in her fiction, to make fine distinctions between a hackneyed Byronic turn and a deeper understanding of Byron's poetry. Harold's *faux* Byronism conceals a darker threat, moreover: the treatment of women as lesser, 'slight things' (p. 175). The 'padded yoke' that Esther fears not only derives from the elegant tedium of Transome Court, but also from the 'stifling oppression' of her suitor's affections (pp. 419, 465). Harold's imperious disregard of his mother culminates in the concluding chapters of the novel when the secret of his illegitimacy is exposed. Despite a belated comprehension of 'the neglected solitariness of his mother's life' (p. 457), Harold's bitterness prevents him from offering Mrs Tansome any emotional relief. Recoiling from the revelation of his mother's past 'sin', an authentically Byronic attitude is glimpsed when 'All the pride of his nature rebelled against his sonship' (p. 458), a desire for sovereignty ultimately tethered to those he sought to dominate. Harold's Byronic inheritance is his mother's outcast state and 'self-absorbed suffering' (p. 371), along with the prospect of being dispossessed from the decaying 'ancestral' seat.[10]

In his final scene with Esther, among the 'saddening relics and new finery of Transome Court' (p. 471), Harold both is and is not the Byronic potentate that Lyddy, the Lyons' maid, takes him for. Harold can be seen, in many ways, as a reworking of the lascivious title character of Byron's drama, *Sardanapalus* (1821), with Felix as the reproving yet prudent counsellor Salemenes. Where an 'unmanly' vanity proves to be the undoing of Byron's protagonist – his imprudent rule reflected in the dishonouring of his wife and an infatuation with a slave that corresponds with Harold's disreputable past with women – he is also capable of eloquence and mercy, much as Harold is capable of generosity when he renounces any claim on Esther in the wake of his own scandal.[11] The opening soliloquy, by Salemenes, speaks to the redeemable failings of both Byron's and Eliot's protagonist:

> In his effeminate heart
> There is a careless courage which corruption
> Has not all quench'd, and latent energies,
> Repress'd by circumstance, but not destroy'd—
> Steep'd, but not drown'd, in deep voluptuousness. (I. i. ll. 9–13)

Harold's 'addict[ion] at once to rebellion and to conformity' is reminiscent of this Byronic hero's irreverent indeterminacy and his predilection for indulgence (p. 110). Like Sardanapalus, Harold is louche but not base, fond of the trappings of rank but not bound by tradition. Eliot draws out Harold's inconsistencies of character, in the following passage, through a succession of semi-colons, sub-clauses, and conjunctions, which modify statements incrementally, like a prose equivalent of Byron's poetic half-lines:

> In fact Harold Transome was a clever, frank, good-natured egoist; not stringently consistent, but without any disposition to falsity; proud, but with a pride that was moulded in an individual rather than an hereditary form; unspeculative, unsentimental, unsympathetic; fond of sensual pleasures, but disinclined to all vice, and attached as a healthy, clear-sighted person, to all conventional morality, construed with a certain freedom, like doctrinal articles to which the public order may require subscription. (pp. 110–11)

This passage also makes clear that Harold is neither the 'dissolute cosmopolitan' derided in the Tory press nor the Liberal's 'intellectual giant and moral lobster' (p. 109). He may divide, or crystallise, viewpoints, but, then, so does Felix, who we are told was 'always thinking himself wiser than other people' (p. 353). Harold is, as Eliot makes clear, both less and more than a revisionary 'hero'.

'[W]holesale generic distinctions break down in the face of the novel's complexity', as Carroll argues ('Giaour's Campaign', p. 248). Both male protagonists subscribe to the contemporary gender ideology that women serve men, whether to gratify desires, in the case of Harold, or as the moral support advocated by Felix.[12] Both men, in their treatment of women, are dictators, with Felix's mastery over the adoring Esther conforming to certain ideas of romantic love that seem to be discredited elsewhere in the novel. Such concerns over gender and generic boundaries are part of a wider debate about masculinity that focuses on, as elsewhere in Eliot's fiction, the figure of the hero. As Esther's notion of a gentleman is found wanting, along similar lines to Margaret Hale's in Gaskell's *North and South*, the path seems clear for a new kind of hero to emerge. Felix, who readily rejects the claims of chivalry, often meditates on the virtuous course of action, gravitating towards a kind of practical heroism that acts, at the very least, as an antidote to Harold's pragmatic politics. Felix urges on himself the following words prior to his impromptu speech on nomination day: 'Not to waste energy, to apply force where it would tell, to do small work close at hand, not waiting for speculative chances of heroism, but preparing for them' (p. 287). As becomes evident in the strike scene, however, Felix's 'large Ideality' (p. 67), when acted upon, lacks the preparedness and insight he advocates. This 'hands on' heroism has consequences that render his position as fallible as Harold's.

It is clear that in setting up her protagonist as an alternative, albeit flawed, hero, Eliot is actively seeking heroism in the unexceptional, part of the author's broader literary project as discussed at the start of Chapter 4. It is also clear, when Tommy Trounsem, the drunken bill-sticker, declares 'himself one of the heroes of the day', that anyone can appropriate, or misappropriate, such ideas (p. 302). Given the various characters who are accorded, or accord themselves, some form of heroic status in the novel, heroism is shown to be both unstable and subjective, a matter of contention, and is therefore unlikely to be embodied by any one man. Eliot is as sceptical of Felix's Wordsworthian agenda, with its aspirations to defend the common man, as she is of the popularist fictional heroes that fall short of the heroine's over-heated imagination.[13] As Harold's calculating ambition is critiqued, so Felix's 'radicalism' is rendered ironic, despite his reformist zeal. *Felix Holt* goes further than staging the simultaneous shortcomings and survival of the romantic hero, and extends beyond what Dramin identifies as 'a conflict between types of Romanticism' ('Romanticism in the Late Novels', p. 276). Eliot's novel exposes the misrepresentation of masculine 'types', including the Byronic hero. The most obviously Byronic character in the novel is, as has been demonstrated above, more mystifying and adaptable than the title character in many ways. As is evident in her earlier work, 'The Lifted Veil' (1859), discussed in the previous chapter, Eliot's fiction not only mediates between the Romantic and the Victorian; it also anticipates, in the figure of Harold Transome, the decadent aestheticism of the *fin-de-siècle*. Eliot's engagements with nineteenth-century models of masculinity – and the fluctuating fortunes of the Byronic hero in particular – become ever more involved and innovative in her final novel.

II

The origins of Eliot's last novel, *Daniel Deronda*, are invariably traced back to an episode at the casino in Homburg where Eliot witnessed 'the play of Miss Leigh, Byron's grand niece, who is only 26 years old, and is completely in the grasp of this mean, money-raking demon. It made me cry to see her young fresh face among the hags and brutally stupid men around her'. Eliot is repelled by the 'monotonous hideousness' of gambling, and fears that there is 'very little dramatic "Stoff" to be picked up by watching or listening'; and yet this incident served as inspiration for one of Eliot's most memorable scenes in which one of her most arresting characters is introduced.[14] As Ruby V. Redinger states, 'the living reminder of Byron's incestuous affair with Augusta Leigh brought into being Gwendolen Harleth, a symbol of what her creator most feared and yet with a vitality of her own that takes possession of the novel'.[15] Eliot's mixed feelings of antipathy and captivation at these scenes of gambling, combined with the recollection of 'that execrable discussion raised in relation to Byron' (the 'desecration of family ties' she feared as a result of the public commentary on incest), are compressed into Gwendolen's lurid gothic visions (21 April 1873; 21 September 1869). Gwendolen's defiance, scorn, and sense of superiority mark her out as the most self-evidently Byronic character in *Daniel Deronda*. And yet her coldness – that is matched, and then mastered, by Grandcourt – and her aversion to sexual intimacy are anything but Byronic. Gwendolen, Byron's fictional heir, is locked in a struggle between predictable and psychologically complex behaviour.

We are told, during Gwendolen's courtship with Grandcourt, that she prefers to reside in uncertainties, remaining open to both the good and the evil proclivities of her character. This possible allusion to Keats serves to recall an earlier reference to *Lamia* when, in the opening chapter, onlookers scrutinise Gwendolen.[16] As Timothy Pace argues, 'That the iridescent Gwendolen Harleth is the most imaginatively alive character in *Daniel Deronda* has been felt by a majority of readers, and surely George Eliot strikes the keynote for this vitality in her description in Chapter One of Gwendolen's lamia-like beauty and power of fascination'.[17] Pace is keen to stress the subtle interplay between a negatively capable state and Eliot's 'religion of humanity' in the novel. But the onlookers in the opening chapter are not debating an ethical conundrum posed by Gwendolen's 'two-sidedness'; they are assessing what kind of beauty is on display and whether the display, her resplendent *'ensemble du serpent'*, is successful (p. 12, original emphasis). In the description of her as a 'Nereid in sea-green robes and silver ornaments, with a pale sea-green feather fastened in silver falling backward over her green hat and light-brown hair' (p. 12), Gwendolen is a more vividly-realised version of her prototype in 'The Lifted Veil' – the Water-Nixie, or 'fatal-eyed woman', in her 'pale-green dress' – and draws on, once again, the 'demon ancestry' (p. 68) of the *femme fatale*.[18] Latimer's warped perception of Bertha in Eliot's short story, as discussed in Chapter 4, invites us to connect the allusions to Keats in this novel with Deronda's caustic observation of Gwendolen at the casino, when his 'eye severe', like the philosopher's in *Lamia*, results in her 'lip-paleness' (p. 10).[19] His visual rebuke, and its effect on Gwendolen's composure, recall the following lines when Apollonius '… Had fixed his eye, without a twinkle or stir/ Full on the alarmèd beauty of the bride,/ Brow-beating her fair form, and troubling her sweet pride' (II. ll. 246–8). Eliot demonstrates, through the reference to Keats's poem and the fate of his heroine, that the 'fixing' of an identity by those transfixed by her 'can be destructive in the case of a nature that is fundamentally complex' (Pace, *'Daniel Deronda* and Keats's "Lamia" ', p. 38). The performative aspect of Gwendolen's character, consciously constructed and then consolidated by those around her, diminishes the 'iridescence' that Eliot endows her with (p. 42). Her stylish serpentine façade, which hides a latent yet 'wonderfully mixed consciousness' (p. 694), is gradually subsumed by the genuinely reptilian Grandcourt.

Gwendolen is constantly adopting and adapting roles, regarding her own 'exceptional' life as that of a princess, a romantic heroine, or an actress on the stage. This role-playing, around which darker shadows form, evolves out of an appetite for fiction. Gwendolen's mother fears for her daughter and her over-active imagination: 'Don't talk in that way, child, for heaven's sake! you do read such books – they give you such ideas of everything. I declare when your aunt and I were your age we knew nothing about wickedness. I think it was better so' (p. 96). Mrs Davilow's reprimand is in response to Gwendolen's imperious fantasies about Grandcourt's prospects and his subjection to her will:

He [Grandcourt] will declare himself my slave – I shall send him round the world to bring me back the wedding-ring of a happy woman – in the meantime all the men who are between him and the title will die of different diseases – he will come back Lord Grandcourt – but without the ring – and fall at my feet. (p. 95)

It is at this point in the novel that Gwendolen, who has been singled out for her 'witching' attractions, is now depicted, more baldly, as a 'witch' engaged in 'wickedness', the narrator's previous indulgence hardening after her merciless treatment of Rex (pp. 38, 77). It is also at this point in the novel, when her ambition is at its most unattractive, that she makes her most catastrophic miscalculation. Gwendolen is, like *Sense and Sensibility*'s Marianne Dashwood before her, 'born to an extraordinary fate. She was born to discover the falsehood of her own opinions, and to counteract, by her conduct, her most favourite maxims'.[20] Yet there is no second love for Eliot's heroine, after Deronda marries Mirah, and her first love is anything but the rascally pretender that Willoughby turns out to be. Although both heroines imagine their future partners as 'the hero of a favourite story', and both are punished for their fiction-fuelled delusions, Gwendolen's error of judgement is conspicuous because of her incentives for accepting Grandcourt and her foreknowledge of his past misdemeanours.

Grandcourt is the ultimate deconstruction of the 'hero' in nineteenth-century realist fiction. If Anne Brontë's Arthur Huntingdon is the Byronic hero denuded of glamour, an exposé of petty maliciousness and frailties, then Grandcourt is, as Marysa Demoor suggests, the 'acme' of the monstrous male in Victorian women's fiction.[21] Unlike Huntingdon, who resorts to bullying his wife, Grandcourt masters Gwendolen through a mesmerising oppression. Grandcourt is presented as the perfect match for Gwendolen in many respects – with the same word, 'peremptory', used to describe the respective will of each (pp. 17, 127) – and yet his egotism is 'exorbitant' and 'fastidious', as opposed to her 'intoxication of youthful egoism' (pp. 319, 278, 355). The energy that animates Gwendolen's ego, and exposes her failings, is consumed and crushed by Grandcourt's barren apathy. He is dehumanised by repeated comparisons with cold-blooded reptiles and lacks the 'better self' that leaves the way open for Gwendolen's possible redemption (p. 262). If Grandcourt's misanthropy is Byronic, akin to the decadent Sardanapalus,[22] then the Byronic has been stripped of fundamental traits: a consciousness of flaws, even if the protagonist lacks the wherewithal to change them, and an ungovernable passion (his 'flaccid' temperament is the antithesis of what is often regarded as Byronic, p. 111). The meticulousness of Grandcourt's behaviour, moreover, lends a studied aspect to his character that communicates an air of disdain. Lush derides his master 'acting like the hero of a ballad', a phrase that satirises romantic conventions in a manner similar to other novels considered in this book (p. 285). Lush's withering remark also speaks to the self-willed 'hoodwinking' of the heroine: 'with all her [Gwendolen's] perspicacity, and all the reading which seemed to her mamma dangerously instructive, her judgment was consciously a little at fault before Grandcourt' (p. 137). Gwendolen is willing to believe, or act out a conviction, in a fantasy that forms, at first, part of her performed identity.

Gwendolen's romantic role-playing holds some initial charm for Grandcourt when he thinks of her as Amaryllis, who 'fleeing desired that her hiding-place should be known; and that love will find out the way "over the mountain and over the wave" may be said without hyperbole in this age of steam' (pp. 157–8). The reference to industry at the close of this saccharine platitude sounds a note of disquiet that reverberates throughout their courtship. At the start of Chapter 13, Eliot depicts an almost Keatsian scene of corn-fields, poppies, and 'soft grey downs' as a backdrop for Gwendolen and Grandcourt's outing, yet modernity intrudes into the romantic rural landscape: 'The road lay through a bit of country where the dairy-farms looked much as they did in the days of our forefathers – where peace and permanence seemed to find a home away from the busy change that sent the railway train flying in the distance' (p. 131). Mrs Davilow's 'uneasy foreboding' at the sight of her daughter and suitor in this episode foreshadows the drama in Cardell Chase. The 'changing scenes of the forest from roofed grove to open glade growing lovelier with the lengthening shadows, and the deeply felt but undefinable gradations of the mellowing afternoon' do not stage the anticipated marriage proposal (p. 150). Rather, the 'ghastly vision' of Mrs Glasher and her children, gripping Gwendolen with the same terror she experiences in previous tableau, shatters the illusion of a picture-perfect moment (p. 152). The heroine's blinkered perspective is reconfirmed when what had been described earlier as a scene that 'a painter would have been glad to look on' is redrawn: 'What horrors of damp huts, where human beings languish, may not become picturesque through aerial distance!' (pp. 147, 155). It is hard not to read into this statement a wider critique of Romanticism, where even Wordsworth, describing idyllic 'pastoral farms' from an elevated vantage point, is found wanting.[23] Wordsworth's poetic vision is here subjected to the social world of Eliot's prose. Eliot's fear of fiction contaminating the imagination, and of being 'left to my own musings and [to] imagine scenes in which I was chief actress' (16 March 1839), resurfaces almost 40 years later when Gwendolen's 'uncontrolled reading' is blamed for 'somehow not prepar[ing] her for this encounter with reality' (p. 155).

Daniel Deronda takes its place in a tradition of nineteenth-century realist novels that contest or satirically reject romance. It would be erroneous to read this novel as straightforwardly romantic *or* realist, however. Gwendolen is not the only character in the novel to indulge in romantic fictions: the Meyrick girls read Daniel and Mirah's relationship in the light of Walter Scott's *Ivanhoe* and the *Arabian Nights*; Hans Meyrick, in one of his more fanciful moods, alludes to Byron by imagining himself as a Giaour; and the 'book-devouring' Isabel populates the story of Gwendolen's marriage with 'a corsair or two to make an adventure that might end well' (p. 708). Although the last point serves to remind us how far removed Grandcourt's jaded cynicism is from the common perception of Byron's romanticised outlaws, similar allusions to the romantic are not as sharply ironic. The Meyricks, in their generosity and genteel poverty, have a 'romantic readiness to believe in innocent need and to help it' (p. 194). The following passage about the family brings to mind Gwendolen's unsettling gothic visions: 'The Meyricks had their little oddities, streaks of eccentricity from the mother's blood as well as the father's, their minds being like mediaeval houses with unexpected recesses and openings from this into that, flights of steps and sudden outlooks' (p. 197). This description emphasises the romantic architecture of Eliot's realist house of fiction and the psychological spaces it accommodates.

'Romantic' scenes often precede Gwendolen's most traumatic episodes and they also precede some of the most instructive scenes in the novel. A 'delicious Sunday morning', when the 'melancholy waning sunshine of autumn rested on the leaf-strown grass and came mildly through the windows in slanting bands of brightness over the old furniture', jars as a setting for Gwendolen's dispiriting interview with Klesmer (p. 250). And yet Daniel and Mirah's shared love of autumn, and of dusk, reaffirms our pleasure in such descriptions. Of greater significance, the following passage, in which the sun's dying rays illuminate a grey day, gives moment and credibility to Daniel and Mordecai's preternatural convergence:

> When the wherry was approaching Blackfriars Bridge, where Deronda meant to land, it was half-past four, and the grey day was dying gloriously, its western clouds all broken into narrowing purple strata before a wide-spreading saffron clearness, which in the sky had a monumental calm, but on the river, with its changing objects, was

reflected as a luminous movement, the alternate flash of ripples or currents, the sudden glow of the brown sail, the passage of laden barges from blackness into colour, making an active response to that brooding glory. (p. 492)

Such passages underline the inaccuracy of considering Eliot as a writer whose realism opposes the romantic. Like Gaskell, in *Wives and Daughters*, various romantic registers are woven into the narrative. The perils of Molly Gibson's ungoverned reading, echoed in Gwendolen's, do not preclude a richer, more vibrant, and life-affirming Romanticism from partnering Roger's Victorian scientific enquiries. Equally, Gwendolen's throwaway lines about the Romantic poets, such as her shallow allusion to Coleridge's aesthetic of the imagination in Chapter 5, do not prevent lines from 'The Rime of the Ancient Mariner' commenting on her later, tortured tale of Grandcourt's death, or the opening lines from his poem 'Love' acting as an appropriate epigraph for Daniel's declaration to Mirah in Chapter 68.[24] Superficial references that mislead or are not comprehended give way to a deeply evocative engagement with Romantic writers and their ideas.

Of all Eliot's novels, 'Byronic influence is strongest in *Daniel Deronda*', as K. M. Newton claims, and it can be felt most strongly in Gwendolen and in the figure of Daniel's estranged mother, the Princess Halm-Eberstein.[25] The latter's 'mingled suffering and defiance' (p. 631), along with her autonomous will, mark out the least forgiving portrait of a Byronic egotist in Eliot's fiction. Where Gwendolen's performative self risks eclipsing any 'real' emotion or empathy, the Alcharisi's stage persona subsumes her entire being. Like Eliot's earlier anti-heroine Armgart, in the verse drama of that name, or Charlotte Brontë's Vashti in *Villette* (1853), 'feeling [...] immediately became matter of conscious representation: experience immediately passed into drama, and she acted her own emotions' (p. 629). The Alcharisi represents a closed circuit of remembered pleasure and present pain, which is perhaps why her character is limited to only two chapters. Her demands for liberty are defended on the basis of her superior talent: 'My nature gave me a charter' (p. 664). Like Armgart, then, the Alcharisi's defiance of a society that sees unmaternal women as monsters serves her own self-empowerment. Where Armgart attempts to make amends after the loss of her voice, however, the Alcharisi remains unrepentant. The forceful rationale behind her rhetoric – 'Had I not a rightful claim to be something more than a mere daughter and mother?' (p. 664) – is diffused by a hyperbole that is contrasted unfavourably against Deronda's keenly-felt emotion.

Eliot would seem to have a singular lack of sympathy for the Princess Halm-Eberstein. This is evident in the description of her as a 'sorceress' (p. 659), whose past returns, like 'spots of memory' (p. 635), as pain rather than as Wordsworthian solace. And yet the hero's repugnance at his mother colours this 'tragic experience' in telling ways (p. 667). In rejecting Deronda's projection of a feminine consciousness, stating categorically 'You are not a woman. You may try – but you can never imagine what it is to have a man's force of genius in you, and yet to suffer the slavery of being a girl' (p. 631), the Alcharisi's coldness – or, in her son's eyes, cruelty – casts a dark shadow over his relationship with Gwendolen and then Mirah. Deronda is unable to rescue his mother, as he is ultimately unable to rescue Gwendolen from the ravages of her repressed memories; he rescues the woman who can, as her name suggests, reflect his nobler self and aspirations. With regards to the Alcharisi, Deronda recoils from a woman he cannot 'read', a mother with an inscrutable physiognomy, a 'face so mobile that the next moment she might look like a different person' (p. 624). Eliot's depiction of the ambitious female artist is, as elsewhere in her fiction, severe, and yet the Alcharisi exposes a constraint on Deronda's sensibility; his search for familial accord blinds him to another's 'equivalent centre of self'.[26] This unflinching portrait of the Byronic egotist serves as a critique, a reality check of sorts, on the limits of human understanding and empathy. Byron is once more instrumental in shaping and refining Eliot's aesthetic.

The extent of Eliot's involvement with her literary ancestors is demonstrated in the cast of characters who reflect varying shades of the Romantic in this novel. As a self-proclaimed Wandering Jew, 'who saw everything and nothing by turns', the 'terrible' Klesmer is notably Byronic, and his conviction in the social value of the artist resembles Shelley (pp. 118, 119).[27] A more compelling example is Mordecai, whose quest can be summarised, or satirised, by Byron's declaration in *Don Juan*, 'I want a hero' (I. i). His febrile consumptiveness evokes Keats, a Romantic presence that is confirmed when Eliot cites the opening lines from 'On Seeing the Elgin Marbles' as the epigraph for Chapter 43. In his feelings of exclusion, 'like a poet among people of a strange speech', and the repulsion that others feel at his 'grasp and speech which assume to dominate', Mordecai comes close to Coleridge's Mariner, as he too is compelled to impart his creed (pp. 529, 500). Eliot is most indebted to Shelley, however, for her characterisation of the Jewish seer. The allusion to Matthew Arnold's famous assessment of Shelley, as a 'beautiful and ineffectual angel, beating in the void his luminous wings in vain', is unmistakeable in Mordecai's declaration: 'the spirit of my youth has been stirred within me, and this body is not strong enough to bear the beating of its wings' (p. 521).[28] The poet is even more persuasively felt in Mordecai's idealism and the priority accorded to inward transformation in affecting social change.

Despite his prominence in this section of the novel, Shelley is subject to the same scepticism as the other Romantic poets who feature in Eliot's fiction. The quotations from *Prometheus Unbound* (1820) that serve as epigraphs in *Daniel Deronda* are complicated by lines from the same poem that are recited in a meeting of the 'Philosophers' Club'. Miller, who is referred to as 'the broad-chested quoter of Shelley' (p. 522), is an educated man who listens to Mordecai, as do the other members, yet cannot empathise with his vision. In this instance, Mordecai's kinship with Shelley is used to highlight, somewhat painfully, how ineffectual he is at communicating ideas even when in the company of fellow intellectuals. Far from acting as a mere literary marker for his character, however, the repeated references to Shelley give strength and value to Mordecai's poetic sensibilities and romantic optimism. In other words, Shelley's presence helps to humanise the spectral Mordecai.

Mordecai remains the true Romantic visionary of the novel. But the title character is also 'a Shelleyan Romantic who longs to devote his life to a higher ideal' (Newton, 'Romanticism', p. 339). Eliot examines what constitutes the 'romantic' through the figure of Daniel Deronda. At the beginning of Chapter 19, Eliot states, 'To say that Deronda was romantic would be to misrepresent him', yet she is quick to modify this declaration in the following description: 'under his calm and somewhat self-repressed exterior there was a fervour which made him easily find poetry and romance among the events of everyday life' (p. 205). She reprises the subject, once more, in Chapter 41: 'And, if you like, he was romantic. That young energy and spirit of adventure which have helped to create the world-wide legends of youthful heroes going to seek the hidden tokens of their birth and its inheritance of tasks, gave him a certain quivering interest in the bare possibility that he was entering on a like track' (p. 515). Deronda's quest for identity and purpose can be read as romantic, quixotic even, but the chivalry that is ascribed to him, in his conduct with women, is unusual. We are told that a sense of heroism is instilled in him because of his doubtful parentage, casting his patient yet pained forbearance as a form of courage. Eliot is careful to reaffirm Deronda's 'manly' qualities – with Sir Hugo even comparing him, teasingly, to the eighteenth-century seducer Lovelace – and yet his femininity is stressed in his seraphic boyishness and a delicacy of feeling that leaves him 'completely unmanned' by Gwendolen's unnerving revelations towards the end of the novel (p. 693). In Deronda, Eliot rethinks the preconceived gendering of the male protagonist, drawing on the strengths of both masculinity and femininity for her atypical hero, while also demonstrating the arbitrariness of such categories.

> This state of feeling was kept up by the mental balance in Deronda, who was moved by an affectionateness such as we are apt to call feminine, disposing him to yield in ordinary details, while he had a certain inflexibility of judgment, and independence of opinion, held to be rightfully masculine. (p. 322)

This new kind of heroism seems far removed from the Byronic hero. And yet Eliot's pioneering protagonist draws on more allusions to the Romantic poets than any other character in the novel. Deronda's private grief over his relations with Sir Hugo is directly compared with 'Byron's susceptibility about his deformed foot' (p. 174),[29] and a broader influence is detectable in Deronda's attempts to 'rescue' both Mirah and Gwendolen. What Dramin refers to as Byron's 'altruistic compassion for persecuted underdogs' (p. 285), most readily evident in his defence of the Luddites and involvement with the Greek War of Independence, is key to understanding Deronda's feelings towards Gwendolen: 'All this implied a nature liable to difficulty and struggle – elements of life which had a predominant attraction for his sympathy, due perhaps to his early pain in dwelling on the conjectured story of his own existence' (p. 324). The hero of Eliot's last novel, in his compassionate search for a cause, is diametrically opposed to the pseudo-Romantic poet in her early story 'The Lifted Veil'. A more significant political parallel between Byron's poetry and *Daniel Deronda* is discernible, as Tischler Millstein argues, in 'the shared memories of pain that Byron captures so eloquently in the *Hebrew Melodies*'. Byron's sympathy with the plight of the Jews corresponds with Deronda's vocation – both are 'connected in an effort to re-awaken English national identity'.[30] Through the character of Deronda, then, Eliot engages with the diverse faces, or facets, of the Byronic hero; his increased agency in the novel withstands an archetypal trajectory of negative egoism to positive self-regulation and altruistic suffering.

Daniel Deronda has close affinities with another Romantic poet. He is directly compared to Shelley, as well as to Byron, but his openness to possibility and doubt indicates Keatsian tendencies that, as we have already seen, remain stifled in Gwendolen's personality. As Jenny Uglow suggests,

Daniel's receptivity is extremely close both to what Keats described as the negative capability of the artist's imagination and to what George Eliot in all her earlier novels described as the essentially 'feminine' capacity to suppress the self in a relationship with another. Daniel is not an artist but he and Mordecai are described as having a 'poetic yearning' in relation to their large political visions (if poets are indirect legislators then legislators may be hidden poets).[31]

Deronda is something of a chameleon poet in his fervent, yet unobtrusive, sympathies, 'an activity of imagination on behalf of others' (p. 178). It is this Keatsian mode of consciousness that immediately precedes his sighting of Mirah:

> He was forgetting everything else in a half-speculative, half-involuntary identification of himself with the objects he was looking at, thinking how far it might be possible habitually to shift his centre till his own personality would be no less outside him than the landscape, – when the sense of something moving on the bank opposite him where it was bordered by a line of willow-bushes, made him turn his glance thitherward. In the first moment he had a darting presentiment about the moving figure; and now he could see the small face with the strange dying sunlight upon it. (p. 189)

Caught in the balanced repetition of 'half' is the interpretative dilemma of whether Deronda's reverie is interrupted by the intrusion of the external world, the urgency of the moment turning his ideological speculations into practical actions; or whether his conscious displacement of self in the identification with his surroundings heightens his sensitivity to Mirah's presence and distressed state. On the one hand, his 'many-sided sympathy' has the effect of cancelling out definite opinions and actions, inducing a state of negative capability that is accompanied, Eliot fears, by a 'meditative numbness' (pp. 364, 365). On the other hand, his 'darting presentiment about the moving figure' suggests anything but indecision or self-absorption. Deronda's cultivation of a Romantic inner life saves another's soul, which serves as a blueprint for, rather than an early draft of, his later deeds. It is Deronda's desire to expand his Romantic sensibility through outward-going sympathies, combined with a personal charisma, that lays the foundation for a mutual accord with Mordecai and becomes the kernel of his later Zionism.

It is Deronda's ability to observe beauty within the mundane, 'feel[ing] the presence of poetry in everyday events' (p. 366), that singles him out as a pioneer. Where Mordecai – who is as poetic as anyone else in the novel – is caught 'floating among cloud-pictures', Deronda comes closest to prizing 'impartial midday falling on commonplace, perhaps half-repulsive, objects which are really the beloved ideas made flesh. Here undoubtedly lies the chief poetic energy' (p. 381). This vision of poetic empathy with the everyday becomes indivisible from a Romantic spirit in the 'Notes on *The Spanish Gypsy*': '... an imagination actively interested in the lot of mankind generally; and these feelings become piety—*i.e.*, loving, willing submission, and *heroic Promethean effort* towards high possibilities, which may result from our individual life'.[32] In effect, it is Deronda's 'advanced Romantic thinking', to use Newton's phrase, that forges the Promethean will into an instrument for the public good.[33] It is not only Mirah who is saved by this new Romantic hero. The Meyricks, Mordecai, and Deronda himself are, in turn, touched by the survival of this song-bird, whose voice will reach a wider Jewish audience with her Keatsian equation of beauty and truth.[34] Mirah demonstrates that the underlying and subtle significance of the Romantic poets intensifies, rather than diminishes, as the novel progresses. Terence Cave argues that 'The readers of *Daniel Deronda* have to learn all over again to read romance, but to read it through, and not against, realism: or, perhaps better, to read it as an evolved or "developed" form of narrative, fusing elements from previous narrative modes'.[35] Eliot graduates from Latimer's erroneous 'connection' with the Romantic poets in 'The Lifted Veil' to an understanding of Romanticism in *Daniel Deronda* that informs and extends the aesthetic claims of realism.

III

The final sections of this chapter, and the conclusion of this book, focus on Eliot's penultimate novel *Middlemarch*, published in serial form between 1871 and 1872. Byron's presence in this novel demonstrates, as with *Daniel Deronda*, that the author's interest in the Byronic hero, and Byronism in general, grew rather than contracted over the course of her writing career. The character of Will Ladislaw, in particular, draws on a number of second-generation Romantic poets, making him, as Carroll Viera states, 'perhaps Latimer's closest kinsman in George Eliot's novels'.[36] Yet, despite their shared literary heritage, Ladislaw has little in common with Latimer's odious self-absorption. The painfully claustrophobic psychology of Latimer's first-person narrative has no place in the sweeping scope and demographic of Eliot's later novels. Ladislaw is not a model hero, as discussed in Part I of the previous chapter, and neither is he immune from Eliot's irony. And yet, as the character closest to an authentic Romantic artist in Eliot's fiction – of whom Mr Brooke predicts 'he may turn out a Byron' (p. 67) – he bears little resemblance to a Byronic egotist. Ladislaw has more in common with the energetic evangelising of Felix Holt and Daniel Deronda than with Harold Transome's exotic potentate and Henleigh Mallinger Grandcourt's malevolence. Still, his evangelising, when voiced with a Romantic sensibility, is mercifully free of the worthiness that mars Eliot's other would-be pioneers. Through Ladislaw, *Middlemarch* harnesses, however tentatively, a Byronic mutability that is invested in the pressing matter of reform. Ladislaw's active participation in the prevailing theme of progress positions him at the ideological core of a novel, set immediately prior to the Reform Act of 1832, where political concerns offset and reflect upon the relative positions and ambitions of male and female characters.

In the acclaimed 1994 BBC adaptation of *Middlemarch*, directed by Anthony Page, Ladislaw takes centre stage.[37] In many ways, the portrayal of Ladislaw, by Rufus Sewell, is a forerunner of Colin Firth's iconic portrayal of Mr Darcy in the BBC adaptation of *Pride and Prejudice*, which was screened a year after *Middlemarch* (both had screenplays by Andrew Davies). The impression made by this adaptation of *Middlemarch* would not become completely clear, however, until a decade later, with the BBC's adaptation of the industrial romance *North and South* in 2004, discussed in Chapter 3. Indeed, John Lyttle's comment on the costume drama, that 'Production values tend to smother political points', is contradicted by screen versions of *Middlemarch* and *North and South* that heighten a sense of historical upheaval and reinforce the male lead's involvement with political issues of representation and accountability.[38] Ladislaw's enhanced Byronic profile in the BBC mini-series of *Middlemarch*, which served as a blueprint for successive screenplays by Davies in the 1990s and 2000s, directs the hero's desire into activism as well as the vagaries of romantic passion. Sewell's Ladislaw, as I will argue in Part IV of this chapter, is an influential reimagining of the Byronic hero from page to screen.

References to the Romantic poets are as embedded in the fabric of this novel as elsewhere in Eliot's fiction. The ever-present Wordsworth, accompanied by William Blake, provides a sympathetic subtext for Dorothea Brooke's epiphany during the latter stages of *Middlemarch*. In particular, stanzas from 'The Divine Image' and a borrowing from 'Tintern Abbey' precipitate her need to do some 'active good' for Lydgate in the wake of the Raffles scandal (p. 625). Lines from 'Ode to Duty' frame one of the most important chapters of the novel when Dorothea acknowledges her own part in a larger 'involuntary, palpitating life', and resolves to comfort Rosamond (p. 648). Brooke is, however, the first character to mention Wordsworth, along with a host of other poets including Byron. His allusions to Robert Southey prove equally instructive. Brooke's attempts to draw out Casaubon with a literary conversation about Southey's *History of the Peninsular War* (1823–32) demonstrate an inability to comprehend his taciturn dinner guest. His taste for Southey's later prose works may not be as damning as Mrs Transome's delight in his exotic poems in *Felix Holt*, but it provides an occasion for Casaubon to exercise his intellectual poise at the expense of 'good Mr Brooke's scrappy slovenliness' (p. 14).[39] As most of the references to the Romantic poets are made by the bumbling Brooke, the reader remains guarded about their function and significance in the novel.

Other characters that display an interest in or familiarity with Romantic writers add to our cautionary regard. Rosamond Vincy is well versed in the popular literature of the day. Somewhat predictably, her favourite is Thomas Moore's *Lalla Rookh: An Oriental Romance* (1817), a poem that the short-sighted Mrs Steene also knows by heart in Eliot's early story 'Brother Jacob'. 'Her [Rosamond's] romanticism', as Stone comments, 'is of the shallow nature that delights in Thomas Moore's poetry and that sees in her husband-to-be a dashing outsider with aristocratic connections straight out of a silver-fork novel' (*Romantic Impulse*, p. 236). Conversely, steady Mary Garth shares with Fred Vincy an enjoyment of reading Walter Scott. Eliot composes a sonnet on 'her longest-venerated and best-loved Romanticist' as an epigraph for Chapter 57, which opens with a scene of Mary's siblings enjoying *Ivanhoe* (1820), 'reading aloud from that beloved writer who has made a chief part in the happiness of many young lives' (p. 469).[40] The reading of Romantic writers is more than a satirical device; it is the manner in which they are read – with Scott shared communally, for instance – that registers on Eliot's cultural and aesthetic barometer.

With a 'quick and pliable' mind (p. 174), Ladislaw is, as Barbara Hardy comments, 'the nearest thing in the novel to a portrait of the artist, and a Romantic artist at that'.[41] His comment to Dorothea that 'I should never succeed in anything by dint of drudgery. If things don't come easily to me I never get them' is notably Keatsian (p. 172), echoing the poet's famous pronouncement 'That if Poetry comes not as naturally as the Leaves to a tree it had better not come at all'.[42] Yet it is Ladislaw's resemblance to Shelley that has been noted by critics.[43]

Eliot was influenced by George Henry Lewes's enthusiasm for Shelley and his conviction that this Romantic poet was 'the original man, the hero'.[44] Lewes continues a tradition of seeing Shelley as the consummate poet, which begins with John Stuart Mill and extends to W. B. Yeats. It is Brooke, once again, who makes the connection between Ladislaw and a Romantic poet explicit: 'He seems to me a kind of Shelley'. And, in his cautious endorsement of 'liberty, freedom, emancipation – a fine thing under guidance', Brooke voices a Victorian liberal's response to Shelley (p. 296).[45] Brooke is careful to separate himself, and Ladislaw, from the 'laxities or atheism' that had become part of Shelley's posthumous reputation, and Eliot is equally careful on the subject of Ladislaw's progressive radicalism. Lydgate may associate his friend with 'a romantic disregard of your own worldly interests', and yet this spirit of Romanticism is tempered by practical concerns: Ladislaw's attitude towards political change is both pragmatic, 'If you go in for the principle of Reform, you must be prepared to take what the situation offers', and expedient, as it offers an outlet for his ardency and 'literary refinements' (pp. 385, 379).

Eliot is not only interested in a sanitised Shelley. For Dorothea, a more profoundly Shelleyan figure than Ladislaw in some respects, her grander ideals may founder, yet she retains an ardour for improving the lives of others. More importantly, she learns to be guided by a fervency of feeling that is not channelled solely into social utopianism. The following passage, where Dorothea speculates on Will's prospects as a poet, illuminates Eliot's admiration for Shelley and stages a dialogue between the speakers' respective attitudes towards art. It also tests Ladislaw's 'poetic metal'[46] in the measured flow of prose:

> 'To be a poet is to have a soul so quick to discern, that no shade of quality escapes it, and so quick to feel, that discernment is but a hand playing with finely ordered variety on the chords of emotion – a soul in which knowledge passes instantaneously into feeling, and feeling flashes back as a new organ of knowledge. One may have that condition by fits only.'[47]
>
> 'But you leave out the poems,' said Dorothea. 'I think they are wanted to complete the poet. I understand what you mean about knowledge passing into feeling, for that seems to be just what I experience. But I am sure I could never produce a poem.'
>
> 'You *are* a poem – and that is to be the best part of a poet what makes up the poet's consciousness in his best moods,' said Will,

showing such originality as we all share with the morning and the spring-time and other endless renewals.

'I am very glad to hear it,' said Dorothea, laughing out her words in a birdlike modulation, and looking at Will with playful gratitude in her eyes. 'What very kind things you say to me!' (p. 186, original emphasis)

The paraphrased passage from 'A Defence of Poetry' is met by Dorothea's unassuming observation that Ladislaw has missed out a vital ingredient in his philosophy of the poet – the poems. His subsequent idealisation of her as an embodied poem is similarly met with a blithe, yet flirtatious, affection that accords with Eliot's own indulgent regard for this suitor. Animated by the cross-fertilisation and conflicts between ideology and audience, lyric performance and narrative commentary, this exchange speaks to and complicates Margaret Homans's statement about the 'generic incompatibility between a poet's vision and the form of the novel'.[48] What I take to be the interfused frictions over genre and aesthetics in this passage capture a Shelleyan duality: poetry as personal epiphany and poetry as an effective mode of public address. Shelley, in this sense, serves as a poet for those invested in an abstract ideal of beauty at the same time as he heralds the promise of a poet for the masses.

Nancy Henry may be right to contend that 'the only poet in her [Eliot's] fiction is more enamored with the myth of the poet than with writing poetry', but Ladislaw's shortcomings in this regard signal a broader political use for his proselytising about art.[49] The purpose that Shelley serves here is not necessarily to bequeath a lyric heir or to provide hidden Theresas with a voice – the 'sacred poet' – they lack (p. 3). It is, I would argue, to highlight Will and Dorothea's shared fate, 'a certain spiritual grandeur ill-matched with the meanness of opportunity', and a common bond of feeling that will, in time, unite their vision of public service. In addition to guiding him towards a vocation that will suit his talents, Ladislaw inherits from Shelley a susceptibility to external stimuli; he is open, in contrast to Casaubon, to changeable sensations and possibilities. 'Will', we are told, 'was made of very impressible stuff. The bow of a violin drawn near him cleverly, would at one stroke change the aspect of the world for him, and his point of view shifted as easily as his mood' (p. 320). Likewise, Ladislaw's association of Dorothea with the Romantic trope of the Æolian harp not only speaks to his lyricising, but to the impressible cadences of her heart and soul (p. 174).[50] Their affinity is established in the novel through the unconscious effect they have on each other: 'the smile [Ladislaw's] was irresistible, and shone back from her face too' (p. 171). Dorothea is as enthused by Ladislaw's opinions and feelings as he is about hers. When, for example, he is compelled, 'mysteriously forced', to be receptive to her, she also flourishes: 'Each looked at the other as if they had been two flowers which had opened then and there' (p. 299).

Middlemarch was published, as Frances Wilson notes, 'when the climate against Byron was at its height in 1872'.[51] However, as ascertained in the previous chapter, Eliot's interest in Byron's poetry, his political activism, and the vicissitudes of his fame increased, if anything, in the wake of her outrage at allegations over the poet's incest with his half-sister. In coupling together Shelley and Byron in *Middlemarch's* Ladislaw, Eliot comes close to the Marxist writer and social philosopher, Friedrich Engels. Engels, in *The Condition of the Working Class in England* (1845), claimed that both Shelley and Byron were avidly read and appreciated by a working class who were open to a more progressive literature than the middle classes: 'Shelley's prophetic genius has caught their [the workers'] imagination, while Byron attracts their sympathy by his sensuous fire and by the virulence of his satire against the existing social order'.[52] A Byronic 'sympathy' and 'sensuous fire' takes hold in Eliot's novel as Dorothea imbibes Ladislaw's rejuvenating potency. Continuing the flower analogy considered above in relation to a Shelleyan sensibility, she responds to his presence, 'her face brightening and her head becoming a little more erect on its beautiful stem' (p. 664), while Rosamond's reaction to a letter from Will is strikingly similar: 'her face looked like a reviving flower – it grew prettier and more blooming' (p. 620). Ladislaw's Byronic fertility is evident in the walks that take him through the Edenic setting of Halsell Common, 'where the sunlight fell broadly under the budding boughs, bringing out the beauties of moss and lichen, and fresh green growths piercing the brown' (p. 388); in the 'warm activity and fellowship' that draws a 'troop of droll children' to him, like the Pied Piper of Middlemarch, for impromptu Punch and Judy shows (pp. 392, 381); and, most notably, in the description of him as 'an incarnation of the spring whose spirit filled the air – a bright creature, abundant in uncertain promises' (p. 389). Ladislaw's 'uncertain promises' combine Shelleyan stimulus with Byronic incandescence and intensity, as well as personifying what Barbara Hardy refers to as 'The unplayed possibilities [that] emerge everywhere in *Middlemarch*'.[53]

Ladislaw's Byronic vitality is also palpable in his sense of political maturation. When the Reform Bill is debated in the House of Commons,

Will foretells that 'Things will grow and ripen as if it were a comet year' (p. 378). His potential for 'endless renewals', quoted in the long passage above, harnesses a pressing and elastic vigour that recalls Keats's 'Hyperion' poems and Shelley's *Prometheus Unbound*.[54] The debates over reform in the novel not only provide a platform for the 'virulence of [Byron's] satire against the existing social order' that Engels identifies; political polemic is indivisible from the battle fought in Middlemarch between 'Old and Young', the title of Book 2. As if to emphasise this Titanic conflict, Ladislaw, described by Brooke as 'that youngster' and by Casaubon as 'a young relative of mine', is first observed at Lowick, 'conspicuous on a dark background of evergreens', as Dorothea and her party approach 'a fine yew-tree' in the grounds (p. 64): Casaubon, conversely, is found dead in the Yew-Tree Walk.[55] The reader is taken back to the setting for this symbolic struggle between Casaubon and Ladislaw as 'Old and Young' when Ladislaw and Dorothea look out upon the same prospect during the storm in Chapter 83; their spontaneous avowal of love reaffirms youth and progress. The hybridisation of Shelley's vision and Byron's 'virulence' culminates in Ladislaw's union with Dorothea and channels the novel's 'unpredictable and contradictory energy' into broadly positive if poignant ends.[56] In short, Ladislaw's heroic potential derives from Eliot's regard for and engagements with the later Romantic poets.

More explicitly Byronic is Ladislaw's scandalous connections with more than one married woman. Yet, equally Byronic, Ladislaw adores only one woman – like Conrad in *The Corsair*, 'for him earth held but her alone' (I. l. 480) – and his treatment of 'other' women can be unguarded and callous. When he is discovered comforting Lydgate's wife in Chapter 77, his language is marked by an uncharacteristic violence; words are visceral 'knife-wound[s]', intended to 'lacerat[e]' the recipient with his rage (pp. 656, 651). Ladislaw's brutal rejection of Rosamond is restated when he confirms the depth of his passion for Dorothea: 'No other woman exists by the side of her. I would rather touch her hand if it were dead, than I would touch any other woman's living' (p. 640). Evidence of his emotional complexity is apparent immediately after this scene, however, when we are told of his 'delicate generosity' to another (in not disclosing Bulstrode's offer of reparation, p. 643) and the quick repentance of his cruelty to Rosamond. Earlier in the novel, Ladislaw proves capable of charming Casaubon over dinner in Rome to then reveal, somewhat petulantly, the futility of his cousin's life's work. Ladislaw fluctuates, in Chapter 22 alone, between kindness and anger, ardour and obstinacy, mental agility and dreariness. Within the space of a single paragraph, at the start of Chapter 39, Ladislaw moves from the Byronic 'depths of boredom' to practical concerns over his lodgings and 'a tickling vision of a sheep-stealing epic written with Homeric particularity' (p. 319).[57] Ladislaw's countenance, as capricious as his disposition, is described as being as changeable as the weather, an analogy that generates parallels with the 'extremes of expression' that Thomas Moore emphasises in his life of Byron.[58] The 'uncertainty of his [Ladislaw's] changing expression', where even his features seem to alter, signal for Eliot a capacity for 'metamorphosis' (p. 174), a term that Charlotte Brontë also used to describe her mercurial hero, Mr Rochester, towards the end of *Jane Eyre* (1847).

IV

Commenting on the 1994 BBC mini-series of *Middlemarch*, which will be discussed in more detail shortly, Ian MacKillop and Alison Platt raise a common objection levelled at screen adaptations – the 'flattening' of character. In this instance, they argue, 'there is not much more to Ladislaw than the drop-dead-gorgeousness of his appearance'.[59] Bernard O'Keefe's question, 'Would George Eliot have approved of the smouldering Ladislaw?', seems to be answered by Anne D. Wallace: 'I even liked the Byronic Ladislaw, although I knew Eliot would disapprove'.[60] The fair features and 'light-brown curls' of Eliot's hero are exchanged on screen for dark features and his geniality is replaced with a scowl (p. 63).[61] Rather than the 'very pretty sprig' that Mrs Cadwallader describes, or the frivolous *dilettante* that critics have objected to, Ladislaw's presence is now imposing (p. 271). As MacKillop and Platt note, 'He [Ladislaw] grows up during the course of the novel. On the screen, however, he dominates: he is fully formed, glowing and glowering' ('Television and the Illustration of *Middlemarch*', p. 82). It is worth remembering, however, that when Dorothea first meets Ladislaw in the novel, he is brooding with 'discontent' and he displays a 'threatening aspect' that disturbs both the heroine and the reader (p. 65). Later passages describe a delicate profile and 'defiant curves of lip and chin' that recall the trademark features of the Byronic hero (p. 299). With his Byronic 'look' and pose of the poet, without the poems, Ladislaw could be mistaken for what Matthew Arnold dubbed the 'theatrical' Byron, or what Thomas Carlyle referred to as 'a huge *sulky Dandy*'.[62] What should also be remembered is that while Arnold expressed contempt for those who neglected the poetry in an outward show of Byronism, he was impressed by Byron's energetic opposition to society's 'mind-forg'd

manacles'[63], noting with approval that 'The falsehood, cynicism, insolence, misgovernment, oppression, with their consequent unfailing
crop of human misery, which were produced by this state of things,
roused Byron to irreconcilable revolt and battle' ('Essay on Byron',
p. 400). Ladislaw's Byronic colouring is a surface gloss that also permeates the political cast of his character.

When Mrs Cadwallader describes Ladislaw as 'A sort of Byronic hero –
an amorous conspirator' (p. 313), Eliot is not only dramatising 'the
Victorians' hyperbolic, tabloid image of Byron' (Dramin, 'Romanticism
in the Late Novels', p. 296). What appears to be nothing more than
wry gossip bears further scrutiny. Eliot is aligning her own hesitant
regard for this figure, reflected in 'sort of', with the public perception of Byron's scandalous persona; she is simultaneously positioning
Ladislaw's local involvement with reform alongside Byron's political
pursuits. This impetuous youth is accorded a certain gravitas by association with the 'honest and energetic efforts for his fellow-men' that Eliot
revered about the poet.[64] Conflating trivia and penetrating observation
in this way indicates that neither the presence of Byron in the novel
nor the tittle-tattle of Middlemarch society should be underestimated.
In addition to this association with sedition and sexual intrigue, Eliot
emphasises Ladislaw's pride, his 'gnashing impetuosity' (p. 181), and
his frequently irritable temper (Lydgate describes him as being 'like a
bit of tinder', for instance, p. 385). Relishing spontaneity, in his Grand
Tour of Europe, Ladislaw resembles the wandering Childe Harold; his
experiments with wine and opium, albeit ironically deflated by Eliot,
also recall the Byronic hero's desire for sensation to revitalise a sated
soul. Ladislaw is undeniably more sociable and less morbid than many
of Byron's protagonists, and yet his feelings for Dorothea, and their for-
bidden love, are distinctly Byronic. Indeed, the course of their relationship makes good the Giaour's claim that 'love will find its way/ Through
paths where wolves would fear to prey' (*The Giaour*, ll. 1048–9).

Ladislaw's fondness for romantic rhetoric, envisaging himself engaged
in 'an unavoidable feat of heroism', is often the subject of mild mockery, however (p. 174).

> Will did not know what to say, since it would not be useful for him
> to embrace her slippers, and tell her that he would die for her: it was
> clear that she required nothing of the sort. (p. 184)

As Barbara Hardy states, 'worship, adoration, higher love-poetry, queens,
and foot-stools are inappropriate images for love in the quotidian world

of *Middlemarch*' ('*Middlemarch* and the Passions', p. 16). But Ladislaw is never rendered ridiculous. The narrator's polyphonic voice – absorbing, melding, and shaping the consciousness of characters – is infused, on occasion, with Ladislaw's overblown language. The deflation of his endearingly inappropriate idealisation of Dorothea as a goddess or a work of art is comparable with the narrator's increasing scepticism at such untenable image-worship in the Prelude. In other words, Ladislaw is guilty of the narrator's former imprudence. Furthermore, the hero himself comments on how 'Worship is usually a matter of theory rather than of practice. But I am practising it to excess just at this moment', suggesting that his infatuation is determined by a Romantic model that he both subscribes to and scrutinises (p. 359). Ladislaw not only benefits from the author's preferential treatment, much to the continuing consternation of critics; he also displays a disarming self-awareness of his own flaws.

This playfully ironic regard for Will's tendency to romantic melodrama is somewhat lost in the BBC adaptation.[65] Omitting all dialogue from the final love scene, doubt and reticence are replaced by Dorothea symbolically deadheading flowers – a strong visual sign of renewal – and Ladislaw striding across lush green grounds (reminding the viewer, once again, of his 'manly' vigour). The 'uncertain promises' (p. 389) heralded by the hero and his relationship with Dorothea, as discussed above, are resolved rapidly and unambiguously – passion presumably transcending the need for words. The inherent drama of Eliot's original scene, in which the lovers attempt to reconcile themselves to separation, renders Davies's revision curiously underwhelming. As MacKillop and Platt comment,

> In the novel Ladislaw and Dorothea only just make it. Her release from paralysis, her sobbing admission that she hates her wealth, might have been kept in check until after Ladislaw's departure. The BBC offers a muffled cry where there could have been a roar. ('Television and the Illustration of *Middlemarch*', p. 78)

The scene in the adaptation takes place on a tranquil sunny day as opposed to the storm in Eliot's novel that symbolises Ladislaw and Dorothea's profound yet unresolved emotions and animates their feelings for one another.[66] The tempestuous weather also sounds a note of disquiet. Ladislaw's romantic posturing, presenting himself as 'one on the brink of the grave', does not elicit the intended response from Dorothea (p. 665). Recalling the couple's first meeting, when Dorothea confesses that Ladislaw's is a 'language I do not understand', she now checks his hyperbole: 'No – don't say that – your life need not be maimed' (pp. 65, 666). Ladislaw's emotional outpouring, which gives voice to the 'angry spirit' of the storm, is both fervent and trembling; yet he is blind, as he has often been, to Dorothea's needs (p. 666). She pulls away from his embrace to comfort herself with practical plans, recognising, in Barbara Hardy's words, 'the limits of adoration' (*'Middlemarch* and the Passions', p. 16). That said, this impulsive union – which raises the question of whether Dorothea is temporarily responding to Ladislaw's spontaneous energy (as Rosamond has previously responded to hers) – also anticipates the sense of unpredictable, or alternative, futures captured in the novel's conclusion. Marriages, the narrator tells us, are great beginnings as well as endings, and the Finale speculates upon rather than dictates the possible destinies of the central characters.[67]

In addition to the altered ending, Ladislaw is portrayed from the start of the adaptation as the 'ardent public man' he is to become in Eliot's Finale (p. 686). His investment in reform is not portrayed as a whim; Episode 3 begins with Ladislaw at the centre of local talk about emancipation, for example. The opening scene draws attention to the rapid progress and displacement associated with modern forms of transport, accompanied by Lydgate's animated exclamation – 'the future' – but it is Ladislaw who provides a focal point for change amidst the historical flux of Eliot's setting. In direct contrast to Leslie Stephen's comment that the character of Ladislaw in Eliot's novel 'had not the moral force to be a leader in thought or action' (imagining him as a journalist rather than a politician), the BBC adaptation propels him into the limelight and casts him as a moral centre of the story.[68] This elevation of Ladislaw from embryonic to 'fully formed' hero provoked controversy amongst reviewers who argued that Dorothea, as well as the voice of the narrator, had been eclipsed as the formidable nexus of the novel.[69]

Ladislaw carries equal top billing, metaphorically, in a costume drama that is keen to emphasise political moment. This adaptation serves to identify a central tension in the novel rather than presenting a flawed or erroneous depiction of Dorothea's second husband. Through Ladislaw, Eliot, in effect, forms an alliance between the Byronic hero and Carlyle's hero-reformer, both of whom have an innate authority and command allegiance. Depicted, somewhat divisively, as an 'agitator', Ladislaw may be, like Byron's Giaour, a 'stray renegade'.[70] Yet this 'constitutional rebel' ('Television and the Illustration of *Middlemarch*', p. 82) works towards the general good: 'His nature warmed easily in the presence of subjects which were visibly mixed with life and action, and the easily-stirred rebellion in him helped the glow of public spirit' (p. 380). Here, then, are the 'disruptive energies' of the Byronic hero – which, as discussed in relation to Gaskell in Chapter 3, both fascinated and repelled Carlyle – governed by an altruistic agency (Stone, *Romantic Impulse*, p. 23). Channelling Byronic satire and political dissent into a Carlylean social cause goes some way to explaining Eliot's partial if ambivalent regard for this 'miscellaneous and *bric-à-brac*' fellow (p. 359, original emphasis). Her commitment to this impassioned public speaker with an artist's sensibility is most evident when his propensity towards a 'spontaneous overflow of powerful feelings' graduates into 'emotion recollected in tranquillity'[71]: '[Will] work[ed] well in those times when reforms were begun with a young hopefulness of immediate good which has been much checked in our days, and getting at last returned to Parliament by a constituency who paid his expenses' (Finale, p. 686). This Byronic hero-reformer is, in many ways, a literary experiment. But it is important to note that, in Will Ladislaw, Eliot comes closest to realising what she grapples with in her previous novel, *Felix Holt*, and in her last novel, *Daniel Deronda*: 'a social reformer who finds a vocation which can use his romantic vision'.[72] It is not simply the case that Ladislaw's Romantic posturing is appropriated and repurposed for a civic-minded Victorianism, however. His Byronic inheritance accords with and becomes enmeshed within the Carlylean figure of the 'Ablest Man'.

Middlemarch is not, therefore, a novel with a restricted sense of heroism. What makes a hero, the adaptation reminds us, changes under historical pressure and can come to encompass unexpected, modified, and even Romantic ideals. Ladislaw's ambition that his 'public exertions' might be seen as 'heroic' are fulfilled, I would argue, in a Finale where 'channels which had no great name on the earth' are part of, in Dorothea's evolving worldview, 'widening the skirts of light' (pp. 387, 688, 323). This Romantic reformer's modest achievements do not constitute the failure of idealism, but the reconfiguration of heroism on an 'unhistoric' scale. Quite apart from the perennial objections to period drama that revolve around authenticity, the BBC adaptation of *Middlemarch* expands upon the Byronic hero's capacity for renewal as it re-codifies masculinity in relation to wider issues of community, politics, and progress. It is not Byron's infamy that accounts for his appeal to nineteenth-century women writers. In fact, as we have seen, after denouncing the scandal that had become synonymous with Byron's reputation, Eliot's fictional engagements with this Romantic poet moved away from a preoccupation with his notoriety to a profoundly conflicted and sophisticated rethinking of Romantic legacies.

The Byronic hero found a series of unlikely cultural allies among women writers who would seem, on a surface level at least, to resist the profligacy and discord that his presence denotes. The Byronic hero – 'a man of many thoughts,/ And deeds of good and ill, extreme in both' (*Manfred*, II. ii. ll. 34–5) – provided a catalyst for the ideological indeterminacies and the aesthetic challenges of gender and genre that preoccupied the nineteenth-century women writers featured in this book. His presence, under various guises, is persistent if changeable in novels that dramatise his shortcomings and profit from a regenerative potential that destabilises sexual mores and probes the political status quo. Byronic male leads in screen adaptations of the last two decades reinscribe the charged yet creative dialogues between Austen, Gaskell, Eliot, and Byron, setting a contemporary stage for the most recent incarnation of this memorable anti-hero. In this sense, Goethe's statement, in 1823, that 'a character of such eminence had never existed before, and probably would never come again' is apposite in acknowledging the uniqueness of brand Byron.[73] Goethe is short-sighted, however, in not anticipating the cultural force of this phenomenon in fiction and on film over successive generations. The manifold afterlives of the Byronic hero were implanted in the poems that brought him to prominence two centuries ago. The final words of this book are – fittingly and somehow inevitably – Byron's: 'He had (if 'twere not nature's boon) an art/ Of fixing memory on another's heart' (*Lara*, I. ll. 363–4).

Notes

Introduction

1. Elizabeth Barrett Browning, *Stanzas on the Death of Lord Byron*, ll. 29–30, 34, in *Aurora Leigh and Other Poems*, ed. by John Robert Glorney Bolton and Julia Bolton Holloway (London: Penguin, 1995). Subsequent line references will be given in the text.
2. Letitia Landon (L.E.L.), *The Portrait of Lord Byron at Newstead Abbey*, ll. 13–21, in *Fisher's Drawing Room Scrap-Book* (London: Fisher, Son, & Co., 1840), pp. 11–14.
3. A similar cocktail of controversy surrounds James Bond (on screen and on the page) as surrounds Byron and his legacy. Most recently, Daniel Craig has played the eponymous spy as a case-hardened hit man in a series of 'grittier' Bond films, including *Casino Royale* (2006), *Quantum of Solace* (2008), and *Skyfall* (2012). The latter film begins with the self-imposed exile of 007 and ends with the return to his ancestral seat, the site of childhood trauma, to face his deformed nemesis.
4. Of this defining moment, Byron famously proclaimed, 'I awoke one morning and found myself famous'. Byron's celebrity has been the subject of recent studies, including Ghislaine McDayter, *Byromania and the Birth of Celebrity Culture* (Albany, NY: State University of New York Press, 2009), and Tom Mole, *Byron's Romantic Celebrity: Industrial Culture and the Hermeneutic of Intimacy* (Basingstoke: Palgrave, 2007).
5. Andrew Elfenbein, *Byron and the Victorians* (Cambridge: Cambridge UP, 1995), p. 8.
6. *Twilight* is a series of four vampire fantasy novels, written by Stephenie Meyer, and published between 2005 and 2008. Film versions of the novels, *The Twilight Saga*, were released between 2008 and 2012. The *Fifty Shades* trilogy, written by E. L. James, was published in 2011–12, with a film version of the first novel released in 2015. The Byronic hero is not only evident in contemporary fan fiction. A Byronic subtext emerges in J. M. Coetzee's *Disgrace* (1999), the Booker Prize winning novel about racial politics in South Africa, for instance. See Jonathan Gross, '"I have a penchant for black": Race and Orphic Dismemberment in Byron's *The Deformed Transformed* and J. M. Coetzee's *Disgrace*', in *Byron and the Politics of Freedom and Terror*, ed. by Matthew J. A. Green and Piya Pal-Lapinski (Basingstoke: Palgrave, 2011), pp. 167–81.
7. Cited in Deborah Kaplan, 'Mass Marketing Jane Austen: Men, Women, and Courtship in Two Film Adaptations', in *Jane Austen in Hollywood*, ed. by Linda Troost and Sayre Greenfield, 2nd edn (Lexington, KY: University Press of Kentucky, 2001), pp. 177–87 (p. 176).
8. Of Barbara Cartland, the 'literary magpie', Roger Sales states: 'although her heroes may well have tinges of Byron about them, they also resemble other heroes from a wide range of other texts'. The heroes of popular romance often lack the self-scrutiny and wit of Byron's protagonists and their more

memorable literary offspring. See Sales, 'The Loathsome Lord and the Disdainful Dame: Byron, Cartland and the Regency Romantic', in *Byromania: Portraits of the Artist in Nineteenth- and Twentieth-Century Culture*, ed. by Frances Wilson (Basingstoke: Macmillan, 1999), pp. 166–83 (p. 179).

9. Drawn from Milton's Satan and distilled through the Gothic villain and the Marquis de Sade, Byron realised the rebel 'type' and made 'vampirism' fashionable. See Mario Praz, *The Romantic Agony*, 2nd edn, trans. by Angus Davidson (Oxford: Oxford UP, 1951), p. 77.

10. *The Diary of Virginia Woolf*, ed. by Anne Olivier Bell with Andrew McNellie, 5 vols (London: Hogarth Press, 1977–84), III, p. 288; *The Essays of Virginia Woolf*, ed. by Andrew McNellie, 4 vols (London: Hogarth Press, 1986–94), III, p. 482. For a more extensive discussion of Woolf's literary regard for Byron and Byronism, see Julia Briggs, 'Reading People, Reading Texts: "Byron and Mr Briggs"', in *Reading Virginia Woolf* (Edinburgh: Edinburgh UP, 2006), pp. 63–79.

11. Frances Wilson, 'Introduction: Byron, Byronism and Byromaniacs', in *Byromania*, pp. 1–23 (pp. 1, 2).

12. Peter L. Thorslev Jr., *The Byronic Hero: Types and Prototypes* (Minneapolis, MN: University of Minnesota Press, 1962), p. 3.

13. See Mario Praz, *The Hero in Eclipse in Victorian Fiction*, trans. by Angus Davidson (London, New York, and Toronto: Oxford UP, 1956).

14. Thomas Babington Macaulay mistakenly predicted the demise of 'that magical potency which once belonged to the name of Byron', in his review of Thomas Moore's *Letters and Journals of Lord Byron: With Notices of his Life* for the *Edinburgh Review* in June 1831. Over 30 years later, in November 1864, Walter Bagehot opined that 'the cause of his momentary fashion is the cause also of his lasting oblivion'. Both Macaulay and Bagehot are cited in *Byron: The Critical Heritage*, ed. by Andrew Rutherford (London: Routledge, 1970), pp. 295–316, pp. 365–7 (pp. 316, 365). Rutherford presents a selection of the ongoing debates about Byron's poetry and the fashion for Byronism that extended throughout the nineteenth century. In addition, Samuel Chew's invaluable study charts the peaks and troughs of Byron's posthumous reputation and is a testament to the poet's undimmed presence in the century following his death. The book includes a 54 page bibliographic list of Byroniana. See Samuel C. Chew, *Byron in England: His Fame and After-Fame* (London: John Murray, 1924).

15. William D. Brewer, 'Introduction', in *Contemporary Studies on Lord Byron*, ed. by William D. Brewer (Lewiston, NY: Edwin Mellen Press, 2001), p. 3.

16. Atara Stein, *The Byronic Hero in Film, Fiction, and Television* (Carbondale, IL: Southern Illinois UP, 2004), p. 213. See, also, Stein, 'Immortals and Vampires and Ghosts, Oh My!: Byronic Heroes in Popular Culture', in *Romanticism and Contemporary Culture*, ed. by Laura Mandell and Michael Eberle-Sinatra. Special issue of *Romantic Circles Praxis Series* (February 2002), http://www.rc.umd.edu/praxis/contemporary/stein/stein.html, accessed 8 April 2002, 9pp. In addition, Karen McGuire considers the parallels between Byron's celebrity and the late twentieth-century megastar, Michael Jackson, in 'Byron Superstar: The Poet in Neverland', *Contemporary Studies on Lord Byron*, pp. 141–59.

17. Dickens's complex regard for Byron is the subject of William R. Harvey, 'Charles Dickens and the Byronic Hero', *Nineteenth-Century Fiction*, 24:3 (1969), pp. 305–16, and Vincent Newey, 'Rival Cultures: Charles Dickens and the Byronic Legacy', in *Romantic Echoes in the Victorian Era*, ed. by Andrew Radford and Mark Sandy (Aldershot: Ashgate, 2008), pp. 67–83. Byronic Romanticism held a 'deep fascination' for Dickens, especially with regards to social and political satire, according to Newey (p. 68). Richard Lansdown also notes the prevalence of Byronic heroines in Dickens's novels. See Lansdown, 'The Byronic Hero and the Victorian Heroine', *Critical Review*, 41 (2001), pp. 105–16. Deborah Lutz observes the 'punishing' treatment of Byron and Byronism in Anthony Trollope's novels, *The Eustace Diamonds* and *The Last Chronicle of Barset*. See Lutz, 'The Pirate Poet in the Nineteenth Century', in *Pirates and Mutineers of the Nineteenth Century: Swashbucklers and Swindlers*, ed. by Grace Moore (Farnham: Ashgate, 2011), pp. 23–39 (p. 24).

18. *Byron and the Victorians*, p. 168. Elfenbein recognises that women readers and writers were part of the construction of Byronism, and discusses the Brontë siblings in his chapter on Emily Brontë.

19. Byron's cultural reach (extending to art and music as well as literature) spread far and wide across Europe, from France and Spain to Greece and Romania, as is well documented in *The Reception of Byron in Europe*, ed. by Richard A. Cardwell, 2 vols (London: Thoemmes Continuum, 2004). For a discussion of Byron's impact in the US, see Peter X. Accardo, 'Byron in America to 1830', *Harvard Library Bulletin*, 9:2 (1998), pp. 5–60, and William E. Leonard, *Byron and Byronism in America* (New York: Columbia UP, 1907).

20. 'Few women figure in the history of Byron criticism', according to Samuel Chew, in his otherwise excellent and entertaining study of Byron's afterlives, published a century after the poet's death (*Byron in England*, p. 319).

21. See, for instance, *Fellow Romantics: Male and Female British Writers, 1790–1835*, ed. by Beth Lau (Farnham: Ashgate, 2009), and Caroline Franklin, *The Female Romantics: Nineteenth-Century Women Novelists and Byronism* (New York and Abingdon: Routledge, 2013).

22. See Paul A. Cantor, 'Mary Shelley and the Taming of the Byronic Hero: "Transformation" and *The Deformed Transformed*', in *The Other Mary Shelley: Beyond Frankenstein*, ed. by Audrey A. Fisch, Anne K. Mellor, and Esther H. Schor (Oxford: Oxford UP, 1993), pp. 89–106, and Susan J. Wolfson, 'Hemans and the Romance of Byron', in *Felicia Hemans: Reimagining Poetry in the Nineteenth Century*, ed. by Nanora Sweet, Julie Melnyk, and Marlon B. Ross (Houndmills: Palgrave, 2001), pp. 155–80. For Cantor, Mary Shelley's work typifies contemporary concerns over 'the new Romantic premium on the self' (p. 104). Shelley rehabilitates the Byronic hero in 'Transformation' (1831), her reimagining of Byron's drama, *The Deformed Transformed* (1824). Franklin includes chapters on Mary Shelley and Lady Caroline Lamb in *Female Romantics*.

23. Letitia Landon (L.E.L.), 'Stanzas, Written beneath the Portrait of Lord Byron, painted by Mr. West', in *The Literary Souvenir; or, Cabinet of Poetry and Romance*, ed. by Alaric A. Watts (London: Longman et al., 1827), pp. 33–6 (l. 1). Susan Wolfson considers L.E.L. as a 'Byronic she-artist' who 'doesn't just channel Byronic lava but produces its pulse and flow for female veins',

in *Romantic Interactions: Social Being & the Turns of Literary Action* (Baltimore, MD: Johns Hopkins UP, 2010), pp. 259, 278.

24. *Female Romantics*, p. 1. The emphasis of Franklin's study is on nineteenth-century women writers who embarked upon the 'challenge of Byronism' for political ends (p. 2). Byron's legacy functions as the ingredient that activates a narrative of liberal feminism.

25. Elizabeth Barrett Browning refers to 'a sort of novel-poem' in a letter written to Robert Browning in February 1845. For Marjorie Stone, Barrett Browning is a Romantic Victorian for whom Byron was a formative and lasting influence. See Stone, 'Elizabeth Barrett Browning and Victorian Versions of Byron and Wollstonecraft: Romantic Genealogies, Self-Defining Memories and the Genesis of *Aurora Leigh*', in *Romantic Echoes*, pp. 123–41 (p. 140). See, also, Dorothy Mermin, 'Beginning to Write', in *Godiva's Ride: Women of Letters in England, 1830–1880* (Bloomington and Indianapolis: Indiana UP, 1993), pp. 3–19.

26. Byron is 'salt as life' in 'A Vision of Poets', published in *Poems* 1844 (l. 413). Jane Stabler discusses the allure of Byron for Barrett Browning – 'pungent, physical, and erotic' – and her shifting regard for Shelley in 'Romantic and Victorian Conversations: Elizabeth Barrett and Robert Browning in Dialogue with Byron and Shelley', in *Fellow Romantics*, pp. 231–53 (p. 236).

27. The Brontë sisters were steeped in Byron's poetry, Thomas Moore's *Life of Byron*, and Finden's engravings, which were diligently copied out in their own drawings (for evidence of the latter, see *The Art of the Brontës*, ed. by Christine Alexander and Jane Sellars [Cambridge: Cambridge UP, 1995]). Tom Winnifrith contends, with regards to their early writings, that 'the Brontës' juvenilia provides confirmatory evidence of the sisters' preoccupation with [...] the Byronic hero, beautiful but damned'. See *The Brontës and Their Background: Romance and Reality* (London and Basingstoke: Macmillan, 1973), p. 5. On Charlotte Brontë's formative immersion in the Byronic, see Christine Alexander, *The Early Writings of Charlotte Brontë* (Oxford: Basil Blackwell, 1983). For Byron's influence on the Brontës' later works, especially on the 'timeless twin-ness' of Byron and Emily Brontë, see, among others, Margiad Evans, 'Byron and Emily Brontë: An Essay', *Life and Letters*, 57 (1948), pp. 193–216 (p. 196); Helen Brown, 'The Influence of Byron on Emily Brontë', *Modern Language Review*, 34 (1939), pp. 374–81; and F. B. Pinion, 'Byron and *Wuthering Heights*', *Brontë Society Transactions*, 21 (1995), pp. 195–201. See, also, Irene Tayler, *Holy Ghosts: The Male Muses of Emily and Charlotte Brontë* (New York: Columbia UP, 1990). For a discussion of Byronic presences in screen adaptations of the Brontës' fiction, see Lucasta Miller, *The Brontë Myth* (London: Jonathan Cape, 2001); Patsy Stoneman, *Brontë Transformations: The Cultural Dissemination of 'Jane Eyre' and 'Wuthering Heights'* (London: Prentice Hall/ Harvester-Wheatsheaf, 1996); and Sarah Wootton, '"Picturing in me a hero of romance": The Legacy of *Jane Eyre*'s Byronic Hero', in *A Breath of Fresh Eyre: Intertextual and Intermedial Reworkings of 'Jane Eyre'*, ed. by Margarete Rubik and Elke Mettinger-Schartmann (Amsterdam and New York: Rodopi, 2007), pp. 229–241.

28. Winifred Gérin reads the Brontës' heroes, Rochester and Heathcliff, as 'proof that the influence of Byron was no shallow thing, no slavish imitation of a literary model'. See 'Byron's Influence on the Brontës', *Keats-Shelley Memorial*

Bulletin, 17 (1966), pp. 1–19 (p. 5). Later critics who argue for the Brontës' indebtedness to and movement away from Byron include Nina Auerbach, 'This Changeful Life: Emily Brontë's Anti-Romance', in *Shakespeare's Sisters: Feminist Essays on Women Poets*, ed. by Sandra M. Gilbert and Susan Gubar (Bloomington and London: Indiana UP, 1979), pp. 48–64; Andrew Elfenbein, *Byron and the Victorians*, especially his chapter on Emily Brontë; and Inga-Stina Ewbank, *Their Proper Sphere: A Study of the Brontë Sisters as Early-Victorian Female Novelists* (London: Edward Arnold, 1966).

29. Anne Brontë asserts, when justifying the publication of her novel in the 'Preface to the Second Edition', that 'I wished to tell the truth, for truth always conveys its own moral to those who are able to receive it'. See *The Tenant of Wildfell Hall*, ed. by Stevie Davies (London: Penguin, 1996), p. 3.

30. Emily Brontë, *Wuthering Heights*, ed. by David Daiches, rpt (London: Penguin Classics, 1985), p. 187. Subsequent references will be given in the text.

31. Charlotte Brontë, *Jane Eyre* (London: Penguin, 2002), pp. 150–1, 156. Subsequent references will be given in the text.

32. Atara Stein, '"I Loved Her and Destroyed Her": Love and Narcissism in Byron's *Manfred*', *Philological Quarterly*, 69:2 (1990), pp. 189–215 (p. 197).

33. Passages from Austen's *Persuasion* and Eliot's *Felix Holt* are included in Rutherford's critical heritage of Byron and constitute a significant proportion of the extracts by women writers.

34. See *Jane Austen's Letters*, ed. by Deirdre Le Faye, 4th edn (Oxford: Oxford UP, 2011), p. 268.

35. See *The George Eliot Letters*, ed. by Gordon S. Haight, 9 vols (London and New Haven: Oxford UP, 1956–78), V, p. 54. Subsequent references will be dated in the text.

36. Matthew Arnold, 'Byron', from *Essays in Criticism: Second Series 1888*, in *Matthew Arnold: Selected Prose*, ed. by P. J. Keating (Harmondsworth: Penguin, 1970), pp. 385–404 (p. 401).

37. An example of this can be found towards the end of William St Clair's otherwise excellent essay, 'The Impact of Byron's Writings: An Evaluative Approach', in *Byron: Augustan and Romantic*, ed. by Andrew Rutherford (Basingstoke: Macmillan, 1990), pp. 1–25. When considering the early Victorian reception of Byron, St Clair states: '… almost everyone seems to have read and admired Byron's poetry, even if they disapproved of the man. But it is the early Byron they like, not *Don Juan*, and it was the women writers, Charlotte Brontë, Elizabeth Barrett Browning, and George Eliot who disliked that poem most' (pp. 23–4). A primary objective of this book is to amend the view that Victorian women writers were Byron's least receptive critics. Eliot, in particular, read, re-read, and made references to *Don Juan* in her writings.

38. Michael O'Neill, '"In the Sea of Life Enisled": Byron and Arnold', in *Byron and the Isles of Imagination: A Romantic Chart*, ed. by Alistair Heys and Vitana Kostadinova (Plovdiv: Plovdiv UP, 2009), pp. 67–87 (p. 78). See, also, O'Neill, '"The burden of ourselves": Arnold as a Post-Romantic Poet', *Yearbook of English Studies*, 36:2 (2006), pp. 109–24; and 'The Romantic Bequest: Arnold and Others', in *The Oxford Handbook of Victorian Poetry*, ed. by Matthew Bevis (Oxford: Oxford UP, 2013), pp. 217–34.

39. Susan Allen Ford, 'Learning Romance from Scott and Byron: Jane Austen's Natural Sequel', *Persuasions*, 26 (2004), pp. 72–88 (p. 77). The unprecedented

sales of Byron's poems are the subject of St Clair, 'The Impact of Byron's Writings'.

40. Jane Austen, *Persuasion*, ed. by Gillian Beer (London: Penguin, 1998), p. 94. Subsequent references will be given in the text.

41. Robert Browning, 'Andrea del Sarto', l. 49, in *Robert Browning: Selected Poems*, intro. and notes by Daniel Karlin (London: Penguin, 1989). Byron was a formative influence on Robert Browning; the speakers of the latter's dramatic monologues share certain features with the former's.

42. Gross, 'Race and Orphic Dismemberment', p. 167. *Jane Eyre*'s Rochester and *Middlemarch*'s Will Ladislaw share a stated capacity for metamorphosis.

43. George Eliot, *Middlemarch: A Study of Provincial Life*, rpt (Ware: Wordsworth Classics, 1995), pp. 174, 176. Subsequent references will be given in the text.

44. Byron presented himself as a conundrum, 'such a strange *mélange* of good and evil, that it would be difficult to describe me'. See Leslie Marchand, *Byron: A Biography*, 3 vols (New York: Alfred A. Knopf, 1957), p. 1066.

45. Jane Austen, *Pride and Prejudice* (Ware: Wordsworth Classics, 1992), p. 197. Subsequent references will be given in the text.

46. Letter of April 1850, in *The Letters of Mrs Gaskell*, ed. by J. A. V. Chapple and Arthur Pollard (Manchester: Manchester UP, 1966).

47. See E. J. Clery, 'Austen and Masculinity', in *A Companion to Jane Austen*, ed. by Claudia L. Johnson and Clara Tuite (Chichester: Wiley-Blackwell, 2012), pp. 332–42.

48. Cited in McGuire, 'Byron Superstar', p. 150.

49. For Victor Brombert, modern anti-heroes resist a single type or description and adopt, as with the Byronic hero, 'a paradoxical, at times provocative, stance'. See Brombert, *In Praise of Antiheroes: Figures and Themes in Modern European Literature, 1830–1980* (Chicago and London: University of Chicago Press, 1999), p. 1.

50. Jerome J. McGann, *Fiery Dust: Byron's Poetic Development* (Chicago: University of Chicago Press, 1968), p. 27.

51. Recorded in Marguerite, Countess of Blessington, *Conversations of Lord Byron with the Countess of Blessington* (London: R. Bentley, 1834), p. 389. Lady Blessington dubbed Byron 'a perfect chameleon', with the capacity 'of taking the colour of whatever touches him' (p. 110).

52. Byron acknowledged that *Childe Harold's Pilgrimage* drew on his own experiences when abroad, yet insisted that the protagonist was a 'child of imagination' in the 'Preface to the First and Second Cantos', for instance. See *Byron: Poetical Works*, ed. by Frederick Page, rev. edn. John Jump (Oxford: Oxford UP, 1970), p. 179. Such disclaimers did little to abate the conflation of the poet and his poetry, as Macaulay testifies: 'Lord Byron never wrote without some reference, direct or indirect, to himself. The interest excited by the events of his life, mingles itself in our minds, and probably in the minds of almost all our readers, with the interest which properly belongs to his works' (cited in *Byron: The Critical Heritage*, pp. 301–2).

53. *The Letters of Mary Wollstonecraft Shelley*, ed. by Betty T. Bennett (Baltimore, MD: Johns Hopkins UP, 1980), I, p. 289.

54. Matthew Arnold, 'Stanzas from the Grande Chartreuse', l. 136, in *Arnold: Poetical Works*, ed. by C. B. Tinker and H. F. Lowry, rpt (London: Oxford UP, 1969). His famous line imitates even as it ironises, as O'Neill argues ('Byron

and Arnold', p. 79). The 'theatrical preludings' that Arnold associates with a narrow understanding of the poet are also insolubly connected with the 'real Byron' that he praises ('Byron', p. 401).

55. *Manfred: A Dramatic Poem*, Act II, scene ii, ll. 97–8. *Byron: Poetical Works*, ed. by Frederick Page, rev. edn. John Jump (Oxford: Oxford UP, 1970). Unless otherwise stated, references to Byron's poetry are taken from this edition and will be given in the text.

56. A selling point for Fiona MacCarthy's substantial biography, *Byron: Life and Legend*, was uncovering the poet's homosexuality and relationships with boys. Rather than being 'hidden', Byron's sexual predilections have been the subject of much speculation, including an appendix, 'Byron's Sexual Ambivalence', in Doris Langley Moore, *Lord Byron: Accounts Rendered* (London: John Murray, 1974). MacCarthy's biography considers Byron's fame and aspects of his posthumous reputation, with a concluding section devoted to 'The Byron Cult'. See MacCarthy, *Byron: Life and Legend* (London: John Murray, 2002).

57. *Byron*, directed by Julian Farino, screenplay by Nick Dear (BBC, 2003). Nick Dear also wrote the screenplay for the 1995 film version of *Persuasion*, which is discussed in Chapter 2. This book is not concerned with the films and fiction that feature Byron himself as a character. On this subject, see Ramona M. Ralston and Sidney L. Sondergard, 'Screening Byron: The Idiosyncrasies of the Film Myth', and Alex Alec-Smith, 'Appendix: Byron in Fiction: A List of Books', in *Byromania*. See, also, G. Todd Davis, 'Fictions of Byron: An Annotated Bibliography', *Romantic Circles* (January 2006), http://www.rc.umd.edu/reference/byron-fictions/index.html, accessed 28 July 2014.

58. Jane Tranter's comments are a part with the BBC's drive at that time to make period dramas 'relevant' and 'racy'. The biopic attracted attention for explicit sex scenes, with a piece in *The Sun* newspaper headed 'You Dirty Ode Man!'; Byron was branded 'Britain's most famous bonking bard'. See Tom Leonard, 'BBC to portray Byron as a "sex-god aristo"', http://www.telegraph.co.uk/news/uknews/1412508/BBC-to-portray-Byron-as-a-sex-god-aristo.html, accessed 12 March 2002; and Giovanna Iozzi, 'You Dirty Ode Man!: Byron Laid Bare in TV Sizzler', *The Sun*, 27 September 2003, p. 15.

59. Ian MacKillop and Alison Platt, '"Beholding in a Magic Panorama": Television and the Illustration of *Middlemarch*', in *The Classic Novel: From Page to Screen*, ed. by Robert Giddings and Erica Sheen (Manchester: Manchester UP, 2000), pp. 71–92 (p. 82).

60. Luaine Lee, 'Colin Firth Inhabits a Few Darcys', *Scripps Howard News Service*, 30 April 2001.

61. Victorian Coren, 'Don't Call Me Darcy', *Evening Standard*, 9 June 2000. A recurring theme of publicity for the film of *Bridget Jones's Diary* was the extent to which Firth had become typecast. A sample of articles from 2000 includes: 'There's No Escaping Mr Darcy'; 'No More Mr Darcy'; 'Forever Darcy'. The film was based on Helen Fielding's newspaper column turned novel, *Bridget Jones's Diary* (1996), which took inspiration from both Austen's *Pride and Prejudice* and the 1995 BBC adaptation.

62. Jean Hall, 'The Evolution of the Surface Self: Byron's Poetic Career', *Keats-Shelley Journal*, 36 (1987), pp. 134–57 (pp. 157, 140, 141). Andrew Rutherford offers a useful summary of writers who were sceptical of Byron's most

successful poems in *Byron The Best-Seller*, The Byron Foundation Lecture (Nottingham: University of Nottingham, 1964).

63. On the 'process of [Byron's] self-presentation and representations', see Christine Kenyon Jones, 'Fantasy and Transfiguration: Byron and His Portraits', in *Byromania*, pp. 109–36 (p. 110). See, also, *Byron: The Image of the Poet*, ed. by Christine Kenyon Jones (Newark, NJ: University of Delaware Press, 2008).

64. Diego Saglia, 'Touching Byron: Masculinity and the Celebrity Body in the Romantic Period', in *Performing Masculinity*, ed. by Rainer Emig and Antony Rowland (Basingstoke: Palgrave Macmillan, 2010), pp. 13–27 (pp. 14, 25).

65. *Marino Faliero, Doge of Venice*, Act II, scene i, l. 36. The phrase 'ungovernable temper' is taken from Byron's preface to the work (p. 407).

66. Some of the ideas presented here on *Marino Faliero* were formulated in response to a research paper given by Madeleine Callaghan at Durham University on 28 January 2015. Callaghan considers Byron's Cain as another hero figure engaged in a battle of semantics. See '"Stumbling Stanzas": Flawed Heroism and the Struggle with Language in Byron's *Cain*', *Byron Journal*, 38:2 (2010), pp. 125–35.

67. On the subject of historical transmission in Byron's Venetian plays, see Chapter 3 of Carla Pomarè's book, *Byron and the Discourses of History* (Farnham: Ashgate, 2013).

68. The phrase is taken from Keats's poem, 'La Belle Dame sans Merci', l. 27, in *John Keats: The Complete Poems*, ed. by John Barnard, 3rd edn (London: Penguin, 1988).

69. See *Byron: The Critical Heritage*, pp. 2–3.

70. Cited in *Byron: The Critical Heritage*, p. 288.

71. Susan J. Wolfson, '"Their She Condition": Cross-Dressing and the Politics of Gender in *Don Juan*', *ELH*, 54:3 (1987), pp. 585–617. See, also, Wolfson, '"A Problem Few Dare Imitate": *Sardanapalus* and "Effeminate Character"', *ELH*, 58:4 (1991), pp. 867–902. For Jonathan Gross, the narrator's homoerotic engagement with the hero is political: 'it is the gay aspect of his [the narrator's] bisexual identity that accounts for some of the most subversive, carnivalesque qualities of his poem'. See Gross, '"One Half What I Should Say": Byron's Gay Narrator in *Don Juan*', *European Romantic Review*, 9:3 (1998), pp. 323–50 (p. 324).

72. See Cantor, 'Mary Shelley and the Taming of the Byronic Hero'. Steven Bruhm detects a transgressive queerness throughout the poetry: 'Byron is queer in that he forces us to reevaluate our very notion of what Romantic male sexuality might be'. Bruhm, 'Reforming Byron's Narcissism', in *Lessons of Romanticism: A Critical Companion*, ed. by Thomas Pfau and Robert F. Gleckner (Durham, NC and London: Duke UP, 1998), pp. 429–47 (p. 438). See, also, Bruhm, *Reflecting Narcissus: A Queer Aesthetic* (Minneapolis, MN and London: University of Minnesota Press, 2001). Gross situates Byron more broadly within a homosocial sphere in which public relationships with women enhanced his prestige with other men. See Jonathan Gross, 'Epistolary Engagements: Byron, Annabella, and the Politics of 1813', in *Contemporary Studies on Lord Byron*, pp. 17–36.

73. Jacqueline M. Labbe, *The Romantic Paradox: Love, Violence and the Uses of Romance, 1760–1830* (Basingstoke: Macmillan, 2000).

74. According to Sedgwick, relationships between men, however hostile, are orchestrated through and supplant the significance of women in the nineteenth-century novel. See Eve Kosofsky Sedgwick, *Between Men: English Literature and Male Homosocial Desire* (New York and Chichester: Columbia UP, 1985).

75. Caroline Franklin argues for the range of Byron's female characters, 'from the eroticized passive victim of patriarchal force to the masculinized woman-warrior, from the romantic heroine of sentiment to the sexually voracious virago or the chaste republican matron, and so the list goes on. Byron was constantly experimenting with the representation of women'. See Franklin, *Byron's Heroines* (Oxford: Clarendon Press, 1992), p. 1.

76. Andrew Elfenbein, 'Byronism and the Work of Homosexual Performance in Early Victorian England', *Modern Language Quarterly*, 54:4 (1993), pp. 535–66 (p. 537). Saglia considers the importance of Byron's body to the silver-fork and dandy novelists, Bulwer-Lytton and Disraeli, in 'Touching Byron'.

77. Both men served as Conservative MPs (Bulwer-Lytton in later life) and Disraeli twice served as a Tory Prime Minister. A useful contrast between Bulwer-Lytton and Dickens, in terms of their respective treatment of Byronism, can be found in Newey, 'Rival Cultures'.

78. '[T]he scandal of Byron's marriage [and] how serial reactivation of it impacted on the twin history of feminism and women's fiction' is a primary concern for Franklin in *Female Romantics* (p. 4). See, also, Chapter 7 of Wolfson, *Romantic Interactions*.

79. Caroline Franklin, *Byron and Women Novelists*, The Byron Foundation Lecture (Nottingham: University of Nottingham, 2001), p. 37.

80. 'Hemans and the Romance of Byron', p. 172. Hemans's involved dialogues with Byron culminate, for Wolfson, in a 'poetry of female heroics' (p. 155).

81. Malcolm Kelsall discusses Byron's sexual politics in 'Byron and the Romantic Heroine', in *Byron: Augustan and Romantic*, pp. 52–62 (p. 52). Carlyle is cited in *Byron: The Critical Heritage*, p. 291.

82. Elizabeth Gaskell, *North and South*, ed. by Angus Easson, rpt (Oxford: Oxford UP, 1982), p. 64.

83. George Eliot, 'Evangelical Teaching: Dr Cumming', *Westminster Review*, lxiv (October 1855), pp. 436–62, in *George Eliot: Selected Critical Writings*, ed. by Rosemary Ashton, rpt (Oxford: Oxford UP, 2000), pp. 138–70 (p. 148). Eliot's comments come close to Barrett Browning's earlier paean to Byron as the poet of liberty in *Stanzas on the Death of Lord Byron*: 'That generous heart where genius thrill'd divine,/ Hath spent its last most glorious throb for thee—/ Then sank amid the storm that made thy children free!' (ll. 16–18).

84. Sydney Carton, in Charles Dickens's *A Tale of Two Cities* (1859), can be considered a Byronic hero whose self-sacrifice ennobles his death. The novel closes on a note of Byronic pathos that channels the protagonist's introspection into a moment of civic good.

85. Davies's comment is made in the BBC documentary, *Pride and Prejudice Revisited*, narrated by Emilia Fox and directed by John Hay (2005).

86. Davies was keen to distinguish his mini-series of *Sense and Sensibility* from the successful film version directed by Ang Lee, with screenplay by Emma Thompson (Columbia Pictures, 1995). For Davies's commentary on his television adaptation, see the interview with him as part of the DVD's Special

Features. *Sense and Sensibility*, directed by John Alexander, screenplay by Andrew Davies (BBC, 2008).

87. Umberto Eco, cited in Patsy Stoneman, 'The Brontë Legacy: *Jane Eyre* and *Wuthering Heights* as Romance Archetypes', *Rivista di Studi Vittoriani*, 3:5 (1998), pp. 5–24 (p. 9). For Russell, the artifice of Byron's Romanticism was overlooked, 'omitting the element of pose in his cosmic despair and professed contempt for mankind. Like many other prominent men, he was more important as a myth than as he really was. As a myth, his importance, especially on the Continent, was enormous'. See Bertrand Russell, *A History of Western Philosophy* (London: Routledge Classics, 2004), p. 680.

88. William Wordsworth, 'Lines Written a Few Miles above Tintern Abbey, on Revisiting the Banks of the Wye during a Tour, July 13, 1798', l. 97. *William Wordsworth: The Pedlar, Tintern Abbey and the Two-Part Prelude*, ed. by Jonathan Wordsworth (Cambridge: Cambridge UP, 1985).

89. '[C]ritics', Denise Tischler Millstein argues, often 'miss the significance of Byron's presence or ignore that Byronic heroes find particular shape in Eliot's characters', in 'Lord Byron and George Eliot: Embracing National Identity in *Daniel Deronda*', *Forum: University of Edinburgh Postgraduate Journal of Culture & the Arts*, 1 (Autumn 2005), http://www.forumjournal.org/site/issue/01/denise-tischler-millstein, accessed 20 July 2012.

1   Jane Austen's Byronic Heroes I: *Northanger Abbey* and *Sense and Sensibility*

1. Rachel M. Brownstein, 'Romanticism, A Romance: Jane Austen and Lord Byron, 1813–1815', *Persuasions*, 16 (1994), pp. 175–84 (p. 176). Brownstein reflects critically on this polarisation in a later essay, stating 'When their names turn up on the same page today, it is usually to suggest the range of Romantic period writing and/or the binary opposition between genders and genres: compare and contrast the maiden novelist who signed herself "A Lady" with that exhibitionist rake, the Noble Poet'. See Rachel M. Brownstein, 'Endless Imitation: Austen's and Byron's Juvenilia', in *The Child Writer from Austen to Woolf*, ed. by Christine Alexander and Juliet McMaster (Cambridge: Cambridge UP, 2005), pp. 122–37 (p. 122). For Shobhana Bhattacharji, contrasts between Austen and Byron provide a starting point for exploring genre and mood, as well as travel and pilgrimage. See Bhattacharji, 'The Gloom and Cheerfulness of Childe Harold and Elizabeth Bennet', in *Byron: Heritage and Legacy*, ed. by Cheryl A. Wilson (New York and Basingstoke: Palgrave, 2008), pp. 151–63.

2. A number of authors and critics have noted the proximity of Austen and Byron in terms of satire. Doucet Devin Fischer claims that 'Austen's awareness of the multiple ironies that Byron chose to compress into one clever pun is diffused throughout her fictions', in 'Byron and Austen: Romance and Reality', *Byron Journal*, 21 (1993), pp. 71–9 (pp. 73–4). See, also, William Galperin, 'Byron, Austen, and the "Revolution" of Irony', *Criticism*, 32:1 (1990), pp. 51–80. W. H. Auden, when contemplating Austen as the recipient of his 'Letter to Lord Byron' (1937), the 'one other author in my pack', offers a pastiche of her audacious satire:

> You could not shock her more than she shocks me;
> Beside her Joyce seems innocent as grass.
> It makes me most uncomfortable to see
> An English spinster of the middle-class
> Describe the amorous effects of 'brass',
> Reveal so frankly and with such sobriety
> The economic basis of society.

W. H. Auden, *The English Auden: Poems, Essays and Dramatic Writings, 1927–1939*, ed. by Edward Mendelson, rpt (London: Faber and Faber, 1989), p. 171. Subsequent page references will be given in the text.

3. See Beth Lau, 'Placing Jane Austen in the Romantic Period: Self and Solitude in the Works of Austen and the Male Romantic Poets', *European Romantic Review*, 15:2 (June 2004), pp. 255–67 (p. 264); and 'Home, Exile, and Wanderlust in Austen and the Romantic Poets', *Pacific Coast Philology*, 41 (2006), pp. 91–107 (p. 91). See, also, *Fellow Romantics: Male and Female British Writers, 1790–1835*, ed. by Beth Lau (Farnham: Ashgate, 2009); Nina Auerbach, 'Jane Austen and Romantic Imprisonment', in *Jane Austen in a Social Context*, ed. by David Monaghan (London: Macmillan, 1981), pp. 9–27; and Susan Morgan, 'Jane Austen and Romanticism', in *The Jane Austen Companion*, ed. by J. David Grey (New York: Macmillan, 1986), pp. 364–8. Austen's prominence, in terms of critical reception and popular culture, can be explained if her novels are viewed as specifically Romantic productions, according to Clara Tuite. See *Romantic Austen: Sexual Politics and the Literary Canon* (Cambridge: Cambridge UP, 2002).

4. '[H]ints of common ground dissolve into a basis of significant dissimilarlity', argued L. J. Swingle in 'The Perfect Happiness of the Union: Jane Austen's *Emma* and English Romanticism', *Wordsworth Circle*, 7:4 (1976), pp. 312–19 (p. 312). This article was published in a special issue of *The Wordsworth Circle* devoted to the topic of Austen as a Romantic writer. Swingle's later essay, for the same journal, argued for a link between Austen and her contemporaries in terms of an 'almost obsessive preoccupation with contrarieties'. See 'The Poets, the Novelists, and the English Romantic Situation', *Wordsworth Circle*, 10:2 (Spring 1979), pp. 218–27 (p. 220).

5. Elizabeth Barrett Browning, *Aurora Leigh*, Book VII, l. 150. See *Aurora Leigh and Other Poems*, ed. by John Robert Glorney Bolton and Julia Bolton Holloway (London: Penguin, 1995). Subsequent references to Barrett Browning's poetry will be given in the text. Anne Mellor, among others, has argued for 'at least *two* romanticisms, the men's and the women's' in an effort to shift the study of Romanticism away from a presiding group of male poets. Anne K. Mellor, 'Why Women Didn't Like Romanticism: The Views of Jane Austen and Mary Shelley', in *The Romantics and Us: Essays on Literature and Culture*, ed. by Gene W. Ruoff (New Brunswick, NJ: Rutgers UP, 1990), pp. 274–87 (p. 285). See, also, Anne K. Mellor, *Romanticism & Gender* (New York and London: Routledge, 1993).

6. The following represents a brief selection of the critical studies that have reframed the debates over Romantic dialogues and legacies in recent years: Beth Lau, ed., *Fellow Romantics: Male and Female British Writers, 1790–1835* (Farnham: Ashgate, 2009); Michael O'Neill, *The All-Sustaining Air: Romantic Legacies and Renewals in British, American, and Irish Poetry*

since 1900 (Oxford: Oxford UP, 2007); 'Romanticism and its Legacies', special issue of *Romanticism*, 14:1 (2008), guest ed. Michael O'Neill; Andrew Radford and Mark Sandy, eds., *Romantic Echoes in the Victorian Era* (Aldershot: Ashgate, 2008); Mark Sandy, ed., *Romantic Presences in the Twentieth Century* (Aldershot: Ashgate, 2012); 'Modelling the Self: Subjectivity and Identity in Romantic and Post-Romantic Thought and Culture', special issue of *Romanticism and Victorianism on the Net*, 51 (August 2008), guest eds. Mark Sandy and Sarah Wootton, http://www.erudit.org/revue/ravon/2008/v/n51/index.html?lang=en; Susan J. Wolfson, *Romantic Interactions: Social Being & the Turns of Literary Action* (Baltimore, MD: Johns Hopkins UP, 2010); and Sarah Wootton, *Consuming Keats: Nineteenth-Century Representations in Art and Literature* (Basingstoke: Palgrave Macmillan, 2006). See, also, Carmen Casaliggi and Paul March-Russell, eds., *Legacies of Romanticism: Literature, Culture, Aesthetics* (New York and Abingdon: Routledge, 2012).

7. Jane Austen, *Pride and Prejudice* (Ware: Wordsworth Classics, 1992), pp. 20, 21. Subsequent references will be given in the text.

8. See Gaye King, 'Catton Hall', *Transactions of the Jane Austen Society*, 2 (1991), pp. 61–3 (p. 62). For details of the poet's involvement in Lord Portsmouth's scandalous second marriage, see Claire Tomalin, *Jane Austen: A Life* (London: Viking, 1997), pp. 87–9, and Brownstein, 'Romanticism, A Romance', pp. 182–3.

9. When unable to find a likeness for her heroine, Austen speculates that Darcy 'prizes any Picture of her too much to like it should be exposed to the public eye.—I can imagine he wd have that sort [of] feeling—that mixture of Love, Pride & Delicacy'. Letter to Cassandra Austen, dated 24 May 1813, in *Jane Austen's Letters*, ed. by Deirdre Le Faye, 4th edn (Oxford: Oxford UP, 2011), p. 222. Subsequent references to Austen's letter are taken from this edition and will be dated in the text.

10. John Gibson Lockhart [John Bull], 'Letter to the Right Hon. Lord Byron' (London: William Wright, 1821). http://lordbyron.cath.lib.vt.edu/doc.php?choose=JoLockh.1821.JohnBull.xml, accessed 22 June 2013, pp. 29–30. Lockhart lampoons what he sees as the affected melancholy of *Childe Harold's Pilgrimage* and praises 'the sweet, fiery, rapid, easy—beautifully easy, anti-humbug style of *Don Juan*' (p. 42).

11. *Byron*, directed by Julian Farino, screenplay by Nick Dear (BBC, 2003).

12. The responses to Austen's novels, by both Annabella Milbanke and Lady Bessborough, are cited in Elizabeth Barry, 'Jane Austen and Lord Byron: Connections', *Persuasions*, 8 (1986), pp. 39–41 (p. 39).

13. Michael Williams, 'Jane Austen and Lord Byron: A View of Regency London', *Unisa English Studies*, 21 (1983), pp. 11–16 (p. 15).

14. John Halperin, *The Life of Jane Austen* (Baltimore, MD: Johns Hopkins UP, 1984), p. 252; Brownstein, 'Romanticism, a Romance', p. 175.

15. Jane Stabler, 'Literary Influences', in *Jane Austen in Context*, ed. by Janet Todd (Cambridge: Cambridge UP, 2005), pp. 41–50 (p. 49). Richard Cronin's comment appears in the chapter entitled 'Literary Scene' in the same collection (see p. 292).

16. William Deresiewicz, *Jane Austen and the Romantic Poets* (New York: Columbia UP, 2004), p. 7.

17. For further discussion of Austen's eclectic reading habits and her familiarity with Richardson, see the section entitled 'Nice Affecting Stories', in David

Nokes, *Jane Austen: A Life* (London: Fourth Estate, 1997), pp. 102–17 (p. 109). Gerarda Maria Kooiman-Van Middendorp notes that Austen was 'well-acquainted with contemporary authors', yet she reserved a special status for Richardson. See the chapter on Jane Austen in *The Hero in the Feminine Novel* (Middleburg: G. Widen Boer, 1931), pp. 49–59 (p. 49). For a commentary on allusions to Richardson in Austen's fiction, as well as the influence of Milton and Shakespeare on her work, see Jocelyn Harris, 'Jane Austen and the Burden of the (Male) Past: The Case Reexamined', in *Jane Austen and Discourses of Feminism*, ed. by Devoney Looser (Basingstoke: Macmillan, 1995), pp. 87–100 (pp. 92–3). See, also, Joe Bray, 'The Source of "Dramatized Consciousness": Richardson, Austen, and Stylistic Influence', *Style*, 35 (Spring 2001), pp. 18–33.

18. Jane Austen, *Northanger Abbey and Other Works*, ed. by James Kinsley and John Davie, intro. by Claudia L. Johnson (Oxford: Oxford UP, 2003), p. 26. Subsequent references will be given in the text.

19. David Gilson, 'Jane Austen's Verses', *The Book Collector*, 33 (1984), pp. 25–37 (p. 37). Here Gilson provides bibliographic details for some of Austen's occasional verse. In an essay on Austen's poetry, David Selwyn argues for 'a tradition of family verse-writing', and reminds us that her final written words were a poem. See Selywn, 'Poetry', in *Jane Austen in Context*, pp. 59–67 (p. 59).

20. Deresiewicz states that there are only five known occasions when Austen copied out another writer's verse (*Austen and the Romantic Poets*, p. 7).

21. Quotations from Byron's poem, 'Napoleon's Farewell', are taken from *Lord Byron: The Complete Poetical Works*, ed. by Jerome J. McGann, 7 vols (Oxford: Clarendon Press, 1981), III, pp. 312–3. Quotations from Austen's copy, 'Lines of Lord Byron, in the Character of Buonaparté', are taken from the original manuscript, MS8/A0174, housed in the University of Southampton Library. I would like to thank the Senior Archivist, Karen Robson, for her assistance.

22. William Shakespeare, *The Life of Henry the Fifth*, Act III, scene i, l. 1, in *The Complete Oxford Shakespeare*, ed. by Stanley Wells and Gary Taylor, 3 vols (London: Guild Publishing, by arrangement with Oxford UP, 1987), I.

23. Corin Throsby, 'Byron, Commonplacing and Early Fan Culture', in *Romanticism and Celebrity Culture, 1750–1850*, ed. by Tom Mole (Cambridge: Cambridge UP, 2009), pp. 227–44 (p. 228). Throsby gives details of the Byron poems that were frequently quoted from in commonplace books of the period.

24. References to this group of poems are taken from Lord Byron, *Poems 1816*, intro. by Jonathan Wordsworth (Oxford: Woodstock Books, 1990), pp. 25–38.

25. See Austen's letter to her sister, dated 4 February 1813.

26. Darryl Jones, *Jane Austen* (Basingstoke: Palgrave, 2004), p. 171.

27. Deresiewicz, *Austen and the Romantic Poets*, p. 146. Todd argues for the contemporary significance of literature inspired by the Battle of Waterloo for the genesis of *Persuasion*. See her 'Introduction' to Jane Austen, *Persuasion*, ed. by Janet Todd and Antje Blank (Cambridge: Cambridge UP, 2006). In addition, David Nokes associates the completion of *Emma* with Napoleon's previous escape from Elba and conflates the success of these endeavours: 'By the end of March, when the French Emperor resumed power in Paris, she had finished the book' (*Austen: A Life*, p. 459).

28. The extent to which Byron was influenced by and departed from the eighteenth-century libertinism of Pierre Choderlos de Laclos's *Les Liaisons dangereuses* is the subject of Jonathan Gross's essay 'Epistolatory Engagements: Byron, Annabella, and the Politics of 1813', in *Contemporary Studies on Lord Byron*, ed. by William D. Brewer (Lewiston, NY: Edwin Mellen Press, 2001), pp. 17–36.

29. Jason Solinger, 'Modern Masculinities', *Novel*, 42:1 (2009), pp. 5. http://lion.chadwyck.co.uk, accessed 29 August 2012.

30. Kenneth L. Moler argues that the figure of Mr Darcy incorporates and critiques aspects of a character-type from Samuel Richardson's and Fanny Burney's fiction. See Moler, '*Pride and Prejudice*: Jane Austen's "Patrician Hero" ', *Studies in English Literature, 1500–1900*, 7:3 (1967), pp. 491–508.

31. Joseph Kestner, 'Jane Austen: Revolutionizing Masculinities', *Persuasions*, 16 (1994), pp. 147–60 (p. 148).

32. Isabelle Bour detects the influence of John Locke's *Some Thoughts Concerning Education* on *Pride and Prejudice*. Locke argues that civility can be demonstrated through the social activity of dancing. See Bour, 'Locke, Richardson, and Austen: Or, How to Become a Gentleman', *Persuasions*, 30 (2008), pp. 159–69 (pp. 164–5).

33. As John Tosh observes, '"Character" was in effect taking over some of the ground previously occupied by birth and rank as markers of social status'. See 'The Old Adam and the New Man: Emerging Themes in the History of English Masculinities, 1750–1850', in *English Masculinities 1660–1800*, ed. by Tim Hitchcock and Michèle Cohen (London and New York: Longman, 1999), pp. 217–38 (p. 235).

34. Michael Kramp, *Disciplining Love: Austen and the Modern Man* (Columbus, OH: Ohio State UP, 2007). Criticism that has previously argued for a renewed focus on masculinities in Austen's fiction includes: Claudia L. Johnson's 'Afterword', entitled 'Remaking English Manhood in *Emma*', in *Equivocal Beings: Politics, Gender, and Sentimentality in the 1790s: Wollstonecraft, Radcliffe, Burney, Austen* (Chicago: University of Chicago Press, 1995), pp. 191–203; Joseph Kestner, 'Jane Austen: Revolutionizing Masculinities', *Persuasions*, 16 (1994), pp. 147–60; and Devoney Looser, 'Jane Austen "Responds" to the Men's Movement', *Persuasions*, 18 (1996), pp. 159–70. See, also, Claudia L. Johnson, 'Austen Cults and Cultures', in *The Cambridge Companion to Jane Austen*, ed. by Edward Copeland and Juliet McMaster (Cambridge: Cambridge UP, 1997), pp. 211–26.

35. Sarah Frantz, 'Jane Austen's Heroes and the Great Masculine Renunciation', *Persuasions*, 25 (2003), pp. 165–75 (p. 169).

36. For a further discussion of Byron's attention to appearance, see Christine Kenyon Jones, 'Fantasy and Transfiguration: Byron and His Portraits', in *Byromania: Portraits of the Artist in Nineteenth- and Twentieth-Century Culture*, ed. by Frances Wilson (Basingstoke: Macmillan, 1999), pp. 109–36.

37. Martine Voiret, 'Books to Movies: Gender and Desire in Jane Austen's Adaptations', in *Jane Austen and Co.: Remaking the Past in Contemporary Culture*, ed. by Suzanne R. Pucci and James Thompson (Albany, NY: State University of New York Press, 2003), pp. 229–45 (pp. 232–3).

38. Herbert Sussman, *Victorian Masculinities: Manhood and Masculine Poetics in Early Victorian Literature and Art* (Cambridge: Cambridge UP, 1995), p. 10.

39. Cited in Bour, 'Locke, Richardson, and Austen', p. 164.
40. Jane Austen, *Emma*, ed. by Ronald Blythe, rpt (London: Penguin, 1985), p. 432. Subsequent references will be given in the text. This 'true English style' is also associated with Byron (p. 122). In his 'Letter to Lord Byron', Lockhart praises the poet's unrivalled understanding of the English lady and gentleman, contending 'I will tell you, Lord Byron: England is yours, if you choose to make it so.—I do not, speak of the England of days past, or of the England of days to come, but of the England of the day that now is' ('Letter to Lord Byron', p. 46). The later cantos of *Don Juan*, published after Lockhart hailed the poem as a standard of unaffected brilliance, shift attention to English society.
41. For Judith Wilt, 'Frank Churchill is thoroughly alive, and thoroughly a serious character, a moral conundrum, in the way that Wickham and William Elliot are not'. See 'Jane Austen's Men: Inside/Outside "the Mystery"', in *Men by Women*, ed. by Janet Todd (New York and London: Holmes and Meier, 1981), pp. 59–76 (pp. 66, 71–2).
42. 'Churchill to Knightley is', Kestner argues, 'gallant only in a debased manner' ('Revolutionizing Masculinities', p. 150).
43. John Lauber, 'Heroes and Anti-Heroes in Jane Austen's Novels', *The Dalhousie Review*, 51:4 (Winter 1971–72), pp. 489–503 (p. 499).
44. Michèle Cohen, ' "Manners" Make the Man: Politeness, Chivalry, and the Construction of Masculinity, 1750–1830', *Journal of British Studies*, 44 (2005), http://lion.chadwyck.co.uk, accessed 28 February 2006.
45. Byron, Coleridge, and Wordsworth influence the complexity and depth of intimate relationships in this novel, according to Deresiewicz. See Chapter 4, '*Emma*: Ambiguous Relationships', in *Austen and the Romantic Poets*.
46. Mario Praz, 'The Metamorphoses of Satan', in *The Romantic Agony*, 2nd edn, trans. by Angus Davidson (Oxford: Oxford UP, 1951), pp. 55–94 (p. 68). Janet Todd observes that Byron 'modeled his image on Ann Radcliffe's work, on her magnetic monsters, Schedoni and Montoni', in *Men by Women*, p. 4. See, also, *The Gothic Byron*, ed. by Peter Cochran (Newcastle upon Tyne: Cambridge Scholars, 2009).
47. See the chapters on 'The Gothic Villain', 'Four Turkish Tales', and 'Two Metaphysical Dramas', in Peter L. Thorslev, *The Byronic Hero: Types and Prototypes* (Minneapolis, MN: University of Minnesota Press, 1962).
48. The novel was revised and completed in 1803; it was published posthumously in 1818 with *Persuasion*. See 'Jane Austen and the *Northanger* Novelists' for a discussion of the 'horrid' books that Isabella Thorpe recommends to Catherine Morland, in *Gothic Writers: A Critical and Bibliographical Guide*, ed. by Douglass H. Thomson, Jack G. Voller, and Frederick S. Frank (London: Greenwood Press, 2002).
49. The formative fragment 'Catharine, or the Bower', Austen's prototype for *Northanger Abbey* (and *Sense and Sensibility* in some respects), stages a conversation over Charlotte Smith's novels that reveals the heroine's indiscriminate reading habits as well as the superficial pronouncements of her friend, Camilla Stanley, an early version of Isabella Thorpe. Their exchange offers a foretaste of the fraught subject of women writers, women readers, and genre in *Northanger Abbey*, although this Catherine is quick to rebuff a young woman who 'professed a love of Books without Reading'. John

Thorpe, Isabella's brother, is a revision of Camilla's thoughtless yet entertaining brother, Edward Stanley. See Jane Austen, *Juvenilia*, ed. by Peter Sabor (Cambridge: Cambridge UP, 2006), p. 248.

50. Henry Tilney is, as Margaret Kirkham argues, a 'young peacock' who also deflates 'male delusions of heroic superiority'. See Kirkham, 'Henry Tilney: The Clever Hero of *Northanger Abbey*', *Transactions of the Jane Austen Society*, 6 (1995), pp. 24–30 (p. 29). Albert Sears confirms, by examining booksellers' records from the 1790s, that Tilney's enjoyment of Radcliffe's *The Mysteries of Udolpho* would not have been uncommon. See Albert C. Sears, 'Male Novel Reading of the 1790s, Gothic Literature, and *Northanger Abbey*', *Persuasions*, 21 (1999), pp. 106–12.

51. Waldo S. Glock, 'Catherine Morland's Gothic Delusions: A Defense of *Northanger Abbey*', *Rocky Mountain Review of Language and Literature*, 32:1 (1978), pp. 33–46 (pp. 41, 34).

52. Ann Radcliffe, *The Mysteries of Udolpho*, ed. by Bonamy Dobrée, intro. by Terry Castle, rpt (Oxford: Oxford UP, 2008), p. 342. Subsequent references will be given in the text.

53. Both John A. Dussinger and Diane Long Hoeveler detect a sexual frisson between the hero's father and the heroine in *Northanger Abbey*, raising the Gothic and, of course, Byronic theme of incest. See John A. Dussinger, 'Parents Against Children: General Tilney as Gothic Monster', *Persuasions*, 20 (1998), pp. 165–74; and Diane Long Hoeveler, *Gothic Feminism: The Professionalization of Gender from Charlotte Smith to the Brontës* (University Park, PA: Pennsylvania State Press, 1998).

54. Sonia Hofkosh explores the captivating effects of Austen's realism in 'The Illusionist: *Northanger Abbey* and Austen's Uses of Enchantment', in *A Companion to Jane Austen*, ed. by Claudia L. Johnson and Clara Tuite (Chichester: Wiley-Blackwell, 2012), pp. 101–11.

55. See Beth Lau, 'Madeline at Northanger Abbey: Keats's Antiromances and Gothic Satire', *Journal of English and Germanic Philology*, 84:1 (1985), pp. 30–50. Lau argues persuasively for Keats as an important literary counterpart to Austen in 'The Uses and Abuses of Imagination in Jane Austen and the Romantic Poets', in *Fellow Romantics*, pp. 179–210.

56. 'The Eve of St Agnes', l. 300. The edition referred to is *John Keats: The Complete Poems*, ed. by John Barnard, 3rd edn (London: Penguin, 1988).

57. Karl Kroeber, 'Jane Austen, Romantic', *Wordsworth Circle*, 7:4 (1976), pp. 291–6 (p. 295).

58. *Northanger Abbey*, directed by Jon Jones, screenplay by Andrew Davies (ITV, 2007).

59. Lisa Hopkins, *Relocating Shakespeare and Austen on Screen* (Basingstoke: Palgrave Macmillan, 2009), pp. 152–3.

60. The 1987 BBC adaptation of *Northanger Abbey* includes similar scenes of Catherine's garish Gothic fantasies. Although the 2007 adaptation is not as camp as the 1987 adaptation, the final scene of General Tilney stalking his grounds as lightning strikes the Abbey indulges in a moment of filmic cliché. For a discussion of the 1987 adaptation, see Bruce Stovel, '*Northanger Abbey* at the Movies', *Persuasions*, 20 (1998), pp. 236–47; and Marilyn Roberts, 'Catherine Morland: Gothic Heroine After All?', *Topic*, 48 (1997), pp. 22–30.

61. Cates Baldridge contends that 'Austen's text [is] changed by – in some sense changed into – the kind of discourse it would have us reject, and the result is an interpenetration of styles and plot lines that leaves neither Gothicism nor moral realism untouched, a mutual illumination that can genuinely merit the label "dialogic" '. See *The Dialogics of Dissent in the English Novel* (Hanover and London: University Press of New England, 1994), p. 61.

62. *Persuasion*, directed by Adrian Shergold, screenplay by Simon Burke (BBC, 2007).

63. Sarah Ailwood, ' "Too much in the common Novel style": Reforming Masculinities in Jane Austen's *Sense and Sensibility*', in *Women Constructing Men: Female Novelists and Their Male Characters, 1750–2000*, ed. by Sarah S. G. Frantz and Katharina Rennhak (Plymouth: Lexington Books, 2010), pp. 67–82 (pp. 67, 73).

64. Jane Austen, *Sense and Sensibility*, ed. by Ros Ballaster (London: Penguin Classics, 1995), p. 15. Subsequent references will be given in the text.

65. Emily Brontë, *Wuthering Heights*, ed. by David Daiches, rpt (London: Penguin Classics, 1985), pp. 171, 195.

66. *Alastor; or, The Spirit of Solitude*, l. 153, in *Percy Bysshe Shelley: The Major Works*, ed. by Zachary Leader and Michael O'Neill, rpt (Oxford: Oxford UP, 2009).

67. Conversely, according to Auerbach, Marianne's 'questing spirit is bowed down by indelible manacles' in submitting to the 'confederacy against her' (p. 321) and accepting the unsatisfying mediocrity offered by Colonel Brandon. See 'Jane Austen and Romantic Imprisonment', p. 26.

68. William Wordsworth's famous comment, that 'all good poetry is the spontaneous overflow of powerful feelings', is taken from 'Preface to *Lyrical Ballads, with Pastoral and Other Poems* (1802)', in *William Wordsworth: The Major Works*, ed. by Stephen Gill, rpt (Oxford: Oxford UP, 2008), pp. 595–615 (p. 598).

69. *Sense and Sensibility*, directed by Ang Lee, screenplay by Emma Thompson (Columbia Pictures, 1995).

70. For Penny Gay's reading of this scene, see '*Sense and Sensibility* in a Postfeminist World: Sisterhood is Still Powerful', in *Jane Austen on Screen*, ed. by Gina Macdonald and Andrew Macdonald (Cambridge: Cambridge UP, 2003), pp. 90–110 (pp. 96, 93).

71. Cheryl L. Nixon, 'Balancing the Courtship Hero: Masculine Emotional Display in Film Adaptations of Austen's Novels', in *Jane Austen in Hollywood*, ed. by Linda Troost and Sayre Greenfield, 2nd edn (Lexington, KY: University Press of Kentucky, 2001), pp. 22–43 (p. 23).

72. Mrs Dashwood contrasts Brandon's 'manly unstudied simplicity' with Willoughby's contrived manners towards the end of the novel (p. 287).

73. 'Austen's characters are [...] often placed by their command of books and allusion, or by books neglected, misquoted, unread', as Patricia C. Brückmann argues, in '"Such days as these": Books, Readers, and Libraries in *Persuasion*', in *New Windows on a Woman's World: Essays for Jocelyn Harris*, ed. by Colin Gibson and Lisa Marr, 2 vols (Dunedin, New Zealand: University of Otago, 2005), II, pp. 9–28 (p. 9).

74. Arthur F. Marotti and Marcelle Freiman, 'The English Sonnet in Manuscript, Print and Mass Media', in *The Cambridge Companion to The Sonnet*, ed. by

A. D. Cousins and Peter Howarth (Cambridge: Cambridge UP, 2011), pp. 66–83 (p. 80).

75. *Sense and Sensibility*, directed by John Alexander, screenplay by Andrew Davies (BBC, 2008). The series was originally broadcast over three episodes in January 2008.

76. Lines 1–4. Although Byron's poem was composed some months before Austen died in 1817, it was years after the publication of *Sense and Sensibility* in 1811. The poem was not published until 1830.

77. Arnold argued that the fashion for the Byronic missed what was exceptional in his poetry. See Matthew Arnold, 'Byron', from *Essays in Criticism: Second Series 1888*, in *Matthew Arnold: Selected Prose*, ed. by P. J. Keating (Harmondsworth: Penguin, 1970), pp. 385–404 (p. 401). Michael O'Neill argues persuasively for Arnold's preoccupation with Byron's poetry. See '"In the Sea of Life Enisled": Byron and Arnold', in *Byron and the Isles of Imagination: A Romantic Chart*, ed. by Alistair Heys and Vitana Kostadinova (Plovdiv: Plovdiv UP, 2009), pp. 67–87.

78. Davies's screenplay developed the stories of all three male suitors, including Colonel Brandon's. He was particularly keen that Edward Ferrars should appear more 'manly' and be engaged in physical activity. The Byronic colouring of Willoughby and Brandon extends to Dan Stevens's Edward when he admits that he's 'prone to these dark moods'. For Davies's commentary on the adaptation, cited here and elsewhere in this chapter, see the interview with him on the DVD's Special Features.

79. Kate Harwood, BBC Head of Drama, on http://www.bbc.co.uk/drama/senseandsensibility/.

80. William Wordsworth, 'Lines Written a Few Miles above Tintern Abbey, on Revisiting the Banks of the Wye during a Tour, July 13, 1798', ll. 89–99. *William Wordsworth: The Pedlar, Tintern Abbey and the Two-Part Prelude*, ed. by Jonathan Wordsworth (Cambridge: Cambridge UP, 1985). The phrase, 'chastening thoughtfulness', is taken from the editorial notes to this edition (p. 37).

81. These lines are taken from Elizabeth Barrett Browning's poem, 'Lady Geraldine's Courtship' (ll. 163, 166). The phrase 'veined humanity' refers to Robert Browning's poetry; her evocative praise of his series, *Bells and Pomegranates*, as 'some "Pomegranate," which, if cut deep down the middle,/ Shows a heart within blood-tinctured, of a veined humanity!—' (ll. 165–6), attracted his admiration.

82. Ballaster, intro., *Sense and Sensibility*, p. xviii (original emphasis).

2   Jane Austen's Byronic Heroes II: *Persuasion* and *Pride and Prejudice*

1. See Jane Austen, *Persuasion*, ed. by Janet Todd and Antje Blank (Cambridge: Cambridge UP, 2006), p. lviii.

2. Marilyn Butler, *Jane Austen and the War of Ideas* (Oxford: Clarendon, 1975), p. 290. A volume of Byron's poetry appeared alongside editions of Scott's *Marmion* and *The Lady of the Lake* in an exhibition of Jane Austen's reading at Chawton House Library in 2009.

3. P. D. James's sequel to *Pride and Prejudice*, the murder mystery *Death Comes to Pemberley* (2011), was televised by the BBC, over three nights, during Christmas 2013. Matthew Rhys commented on the 'nightmare' of playing Mr Darcy, and the close association of Colin Firth with the role, for a BBC video blog, http://www.bbc.co.uk/blogs/tv/entries/11866388-9f15-3653-abef-470355092f63, accessed 23 March 2015.

4. Jane Austen, *Persuasion*, ed. by Gillian Beer (London: Penguin, 1998), p. 94. Subsequent references will be given in the text.

5. Susan Allen Ford, 'Learning Romance from Scott and Byron: Jane Austen's Natural Sequel', *Persuasions*, 26 (2004), pp. 72–88 (p. 73).

6. John Halperin, *The Life of Jane Austen* (Baltimore, MD: Johns Hopkins UP, 1984), p. 303.

7. Patricia C. Brückmann, '"Such Days as These": Books, Readers, and Libraries in *Persuasion*', in *New Windows on a Woman's World: Essays for Jocelyn Harris*, ed. by Colin Gibson and Lisa Marr, 2 vols (Dunedin, New Zealand: University of Otago, 2005), II, pp. 9–28 (pp. 15–16).

8. Bakhtin defines the 'hybrid construction' as 'an utterance that belongs, by its grammatical (syntactic) and compositional markers, to a single speaker, but that actually contains mixed within it two utterances, two speech manners, two styles, two "languages," two semantic and axiological belief systems'. See 'Discourse in the Novel', in *The Dialogic Imagination: Four Essays by M. M. Bakhtin*, ed. by Michael Holquist, trans. by Caryl Emerson and Michael Holquist (Austin, TX: University of Texas Press, 1981), p. 304.

9. Jane Austen, *Northanger Abbey and Other Works*, ed. by James Kinsley and John Davie, intro. by Claudia L. Johnson (Oxford: Oxford UP, 2003), p. 323. Subsequent references will be given in the text. In many respects, *Sanditon* represents a culmination of Austen's literary dialogues with past and present authors – making allusions to Cowper, Burney, Scott, and Wordsworth, among others – and it also extends her concerns over the undiscerning reader and the value of the novel.

10. 'The truth was that Sir Edward whom circumstances had confined very much to one spot had read more sentimental Novels than agreed with him. His fancy had been early caught by all the impassioned, and most exceptionable parts of Richardsons; and such Authors as have since appeared to tread in Richardson's steps, so far as Man's determined pursuit of Woman in defiance of every opposition of feeling and convenience is concerned, had since occupied the greater part of his literary hours, and formed his Character' (*Sanditon*, p. 327).

11. William Hazlitt, 'Lord Byron', in *The Spirit of the Age* (UK: Dodo Press, 2007), p. 63. The specific phrase 'first-rate' also anticipates Charlotte Brontë's eager recommendation of Byron's and Scott's poetry, as well as Thomas Moore's *Life of Byron*, to a friend. See *The Letters of Charlotte Brontë: With a Selection of Letters by Family and Friends*, ed. by Margaret Smith, 3 vols (Oxford: Clarendon Press, 1995), I, pp. 130–1. Brontë, along the lines of Captain Benwick, 'devoured the works of Scott and Byron with something bordering on obsession'. See *An Edition of the Early Works of Charlotte Brontë*, ed. by Christine Alexander, 3 vols (Oxford: Basil Blackwell, 1991), II. i, p. xxi.

12. Austen wrote occasional verses and amusing impromptu rhymes, as did her mother, while her brother James 'took the writing of poetry seriously'.

See David Selywn, 'Poetry', in *Jane Austen in Context*, ed. by Janet Todd (Cambridge: Cambridge UP, 2005), pp. 59–67 (p. 62).

13. Nina Auerbach, 'O Brave New World: Evolution and Revolution in *Persuasion*', *ELH*, 39:1 (1972), pp. 112–28 (p. 116).

14. John Wiltshire, *Recreating Jane Austen* (Cambridge: Cambridge UP, 2001), p. 92.

15. It would be tempting, although anachronistic, to suggest that Austen had the following image of caves as 'deep/ And dark-green chasms' in mind from the final canto of Shelley's *The Revolt of Islam*. See *The Complete Poetry of Percy Bysshe Shelley*, ed. by Donald H. Reiman and Neil Fraistat, 3 vols (Baltimore, MD: John Hopkins UP, 2000-), III, ll. 4770–1. *Persuasion* was completed about a year before Shelley wrote this poem, however. Keith G. Thomas reads Anne as the poet-figure from *Alastor*, who remains steadfast to ideals despite disappointment and loss: she too is a solitary figure – often disregarded or denigrated. See Thomas, 'Jane Austen and the Romantic Lyric: *Persuasion* and Coleridge's Conversation Poems', *ELH*, 54 (1987), pp. 893–924 (pp. 893–4). Peter Robinson suggests an alternative Romantic echo in the 'deep romantic chasm' of Coleridge's 'Kubla Khan'. See Peter Robinson, 'Captain Benwick's Reading', *Essays in Criticism*, 57:2 (2007), pp. 147–70 (p. 149). It is just as likely that Austen is alluding to Ann Radcliffe or Walter Scott, or that she is invoking the language of Romantic writers more generally. Todd and Blank note the similarities between Austen's and Fanny Burney's descriptions of Lyme and its surroundings, and also offer William Gilpin's *Observations on the Western Parts of England, Relative Chiefly to Picturesque Beauty* as a possible source for the passage. See *Persuasion*, ed. by Todd and Blank, pp. 362–3.

16. 'Jane Austen and the Romantic Lyric', p. 917. For Thomas, *Persuasion* shares affinities with the elegiac lyrics of Keats, Shelley, Wordsworth, and, most especially, Coleridge. Auerbach previously noted the proximity of Austen's last novel to the poetry of Keats and Shelley in 'O Brave New World', p. 128.

17. Darryl Jones argues that Wentworth's letter writing represents an 'ideological fissure'. The hero is so overcome by his emotions that the 'pen of patriarchal authority falls from his hands', thereby permitting a romantic resolution. See Darryl Jones, *Jane Austen* (Basingstoke: Palgrave, 2004), pp. 185, 187.

18. References to the cancelled chapters are taken from *Persuasion*, ed. by Todd and Blank, pp. 322, 318, 321.

19. *Persuasion*, directed by Roger Michell, screenplay by Nick Dear (BBC and WGBH, 1995).

20. The 1995 film of *Persuasion* is particularly successful in conveying Anne Elliot's raw yet subdued passions through an autumnal setting.

21. Keats refers to '"The vale of Soul-making"' in his letter to George and Georgiana Keats, dated 14 February – 3 May 1819, in *Letters of John Keats*, ed. by Robert Gittings, rpt (Oxford: Oxford UP, 1992), pp. 210–56 (p. 249). Janet Todd suggests sources for Anne's 'musings and quotations', as well as offering Charlotte Smith's *Elegiac Sonnets* as a possible source for the 'tender sonnet' she recalls (pp. 78–9), in *The Cambridge Introduction to Jane Austen* (Cambridge: Cambridge UP, 2006), p. 124; and, with Blank, in *Persuasion*, pp. 360–1. Smith's novels are discussed in Austen's early work, 'Catharine, or the Bower'.

22. Charles J. Rzepka argues for a correlation between the social position of women and the 'ever-increasing marginalization of male poets', in 'Making it in a Brave New World: Marriage, Profession, and Anti-Romantic *Ekstasis* in Austen's *Persuasion*', *Studies in the Novel*, 26:2 (1994), 37 pp. (p. 27), http://lion.chadwyck.co.uk. Doucet Devin Fischer comments on contrasting views of Austen and Byron, with regards to their depictions of women, in 'Byron and Austen: Romance and Reality', *Byron Journal*, 21 (1993), pp. 71–9.

23. *Cambridge Introduction to Jane Austen*, pp. 128–9. *The Prisoner of Chillon* was written in the summer of 1816 – when Austen was completing *Persuasion* – and published in December of that year.

24. Beth Lau also detects a shared sense of solitude, restlessness, and dislocation in Romantic writing. Home is often a place where the protagonist is not, and nostalgically yearns for, in the fiction of both Austen and Byron. See 'Placing Jane Austen in the Romantic Period: Self and Solitude in the Works of Austen and the Male Romantic Poets', *European Romantic Review*, 15:2 (June 2004), pp. 255–67; and 'Home, Exile, and Wanderlust in Austen and the Romantic Poets', *Pacific Coast Philology*, 41 (2006), pp. 91–107.

25. Nina Auerbach, 'Jane Austen and Romantic Imprisonment', in *Jane Austen in a Social Context*, ed. by David Monaghan (London: Macmillan, 1981), pp. 9–27 (p. 10).

26. See *Persuasion*, p. 245, n. 8. This presupposes that Austen read at least the first two cantos of *Childe Harold's Pilgrimage*.

27. In drawing on 'the historical paradigms of Nelson and Wellington', Wentworth's character highlights the 'dessicated concept of masculinity' presented by Sir Walter and William Elliot. This, according to Joseph Kestner, is 'a sign of the democratizing process of the nineteenth century'. See 'Jane Austen: Revolutionizing Masculinities', *Persuasions*, 16 (1994), pp. 147–60 (p. 158).

28. The central episode in Lyme is a hymn to the sea-faring life, as the group bask, before Louisa's accident, in the light reflected from the water. This adaptation focuses on the sea as a source of employment not only for sailors, but for fishermen and the women who dress the catch. The activity on the Cobb is contrasted against the agricultural workers at Kellynch who lose their livelihoods as a result of Sir Walter's extravagance.

29. Rzepka offers a robust critique of Auerbach's reading of the Navy's 'enormous revolutionary potential [in *Persuasion*], as it brings mobility to a static society and emotional release to a suppressed heroine' ('O Brave New World', p. 119). Wentworth's entrepreneurship is underpinned by 'accumulating capital in a literally cut-throat competition', and Anne will most likely end up as another Mrs Harville rather than another trail-blazing Mrs Croft. Although Rzepka is right to direct the reader to Anne's 'emotionally exposed position at the end of the book', it should also be noted that anxieties over a future war are ascribed to her friends; the heroine's tender disposition, we are told, is amply rewarded by her sea-faring husband's affection. See 'Making it in a Brave New World', pp. 14, 13.

30. For William Deresiewicz, it is the aftermath of loss that offers the strongest connection between Austen and Byron in *Persuasion*. See *Jane Austen and the Romantic Poets* (New York: Columbia UP, 2004), p. 130.

31. Mary Waldron, *Jane Austen and the Fiction of her Time* (Cambridge: Cambridge UP, 1999), pp. 147–8.

32. After Wentworth's arrival in the neighbourhood, the Musgrove sisters are giddy with excitement, 'their heads were both turned by him' (p. 51).

33. For Swinburne, Byron's resistance to critical attacks 'are enough of themselves to embalm and endear his memory in the eyes of all who are worthy to pass judgment upon him'. See 'Swinburne's Defence of Byron [1866]', in *Byron: The Critical Heritage*, ed. by Andrew Rutherford (London: Routledge, 1970), p. 374.

34. Margaret Madrigal Wilson, 'The Hero and the Other Man in Jane Austen's Novels', *Persuasions*, 18 (1996), pp. 182–5 (p. 184).

35. Jason D. Solinger, *Becoming the Gentleman: British Literature and the Invention of Modern Masculinity, 1660–1815* (New York: Palgrave Macmillan, 2012), p. 94.

36. Philip Mason refers to Wentworth as 'perfect' in *The English Gentleman: The Rise and Fall of an Ideal* (London: André Deutsch, 1982), p. 78.

37. *Persuasion*, directed by Adrian Shergold, screenplay by Simon Burke (ITV, 2007).

38. W. Paul Elledge, 'Talented Equivocation: Byron's "Fare Thee Well"', *Keats-Shelley Journal*, 35 (1986), pp. 42–61 (pp. 42, 43).

39. Tom Hoberg, 'Her First and Her Last: Austen's *Sense and Sensibility*, *Persuasion*, and Their Screen Adaptations', in *Nineteenth-Century Women at the Movies: Adapting Classic Women's Fiction to Film*, ed. by Barbara Tepa Lupack (Bowling Green, OH: Bowling Green State University Popular Press, 1999), pp. 140–66 (pp. 153–4).

40. Serajul Islam Choudhury, 'Jane Austen's Heroes: Are They Adequate?', *Dacca University Studies*, 10 (1961), pp. 113–34 (p. 126).

41. Sidney Gottlieb applauds Roger Michell's 'revisionary aesthetic' in 'Persuasion and Cinematic Approaches to Jane Austen', *Literature/Film Quarterly*, 30 (2002), http://lion.chadwyck.co.uk.

42. Rachel M. Brownstein, 'Romanticism, A Romance: Jane Austen and Lord Byron, 1813–1815', *Persuasions*, 16 (1994), pp. 175–84 (p. 179).

43. D. W. Harding, 'The Character of Literature from Blake to Byron', *The Pelican Guide to English Literature*, ed. by Boris Ford (London: Penguin, 1982), V, pp. 35–68 (p. 51).

44. Jane Austen, *Pride and Prejudice* (Ware: Wordsworth Classics, 1992), pp. 41, 254, original emphasis. Subsequent references will be given in the text.

45. Gerarda Maria Kooiman-Van Middendorp, *The Hero in the Feminine Novel* (Middleburg: G. Widen Boer, 1931), p. 50.

46. Atara Stein, 'Immortals and Vampires and Ghosts, Oh My!: Byronic Heroes in Popular Culture', *Romanticism and Contemporary Culture*, ed. by Laura Mandell and Michael Eberle-Sinatra. Special issue of *Romantic Circles Praxis Series* (February 2002), http://www.rc.umd.edu/praxis/contemporary/stein/stein.html, accessed 8 April 2002, 9pp. (p. 3).

47. Jerome J. McGann, 'Hero with a Thousand Faces: The Rhetoric of Byronism', *Studies in Romanticism*, 31 (1992), pp. 295–313 (p. 302).

48. Edmund Burke, *Reflections on the Revolution in France 1790*, ed. by L. G. Mitchell (Oxford: Oxford UP, 1999), p. 34. The phrase 'rational and manly freedom', quoted in the next paragraph, is taken from this edition (p. 35).

49. Review of Thomas Moore's *Letters and Journals of Lord Byron: With Notices of his Life*, *Edinburgh Review*, 53 (June 1831), pp. 544–72. Cited in *Byron: The Critical Heritage*, pp. 295–316 (p. 297).

50. Paul Giles, 'The Gothic Dialogue in *Pride and Prejudice*', *Text and Context*, 2 (1988), pp. 68–75 (p. 70).

51. The 'liberal descent', of a man like Darcy, 'inspires us with a sense of habitual native dignity, which prevents that upstart insolence almost inevitably adhering to and disgracing those who are the first acquirers of any distinction', argues Burke, in *Reflections on the Revolution*, p. 34.

52. Austen wrote of her niece's response to *Pride and Prejudice*: 'Her liking Darcy & Eliz^th is enough. She might hate all the others, if she would'. Letter to Cassandra Austen, dated 9 February 1813, in *Jane Austen's Letters*, ed. by Deirdre Le Faye, 4th edn (Oxford: Oxford UP, 2011), p. 214. The phrase 'Love, Pride & Delicacy' appears in a letter dated 24 May 1813 (p. 222).

53. Michèle Cohen, '"Manners" Make the Man: Politeness, Chivalry, and the Construction of Masculinity, 1750–1830', *Journal of British Studies*, 44 (2005) http://lion.chadwyck.co.uk accessed 28 February 2006. The phrase 'chivalry's plural meanings', quoted later in the paragraph, is taken from this article.

54. H. Elisabeth Ellington argues for the influence of William Gilpin in *Pride and Prejudice* and for Capability Brown's improvements at Chatsworth as a source of inspiration for Pemberley. Ellington, '"A Correct Taste in Landscape": Pemberley as Fetish and Commodity', in *Jane Austen in Hollywood*, ed. by Linda Troost and Sayre Greenfield, 2nd edn (Lexington, KY: University Press of Kentucky, 2001), pp. 90–110 (p. 90).

55. Letter dated 27 October 1854, original emphasis. See *The Letters of Mrs Gaskell*, ed. by J. A. V. Chapple and Arthur Pollard (Manchester: Manchester UP, 1966).

56. Deborah Lutz, 'The Pirate Poet in the Nineteenth Century', in *Pirates and Mutineers of the Nineteenth Century: Swashbucklers and Swindlers*, ed. by Grace Moore (Farnham: Ashgate, 2011), pp. 23–39 (p. 33).

57. The importance of Darcy's letter as an 'alternative narrative' is discussed in Susan J. Wolfson, 'Re: Reading *Pride and Prejudice*: "What Think You of Books?"', in *A Companion to Jane Austen*, ed. by Claudia L. Johnson and Clara Tuite (Chichester: Wiley-Blackwell, 2012), pp. 112–22 (p. 119).

58. C. E. Brock captures Lizzie's discomfort when in company with Darcy in his illustration of 1895, 'He could even listen to Sir William Lucas'.

59. E. J. Clery, 'Austen and Masculinity', in *A Companion to Jane Austen*, pp. 332–42 (p. 339). The phrase 'epistemological chasm', quoted at the end of the paragraph, appears on p. 340.

60. Letter of John Keats, dated 21–27 December 1817.

61. *Pride and Prejudice*, directed by Simon Langton, screenplay by Andrew Davies (BBC, 1995). The television series was originally screened over six successive Sunday evenings between 24 September 1995 and 29 October 1995.

62. For a discussion of Austen's widespread appeal and the consequent anxiety for scholars, see Claudia L. Johnson, 'Austen Cults and Cultures', in *The Cambridge Companion to Jane Austen*, ed. by Edward Copeland and Juliet McMaster (Cambridge: Cambridge UP, 1997), pp. 211–26. Johnson considers Austen's critical reception and focuses on Rudyard Kipling's short story, 'The Janeites'.

63. For further information on the popularity of the BBC adaptation, see Ronnie Jo Sokol, 'The Importance of Being Married: Adapting *Pride and Prejudice*', in

Nineteenth-Century Women at the Movies: Adapting Classic Women's Fiction to Film, pp. 78–105 (p. 78).

64. Both comments are cited in Emily Auerbach, 'Pride and Proliferation', in *The Cambridge Companion to Pride and Prejudice*, ed. by Janet Todd (Cambridge: Cambridge UP, 2013), pp. 186–97 (pp. 186–7).

65. See http://www.bbc.co.uk/arts/bigread/top100.shtml, accessed 18 April 2013. *Pride and Prejudice* topped another poll, conducted in the same year, to find the greatest book by a woman writer. Helen Fielding's newspaper column turned novel, *Bridget Jones's Diary* (1996), which shared twenty-third place with *Sense and Sensibility* in the Orange poll, took inspiration from both Austen's *Pride and Prejudice* and the 1995 BBC adaptation. Mark Darcy, the hero, was based on Colin Firth's performance; Firth then played the role of Mark Darcy in the film versions, *Bridget Jones's Diary* (2001) and *Bridget Jones: The Edge of Reason* (2004).

66. Cheryl L. Nixon, 'Balancing the Courtship Hero: Masculine Emotional Display in Film Adaptations of Austen's Novels', in *Jane Austen in Hollywood*, pp. 22–43 (p. 31). '[T]he BBC adaptation rewrites Austen', according to Nixon, 'by adding physical self-expression to a character notorious for his inability to express himself verbally' (p. 24).

67. Diego Saglia, 'Touching Byron: Masculinity and the Celebrity Body in the Romantic Period', in *Performing Masculinity*, ed. by Rainer Emig and Antony Rowland (Basingstoke: Palgrave Macmillan, 2010), pp. 13–27 (pp. 19, 15). Disraeli's retelling of the storm incident is cited on p. 19.

68. *Lost in Austen*, directed by Dan Zeff, screenplay by Guy Andrews (ITV, 2008).

69. Interview with Colin Firth on NPR's *Fresh Air*, 7 May 2001, http://www.firth.com/int/fa5701.html, accessed 28 April 2013.

70. Posy Simmonds, 'Voices from the Other Side', *The Guardian*, 31 May 2003. Her 'Literary Life' series ran from November 2002 to December 2004, with a selection published in 2003 by Jonathan Cape. See, also, *The Guardian* archive, http://books.guardian.co.uk/posysimmonds/archive, accessed 22 April 2013.

71. *Recreating Jane Austen*, p. 122. Davies's comment is made in the BBC documentary, *Pride and Prejudice Revisited*, narrated by Emilia Fox, directed by John Hay (BBC, 2005).

72. Jean Domarchi, *Cahiers du Cinéma* (1963), cited in George Lellis and H. Philip Bolton, 'Pride but No Prejudice', in *The English Novel and the Movies*, ed. by Michael Klein and Gillian Parker (New York: Frederick Ungar, 1981), pp. 44–51 (p. 44, added emphasis).

73. Laura Thompson, 'Austen's Power', *The Daily Telegraph*, 1 July 2006.

74. Devoney Looser, 'The Cult of *Pride and Prejudice* and its Author', in *The Cambridge Companion to Pride and Prejudice*, pp. 174–85 (pp. 174, 185). See, also, for a further discussion of Austen's continuing cult status and her acolytes.

75. *Pride and Prejudice*, directed by Robert Z. Leonard, screenplay by Aldous Huxley and Jane Murfin (MGM, 1940). Sokol cites a contemporary reviewer, Philip T. Hartung, for praising 'Darcy's invulnerability and impassive disdain, though he found "perhaps a little too much fluttering of hands even

for a comedy of artificial manners"' ('Importance of Being Married', p. 90). Olivier's theatrical gestures may be explained, in part, by the fact that the script was based on a stage play.

76. *Pride and Prejudice*, directed by Cyril Coke, screenplay by Fay Weldon (BBC, 1980). Mrs Gardiner calls Darcy 'stately' even when warming to him in this adaptation. This version, when compared with Davies's version (both screened over six episodes), is more sceptical about the dynamics of adult relationships. Charlotte Lucas takes a prominent role in the early episodes, acting as a sobering counterbalance to the heroine's romantic hopes.

77. William Leith, 'True Romance', *The Observer*, 9 April 2000.

78. Ellen Belton, 'Reimaging Jane Austen: The 1940 and 1995 Film Versions of *Pride and Prejudice*', in *Jane Austen on Screen*, ed. by Gina Macdonald and Andrew Macdonald (Cambridge: Cambridge UP, 2003), pp. 175–96 (p. 192).

79. Virginia L. Blum, 'The Return to Repression: Filming the Nineteenth Century', in *Jane Austen and Co.: Remaking the Past in Contemporary Culture*, ed. by Suzanne R. Pucci and James Thompson (Albany: State University of New York Press, 2003), pp. 157–78 (pp. 166, 165). The gentler, unobtrusive masculinity of Hugh Grant's performance as Edward Ferrars, in the 1995 film of *Sense and Sensibility*, was read in terms of a late twentieth-century liberal feminist idea of the 'New Man'.

80. For Belton, the BBC adaptation realises the 'utopian ideal [of] the post-feminist project' ('Reimagining Jane Austen', p 194). See, also, Lisa Hopkins, 'Mr. Darcy's Body: Privileging the Female Gaze', in *Jane Austen in Hollywood*, pp. 111–21.

81. Linda Troost and Sayre Greenfield, 'Introduction: Watching Ourselves Watching', in *Jane Austen in Hollywood*, pp. 1–12 (p. 4).

82. *Reader, I Married Him* (BBC, 2007). Part 2, on 'Heroes', was screened on 23 May 2007. Daisy Goodwin singled out Darcy as having the 'ideal C.V. for a romantic hero'.

83. Kathy Passero, 'Pride, Prejudice and a Little Persuasion', *A&E Monthly*, December 1996.

84. See Fiona Morrow, 'Still Sitting Pretty', *The Independent*, 19 December 2003.

85. *Pride and Prejudice*, directed by Joe Wright, screenplay by Deborah Moggach (Universal Pictures, 2005).

86. Deborah Moggach, in *Reader, I Married Him*.

87. Dawn frames an adaptation that employs lighting effects to convey atmosphere and a sense of time passing. The interplay of light and shadow also stages the hero and heroine's mental manoeuvrings and awakening desires.

88. Cosmo Landesman, 'In Need of True Grit', review of *Pride and Prejudice*, directed by Joe Wright, *The Sunday Times*, 18 September 2005.

89. *Pride and Prejudice Revisited*; Joanna Briscoe, 'A Costume Drama with Muddy Hems', *The Sunday Times*, 31 July 2005.

90. Briscoe sees Wright's film of *Pride and Prejudice* as akin to 'a rowdy Victorian adaptation', with scenery reminiscent of *Tess of the d'Urbervilles* ('A Costume Drama with Muddy Hems'). Penny Gay argues that *Emma*

Thompson's screenplay for the 1995 film of *Sense and Sensibility* anticipates an audience conversant with *Wuthering Heights* and *Jane Eyre*. I would add that this audience is keyed into screen adaptations of these novels. See Gay, '*Sense and Sensibility* in a Postfeminist World: Sisterhood is Still Powerful', in *Jane Austen on Screen*, pp. 90–110.

91. Monomania, as 'a form of mental illness characterized by a single pattern of repetitive and intrusive thoughts or actions' (*OED*), came into use as a psychiatric term in the early nineteenth century. While a number of Byron's protagonists seem to suffer from this or a similar condition, the term is not widely used in literature until the mid-Victorian period. Nelly Dean, towards the end of Emily Brontë's novel *Wuthering Heights* (1847), surmises that Heathcliff 'might have had a monomania on the subject of his departed idol [Cathy]'. Emily Brontë, *Wuthering Heights*, ed. by David Daiches, rpt (London: Penguin Classics, 1985), p. 354.

92. Janet Todd identifies Darcy's heirs in twentieth-century novels by, among others, Daphne du Maurier, Barbara Cartland, and Georgette Heyer. See 'The Romantic Hero', in *The Cambridge Companion to Pride and Prejudice*, pp. 150–61. On the fate of the Byronic hero in Cartland's romances, see Roger Sales, 'The Loathsome Lord and the Disdainful Dame: Byron, Cartland and the Regency Romance', in *Byromania: Portraits of the Artist in Nineteenth- and Twentieth-Century Culture*, ed. by Frances Wilson (Basingstoke: Macmillan, 1999), pp. 166–83.

93. Clara Tuite, *Romantic Austen: Sexual Politics and the Literary Canon* (Cambridge: Cambridge UP, 2002), p. 19.

3   Elizabeth Gaskell's Byronic Heroes: *Wives and Daughters* and *North and South*

1. See, also, Caroline Franklin, *Byron and Women Novelists*, The Byron Foundation Lecture (Nottingham: University of Nottingham, 2001).

2. *Don Juan*, I. i; J. R. Watson, 'Elizabeth Gaskell: Heroes and Heroines, and *Sylvia's Lovers*', *Gaskell Society Journal*, 18 (2001), pp. 81–94 (p. 81).

3. Thomas Carlyle, *Sartor Resartus*, ed. by Kerry McSweeney and Peter Sabor (Oxford: Oxford UP, 2008), p. 146 (original emphasis); *On Heroes, Hero-Worship, and the Heroic in History* (London and Glasgow: Collins' Clear-Type Press, no date), p. 126. Subsequent page references will be given in the text.

4. Andrew Elfenbein, *Byron and the Victorians* (Cambridge: Cambridge UP, 1995), p. 91. Elfenbein examines the cultural politics of Carlyle's apparent anti-Byronism in Chapter 3 of his study.

5. Donald D. Stone, *The Romantic Impulse in Victorian Fiction* (Cambridge, MA and London: Harvard UP, 1980), p. 23.

6. Carlyle cited in *Byron: The Critical Heritage*, ed. by Andrew Rutherford (London: Routledge, 1970), p. 291.

7. Kristen Guest, 'Dyspeptic Reactions: Thomas Carlyle and the Byronic Temper', in *Nervous Reactions: Victorian Recollections of Romanticism*, ed. by Joel Faflak and Julia M. Wright (Albany, NY: State University of New York Press, 2004), pp. 141–61 (p. 143).

8. Andrew M. Stauffer, 'Byronic Anger and the Victorians', in *Byron: Heritage and Legacy*, ed. by Cheryl A. Wilson (New York and Basingstoke: Palgrave Macmillan, 2008), pp. 197–205 (p. 203).

9. Joseph Kestner, 'Men in Female Condition of England Novels', in *Men by Women*, ed. by Janet Todd (New York and London: Holmes and Meier, 1981), pp. 77–100 (p. 78).

10. Lisa Surridge, 'Working-Class Masculinities in *Mary Barton*', *Victorian Literature and Culture* (2000), pp. 331–43 (p. 333).

11. Elizabeth Gaskell, *North and South*, ed. by Angus Easson, rpt (Oxford: Oxford UP, 1982), p. 334. Subsequent references will be given in the text.

12. Catherine Barnes Stevenson, 'Romance and the Self-Made Man: Gaskell Rewrites Brontë', *Victorian Newsletter*, 91 (Spring 1997), pp. 10–16 (p. 10).

13. Michiel Heyns, 'The Steam-Hammer and the Sugar-Tongs: Sexuality and Power in Elizabeth Gaskell's "North and South" ', *English Studies in Africa*, 32:2 (1989), pp. 79–94 (p. 81). Heyns outlines several similarities between Gaskell's *North and South* and Austen's *Pride and Prejudice*, parallels that re-emerge in relation to the BBC adaptations of these novels, screened in 1995 and 2004 respectively. He concludes, however, that change is far more significant and pervasive in Gaskell's novel.

14. Letter to Lady Kay-Shuttleworth, dated 14 May 1850, original emphasis. See *The Letters of Mrs Gaskell*, ed. by J. A. V. Chapple and Arthur Pollard (Manchester: Manchester UP, 1966), p. 116. Subsequent references to Gaskell's letters will be dated in the text.

15. Rosemarie Bodenheimer, '*North and South*: A Permanent State of Change', *Nineteenth-Century Fiction*, 34:3 (1979), pp. 281–301 (p. 282).

16. Timothy J. Wandling, 'Early Romantic Theorists and the Fate of Transgressive Eloquence: John Stuart Mill's Response to Byron', in *Nervous Reactions*, pp. 123–40 (p. 124).

17. Elizabeth Gaskell, *Mary Barton*, ed. by Stephen Gill (Harmondsworth: Penguin, 1970), pp. 37–8.

18. Cited in Wandling, 'Early Romantic Theorists', p. 128.

19. Following the publication of *Mary Barton*, Gaskell wrote to Edward Chapman that she 'had no idea it would have proved such a fire brand' (1 January 1849).

20. Shirley Foster suggests that her time at 'the Misses Byerleys' laid the foundation for [Gaskell's] later reading'. See Foster, *Elizabeth Gaskell: A Literary Life* (Basingstoke: Palgrave Macmillan, 2002), p. 15.

21. The edition of Gaskell's short stories referred to is *Journalism, Early Fiction and Personal Writings*, ed by Joanne Shattock, in *The Works of Elizabeth Gaskell*, ed. by Joanne Shattock, 10 vols (London: Pickering & Chatto, 2005–06), I. 'The Heart of John Middleton' was published in *Household Words* shortly after Christmas 1850; 'The Sexton's Hero' was published in *Howitt's Journal* in September 1847, although the story may have been written as early as 1841.

22. Mariaconcetta Costantini, 'The Sexton's Hero', *Gaskell Society Journal*, 2 (1997), pp. 77–85 (p. 79). Costantini extends the comparison in a note: 'Though published in the same year as 'The Sexton's Hero', Brontë's *Wuthering Heights* is centred on the devilish character of Heathcliff, whose Romantic legacy is in direct opposition to Gaskell's innovative concept of Christian heroism' (p. 84).

23. Foster argues that her brother was pleased with the criticism on Byron because it 'suggest[ed] that she was taking seriously both his and her father's advice about her studies' (*Literary Life*, p. 9). A letter written by John Gaskell to Elizabeth while at sea, dated 16 July 1827, begins with lines from *Childe Harold's Pilgrimage*: 'Once more upon the waters! yet once more! ...' (III. ii). See John Chapple, *Elizabeth Gaskell: The Early Years* (Manchester and New York: Manchester UP, 1997), pp. 285, 311.

24. Cited in Jenny Uglow, *Elizabeth Gaskell: A Habit of Stories* (London: Faber & Faber, 1993), p. 99 (original emphasis). See, also, Angus Easson, *Elizabeth Gaskell* (London: Routledge and Kegan Paul, 1979), p. 22.

25. See Uglow, pp. 39–42. In a letter to her sister, dated 5 March 1814, Austen wrote: 'I have read the Corsair, mended my petticoat, & have nothing else to do'. *Jane Austen's Letters*, ed. by Deirdre Le Faye, 4th edn (Oxford: Oxford UP, 2011), p. 268. Austen's literary engagements with Byron are far more complex and significant than this quotation suggests, as previous chapters in this book establish. See, also, Sarah Wootton, 'The Byronic in Austen's *Persuasion* and *Pride and Prejudice*', *Modern Language Review*, 102:1 (2007), pp. 26–39.

26. Elizabeth Gaskell, *Cranford*, ed. by Patricia Ingham (London: Penguin, 2005), p. 41. Subsequent references will be given in the text.

27. Literary preferences cause friction between Miss Matty's sister – Miss Jenkyns – and Captain Brown at the end of Chapter 1. The latter insists on reading a passage from Charles Dickens's *The Pickwick Papers* and the former retaliates with a passage from Samuel Johnson's *Rasselas*. This heated exchange not only illustrates a conflict of character, in the contrast between a serious-minded classic and a hugely popular comedy issued in serial form, but also comments, more broadly, on the reluctance of Cranford's women to engage directly with the contemporary.

28. Miss Matty's brother, Peter, the exile who comes home, could also be read as a Romantic character. The story of Peter's flight from Cranford emphasises his singularity and inability to fit in. Furthermore, his exotic wanderings, his tall tales, and penchant for cross-dressing suggest Byronic influences.

29. Elizabeth Gaskell, *Wives and Daughters*, ed. by Pam Morris (London: Penguin, 1996), p. 27. Subsequent references will be given in the text.

30. Gaskell's interest in Wordsworth has long been accepted by critics, as I note in this chapter, as have the connections between *Wives and Daughters* and Maria Edgeworth's fiction. See, for instance, Marilyn Butler, 'The Uniqueness of Cynthia Kirkpatrick: Elizabeth Gaskell's *Wives and Daughters* and Maria Edgeworth's *Helen*', *Review of English Studies*, 23 (1972), pp. 278–90; and Eva Ashberg Borromeo, 'Maria Edgeworth, Frederika Bremer and Elizabeth Gaskell: Sources for *Wives and Daughters*', *Gaskell Society Journal*, 6 (1992), pp. 73–6.

31. The specific lines I am referring to are: 'these pastoral farms/ Green to the very door, and wreathes of smoke/ Sent up in silence...'. William Wordsworth, 'Lines Written a Few Miles above Tintern Abbey, on Revisiting the Banks of the Wye during a Tour, July 13, 1798', ll. 17–19. The edition used is *William Wordsworth: The Pedlar, Tintern Abbey and the Two-Part Prelude*, ed. by Jonathan Wordsworth (Cambridge: Cambridge UP, 1985). Subsequent references will be given in the text.

32. Bonnie Gerard, 'Victorian Things, Victorian Words: Representation and Redemption in Gaskell's *North and South'*, *The Victorian Newsletter*, 92 (Fall 1997), pp. 21–4 (p. 22).

33. Morris, intro., *Wives and Daughters*, p. 660.

34. Julia M. Wright, ' "Growing Pains": Representing the Romantic in Gaskell's *Wives and Daughters'*, in *Nervous Reactions*, pp. 163–85, (p. 165).

35. Dorothy Mermin, *Godiva's Ride: Women of Letters in England, 1830–1880* (Bloomington and Indianapolis: Indiana UP, 1993), p. 14.

36. Review of Thomas Moore's *Letters and Journals of Lord Byron: With Notices of his Life*, in *Edinburgh Review*, 53 (June 1831), pp. 544–72. Cited in *Byron: The Critical Heritage*, pp. 295–316 (pp. 315–16).

37. 'Ode to Napoleon Buonaparte', stanzas iii and xii. Use of the word clay, to denote the physicality of existence, recurs throughout Byron's poetry. In *Manfred*, for example, the eponymous hero decries his connection with mankind and the spirits taunt him with reminders of his mortality: 'What wouldst thou, Child of Clay! with me?'; 'Prostrate thyself, and thy condemned clay,/ Child of the Earth! or dread the worst' (I. i. l. 131; II. iv. ll. 34–5).

38. Jennifer Panek, 'Constructions of Masculinity in *Adam Bede* and *Wives and Daughters'*, *Victorian Review*, 22 (1996), pp. 127–51 (pp. 147–8).

39. Wordsworth's influence is discernible throughout this passage. The opening paragraphs of the chapter also contain a direct reference to his poem, 'Composed upon Westminster Bridge'.

40. Mr Gibson is depicted as intense and somewhat formidable in the illustrations for the Folio Society edition of the novel, published in 2002. An illustration to the lines, 'It was a brilliantly hot summer's morning; men in their shirt-sleeves were in the fields getting in the early harvest' (p. 109), shows Gibson as a dark, obscure figure watching the labourers work in the sunny field. By contrast, Osborne looks more Shelleyan than Byronic, and he is decidedly boyish in the illustration that depicts his death. See Elizabeth Gaskell, *Wives and Daughters*, intro. Victoria Glendinning, illustrated by Alexy Pendle (London: Folio Society, 2002).

41. John Keats, 'Ode to a Nightingale', ll. 69, 9. The edition referred to is *John Keats: The Complete Poems*, ed. by John Barnard, 3rd edn (London: Penguin, 1988). Such moments of Romantic transport often occur when Molly is situated at a window, a prominent feature of George Du Maurier's illustrations for the serialisation of the novel in *The Cornhill Magazine*. 'Væ Victis' shows Molly seated in a bay window, with a book open on her lap, looking at Roger and his father in the garden, for example. The illustration conveys Molly's isolation from the male sphere outside, as Mary Elizabeth Leighton and Lisa Surridge argue. It also indicates that the heroine's transition into womanhood is partly informed by what she reads and the sensations she derives from Romantic literature. For a more detailed discussion of Du Maurier's illustrations to Gaskell's work, see Bill Ruddick, 'George Du Maurier: Illustrator and Interpreter of Mrs Gaskell', *Gaskell Society Journal*, 1 (1987), pp. 48–54; and Mary Elizabeth Leighton and Lisa Surridge, 'The Plot Thickens: Toward a Narratological Analysis of Illustrated Serial Fiction in the 1860s', *Victorian Studies*, 51 (Autumn 2008), pp. 65–101.

42. Andrew Davies, 'Adapting *Wives and Daughters'*, *Gaskell Society Newsletter*, 29 (2000), pp. 2–5 (p. 4). *Wives and Daughters*, directed by Nicholas Renton,

screenplay by Andrew Davies (BBC, 1999). For a further discussion of Davies's adaptation, see Patsy Stoneman, '*Wives and Daughters* on Television', *Gaskell Society Journal*, 14 (2000), pp. 85–100.

43. Where the weather plays an instrumental role in these scenes, Davies omits the turbulent storm that acts as a backdrop to the romantic resolution between Dorothea Brooke and Will Ladislaw in Eliot's *Middlemarch* for his BBC adaptation, screened in 1994, a point that will be discussed further in Chapter 5.

44. Felicia Hemans and Walter Scott are both mentioned in Episode 4, but Davies invariably expands upon and introduces additional allusions to Byron and the Byronic in his screenplays of nineteenth-century novels.

45. *North and South*, p. 197. The quotation is taken from Byron's *The Island; or, Christian and his Comrades*, I. ll. 202–4.

46. Jeffrey E. Jackson, 'Elizabeth Gaskell and the Dangerous Edge of Things: Epigraphs in *North and South* and Victorian Publishing Practices', *Pacific Coast Philology*, 40:2 (2005), pp. 56–72 (p. 65).

47. Deborah Denenholz Morse, 'Mutiny on the *Orion*: The Legacy of the *Hermione* Mutiny and the Politics of Nonviolent Protest in Elizabeth Gaskell's *North and South*', in *Pirates and Mutineers of the Nineteenth Century: Swashbucklers and Swindlers*, ed. by Grace Moore (Farnham: Ashgate, 2011), pp. 117–31.

48. Grace Moore, 'Introduction', in *Pirates and Mutineers of the Nineteenth Century*, pp. 1–10 (p. 1).

49. Mel Campbell, 'Pirate Chic: Tracing the Aesthetics of Literary Piracy', in *Pirates and Mutineers of the Nineteenth Century*, pp. 11–22 (p. 12).

50. Cited in Jackson, 'Epigraphs in *North and South*', p. 66.

51. The word 'craddy', a variant of 'croddy', is defined as 'a daring feat, a challenge to perform, a difficult or dangerous act; a trick, manœuvre'. See *The English Dialect Dictionary*, ed. by Joseph Wright, 6 vols (Oxford: Henry Frowde, 1898), I, pp. 801–2. Here, as Easson states in the explanatory notes to the Oxford World's Classics edition of *North and South*, it basically means 'a puzzle' (p. 446). William Gaskell makes reference to the term in the first of two lectures that he gave in Manchester in 1854, which were subsequently published as a pamphlet and appended to the fifth edition of *Mary Barton*. See William Gaskell, 'Two Lectures on the Lancashire Dialect', in *The Works of Elizabeth Gaskell*, vol. 5, ed. by Joanne Wilkes, pp. 327–58 (pp. 334–5). I would like to thank Professor Joan Beal for her help with this matter.

52. E. J. Clery, 'Austen and Masculinity', in *A Companion to Jane Austen*, ed. by Claudia L. Johnson and Clara Tuite (Chichester: Wiley-Blackwell, 2012), pp. 332–42 (p. 340).

53. David Kelly, 'In Its Own Light: A View of the BBC's *North & South*', *Sydney Studies in English*, 32 (2006), pp. 83–96 (p. 93).

54. *North and South*, directed by Brian Percival, screenplay by Sandy Welch (BBC, 2004).

55. Sandy Welch states that she wanted the factory interior to be a 'central image of the drama': 'It's about capturing the excitement and the hardship of a modernising city'. See Sarah Shannon, 'Love in a Cold Climate', *The Independent*, Online Edition (10 November 2004), 3pp (p. 2).

56. Margaret is frequently depicted encroaching on traditionally male territories and topics of conversation in both the adaptation and the novel.

57. Margaret Harris, 'Taking Bearings: Elizabeth Gaskell's *North and South* Televised', *Sydney Studies in English*, 32 (2006), pp. 65–82 (p. 71). A number of viewers complained about this scene on the BBC's website (for example, 'Major gripe is the brutalising of Mr. Thornton'). See http://www.bbc.co.uk/northandsouth/episode2_yourreviews, accessed 9 April 2007. Subsequent references to viewers' comments are taken from the BBC's website. The actor who played Thornton comments on the character's 'anger' and reputation for 'ruthlessness with his workers' in the DVD's Special Features section.

58. On the subject of masculinity and class as depicted in the novels of nineteenth-century women writers, see Jessica L. Malay, 'Industrial Heroes: Elizabeth Gaskell and Charlotte Brontë's Constructions of the Masculine', in *Performing Masculinity*, ed. by Rainer Emig and Antony Rowland (Basingstoke: Palgrave Macmillan, 2010), pp. 41–59.

59. See, for example, Nils Clausson, 'Romancing Manchester: Class, Gender and the Conflicting Genres of Elizabeth Gaskell's *North and South*', *Gaskell Society Journal*, 21 (2007), pp. 1–20 (pp. 13–14); and Margaret Oliphant, 'Modern Novelists – Great and Small', *Blackwood's Edinburgh Magazine*, 77 (May 1855), pp. 554–68 (pp. 559–60).

60. Thornton asserts his credentials as a 'man of character' who, according to Stefan Collini, 'possess[ed] the moral collateral which would reassure potential business associates or employers'. Cited in John Tosh, 'The Old Adam and the New Man: Emerging Themes in the History of English Masculinities, 1750–1850', in *English Masculinities 1660–1800*, ed. by Tim Hitchcock and Michèle Cohen (London and New York: Longman, 1999), pp. 217–38 (p. 235).

61. Clausson, 'Romancing Manchester', p. 7. Janine Barchas has argued for reading *North and South* as 'the first full-length reworking of *Pride and Prejudice*'. Convincing parallels are established, ranging from the treatment of regional prejudice and Margaret's Darcyesque pride to illustrations of the novels. See Janine Barchas, 'Mrs Gaskell's *North and South*: Austen's Early Legacy', *Persuasions*, 30 (2008), pp. 53–66 (p. 53).

62. Joseph Campbell's account of the modern hero as a self-determining individual, driven by ego and subdued by personal despair, could be a description of the Byronic hero and his descendants. See the final section of his study, 'The Hero Today', in *The Hero with a Thousand Faces*, 2nd edn (1949; Princeton, NJ: Princeton UP, 1968).

63. 'Romancing Manchester', p. 12. The Radcliffean Montoni is an equally important source for Austen's romantic anti-heroes, as discussed in Chapter 1.

64. The description of Thornton's eyes glowing 'like red embers' is particularly Byronic (p. 360). See, for example, *The Giaour*, ll. 832–45, for a striking depiction of 'that dilating eye' (l. 834).

65. The hero of *The Giaour* exclaims, 'A serpent round my heart was wreathed,/ And stung my every thought to strife' (ll. 1194–5). Similar imagery is evident in Byron's 'The Irish Avatar' – 'See the cold-blooded serpent, with venom full flush'd,/ Still warming its folds in the breast of a king!' (ll. 99–100) – and in 'A Sketch from Private Life':

> If like a snake she steal within your walls,
> Till the black slime betray her as she crawls;

> If like a viper to the heart she wind,
> And leave the venom there she did not find; (ll. 47–50)

66. Margaret's voice-over is an example of why the BBC adaptation was, on the whole, a successful adaptation of the novel. The quotation, which inverts our preconceptions of hell, replicates Gaskell's use of complementary opposites.
67. Armitage's performance in the concluding episode is described by one viewer as 'devastatingly sexy (dare I say more so than the "Mr Darcy emerging from the pond scene" in *Pride and Prejudice*?)'.
68. Cited in Patsy Stoneman, 'The Brontë Legacy: *Jane Eyre* and *Wuthering Heights* as Romance Archetypes', *Rivista di Studi Vittoriani*, 3:5 (1998), pp. 5–24 (p. 9).
69. See, also, Patricia Nicol, 'Move Over, Darcy', *The Sunday Times* ('Culture'), 30 April 2006, pp. 6–7.
70. The connection between Gaskell's and Austen's heroes is reinforced, to comic effect, in the final episodes of the BBC sitcom *The Vicar of Dibley*. Harry Kennedy, the character played by Richard Armitage, is introduced in the appropriately-titled episode 'The Handsome Stranger'. Geraldine, the eponymous vicar, accepts his proposal of marriage after a few Austen-inspired misunderstandings. The 1995 film version of *Sense and Sensibility* serves as a romantic reference point and ironic intertext for the two-part Christmas special. See 'Holy Wholly Happy Ending', *The Vicar of Dibley* (BBC, 2007).
71. See 'More Over, Darcy', p. 7
72. Carlyle coined the term, 'Captains of Industry', in *Past and Present* (1843). Carlyle looked to the middle-class industrialists as a replacement for the aristocracy.
73. One reviewer felt that the BBC mini-series highlighted 'issues that are still relevant, like being undercut by cheap imports from abroad and people moving their mills abroad', while another posting objected to Gaskell's novel being 'used in a political way to justify certain views [...]. The media stereotype of employers as "evil" has pervaded the adaption'.
74. 'In Its Own Light', p. 93. Kelly considers the BBC's *North and South* in the context of wider debates about adaptation, perspective, and visual allusions.

4   George Eliot's Byronic Heroes I: Early Works and Poetry

1. U. C. Knoepflmacher, 'Unveiling Men: Power and Masculinity in George Eliot's Fiction', in *Men by Women*, ed. by Janet Todd (New York and London: Holmes and Meier, 1981), pp. 130–46 (p. 134). Knoepflmacher's argument about Eliot's 'gender dysfunctions' is less convincing (p. 131).
2. See, for example, John R. Reed, 'Soldier Boy: Forming Masculinity in *Adam Bede*', *Studies in the Novel*, 33:3 (2001), pp. 268–84. Eve Kosofsky Sedgwick regards *Adam Bede* as an exemplar of 'the historicity of women's relations to men's bonds', in *Between Men: English Literature and Male Homosocial Desire* (New York and Chichester: Columbia UP, 1985), p. 135.
3. George Eliot, *Adam Bede*, ed. by Margaret Reynolds (London: Penguin, 2008), p. 197. Subsequent references will be given in the text.
4. William Wordsworth, 'Preface to *Lyrical Ballads, with Pastoral and Other Poems* (1802)', in *William Wordsworth: The Major Works*, ed. by Stephen Gill, rpt

(Oxford: Oxford UP, 2008), pp. 595–615 (p. 597). Subsequent references to the Preface are taken from this edition and will be given in the text. Eliot's relationship with the 'incomparable Wordsworth', as she referred to the poet, was 'always ardent', according to Stephen Gill. Eliot wrote of Wordsworth's poetry: 'I have never before met with so many of my own feelings, expressed just as I could like', and purchased a six-volume set of his works a year later when she was 21. His poetry features more frequently in Eliot's epigraphs and chapter headings than any other author except Shakespeare. See Stephen Gill, 'Wordsworth at Full-Length: George Eliot', in *Wordsworth and the Victorians* (Oxford: Clarendon, 2001), pp. 145–67 (pp. 145, 147).

5. Donald D. Stone, *The Romantic Impulse in Victorian Fiction* (Cambridge, MA and London: Harvard UP, 1980), p. 192.

6. William Wordsworth, *The Prelude: 1799, 1805, 1850*, ed. by Jonathan Wordsworth, M. H. Abrams, and Stephen Gill (New York and London: W. W. Norton & Company, 1979), 1850, Book XII, ll. 208, 248–61. In addition to *The Excursion*, which Eliot read and admired in its entirety on a number of occasions, she 'knew *The Prelude* equally well', re-reading the work up until her death (Gill, *Wordsworth and the Victorians*, p. 146). *The Mill on the Floss* (1860), a novel immersed in a Wordsworthian dialogue over childhood, memory, and place, opens with what could be considered a 'spot of time'. Eliot also borrows from *The Excursion* to highlight the history of St Ogg's as 'a town 'familiar with forgotten years''. See *The Mill on the Floss*, ed. by A. S. Byatt, rpt (London: Penguin, 2003), p. 124. Subsequent references will be given in the text.

7. A comparable reliance on negatives, and a Wordsworthian 'dreariness', feature in Eliot's description of Mr Tulliver in *The Mill of the Floss*:

> The pride and obstinacy of millers and other insignificant people, whom you pass *un*noticingly on the road every day, have their tragedy too, but it is of that *un*wept, hidden sort, that goes on from generation to generation and leaves *no* record – such tragedy, perhaps, as lies in the conflicts of young souls, hungry for joy, under a lot made suddenly hard to them, under the *dreariness* of a home where the morning brings *no* promise with it, and where the *un*expectant *discontent* of worn and *disappointed* parents weighs on the children like a damp, thick air in which all the functions of life are *depressed*; or such tragedy as lies in the slow or sudden *death* that follows on a bruised passion, though it may be a *death* that finds only a parish funeral. (p. 207, added emphasis)

8. Margaret Homans cautions that 'it is precisely the literalness of Eliot's transposition of Wordsworthian themes – her effort to be a docile student on the model of Wordsworth's implied sister – that constitutes her subversion of them'. See 'Eliot, Wordsworth, and the Scenes of the Sisters' Instruction', in *Bearing the Word: Language and Female Experience in Nineteenth-Century Women's Writing* (Chicago and London: University of Chicago Press, 1986), pp. 120–52 (p. 122). Gill also notes Eliot's 'resistance', as well as her debt, to Wordsworth, bringing her relationship with this writer more in line with the later Romantic poets who will provide the primary focus of this chapter (*Wordsworth and the Victorians*, p. 161).

9. George Eliot, 'The Sad Fortunes of the Reverend Amos Barton', in *Scenes of Clerical Life*, ed. by Thomas A. Noble, rpt (Oxford: Oxford UP, 2009), p. 36 (added emphasis).

10. 'Worldliness and Other-Worldliness: The Poet Young', *Westminster Review* (January 1857), pp. 1–42, in *George Eliot: Selected Essays, Poems and Other Writings*, ed. by A. S. Byatt and Nicholas Warren (London: Penguin, 1990), pp. 164–213 (p. 209).

11. Mario Praz's chapter on George Eliot appears in *The Hero in Eclipse in Victorian Fiction*, trans. by Angus Davidson (London, New York, and Toronto: Oxford UP, 1956), pp. 319–83 (p. 383).

12. George Eliot, *Middlemarch: A Study of Provincial Life*, rpt (Ware: Wordsworth Classics, 1995), p. 688. Subsequent references will be given in the text.

13. George Eliot, 'Thomas Carlyle', *Leader*, 6 (27 October 1855), pp. 1034–5, in *George Eliot: Selected Critical Writings*, ed. by Rosemary Ashton, rpt (Oxford: Oxford UP, 2000), pp. 187–92 (p. 187). Subsequent references in this paragraph are to this edition, p. 188.

14. Thomas Carlyle, letter dated 28 April 1832, cited in *Byron: The Critical Heritage*, ed. by Andrew Rutherford (London: Routledge, 1970), p. 291.

15. See *Romantic Impulse*, pp. 19–27, for Stone's discussion of Carlyle's 'basic Romanticism' (pp. 21, 22). Eliot paid generous tribute to the impact of Carlyle's work: 'For there is hardly a superior or active mind of this generation that has not been modified by Carlyle's writings; there has hardly been an English book written for the last ten or twelve years that would not have been different if Carlyle had not lived' (*Selected Critical Writings*, pp. 187–8). William Deresiewicz considers Carlyle's and Emerson's influence on *Middlemarch* in 'Heroism and Organicism in the Case of Lydgate', *Studies in English Literature*, 38:4 (1998), pp. 723–40. http://lion.chadwyck.co.uk, accessed 14 August 2006.

16. As Gordon S. Haight has argued, 'His [Lydgate's] idea of a wife's function was little better than Casaubon's'. See 'George Eliot's "eminent failure", Will Ladislaw', in *This Particular Web: Essays on Middlemarch*, ed. by Ian Adam (Toronto and Buffalo: University of Toronto Press, 1975), pp. 22–42 (p. 35).

17. For a more detailed account of Ladislaw's reception, see Haight, 'Eliot's "eminent failure" '.

18. George Levine, 'The Hero as Dilettante: *Middlemarch* and *Nostromo*', in *George Eliot: Centenary Essays and an Unpublished Fragment*, ed. by Anne Smith (London: Vision Press, 1980), pp. 152–80 (p. 159). Virginia Woolf, writing in the *Times Literary Supplement* in 1919, regretted that Dorothea could not have been provided with a better mate. Jane Marie Luecke defended Ladislaw's character against his detractors in 'Ladislaw and the *Middlemarch* Vision', *Nineteenth-Century Fiction*, 19:1 (1964), pp. 55–64; and, later, Juliet McMaster confessed to being 'a long-time admirer of the much maligned hero of *Middlemarch*', in 'Will Ladislaw and Other Italians with White Mice', *Victorian Review*, 16:2 (1990), pp. 1–7 (p. 1).

19. The words 'mixed' and 'mixture' are used four times in the Finale, twice to refer to Ladislaw's ancestry (pp. 687–8).

20. George Eliot, 'Janet's Repentance', in *Scenes of Clerical Life*, p. 229. Subsequent references are taken from this edition and refer to p. 229. It is interesting to note that Eliot was reading *Persuasion*, with its emotionally damaged yet

resilient hero, as she began to write 'Janet's Repentance'. Austen remained a continuing and significant influence for Eliot.

21. Letter dated 21 September 1869 (original emphasis). The edition of Eliot's letters referred to is *The George Eliot Letters*, ed. by Gordon S. Haight, 9 vols (London and New Haven: Oxford UP, 1956–78). Subsequent references will be dated in the text.

22. Cited in *Byron: The Critical Heritage*, p. 291 (original emphasis).

23. Stowe sent Eliot a copy ahead of publication in the *Atlantic Monthly*. See Ruby V. Redinger, *George Eliot: The Emergent Self* (London: Bodley Head, 1975), pp. 45–7.

24. The sonnet sequence, 'Brother and Sister', was published in *The Legend of Jubal and Other Poems* (1874). Denise Tischler Millstein argues for a literary conversation between Eliot's poems and Byron's 'Epistle to Augusta':

> The sonnet sequence, which reads like a letter from a cast-off sister to her brother, is a mirror version of Byron's 'Epistle to Augusta', *from* a beloved brother *to* his cast-off sister. It is almost as if the two poems create a whole when read together, with Eliot as the sister of her poem responding to Byron as the brother of his. (original emphasis)

Tischler Millstein, 'George Eliot's *Felix Holt, The Radical* and Byronic Secrets', in *Victorian Secrecy: Economies of Knowledge and Concealment*, ed. by Albert D. Pionke and Denise Tischler Millstein (Farnham, UK and Burlington, VT: Ashgate, 2010), pp. 135–48 (p. 139). Millstein's essay also includes a useful discussion of the Stowe affair and its after-effects on Byron's reputation. The phrase, 'Byron whirlwind', is quoted in 'Byronic Secrets', p. 136. On the same subject, see Caroline Franklin, *Byron and Women Novelists*, The Byron Foundation Lecture (Nottingham: University of Nottingham, 2001), and Susan J. Wolfson, *Romantic Interactions: Social Being & the Turns of Literary Action* (Baltimore, MD: Johns Hopkins UP, 2010).

25. The phrase, 'socially injurious', echoes her initial response to Stowe: 'I think the discussion of such subjects is injurious socially' (10 December 1869). Eliot had already expressed her views on 'The Separation' scandal to Hennell in the letter dated 21 September 1869: 'As to the Byron subject, nothing can outweigh to my mind the heavy social injury of familiarizing young minds with the desecration of family ties. The discussion of the subject in newspapers, periodicals and pamphlets, is simply odious to me, and I think it a pestilence likely to leave very ugly marks. One trembles to think how easily that moral wealth may be lost which it has been the work of ages to produce, in the refinement and differencing of the affectionate relations'.

26. The separation of the fault from the perpetrator is a 'theological commonplace, susceptible of casuistical interpretation', as Stevie Davies notes, identifying a similar instance in Charlotte Brontë's early story, *Captain Henry Hastings*. See Anne Brontë, *The Tenant of Wildfell Hall*, ed. by Stevie Davies (London: Penguin, 1996), pp. 150, 506.

27. A favourite quotation comes from the final scene of *Manfred* when the protagonist proclaims: 'The dead but sceptred sovereigns, who still rule/ Our spirits from their urns' (III. iv. ll. 40–1). Part of these lines are misquoted in 'The Lifted Veil', a point to which I shall return shortly. In *Middlemarch*, the lines relate to

the profound impression made by Dorothea's 'deep-souled womanhood' on Lydgate. The parenthetical question that follows the allusion to Byron's eulogy – '(is there not a genius for feeling nobly which also reigns over human spirits and their conclusions?)' – draws out the pathos of Lydgate's adjustment to his limited horizons (p. 487). It also prefigures the 'incalculably diffusive' effect ascribed to the heroine in the concluding paragraph of the novel (p. 688). This borrowing illustrates Eliot's regard for, and revision of, Byron's poetry, as Dorothea's importance derives not from grand historic acts, but from a poignantly hidden life.

28. The satirical reference is to Coleridge's *Biographia Literaria* (1817), published the year before Byron started writing the first canto of *Don Juan*.

> And Coleridge, too, has lately taken wing,
>   But like a hawk encumber'd with his hood,—
> Explaining metaphysics to the nation—
> I wish he would explain his Explanation. ('Dedication', ii)

Charles Bray, Eliot's close friend, was nicknamed Don Juan, and John Chapman, the publisher with whom Eliot formed an emotional attachment, also attracted comparisons with Byron.

29. See *The Journals of George Eliot*, ed. by Margaret Harris and Judith Johnston (Cambridge: Cambridge UP, 1998), pp. 26, 234; and Gordon S. Haight, *George Eliot: A Biography* (Oxford: Clarendon, 1968), p. 151.

30. Her interest in Scott is comparable with her interest in Wordsworth. Lewes gave Eliot a 48-volume set of Scott's novels following the success of *Adam Bede*. He wrote in the fly-leaf of the first volume that Scott was 'her longest-venerated and best-loved Romanticist'. See Haight, *Biography*, p. 319.

31. Alicia Carroll, 'The Giaour's Campaign: Desire and the Other in *Felix Holt, The Radical*', *Novel: A Forum on Fiction*, 30:2 (1997), pp. 237–58 (pp. 242, 241).

32. Cited in Dorothy Mermin, *Godiva's Ride: Women of Letters in England, 1830–1880* (Bloomington and Indianapolis: Indiana UP, 1993), p. 6. The description of Eliot's letter as 'singularly priggish', quoted in the next paragraph, is Mermin's (p. 13).

33. See Jenny Uglow, *George Eliot* (London: Virago, 1987), pp. 22–3. Eliot writes, 'My imagination is an enemy that must be cast down ere I can enjoy peace or exhibit uniformity of character' (17 September 1840).

34. K. M. Newton, *George Eliot: Romantic Humanist: A Study of the Philosophical Structure of her Novels* (London: Macmillan, 1981), pp. 50, 28. William Hazlitt and Charles Lamb, among others, identified Byron with the circumscribing limitations of egotism.

35. 'Brother Jacob' was published in the *Cornhill Magazine* in July 1864 after the tale – under the Wordsworthian title 'The Idiot Boy' – was rejected by Sampson Low. See *The Lifted Veil and Brother Jacob*, ed. by Helen Small, rpt (Oxford: Oxford UP, 2009), p. xxxix. Subsequent references will be given in the text.

36. Small, intro., *The Lifted Veil and Brother Jacob*, p. xxxii.

37. George Eliot, 'Evangelical Teaching: Dr Cumming', *Westminster Review*, lxiv (October 1855), pp. 436–62, in *Selected Critical Writings*, pp. 138–70 (p. 148).

38. Elizabeth Barrett Browning, *Stanzas on the Death of Lord Byron*, in *Aurora Leigh and Other Poems*, ed. by John Robert Glorney Bolton and Julia Bolton Holloway (London: Penguin, 1995).

39. The terminology is Newton's – see *Romantic Humanist*, pp. 10–11.

40. Sandra M. Gilbert and Susan Gubar discuss the Romantic heritage and Victorian inheritors of the veil image in the chapter 'Made Keen by Loss: George Eliot's Veiled Vision', in *The Madwoman in the Attic: The Woman Writer and the Nineteenth-Century Literary Imagination*, 2nd edn (New Haven and London: Yale UP, 2000), pp. 443–77. Gilbert and Gubar see Eliot as inheriting a female gothic tradition, from Mary Shelley and Charlotte Brontë, and read Latimer as a proxy for Eliot's gendered anxieties over authorship and the plight of the woman artist more generally.

41. William Wordsworth, 'Lines Written a Few Miles above Tintern Abbey, on Revisiting the Banks of the Wye during a Tour, July 13, 1798', l. 31, in *William Wordsworth: The Pedlar, Tintern Abbey and the Two-Part Prelude*, ed. by Jonathan Wordsworth (Cambridge: Cambridge UP, 1985).

42. 'The Two-Part *Prelude* of 1799', I, l. 290.

43. Frederick Burwick, '*The Lifted Veil*: George Eliot's Experiment with First-Person Narrative', in *Women Constructing Men: Female Novelists and Their Male Characters, 1750–2000*, ed. by Sarah S. G. Frantz and Katharina Rennhak (Plymouth: Lexington Books, 2010), pp. 101–18 (p. 105).

44. As Carroll Viera states, 'In Latimer George Eliot provides her fullest exploration of the hypothesis that visionary powers may lead, not to sincerity and sympathy, but to disenchantment and creative impotence'. See ' "The Lifted Veil" and George Eliot's Early Aesthetic', *Studies in English Literature*, 24:4 (1984), pp. 749–67 (p. 753).

45. 'Worldliness and Other-Worldliness', p. 203. The artistic importance that Eliot placed on reflection is depicted, in Romantic terms, in 'Liszt, Wagner, and Weimar', *Fraser's Magazine*, 52 (July 1855), pp. 48–62. See *Selected Critical Writings*, pp. 82–109. Eliot values Liszt's gentleness, as a man, before considering his music.

46. As Anne D. Wallace argues, 'Through a narrator who aspires to be a Wordsworthian poet, a narrative which repeatedly calls attention to the failure of recollection in both life and art, and a structure which mimics the greater Romantic lyric but does not fulfil its expectations, *The Lifted Veil* runs explicitly counter to Wordsworthian poetics'. See Wallace, ' "Vague Capricious Memories": *The Lifted Veil*'s Challenge to Wordsworthian Poetics', *George Eliot - George Henry Lewes Newsletter*, 18–19 (1991), pp. 31–45 (p. 31).

47. Of Eliot's familiarity with German Romanticism, Newton writes:

> There is ample evidence in George Eliot's letters and essays that she was well read in Romantic writing in English but what perhaps separates her from many of her contemporaries is that her knowledge of European Romantic writing was also extensive. The fact that she accompanied G. H. Lewes to Germany while he was researching his biography of Goethe was a particularly significant experience as this gave her first-hand contact with a German intellectual life that had its roots in Romanticism.

> See K. M. Newton, 'Romanticism', in *Oxford Reader's Companion to George Eliot*, ed. by John Rignall (Oxford: Oxford UP, 2000), pp. 336–9 (p. 337).

48. See Keats's letter to George and Georgiana Keats, dated 14 February–3 May 1819, in *Letters of John Keats*, ed. by Robert Gittings, rpt (Oxford: Oxford UP, 1992). Subsequent references are taken from this edition and will be dated in the text.

49. John Keats, *Lamia*, II. l. 237, in *John Keats: The Complete Poems*, ed. by John Barnard, 3rd edn (London: Penguin, 1988).

50. For further background on *Poetry and Prose from the Notebook of an Eccentric*, see *Essays of George Eliot*, ed. by Thomas Pinney (London: Routledge and Kegan Paul, 1963), pp. 13–14. References are taken from the version of *Poetry and Prose* in this edition and relevant page numbers will be given in the text.

51. Percy Bysshe Shelley, 'On the Medusa of Leonardo da Vinci in the Florentine Gallery', ll. 8, 36, in *The Selected Poetry and Prose of Shelley* (Ware: Wordsworth Editions, 1994).

52. Uglow, *George Eliot*, p. 119. Burwick comments on Latimer's 'compromised masculinity', and states that 'A major constituent of Eliot's construction of Latimer, then, is Latimer's construction of Bertha', in 'Eliot's Experiment', p. 110.

53. Hallam Tennyson, cited in *Tennyson: A Selected Edition*, ed. by Christopher Ricks (Berkeley and Los Angeles: University of California Press, 1989), p. 515.

54. See 'Tennyson's *Maud*', *Westminster Review*, 64 (1855), pp. 596–601, in *Selected Critical Writings*, pp. 171–9 (p. 173). Eliot is at pains to stress that, despite her objections to *Maud*, she considers Tennyson to be 'a poet for all ages' (p. 171).

55. Cited in *Tennyson: A Selected Edition*, p. 514.

56. Keats uses the term 'speculation' in his letter of 27 October 1818, discussed in the main text. Keats explains how he is invariably 'speculating on creations of my own brain'.

57. See James M. Decker, 'Interpreting Latimer: Wordsworthian Martyr or Textual Alchemist?', *George Eliot – George Henry Lewes Newsletter*, 20–21 (1992), pp. 58–62.

58. 'Sonnet ("Lift not the painted veil")', ll. 1, 11, 7, in *Percy Bysshe Shelley: The Major Works*, ed. by Zachary Leader and Michael O'Neill, rpt (Oxford: Oxford UP, 2009). I am grateful to Professor Michael O'Neill for his advice on these Shelley poems.

59. Richard Cronin notes the recurring references to Shelley in Eliot's fiction in 'Shelley and the Nineteenth Century', in *The Oxford Handbook of Percy Bysshe Shelley*, ed. by Michael O'Neill and Anthony Howe, with the assistance of Madeleine Callaghan (Oxford: Oxford UP, 2013), pp. 611–26.

60. 'The pale, the cold, and the moony smile', ll. 19, 24, in *The Complete Poetry of Percy Bysshe Shelley*, ed. by Donald H. Reiman, Neil Fraistat, and Nora Crook, 3 vols (Baltimore, MD: John Hopkins UP, 2000-), III.

61. The arrangement of this poem, alongside companion poems from the 'Graveyard Group', in the *Alastor* volume 'change the tone to a more positive view of life', according to Donald H. Reiman and Neil Fraistat (*Complete Poetry of Percy Bysshe Shelley*, II, p. 382).

62. Stone, *Romantic Impulse*, p. 230. *The Spanish Gypsy* was Eliot's first published poem and her most ambitious. Begun in 1864, she struggled with the work in its initial incarnation as a drama and reworked it after a visit to Spain in 1867. Published in 1868, *The Spanish Gypsy* sold well and encouraged Eliot to write the poems that would appear in *The Legend of Jubal and Other Poems* (1874). Wendy S. Williams considers issues of gender, sexual politics, and religion in relation to Eliot's poetry, in *George Eliot, Poetess* (Farnham: Ashgate, 2014).

63. The edition of Eliot's poems referred to is *Collected Poems*, ed. by Lucien Jenkins (London: Skoob Books, 1989), p. 217. Subsequent page references will be given in the text.

64. Byron's *Cain: A Mystery* (1821) underscores Eliot's later poem, 'The Legend of Jubal' (1870). Eliot's eponymous hero, a shepherd who discovers the art of music along with the pains of mortality, leaves the fellowship of his community on a solitary pilgrimage. Martin Bidney argues that the 'work ethic of Eliot/Jubal consorts oddly with the tragic, alienating quest of the Romantic solitary wanderer [...]. "The Legend of Jubal," we must conclude, is an ideologically conflicted work'. Bidney rightly identifies a 'neo-Romantic' strain in the poem, which encompasses Wordsworth, Shelley, and Byron (with the Byronic hero channelled through Tennyson's 'Ulysses'). But what is read as an incongruous intertextual backdrop can be seen as usefully indicative of Eliot's treatment of Romanticism. Jubal may be the hero of the poem, but his brother, Tubal-Cain, emerges as a second protagonist with an equally striking Romantic provenance. The anti-heroes of 'The Legend of Jubal' serve to illustrate an advanced and revisionary Romanticism that pairs Tubal's formidable autonomy and ambition with an energetic industry, and Jubal's vision of inward enlightenment with an 'external soul' (p. 98). See Bidney, '"The Legend of Jubal" as Romanticism Refashioned: Struggles of a Spirit in George Eliot's Musical Midrash', *George Eliot – George Henry Lewes Studies*, 52–53 (2007), pp. 28–59 (pp. 29, 28).
65. William Blake, 'The Clod & the Pebble', l. 12. *Songs of Innocence and of Experience*, ed. by Andrew Lincoln, Blake's Illuminated Books (Princeton, NJ: Princeton UP for The William Blake Trust, 1991), II.
66. Eliot reiterates this point in her 'Notes on *The Spanish Gypsy* and Tragedy in General': 'Silva presents the tragedy of entire rebellion'. See *George Eliot's Life as Related in her Letters and Journals*, ed. by J. W. Cross, 3 vols (Edinburgh and London: Blackwood and Sons, 1885), III, pp. 41–9 (p. 46).
67. K. M. Newton, 'Byronic Egoism and George Eliot's *The Spanish Gypsy*', *Neophilologus*, 57 (1973), pp. 388–400 (p. 393).
68. For the theory of a triangulated desire in literature, by which the relationship between two men is forged through a woman, see Sedgwick, *Between Men: English Literature and Male Homosocial Desire*.
69. 'The Rime of the Ancient Mariner', ll. 3, 587, in *The Collected Works of Samuel Taylor Coleridge, Volume 16: Poetical Works I: Poems (Reading Text)*, ed. by J. C. C. Mays (Princeton, NJ: Princeton UP, 2001).
70. Quotations are taken from the heroine's polemic speech on the necessity of art to affect social change in *Aurora Leigh*. Elizabeth Barrett Browning, *Aurora Leigh and Other Poems*, ed. by John Robert Glorney Bolton and Julia Bolton Holloway (London: Penguin, 1995), Book II, ll. 479, 480, 483–4, 477–78.
71. Susan J. Wolfson's phrase for Felicia Hemans's absorption of the Byronic into a poetics of domestic affection is taken from 'Hemans and the Romance of Byron', in *Felicia Hemans: Reimagining Poetry in the Nineteenth Century*, ed. by Nanora Sweet, Julie Melnyk, and Marlon B. Ross (Houndmills: Palgrave, 2001), pp. 155–80 (p. 163).
72. Atara Stein compares the figure of the Byronic heroine in Victorian fiction with contemporary Byronic heroines on film in Chapter 5 of *The Byronic Hero in Film, Fiction, and Television* (Carbondale, IL: Southern Illinois UP, 2004).
73. Richard Lansdown traces the genesis of the Byronic heroine from Dickens's Edith Dombey and Lady Dedlock to Eliot's Mrs Transome and Gwendolen

Harleth. Lansdown sees *The Corsair*'s Gulnare as an important precursor to these Victorian heroines; *Don Juan*'s Lady Adeline Amundeville also 'anticipates a great deal in Victorian fiction'. Richard Lansdown, 'The Byronic Hero and the Victorian Heroine', *Critical Review*, 41 (2001), pp. 105–16 (p. 107).

74. For a discussion of Armgart as a strong female hero, see Susan Brown, 'Determined Heroines: George Eliot, Augusta Webster, and Closet Drama by Victorian Women', *Victorian Poetry*, 33:1 (1995), pp. 89–109. Grace Kehler is concerned with the wider context of *Armgart*, reading the dramatic poem as an 'inquiry into and lament for lost or suppressed voices' in the history of music. See Kehler, '*Armgart*'s Voice Problems', *Victorian Literature and Culture*, 34 (2006), pp. 147–66 (p. 148). See, also, Rebecca A. Pope, 'The Diva Doesn't Die: George Eliot's *Armgart*', *Criticism*, 32:4 (1990), pp. 469–83.

75. Charlotte Brontë, *Villette*, ed. by Margaret Smith and Herbert Rosengarten, rpt (Oxford: Oxford UP, 1991), p. 322. Subsequent references will be given in the text. Eliot admired Brontë's novel and, as Louise Hudd details, she attended a performance by Rachel. See Hudd, 'The Politics of a Feminist Poetics: "Armgart" and George Eliot's Critical Response to *Aurora Leigh*', *Essays and Studies*, 49 (1996), pp. 62–83 (pp. 72–3).

76. As Kehler argues, 'Walpurga, speaking openly after the voice crisis, depicts her prima donna cousin as a solipsistic and masculinised woman who, like the worst of the patriarchy, relies upon "slaves" whose individuality she fails to recognize' ('*Armgart*'s Voice Problems', p. 158).

77. Nancy Henry, *The Cambridge Introduction to George Eliot* (Cambridge: Cambridge UP, 2008), p. 87.

78. Tennyson described his monodrama, *Maud*, as a 'little *Hamlet*'. Cited in *Tennyson: A Selected Edition*, p. 515.

79. For Brown, the 'mental theatre' of Romantic verse dramas contrasts unfavourably with the indeterminacy of *Armgart* ('Determined Heroines', p. 105).

5   George Eliot's Byronic Heroes II: Later Works

1. Edward Dramin, ' "A New Unfolding of Life": Romanticism in the Late Novels of George Eliot', *Victorian Literature and Culture*, 26:2 (1998), pp. 273–302 (p. 274).

2. George Eliot, *Felix Holt: The Radical*, ed. by Lynda Mugglestone (London: Penguin, 1995), p. 69. Subsequent references will be given in the text.

3. Barbara Hardy, *The Novels of George Eliot: A Study in Form* (London: Athlone Press, 1963), p. 49. 'The urgency of the critique of Romanticism in Eliot's fiction is, of course, testament to the overwhelming influence on her of its literature', as Caroline Franklin argues in the 'Postscript' of *The Female Romantics: Nineteenth-Century Women Novelists and Byronism* (New York and Abingdon: Routledge, 2013), p. 181.

4. Deborah Lutz, 'The Pirate Poet in the Nineteenth Century', in *Pirates and Mutineers of the Nineteenth Century: Swashbucklers and Swindlers*, ed. by Grace Moore (Farnham: Ashgate, 2011), pp. 23–39 (p. 31).

5. Denise Tischler Millstein, 'George Eliot's *Felix Holt, The Radical* and Byronic Secrets', in *Victorian Secrecy: Economies of Knowledge and Concealment*, ed. by Albert D. Pionke and Denise Tischler Millstein (Farnham, UK and Burlington, VT: Ashgate, 2010), pp. 135–48 (p. 139).

6. Parallels can also be drawn between Byron's poem of thwarted love, marriage, and madness, and Emily Brontë's novel, *Wuthering Heights* (1847).
7. For Tischler Millstein, Byron's presence in *Felix Holt* is associated with temptation and sexuality. The poet functions not only as a 'cultural touchstone', but as a secret code for 'excessive political and sexual liberty' ('Byronic Secrets', pp. 135, 148). Alicia Carroll similarly argues that 'sexual desire and sexual repugnance are clearly at issue in the flare-up over Byron' in Chapter 5 of Eliot's novel. See Carroll, 'The Giaour's Campaign: Desire and the Other in *Felix Holt, The Radical*', *Novel: A Forum on Fiction*, 30:2 (1997), pp. 237–58 (p. 247).
8. Donald D. Stone, *The Romantic Impulse in Victorian Fiction* (Cambridge, MA and London: Harvard UP, 1980), p. 226.
9. Mrs Steene's assumption that the aptly named trickster, Mr Faux, is a corsair is also presented as a result of her misdirected reading in the early work, 'Brother Jacob', discussed in Chapter 4.
10. Eliot's debt to Byron in *Felix Holt* comes via an earlier Victorian novel, Charles Dickens's *Bleak House* (1852–53), according to Richard Lansdown. The atmosphere of Transome Court, with its heavy stagnation, resembles that of Chesney Wold. Mrs Transome, with her hidden secret and despairing fate, resembles the 'remarkably Byronic' Lady Dedlock. Lansdown traces the figure of Lady Dedlock back to both the hero of *The Corsair* and the spurned, transgressive heroine, Gulnare. See Richard Lansdown, 'The Byronic Hero and the Victorian Heroine', *Critical Review*, 41 (2001), pp. 105–16 (p. 111).

    The 'sleepy hum' and 'soft monotony' (p. 13) of Transome Court are also mirrored in Molly Gibson's experiences at Hamley Hall in Gaskell's *Wives and Daughters*. The description of her surroundings, induced by Osborne's romantic poems in the aptly titled chapter 'Drifting into Danger', is noticeably similar to the following description of the grounds at Transome Court, with both passages relying on pathetic fallacy:

    > All round, both near and far, there were grand trees, motionless in the still sunshine, and, like all large motionless things, seeming to add to the stillness. Here and there a leaf fluttered down; petals fell in a silent shower; a heavy moth floated by, and, when it settled, seemed to fall wearily ...

11. On the sexual politics of effeminacy in Byron's play, see Susan J. Wolfson, ' "A Problem Few Dare Imitate": *Sardanapalus* and "Effeminate Character" ', *ELH*, 58:4 (1991), pp. 867–902.
12. In Chapter 10, Felix's call for women to demonstrate more moral fibre for the good of their husbands comes close to Ruskin's views of the 'saintly' sex in his lecture, 'Of Queen's Gardens', which was first published in 1865, while Eliot was writing this novel.
13. Felix's impassioned defence of the common man accords with Wordsworth's Preface to the *Lyrical Ballads*. Wordsworth's presence is foreshadowed in the introduction to the novel not only in the figure of the coachman, who is likened to the Wanderer in *The Excursion*, but through Eliot's vision of a changing England that clings, somewhat nostalgically, to personal memory as a valuable record of human history.
14. Letter to John Blackwood, dated 4 October 1872. The edition of Eliot's letters referred to is *The George Eliot Letters*, ed. by Gordon S. Haight, 9 vols (London

and New Haven: Oxford UP, 1956–78). Subsequent references will be dated in the text.

15. Ruby V. Redinger, *George Eliot: The Emergent Self* (London: Bodley Head, 1975), p. 474.

16. George Eliot, *Daniel Deronda*, ed. by Terence Cave (London: Penguin, 1995), p. 12. Gwendolen is described as having 'a sort of Lamia beauty'. Subsequent references will be given in the text.

17. Timothy Pace, 'Who Killed Gwendolen Harleth? *Daniel Deronda* and Keats's "Lamia" ', *Journal of English and Germanic Philology*, 87:1 (1988), pp. 35–48 (p. 35). Subsequent quotations from this article, 'religion of humanity' and 'two-sidedness', are taken from pp. 40, 39.

18. George Eliot, *The Lifted Veil and Brother Jacob*, ed. by Helen Small, rpt (Oxford: Oxford UP, 2009), p. 12.

19. *Lamia*, II. l. 157, in *John Keats: The Complete Poems*, ed. by John Barnard, 3rd edn (London: Penguin, 1988). Subsequent references will be given in the text.

20. Jane Austen, *Sense and Sensibility*, ed. by Ros Ballaster (London: Penguin Classics, 1995), p. 321. The quotation, 'the hero of a favourite story', is taken from this edition, p. 38.

21. Marysa Demoor, 'Male Monsters or Monstrous Males in Victorian Women's Fiction', in *Exhibited by Candlelight: Sources and Developments in the Gothic Tradition*, ed. by Valeria Tinkler-Villani, Peter Davidson, and Jane Stevenson (Amsterdam and Atlanta, GA: Rodopi, 1995), pp. 173–82 (p. 178).

22. Dramin elaborates on this allusion to Byron's play, *Sardanapalus* (1821), in 'Romanticism in the Late Novels', p. 297. Eliot's heroine, Mirah, recalls Byron's heroine, Myrrha, in her noble self-abnegation and ability to salve the hero's conscience.

23. William Wordsworth, 'Lines Written a Few Miles above Tintern Abbey, on Revisiting the Banks of the Wye during a Tour, July 13, 1798', l. 17, in *William Wordsworth: The Pedlar, Tintern Abbey and the Two-Part Prelude*, ed. by Jonathan Wordsworth (Cambridge: Cambridge UP, 1985). Subsequent references will be given in the text. Shifra Hochberg sees Wordsworth as a literary presence in Deronda's development, in his relationship with women, and in the 'Jewish' sections of the novel. See Hochberg, '*Daniel Deronda* and Wordsworth's *The White Doe of Rylstone*', *English Language Notes*, 31:3 (1994), pp. 43–53.

24. Eliot almost used some lines from 'The Rime of the Ancient Mariner' as an epigraph for Chapter 54 before they were replaced with lines from Shelley's *The Cenci* (see p. 842). Hochberg argues that Eliot's interest in Coleridge has been overshadowed by the study of Wordsworth's influence on her work. When, in *Middlemarch*, Dorothea gazes out of her blue room at Lowick on to a vista of lime trees, Coleridge's 'conversation' poem, 'This Lime-Tree Bower My Prison', comes to mind. The allusion speaks to the confinements of her marriage to Casaubon and also reflects a shift from interior insight to an outwardly focused consciousness. This borrowing demonstrates, as Hochberg argues, that 'Eliot's engagement with the Romantic legacy is far more subtle than has yet been recognized'. See Shifra Hochberg, 'The Vista from Dorothea's Boudoir Window and a Coleridgian Source', *English Language Notes*, 29:3 (1992), pp. 41–6 (p. 45).

25. K. M. Newton, 'Byron', in *Oxford Reader's Companion to George Eliot*, ed. by John Rignall (Oxford: Oxford UP, 2000), p. 44.

26. George Eliot, *Middlemarch: A Study of Provincial Life*, rpt (Ware: Wordsworth Classics, 1995), p. 176. Subsequent references refer to this edition, unless otherwise stated, and will be given in the text.
27. Herr Klesmer, with his fiery passions and formidable presence, bears more than a passing resemblance to Monsieur Paul in Charlotte Brontë's novel *Villette* (1853).
28. Matthew Arnold, 'Byron', from *Essays in Criticism: Second Series 1888*, in *Matthew Arnold: Selected Prose*, ed. by P. J. Keating (Harmondsworth: Penguin, 1970), pp. 385–404 (p. 404). Subsequent references will be given in the text.
29. This sympathetic regard for Byron is reminiscent of a letter, dated 20 February 1874, in which Eliot writes: 'There is a certain set who are titillated by the worst and indifferent to the best. I think this fashion is a disgrace. It is something like the uncovering of the dead Byron's club foot'.
30. Tischler Millstein discusses Byron's presence in Eliot's final novel, noting the similarities between Sir Hugo's Abbey and Byron's ancestral home, for instance. She focuses, specifically, on Byron's *Hebrew Melodies*, a collection of lyrics published in 1815 and set to music by the Jewish composer Isaac Nathan. See Tischler Millstein, 'Lord Byron and George Eliot: Embracing National Identity in *Daniel Deronda*', *Forum: University of Edinburgh Postgraduate Journal of Culture & the Arts*, 1 (Autumn 2005), http://www.forumjournal.org/site/issue/01/denise-tischler-millstein, accessed 20 July 2012.
31. Jenny Uglow, *George Eliot* (London: Virago, 1987), p. 234.
32. 'Notes on *The Spanish Gypsy* and Tragedy in General', in *George Eliot's Life as Related in her Letters and Journals*, ed. by J. W. Cross, 3 vols (Edinburgh and London: Blackwood and Sons, 1885), III, pp. 41–9 (p. 47, added emphasis).
33. For Newton, Eliot's final novel offers some form of 'Romantic resolution'. See K. M. Newton, *George Eliot: Romantic Humanist: A Study of the Philosophical Structure of her Novels* (London: Macmillan, 1981), p. 200.
34. Amy Meyrick says to Mirah, 'you always take what is beautiful as if it were true' (p. 466).
35. Cave, intro., *Daniel Deronda*, p. xxviii.
36. Carroll Viera, ' "The Lifted Veil" and George Eliot's Early Aesthetic', *Studies in English Literature*, 24:4 (1984), pp. 749–67 (p. 765).
37. *Middlemarch*, directed by Anthony Page, screenplay by Andrew Davies (BBC, 1994). On the success of this screen version in the UK and the US, see George V. Griffith, 'George Eliot on the American Screen', in *Nineteenth-Century Women at the Movies: Adapting Classic Women's Fiction to Film*, ed. by Barbara Tepa Lupack (Bowling Green, OH: Bowling Green State University Popular Press, 1999), pp. 299–318.
38. John Lyttle, 'All Dressed up for the Movies', *The Independent*, 26 August 1996, p. 2.
39. Having exhausted the more sensational literature they have been reading, Miss Debarry and Miss Selina in *Felix Holt* are 'thrown back on the last great prose work of Mr Southey' (p. 98), which could be the three-volume history that Brooke refers to here. Brooke's choice shows some discernment – it is not an indicator of a shallow mind – yet his allusion is misplaced and contributes to the complex context that Eliot creates for the reading of the Romantics in *Middlemarch*.
40. George Henry Lewes wrote in the fly-leaf of a 48-volume set of Scott's works, given to Eliot as a gift, that he was 'her longest-venerated and best-loved

Romanticist'. See Gordon S. Haight, *George Eliot: A Biography* (Oxford: Clarendon, 1968), p. 319.

41. Barbara Hardy, '*Middlemarch* and the Passions', in *This Particular Web: Essays on Middlemarch*, ed. by Ian Adam (Toronto and Buffalo: University of Toronto Press, 1975), pp. 3–21 (p. 13).

42. Letter to John Taylor, dated 27 February 1818. The edition referred to is *Letters of John Keats*, ed. by Robert Gittings, rpt (Oxford: Oxford UP, 1992), p. 70. Eliot owned and read aloud from a copy of Richard Monckton Milnes's *Life, Letters, and Literary Remains, of John Keats* (1848), which includes the relevant passage from this letter. She also owned a first edition of *Lamia, Isabella, The Eve of St. Agnes, and Other Poems* (1820), which she annotated and underlined. Eliot referred to this 'delightful duodecimo edition of Keats's poems' in a letter dated 6 March 1874. 'Isabella; or, The Pot of Basil' seems to have preoccupied Eliot: she alludes to the poem in a letter dated 27 June 1868; writes a poem, 'How Lisa Loved the King', adapted from Boccaccio's *Decameron* the following year; and makes a further reference to Keats's poem in the Finale of *Middlemarch* when Lydgate envisages his wife as a basil plant 'flourish[ing] wonderfully on a murdered man's brains' (p. 686).

43. See Roland A. Duerksen, 'Shelley in *Middlemarch*', *Keats-Shelley Journal*, 14 (1965), pp. 23–31. This article also appears under the title 'George Henry Lewes and George Eliot', in Duerksen, *Shelleyan Ideas in Victorian Literature* (London and The Hague: Mouton & Co., 1966), pp. 139–49. On the same subject, see Richard Cronin, 'Shelley and the Nineteenth Century', in *The Oxford Handbook of Percy Bysshe Shelley*, ed. by Michael O'Neill and Anthony Howe, with the assistance of Madeleine Callaghan (Oxford: Oxford UP, 2013), pp. 611–26.

44. For Lewes's exalted estimation of Shelley, see his review in the April 1841 issue of the *Westminster Review*. Although his plan to write a biography, 'Life of Percy Bysshe Shelley', did not come to fruition, he assisted William Michael Rossetti with his *Memoir of Shelley*, published in 1886. John A. Huzzard argues for a connection between Eliot's partner and her portrait of Shelley in *Middlemarch*. See Huzzard, 'Will Ladislaw and George Henry Lewes', *George Eliot Fellowship Review*, 9 (1978), pp. 6–10.

45. Later, in Chapter 51, Brooke considers that there is 'a leaven of Shelley' in Ladislaw (p. 412).

46. Eliot praises Shelley's 'poetic metal' in a letter of 17 September 1840. His poem, 'The Cloud', is contrasted favourably, as 'strong soup', against 'the broth of literature'.

47. Ladislaw's vision of the poet rearticulates the following extracts from Shelley's 'A Defence of Poetry':

> Poetry is not like reasoning, a power to be exerted according to the determination of the will. [...] [F]or the mind in creation is as a fading coal which some invisible influence, like an inconstant wind, awakens to transitory brightness: this power arises from within like the colour of a flower which fades and changes as it is developed [...]. [A poet] is more delicately organized than other men, and sensible to pain and pleasure both his own and that of others in a degree unknown to them.

The edition referred to is *Percy Bysshe Shelley: The Major Works*, ed. by Zachary Leader and Michael O'Neill, rpt (Oxford: Oxford UP, 2009), pp. 696–7, pp. 699–700.

48. Margaret Homans, *Bearing the Word: Language and Female Experience in Nineteenth-Century Women's Writing* (Chicago and London: University of Chicago, 1986), p. 122.

49. Nancy Henry, *The Cambridge Introduction to George Eliot* (Cambridge: Cambridge UP, 2008), p. 88.

50. Dorothea informs her uncle that Casaubon does not possess a piano – 'there is only an old harpsichord at Lowick, and it is covered with books' (p. 53) – which suggests the stifling of her soul.

51. Eliot 'described her proud misanthrope as resembling the newly fashionable Percy Bysshe Shelley, when Ladislaw was really one of the nineteenth century's many Byronic heroes', argues Frances Wilson. See 'Introduction: Byron, Byronism and Byromaniacs', in *Byromania: Portraits of the Artist in Nineteenth- and Twentieth-Century Culture*, ed. by Frances Wilson (Basingstoke: Macmillan, 1999), pp. 1–23 (p. 2).

52. Cited in *Byron: The Critical Heritage*, ed. by Andrew Rutherford (London: Routledge, 1970), p. 368. John Clare noted the sympathy of the working classes for Byron when watching his funeral procession move along Oxford Street in July 1824: 'the common people felt his merits and his power and the common people of a country are the best feelings of a prophecy of futurity'. Cited in Jonathan Bate, *John Clare: A Biography* (London: Picador, 2004), p. 267.

53. Barbara Hardy, 'Possibilities', in *A Century of George Eliot Criticism*, ed. by Gordon S. Haight (Boston, MA: Houghton Mifflin, 1965), pp. 325–38 (p. 333).

54. See the opening of Chapter 20. Keats and Shelley were on Eliot's mind when she visited Rome with Lewes in April 1860. She visited the poets' graves in the Protestant Cemetery, mentioning 'Poor Keats's tombstone, with that despairing bitter inscription' in a letter dated 4 April 1860.

55. Ladislaw's youth is stressed when he first appears in the novel:

> 'Who is that *youngster*, Casaubon?'
> They had come very near when Mr Casaubon answered –
> 'That is a *young* relative of mine, a second cousin: the grandson, in fact,' he added, looking at Dorothea, 'of the lady whose portrait you have been noticing, my aunt Julia.'
> The *younger* man had laid down his sketch-book and risen. His bushy light-brown curls, as well as his *youthfulness*, identified him at once with Celia's apparition.
> 'Dorothea, let me introduce you to my cousin, Mr Ladislaw. Will, this is Miss Brooke.' (p. 64, added emphasis)

Immediately identified as the 'younger' man, Ladislaw's 'sunny brightness' casts further shadows over Casaubon's 'rayless' appearance. Dorothea is 'restore[d to] her former sense of young companionship' in Ladislaw's presence (pp. 174, 297).

The yew, *taxus baccata*, is known as the death tree, as most parts of it are poisonous and it is commonly found in graveyards. But it is also associated with transformation and rebirth, drawing together the dichotomy of Casaubon and Ladislaw as 'Old and Young'.

56. J. Hillis Miller, 'A Conclusion in Which Almost Nothing is Concluded', in *Middlemarch in the Twenty-First* Century, ed. by Karen Chase (Oxford: Oxford UP, 2006), pp. 133–56 (p. 147).

57. Ladislaw's humorous interlude is complicated by an earlier discussion of a sheep-stealer who is to be hanged.

58. Thomas Moore, *The Works of Lord Byron: With his Letters and Journals, and his Life*, 14 vols (London: John Murray, 1832), VI, p. 253.

59. Ian MacKillop and Alison Platt, ' "Beholding in a magic panorama": Television and the Illustration of *Middlemarch*', in *The Classic Novel: From Page to Screen*, ed. by Robert Giddings and Erica Sheen (Manchester: Manchester UP, 2000), pp. 71–92 (p. 82). Trevor Nunn cast Rufus Sewell as Septimus Hodge, a friend of Byron's, in Tom Stoppard's play *Arcadia* at the Royal National Theatre in 1993 because 'he looked so Byronic'. After playing Septimus with a 'Byronic swagger' and Ladislaw as a 'brooding intellectual', Sewell appeared as Seth Starkadder in the 1995 BBC adaptation of Stella Gibbons's romantic comedy, *Cold Comfort Farm*. A year later, in 1996, *Elle* magazine ran a short feature, 'Byronic Man – Rufus Sewell', and *Time Out New York* titled an interview with the actor, 'The Byronic Man', after Sewell played Giles Winterborne in the 1997 film of Thomas Hardy's *The Woodlanders*. See Shane Watson, 'A New Romantic', *Vogue*, June 1993; Jasper Rees, 'Return of the Chameleon', *The Telegraph*, 5 June 2006; 'Rufus Sewell', *Elle*, June 1996; and Eve Claxton, 'The Byronic Man', *Time Out New York*, 5–12 March 1998.

60. Bernard O'Keefe, 'The "Soaping" of *Middlemarch*', *English Review*, 5:2 (1994), pp. 7–12 (p. 11); Anne D. Wallace, contribution to '*Middlemarch* on TV – A Symposium', *George Eliot – George Henry Lewes Studies*, 26–7 (September 1994), pp. 36–81 (pp. 65–6).

61. Eliot specifies that both Will Ladislaw and Felix Holt have grey eyes, the same colour as Byron's in Thomas Moore's description of the poet. See Moore, *Works of Lord Byron*, VI, p. 253.

62. Arnold, 'Byron', p. 401; Carlyle is cited in *Byron: The Critical Heritage*, p. 291.

63. William Blake, 'London', l. 8. *Songs of Innocence and of Experience*, ed. by Andrew Lincoln, Blake's Illuminated Books (Princeton, NJ: Princeton UP for The William Blake Trust, 1991), II.

64. George Eliot, 'Evangelical Teaching: Dr Cumming', *Westminster Review*, lxiv (October 1855), pp. 436–62, in *George Eliot: Selected Critical Writings*, ed. by Rosemary Ashton, rpt (Oxford: Oxford UP, 2000), pp. 138–70 (p. 148).

65. O'Keefe argues, in ' "Soaping" of *Middlemarch*', that 'Although the television camera can use visual juxtaposition to ironic effect it still cannot render an ironic tone' (p. 9).

66. David Gervais states that as a 'classic' BBC adaptation with a budget of over £6m, *Middlemarch* was transformed into 'a seamless patchwork of beautifully finished images'. See Gervais, 'Televising *Middlemarch*', *English*, 43 (1994), pp. 59–64 (p. 59). Ian MacKillop similarly comments on 'the tyranny of the visual' in a 'production [that] is like a grand Folio Society edition'. See MacKillop, 'The BBC *Middlemarch*', *George Eliot Review*, 25 (1994), pp. 73–5 (pp. 75, 73).

67. 'There is a strong and deliberate suggestion of the possible lives her characters might have lived', as Barbara Hardy states ('Possibilities', p. 326).

68. Cited in Gordon S. Haight, 'George Eliot's "eminent failure", Will Ladislaw', in *This Particular Web: Essays on Middlemarch*, ed. by Ian Adam (Toronto and Buffalo: University of Toronto Press, 1975), pp. 22–42 (p. 40).

69. On the issue of Dorothea's and George Eliot's displacement in this screen version, see, for example, Kiku Adatto, 'Missing the Glory: *Middlemarch* by George Eliot', *Commonweal*, 121 (July 1994), pp. 21–3. A number of contributors to the 'Middlemarch on TV' symposium expressed dissatisfaction with the blunted narrative voice. See '*Middlemarch* on TV – A Symposium', *George Eliot – George Henry Lewes Studies*, 26–7 (September 1994).

70. *The Giaour*, l. 812. Mr Keck, the editor of the Tory *Trumpet*, disparagingly refers to Ladislaw as an 'energumen' (p. 381), a term for a fanatic or enthusiast that is associated here with the French Revolution. The following exchange between Brooke and Sir James Chettam about Ladislaw illustrates the divergent responses to reform within the same social class:

> 'With his talent for speaking and drawing up documents, there are few men who could come up to him as an agitator – an agitator, you know.'
> 'Agitator!' said Sir James, with bitter emphasis, feeling that the syllables of this word properly repeated were a sufficient exposure of its hatefulness. (pp. 400–1)

71. William Wordsworth, 'Preface to *Lyrical Ballads, with Pastoral and Other Poems* (1802)', in *William Wordsworth: The Major Works*, ed. by Stephen Gill, rpt (Oxford: Oxford UP, 2008), pp. 595–615 (pp. 598, 611).

72. Lee R. Edwards, 'Women, Energy, and *Middlemarch*', in George Eliot, *Middlemarch*, ed. by Bert G. Hornback, Norton Critical Edition, 2nd edn (New York and London: Norton, 2000), pp. 623–30 (p. 628).

73. Cited in *Byron: The Critical Heritage*, p. 13.

Bibliography

Accardo, Peter X., 'Byron in America to 1830', *Harvard Library Bulletin*, 9:2 (1998), pp. 5–60.

Adatto, Kiku, 'Missing the Glory: *Middlemarch* by George Eliot', *Commonweal*, 121 (July 1994), pp. 21–3.

Ailwood, Sarah, ' "Too much in the common Novel style": Reforming Masculinities in Jane Austen's *Sense and Sensibility*', in *Women Constructing Men: Female Novelists and Their Male Characters, 1750–2000*, ed. by Sarah S. G. Frantz and Katharina Rennhak (Plymouth: Lexington Books, 2010), pp. 67–82.

Alexander, Christine, ed., *An Edition of the Early Works of Charlotte Brontë*, 3 vols (Oxford: Basil Blackwell, 1991), II.

—— *The Early Writings of Charlotte Brontë* (Oxford: Basil Blackwell, 1983).

—— and Jane Sellars, eds., *The Art of the Brontës* (Cambridge: Cambridge UP, 1995).

Arnold, Matthew, 'Byron', in *Essays in Criticism: Second Series 1888*, in *Matthew Arnold: Selected Prose*, ed. by P. J. Keating (Harmondsworth: Penguin, 1970), pp. 385–404.

—— *Poetical Works*, ed. by C. B. Tinker and H. F. Lowry, rpt (London: Oxford UP, 1969).

Ashton, Rosemary, *George Eliot: A Life* (London: Penguin, 1997).

Auden, W. H., *The English Auden: Poems, Essays and Dramatic Writings, 1927–1939*, ed. by Edward Mendelson, rpt (London: Faber and Faber, 1989).

Auerbach, Nina, 'Jane Austen and Romantic Imprisonment', in *Jane Austen in a Social Context*, ed. by David Monaghan (London: Macmillan, 1981), pp. 9–27.

—— 'O Brave New World: Evolution and Revolution in *Persuasion*', *ELH*, 39:1 (1972), pp. 112–28.

—— 'This Changeful Life: Emily Brontë's Anti-Romance', in *Shakespeare's Sisters: Feminist Essays on Women Poets*, ed. by Sandra M. Gilbert and Susan Gubar (Bloomington and London: Indiana UP, 1979), pp. 48–64.

Austen, Jane, *Emma*, ed. by Ronald Blythe, rpt (London: Penguin, 1985).

—— *Juvenilia*, ed. by Peter Sabor (Cambridge: Cambridge UP, 2006).

—— *Northanger Abbey and Other Works*, ed. by James Kinsley and John Davie, intro. by Claudia L. Johnson (Oxford: Oxford UP, 2003).

—— *Persuasion*, ed. by Gillian Beer (London: Penguin, 1998).

—— *Persuasion*, ed. by Janet Todd and Antje Blank (Cambridge: Cambridge UP, 2006).

—— *Pride and Prejudice* (Ware: Wordsworth Classics, 1992).

—— *Sense and Sensibility*, ed. by Ros Ballaster (London: Penguin Classics, 1995).

Bachinger, Katrina, ed., *Byronic Negotiations* (Frankfurt am Main: Peter Lang, 2002).

Baird, John D., Review of Kirstin Olsen's *All Things Austen: An Encyclopedia of Austen's World*, *TLS*, 16 September 2005.

Baldridge, Cates, *The Dialogics of Dissent in the English Novel* (Hanover and London: University Press of New England, 1994).

Barchas, Janine, 'Mrs Gaskell's *North and South*: Austen's Early Legacy', *Persuasions*, 30 (2008), pp. 53–66.

Barnard, John, ed., *John Keats: The Complete Poems*, 3rd edn (London: Penguin, 1988).

Barnes Stevenson, Catherine, 'Romance and the Self-Made Man: Gaskell Rewrites Brontë', *Victorian Newsletter*, 91 (Spring 1997), pp. 10–16.

Barrett Browning, Elizabeth, *Aurora Leigh and Other Poems*, ed. by John Robert Glorney Bolton and Julia Bolton Holloway (London: Penguin, 1995).

Barry, Elizabeth, 'Jane Austen and Lord Byron: Connections', *Persuasions*, 8 (1986), pp. 39–41.

Barton, Anne, 'Byron: The Poetry of It All', *New York Review of Books*, 19 December 2002, http://www.nybooks.com/articles/archives/2002/dec/19/byron-the-poetry-of-it-all/, accessed 27 August 2014.

Bate, Jonathan, *John Clare: A Biography* (London: Picador, 2004).

Beard, Margot, ' "Visions of Romance – Anxieties of Common Life" – Jane Austen's Gothic Novel: A Reading of *Northanger Abbey*', *English Academy Review*, 15 (1998), pp. 130–8.

Beaty, Jerome, 'The Forgotten Past of Will Ladislaw', *Nineteenth-Century Fiction*, 13:2 (1958), pp. 159–63.

Becoming Jane, directed by Julian Jarrold, screenplay by Kevin Hood and Sarah Williams (HanWay Films and UK Film Council, 2007).

Belton, Ellen, 'Reimagining Jane Austen: The 1940 and 1995 Film Versions of *Pride and Prejudice*', in *Jane Austen on Screen*, ed. by Gina Macdonald and Andrew Macdonald (Cambridge: Cambridge UP, 2003), pp. 175–96.

Bennett, Betty T., ed., *The Letters of Mary Wollstonecraft Shelley*, 3 vols (Baltimore, MD: Johns Hopkins UP, 1980–88).

Bhattacharji, Shobhana, 'The Gloom and Cheerfulness of Childe Harold and Elizabeth Bennet', in *Byron: Heritage and Legacy*, ed. by Cheryl A. Wilson (New York and Basingstoke: Palgrave, 2008), pp. 151–63.

Bidney, Martin, '"The Legend of Jubal" as Romanticism Refashioned: Struggles of a Spirit in George Eliot's Musical Midrash', *George Eliot – George Henry Lewes Studies*, 52–53 (2007), pp. 28–59.

Blake, William, *Songs of Innocence and of Experience*, ed. by Andrew Lincoln, Blake's Illuminated Books (Princeton, NJ: Princeton UP for The William Blake Trust, 1991), II.

Blessington, Marguerite, Countess of, *Conversations of Lord Byron with the Countess of Blessington* (London: R. Bentley, 1834).

Blum, Virginia L., 'The Return to Repression: Filming the Nineteenth Century', in *Jane Austen and Co.: Remaking the Past in Contemporary Culture*, ed. by Suzanne R. Pucci and James Thompson (Albany, NY: State University of New York Press, 2003), pp. 157–78.

Bodenheimer, Rosemarie, 'North and South: A Permanent State of Change', *Nineteenth-Century Fiction*, 34:3 (1979), pp. 281–301.

Borromeo, Eva Ashberg, 'Maria Edgeworth, Frederika Bremer and Elizabeth Gaskell: Sources for *Wives and Daughters*', *Gaskell Society Journal*, 6 (1992), pp. 73–6.

Bour, Isabelle, 'Locke, Richardson, and Austen: Or, How to Become a Gentleman', *Persuasions*, 30 (2008), pp. 159–69.

Bray, Joe, 'The Source of "Dramatized Consciousness": Richardson, Austen, and Stylistic Influence', *Style*, 35 (Spring 2001), pp. 18–33.

Brewer, William D., ed., *Contemporary Studies on Lord Byron* (Lewiston, NY: Edwin Mellen Press, 2001).

Briggs, Julia, 'Reading People, Reading Texts: "Byron and Mr Briggs" ', in *Reading Virginia Woolf* (Edinburgh: Edinburgh UP, 2006), pp. 63–79.

Briscoe, Joanna, 'A Costume Drama with Muddy Hems', *The Sunday Times*, 31 July 2005.

Brombert, Victor, *In Praise of Antiheroes: Figures and Themes in Modern European Literature, 1830–1980* (Chicago and London: University of Chicago Press, 1999).

Brontë, Anne, *The Tenant of Wildfell Hall*, ed. by Stevie Davies (London: Penguin, 1996).

Brontë, Charlotte, *Jane Eyre* (London: Penguin, 2002).

—— *Villette*, ed. by Margaret Smith and Herbert Rosengarten, rpt (Oxford: Oxford UP, 1991).

Brontë, Emily, *Wuthering Heights*, ed. by David Daiches, rpt (London: Penguin Classics, 1985).

Brown, Helen, 'The Influence of Byron on Emily Brontë', *Modern Language Review*, 34 (1939), pp. 374–81.

Brown, Pearl L., 'From Elizabeth Gaskell's *Mary Barton* to her *North and South*: Progress or Decline for Women?', *Victorian Literature and Culture* (2000), pp. 345–58.

Brown, Susan, 'Determined Heroines: George Eliot, Augusta Webster, and Closet Drama by Victorian Women', *Victorian Poetry*, 33:1 (1995), pp. 89–109.

Browning, Robert, *Selected Poems*, intro. by Daniel Karlin (London: Penguin, 1989).

Brownstein, Rachel M., 'Endless Imitation: Austen's and Byron's Juvenilia', in *The Child Writer from Austen to Woolf*, ed. by Christine Alexander and Juliet McMaster (Cambridge: Cambridge UP, 2005), pp. 122–37.

—— 'Romanticism, A Romance: Jane Austen and Lord Byron, 1813–1815', *Persuasions*, 16 (1994), pp. 175–84.

Brückmann, Patricia C., ' "Such days as these": Books, Readers, and Libraries in *Persuasion*', in *New Windows on a Woman's World: Essays for Jocelyn Harris*, ed. by Colin Gibson and Lisa Marr, 2 vols (Dunedin, New Zealand: University of Otago, 2005), II, pp. 9–28.

Bruhm, Steven, *Reflecting Narcissus: A Queer Aesthetic* (Minneapolis, MN and London: University of Minnesota Press, 2001).

—— 'Reforming Byron's Narcissism', in *Lessons of Romanticism: A Critical Companion*, ed. by Thomas Pfau and Robert F. Gleckner (Durham, NC and London: Duke UP, 1998), pp. 429–47.

Burke, Edmund, *Reflections on the Revolution in France 1790*, ed. by L. G. Mitchell, rpt (Oxford: Oxford UP, 1999).

Burwick, Frederick, '*The Lifted Veil*: George Eliot's Experiment with First-Person Narrative', in *Women Constructing Men: Female Novelists and Their Male Characters, 1750–2000*, ed. by Sarah S. G. Frantz and Katharina Rennhak (Plymouth: Lexington Books, 2010), pp. 101–18.

Butler, Marilyn, *Jane Austen and the War of Ideas* (Oxford: Clarendon, 1975).

—— 'The Uniqueness of Cynthia Kirkpatrick: Elizabeth Gaskell's *Wives and Daughters* and Maria Edgeworth's *Helen*', *Review of English Studies*, 23 (1972), pp. 278–90.

Byron, Lord (George Gordon), *Byron: Poetical Works*, ed. by Frederick Page, rev. edn. John Jump (Oxford: Oxford UP, 1970).

────── *Lord Byron: The Complete Poetical Works*, ed. by Jerome J. McGann, 7 vols (Oxford: Clarendon Press, 1980–93).

────── *Poems 1816*, intro. by Jonathan Wordsworth (Oxford: Woodstock Books, 1990).

Byron, directed by Julian Farino, screenplay by Nick Dear (BBC, 2003).

Callaghan, Madeleine, ' "Stumbling Stanzas": Flawed Heroism and the Struggle with Language in Byron's *Cain*', *Byron Journal*, 38:2 (2010), pp. 125–35.

Campbell, Joseph, *The Hero with a Thousand Faces*, 2nd edn (1949; Princeton, NJ: Princeton UP, 1968).

Cantor, Paul A., 'Mary Shelley and the Taming of the Byronic Hero: "Transformation" and *The Deformed Transformed*', in *The Other Mary Shelley: Beyond Frankenstein*, ed. by Audrey A. Fisch, Anne K. Mellor, and Esther H. Schor (Oxford: Oxford UP, 1993), pp. 89–106.

Cardwell, Richard A., ed., *The Reception of Byron in Europe* (London: Thoemmes Continuum, 2004).

Carlyle, Thomas, *On Heroes, Hero-Worship, and the Heroic in History* (London and Glasgow: Collins' Clear-Type Press, no date).

────── *Sartor Resartus*, ed. by Kerry McSweeney and Peter Sabor (Oxford: Oxford UP, 2008).

Carroll, Alicia, 'The Giaour's Campaign: Desire and the Other in *Felix Holt, The Radical*', *Novel: A Forum on Fiction*, 30:2 (1997), pp. 237–58.

Casaliggi, Carmen, and Paul March-Russell, eds., *Legacies of Romanticism: Literature, Culture, Aesthetics* (New York and Abingdon: Routledge, 2012).

Chapple, J. A. V., *Elizabeth Gaskell: The Early Years* (Manchester and New York: Manchester UP, 1997).

────── and Arthur Pollard, eds., *The Letters of Mrs Gaskell* (Manchester: Manchester UP, 1966).

Chew, Samuel C., *Byron in England: His Fame and After-Fame* (London: John Murray, 1924).

Choudhury, Serajul Islam, 'Jane Austen's Heroes: Are They Adequate?', *Dacca University Studies*, 10 (1961), pp. 113–34.

Clausson, Nils, 'Romancing Manchester: Class, Gender and the Conflicting Genres of Elizabeth Gaskell's *North and South*', *Gaskell Society Journal*, 21 (2007), pp. 1–20.

Claxton, Eve, 'The Byronic Man', *Time Out New York*, 5–12 March 1998.

Cochran, Peter, ed., *The Gothic Byron* (Newcastle upon Tyne: Cambridge Scholars, 2009).

Cohen, Michèle, ' "Manners" Make the Man: Politeness, Chivalry, and the Construction of Masculinity, 1750–1830', *Journal of British Studies*, 44 (2005), http://lion.chadwyck.co.uk, accessed 28 February 2006.

Coleridge, Samuel Taylor, *The Collected Works of Samuel Taylor Coleridge, Volume 16: Poetical Works I: Poems (Reading Text)*, ed. by J. C. C. Mays (Princeton, NJ: Princeton UP, 2001).

Coren, Victorian, 'Don't Call me Darcy', *Evening Standard*, 9 June 2000.

Costantini, Mariaconcetta, 'The Sexton's Hero', *Gaskell Society Journal*, 2 (1997), pp. 77–85.

Cranford, directed by Simon Curtis, screenplay by Heidi Thomas (BBC, 2007).

Cronin, Richard, 'Shelley and the Nineteenth Century', in *The Oxford Handbook of Percy Bysshe Shelley*, ed. by Michael O'Neill and Anthony Howe, with the assistance of Madeleine Callaghan (Oxford: Oxford UP, 2013), pp. 611–26.

Davies, Andrew, 'Adapting *Wives and Daughters*', *Gaskell Society Newsletter*, 29 (2000), pp. 2–5.

Decker, James M., 'Interpreting Latimer: Wordsworthian Martyr or Textual Alchemist?', *George Eliot – George Henry Lewes Newsletter*, 20–21 (1992), pp. 58–62.

Demoor, Marysa, 'Male Monsters or Monstrous Males in Victorian Women's Fiction', in *Exhibited by Candlelight: Sources and Developments in the Gothic Tradition*, ed. by Valeria Tinkler-Villani, Peter Davidson, and Jane Stevenson (Amsterdam and Atlanta, GA: Rodopi, 1995), pp. 173–82.

Deresiewicz, William, 'Heroism and Organicism in the Case of Lydgate', *Studies in English Literature*, 38:4 (1998), pp. 723–40.

—— *Jane Austen and the Romantic Poets* (New York: Columbia UP, 2004).

Dodd, Valerie A., *George Eliot: An Intellectual Life* (New York: St. Martin's Press, 1990).

Dramin, Edward, ' "A New Unfolding of Life": Romanticism in the Late Novels of George Eliot', *Victorian Literature and Culture*, 26:2 (1998), pp. 273–302.

Duerksen, Roland A., *Shelleyan Ideas in Victorian Literature* (London and The Hague: Mouton & Co., 1966).

——'Shelley in *Middlemarch*', *Keats-Shelley Journal*, 14 (1965), pp. 23–31.

Duguid, Lindsay, 'Pig and Pillow', Review of *Pride and Prejudice*, *TLS*, 23 September 2005.

Dussinger, John A., 'Parents Against Children: General Tilney as Gothic Monster', *Persuasions*, 20 (1998), pp. 165–74.

Easson, Angus, *Elizabeth Gaskell* (London: Routledge and Kegan Paul, 1979).

—— ed., *Elizabeth Gaskell: The Critical Heritage* (London and New York: Routledge, 1991).

Edwards, Lee R., 'Women, Energy, and *Middlemarch*', in George Eliot, *Middlemarch*, ed. by Bert G. Hornback, Norton Critical Edition, 2nd edn (New York and London: Norton, 2000), pp. 623–30.

Elfenbein, Andrew, *Byron and the Victorians* (Cambridge: Cambridge UP, 1995).

—— 'Byronism and the Work of Homosexual Performance in Early Victorian England', *Modern Language Quarterly*, 54:4 (1993), pp. 535–66.

Eliot, George, *Adam Bede*, ed. by Margaret Reynolds (London: Penguin, 2008).

—— *Collected Poems*, ed. by Lucien Jenkins (London: Skoob Books, 1989).

—— *Daniel Deronda*, ed. by Terence Cave (London: Penguin, 1995).

—— *Essays of George Eliot*, ed. by Thomas Pinney (London: Routledge and Kegan Paul, 1963).

—— *Felix Holt: The Radical*, ed. by Lynda Mugglestone (London: Penguin, 1995).

—— *Middlemarch: A Study of Provincial Life*, rpt (Ware: Wordsworth Classics, 1995).

—— 'Notes on *The Spanish Gypsy* and Tragedy in General', in *George Eliot's Life as Related in her Letters and Journals*, ed. by J. W. Cross, 3 vols (Edinburgh and London: Blackwood and Sons, 1885), III, pp. 41–9.

—— *Scenes of Clerical Life*, ed. by Thomas A. Noble, rpt (Oxford: Oxford UP, 2009).

—— *Selected Critical Writings*, ed. by Rosemary Ashton, rpt (Oxford: Oxford UP, 2000).

—— *Selected Essays, Poems, and Other Writings*, ed. by A. S. Byatt and Nicholas Warren (London: Penguin, 1990).

—— *The Lifted Veil and Brother Jacob*, ed. by Helen Small, rpt (Oxford: Oxford UP, 2009).

—— *The Mill on the Floss*, ed. by A. S. Byatt, rpt (London: Penguin, 2003).

Elledge, W. Paul, 'Talented Equivocation: Byron's "Fare Thee Well"', *Keats-Shelley Journal*, 35 (1986), pp. 42–61.

Ellington, H. Elisabeth, ' "A Correct Taste in Landscape": Pemberley as Fetish and Commodity', in *Jane Austen in Hollywood*, ed. by Linda Troost and Sayre Greenfield, 2nd edn (Lexington, KY: University Press of Kentucky, 2001), pp. 90–110.

Evans, Margiad, 'Byron and Emily Brontë: An Essay', *Life and Letters*, 57 (1948), pp. 193–216.

Ewbank, Inga-Stina, *Their Proper Sphere: A Study of the Brontë Sisters as Early-Victorian Female Novelists* (London: Edward Arnold, 1966).

Fischer, Doucet Devin, 'Byron and Austen: Romance and Reality', *Byron Journal*, 21 (1993), pp. 71–9.

Fisher's Drawing Room Scrap-Book (London: Fisher, Son, & Co., 1840).

Ford, Susan Allen, 'How to Read and Why: *Emma*'s Gothic Mirrors', *Persuasions*, 25 (2003), pp. 110–20.

—— 'Learning Romance from Scott and Byron: Jane Austen's Natural Sequel', *Persuasions*, 26 (2004), pp. 72–88.

Foster, Shirley, *Elizabeth Gaskell: A Literary Life* (Basingstoke: Palgrave, 2002).

Franklin, Caroline, *Byron and Women Novelists*, The Byron Foundation Lecture (Nottingham: University of Nottingham, 2001).

—— *Byron's Heroines* (Oxford: Clarendon Press, 1992).

—— *The Female Romantics: Nineteenth-Century Women Novelists and Byronism* (New York and Abingdon: Routledge, 2013).

Frantz, Sarah, 'Jane Austen's Heroes and the Great Masculine Renunciation', *Persuasions*, 25 (2003), pp. 165–75.

Galperin, William, 'Byron, Austen, and the "Revolution" of Irony', *Criticism*, 32:1 (1990), pp. 51–80.

Garrett, Martin, *The Palgrave Literary Dictionary of Byron* (Basingstoke: Palgrave Macmillan, 2010).

Gaskell, Elizabeth, *Cranford*, ed. by Patricia Ingham (London: Penguin, 2005).

—— *Mary Barton*, ed. by Stephen Gill (Harmondsworth: Penguin, 1970).

—— *North and South*, ed. by Angus Easson, rpt (Oxford: Oxford UP, 1982).

—— *The Works of Elizabeth Gaskell*, ed. by Joanne Shattock, 10 vols (London: Pickering & Chatto, 2005–06).

—— *Wives and Daughters*, ed. by Pam Morris (London: Penguin, 1996).

—— *Wives and Daughters*, intro. by Victoria Glendinning, illustrated by Alexy Pendle (London: Folio Society, 2002).

Gay, Penny, '*Sense and Sensibility* in a Postfeminist World: Sisterhood is Still Powerful', in *Jane Austen on Screen*, ed. by Gina Macdonald and Andrew Macdonald (Cambridge: Cambridge UP, 2003), pp. 90–110.

Gerard, Bonnie, 'Victorian Things, Victorian Words: Representation and Redemption in Gaskell's *North and South*', *The Victorian Newsletter*, 92 (Fall 1997), pp. 21–4.

Gérin, Winifred, 'Byron's Influence on the Brontës', *Keats-Shelley Memorial Bulletin*, 17 (1966), pp. 1–19.

Gervais, David, 'Televising *Middlemarch*', *English*, 43 (1994), pp. 59–64.

Gilbert, Sandra M., and Susan Gubar, *The Madwoman in the Attic: The Woman Writer and the Nineteenth-Century Literary Imagination*, 2nd edn (New Haven and London: Yale UP, 2000).

Giles, Paul, 'The Gothic Dialogue in *Pride and Prejudice*', *Text and Context*, 2 (1988), pp. 68–75.

Gill, Stephen, ed., *William Wordsworth: The Major Works*, rpt (Oxford: Oxford UP, 2008).

—— *Wordsworth and the Victorians* (Oxford: Clarendon, 2001).

Gilson, David, *A Bibliography of Jane Austen* (Oxford: Clarendon Press, 1982).

—— 'Jane Austen's Verses', *The Book Collector*, 33 (1984), pp. 25–37.

Gittings, Robert, ed., *Letters of John Keats*, rpt (Oxford: Oxford UP, 1992).

Glock, Waldo S., 'Catherine Morland's Gothic Delusions: A Defense of *Northanger Abbey*', *Rocky Mountain Review of Language and Literature*, 32:1 (1978), pp. 33–46.

Gottlieb, Sidney, '*Persuasion* and Cinematic Approaches to Jane Austen', *Literature/Film Quarterly*, 30 (2002), http://lion.chadwyck.co.uk.

Greenberg, Robert A., 'The Heritage of Will Ladislaw', *Nineteenth-Century Fiction*, 15:4 (1961), pp. 355–8.

Griffith, George V., 'George Eliot on the American Screen', in *Nineteenth-Century Women at the Movies: Adapting Classic Women's Fiction to Film*, ed. by Barbara Tepa Lupack (Bowling Green, OH: Bowling Green State University Popular Press, 1999), pp. 299–318.

Gross, Jonathan David, ' "I have a penchant for black": Race and Orphic Dismemberment in Byron's *The Deformed Transformed* and J. M. Coetzee's *Disgrace*', in *Byron and the Politics of Freedom and Terror*, ed. by Matthew J. A. Green and Piya Pal-Lapinski (Basingstoke: Palgrave, 2011), pp. 167–81.

—— ' "One Half What I Should Say": Byron's Gay Narrator in *Don Juan*', *European Romantic Review*, 9:3 (1998), pp. 323–50.

Gross, Terry, Interview with Colin Firth, *NPR's Fresh Air*, 7 May 2001, http://www.spring.net/karenr/int/fa5701.html, transcript accessed 28 April 2013.

Grundy, Isobel, 'Jane Austen and Literary Traditions', in *The Cambridge Companion to Jane Austen*, ed. by Edward Copeland and Juliet McMaster (Cambridge: Cambridge UP, 1997), pp. 189–210.

Guest, Kristen, 'Dyspeptic Reactions: Thomas Carlyle and the Byronic Temper', in *Nervous Reactions: Victorian Recollections of Romanticism*, ed. by Joel Faflak and Julia M. Wright (Albany, NY: State University of New York Press, 2004), pp. 141–61.

Haight, Gordon S., *George Eliot: A Biography* (Oxford: Clarendon, 1968).

——'George Eliot's "eminent failure", Will Ladislaw', in *This Particular Web: Essays on Middlemarch*, ed. by Ian Adam (Toronto and Buffalo: University of Toronto Press, 1975), pp. 22–42.

—— ed., *The George Eliot Letters*, 9 vols (London and New Haven: Oxford UP, 1956–78).

Hall, Jean, 'The Evolution of the Surface Self: Byron's Poetic Career', *Keats-Shelley Journal*, 36 (1987), pp. 134–57.

Halperin, John, 'Jane Austen's Anti-Romantic Fragment: Some Notes on *Sanditon*', *Tulsa Studies in Women's Literature*, 2 (1983), pp. 183–91.

────── *The Life of Jane Austen* (Baltimore, MD: Johns Hopkins UP, 1984).

Harding, D. W., 'The Character of Literature from Blake to Byron', in *The Pelican Guide to English Literature*, ed. by Boris Ford (London: Penguin, 1982), V, pp. 35–68.

Hardy, Barbara, '*Middlemarch* and the Passions', in *This Particular Web: Essays on Middlemarch*, ed. by Ian Adam (Toronto and Buffalo: University of Toronto Press, 1975), pp. 3–21.

────── 'Possibilities', in *A Century of George Eliot Criticism*, ed. by Gordon S. Haight (Boston, MA: Houghton Mifflin, 1965), pp. 325–38.

────── *The Novels of George Eliot: A Study in Form* (London: Athlone Press, 1963).

Hardy, Thomas, *Tess of the d'Urbervilles: A Pure Woman*, ed. by David Skilton (London: Penguin Classics, 1985).

Harman, Claire, 'Partiality and Prejudice', *TLS*, 1 February 2008.

Harmsel, Henrietta Ten, 'The Villain-Hero in *Pamela* and *Pride and Prejudice*', *College English*, 23 (1961), pp. 104–8.

Harris, Jocelyn, 'Jane Austen and the Burden of the (Male) Past: The Case Reexamined', in *Jane Austen and Discourses of Feminism*, ed. by Devoney Looser (Basingstoke: Macmillan, 1995), pp. 87–100.

Harris, Margaret, 'Taking Bearings: Elizabeth Gaskell's *North and South* Televised', *Sydney Studies in English*, 32 (2006), pp. 65–82.

────── 'Whose *Middlemarch*? The 1994 British Broadcasting Corporation Television Production', *Sydney Studies in English*, 21 (1995), pp. 95–102.

────── and Judith Johnston, eds., *The Journals of George Eliot* (Cambridge: Cambridge UP, 1998).

Harvey, William R., 'Charles Dickens and the Byronic Hero', *Nineteenth-Century Fiction*, 24:3 (1969), pp. 305–16.

Hassler, Donald M., '*Marino Faliero*, the Byronic Hero, and *Don Juan*', *Keats-Shelley Journal*, 14 (1965), pp. 55–64.

Henry, Nancy, *The Cambridge Introduction to George Eliot* (Cambridge: Cambridge UP, 2008).

Hermansson, Casie, 'Neither *Northanger Abbey*: The Reader Presupposes', *Papers on Language and Literature*, 36:4 (2000), http://lion.chadwyck.co.uk, accessed 28 February 2006.

Heyns, Michiel, 'The Steam-Hammer and the Sugar-Tongs: Sexuality and Power in Elizabeth Gaskell's "North and South" ', *English Studies in Africa*, 32 (1989), pp. 79–94.

Hillis Miller, J., 'A Conclusion in Which Almost Nothing is Concluded', in *Middlemarch in the Twenty-First Century*, ed. by Karen Chase (Oxford: Oxford UP, 2006), pp. 133–56.

Hoberg, Tom, 'Her First and Her Last: Austen's *Sense and Sensibility*, *Persuasion*, and Their Screen Adaptations', in *Nineteenth-Century Women at the Movies: Adapting Classic Women's Fiction to Film*, ed. by Barbara Tepa Lupack (Bowling Green, OH: Bowling Green State University Popular Press, 1999), pp. 140–66.

Hochberg, Shifra, '*Daniel Deronda* and Wordsworth's *The White Doe of Rylstone*', *English Language Notes*, 31:3 (1994), pp. 43–53.

────── 'The Vista from Dorothea's Boudoir Window and a Coleridgian Source', *English Language Notes*, 29:3 (1992), pp. 41–6.

Hoeveler, Diane Long, *Gothic Feminism: The Professionalization of Gender from Charlotte Smith to the Brontës* (University Park, PA: Pennsylvania State Press, 1998).

Holquist, Michael, ed., *The Dialogic Imagination: Four Essays by M. M. Bakhtin*, trans. by Caryl Emerson and Michael Holquist (Austin, TX: University of Texas Press, 1981).

Homans, Margaret, *Bearing the Word: Language and Female Experience in Nineteenth-Century Women's Writing* (Chicago and London: University of Chicago Press, 1986).

Hopkins, Lisa, 'Mr. Darcy's Body: Privileging the Female Gaze', in *Jane Austen in Hollywood*, ed. by Linda Troost and Sayre Greenfield, 2nd edn (Lexington, KY: University Press of Kentucky, 2001), pp. 111–21.

—— *Relocating Shakespeare and Austen on Screen* (Basingstoke: Palgrave Macmillan, 2009).

Hopkins, Robert, 'General Tilney and Affairs of State: The Political Gothic of *Northanger Abbey*', *Philological Quarterly*, 57 (1978), pp. 213–24.

Hudd, Louise, 'The Politics of a Feminist Poetics: "Armgart" and George Eliot's Critical Response to *Aurora Leigh*', *Essays and Studies*, 49 (1996), pp. 62–83.

Huzzard, John A., 'Will Ladislaw and George Henry Lewes', *George Eliot Fellowship Review*, 9 (1978), pp. 6–10.

Iozzi, Giovanna, 'You Dirty Ode Man!: Byron Laid Bare in TV Sizzler', *The Sun*, 27 September 2003, p. 15.

Jackson, Jeffrey E., 'Elizabeth Gaskell and the Dangerous Edge of Things: Epigraphs in *North and South* and Victorian Publishing Practices', *Pacific Coast Philology*, 40:2 (2005), pp. 56–72.

Johnson, Claudia L., 'Austen Cults and Cultures', in *The Cambridge Companion to Jane Austen*, ed. by Edward Copeland and Juliet McMaster (Cambridge: Cambridge UP, 1997), pp. 211–26.

—— *Equivocal Beings: Politics, Gender, and Sentimentality in the 1790s: Wollstonecraft, Radcliffe, Burney, Austen* (Chicago: University of Chicago Press, 1995).

—— and Clara Tuite, eds., *A Companion to Jane Austen* (Chichester: Wiley-Blackwell, 2012).

Jones, Darryl, *Jane Austen* (Basingstoke: Palgrave, 2004).

Kaplan, Deborah, 'Mass Marketing Jane Austen: Men, Women, and Courtship in Two Film Adaptations', in *Jane Austen in Hollywood*, ed. by Linda Troost and Sayre Greenfield, 2nd edn (Lexington, KY: University Press of Kentucky, 2001), pp. 177–87.

Kehler, Grace, '*Armgart's* Voice Problems', *Victorian Literature and Culture*, 34 (2006), pp. 147–66.

—— 'Between Action and Inaction: The "Performance" of the Prima Donna in Eliot's Closet Drama', in *Nervous Reactions: Victorian Recollections of Romanticism*, ed. by Joel Faflak and Julia M. Wright (Albany, NY: State University of New York Press, 2004), pp. 65–91.

Kelly, David, 'In Its Own Light: A View of the BBC's *North & South*', *Sydney Studies in English*, 32 (2006), pp. 83–96.

Kelsall, Malcolm, 'Byron and the Romantic Heroine', *Byron: Augustan and Romantic*, ed. by Andrew Rutherford (Basingstoke: Macmillan, 1990), pp. 52–62.

Kenyon Jones, Christine, ed., *Byron: The Image of the Poet* (Newark, NJ: University of Delaware Press, 2008).

Kestner, Joseph, 'Jane Austen: Revolutionizing Masculinities', *Persuasions*, 16 (1994), pp. 147–60.

—— 'Jane Austen: The Tradition of the English Romantic Novel, 1800–1832', *Wordsworth Circle*, 7:4 (1976), pp. 297–311.

—— 'Men in Female Condition of England Novels', in *Men by Women*, ed. by Janet Todd (New York and London: Holmes and Meier, 1981), pp. 77–100.

King, Gaye, 'Catton Hall', *Transactions of the Jane Austen Society*, 2 (1991), pp. 61–3.

Kirkham, Margaret, 'Henry Tilney: The Clever Hero of *Northanger Abbey*', *Transactions of the Jane Austen Society*, 6 (1995), pp. 24–30.

Knoepflmacher, U. C., 'Unveiling Men: Power and Masculinity in George Eliot's Fiction', in *Men by Women*, ed. by Janet Todd (New York and London: Holmes and Meier, 1981), pp. 130–46.

Knox-Shaw, Peter, '*Persuasion*, Byron, and the Turkish Tale', *Review of English Studies*, 44 (1993), pp. 47–69.

Kooiman-Van Middendorp, Gerarda Maria, *The Hero in the Feminine Novel* (Middleburg: G. Widen Boer, 1931).

Kramp, Michael, *Disciplining Love: Austen and the Modern Man* (Columbus, OH: Ohio State UP, 2007).

Kroeber, Karl, 'Jane Austen, Romantic', *Wordsworth Circle*, 7:4 (1976), pp. 291–6.

Labbe, Jacqueline M., *The Romantic Paradox: Love, Violence and the Uses of Romance, 1760–1830* (Basingstoke: Macmillan, 2000).

Landesman, Cosmo, 'In Need of True Grit', Review of *Pride and Prejudice*, *The Sunday Times*, 18 September 2005.

Lansdown, Richard, 'The Byronic Hero and the Victorian Heroine', *Critical Review*, 41 (2001), pp. 105–16.

Lau, Beth, ed., *Fellow Romantics: Male and Female British Writers, 1790–1835* (Farnham: Ashgate, 2009).

—— 'Home, Exile, and Wanderlust in Austen and the Romantic Poets', *Pacific Coast Philology*, 41 (2006), pp. 91–107.

—— 'Madeline at Northanger Abbey: Keats's Antiromances and Gothic Satire', *Journal of English and Germanic Philology*, 84:1 (1985), pp. 30–50.

—— 'Placing Jane Austen in the Romantic Period: Self and Solitude in the Works of Austen and the Male Romantic Poets', *European Romantic Review*, 15:2 (June 2004), pp. 255–67.

Lauber, John, 'Heroes and Anti-Heroes in Jane Austen's Novels', *The Dalhousie Review*, 51:4 (Winter 1971–72), pp. 489–503.

Leader, Zachary, and Michael O'Neill, eds., *Percy Bysshe Shelley: The Major Works*, rpt (Oxford: Oxford UP, 2009).

Lee, Luaine, 'Colin Firth Inhabits a Few Darcys', *Scripps Howard News Service*, 30 April 2001.

Le Faye, Deirdre, ed., *Jane Austen's Letters*, 4th edn (Oxford: Oxford UP, 2011).

Leighton, Mary Elizabeth, and Lisa Surridge, 'The Plot Thickens: Toward a Narratological Analysis of Illustrated Serial Fiction in the 1860s', *Victorian Studies*, 51 (Autumn 2008), pp. 65–101.

Leith, William, 'True Romance', *The Observer*, 9 April 2000.

Lellis, George, and H. Philip Bolton, 'Pride but No Prejudice', in *The English Novel and the Movies*, ed. by Michael Klein and Gillian Parker (New York: Frederick Ungar Publishing, 1981), pp. 44–51.

Leonard, Tom, 'BBC to Portray Byron as a "sex-god aristo" ', http://www.telegraph.co.uk, accessed 12 March 2002.

Leonard, William E., *Byron and Byronism in America* (New York: Columbia UP, 1907).

Levine, George, 'The Hero as Dilettante: *Middlemarch* and *Nostromo*', in *George Eliot: Centenary Essays and an Unpublished Fragment*, ed. by Anne Smith (London: Vision Press, 1980), pp. 152–80.

Lockhart, John Gibson [John Bull], 'Letter to the Right Hon. Lord Byron' (London: William Wright, 1821), http://lordbyron.cath.lib.vt.edu/doc.php?choose=JoLockh.1821.JohnBull.xml, accessed 22 June 2013.

Looser, Devoney, 'Jane Austen "Responds" to the Men's Movement', *Persuasions*, 18 (1996), pp. 159–70.

Lost in Austen, directed by Dan Zeff, screenplay by Guy Andrews (ITV, 2008).

Luecke, Jane Marie, 'Ladislaw and the *Middlemarch* Vision', *Nineteenth-Century Fiction*, 19:1 (1964), pp. 55–64.

Lutz, Deborah, *The Dangerous Lover: Gothic Villains, Byronism, and the Nineteenth-Century Seduction Narrative* (Columbus, OH: Ohio State UP, 2006).

Lyttle, John, 'All Dressed up for the Movies', *The Independent*, 26 August 1996.

MacCarthy, Fiona, *Byron: Life and Legend* (London: John Murray, 2002).

—— 'Poet of all the Passions', *The Guardian Review*, 9 November 2002, pp. 4–6.

MacKillop, Ian, and Alison Platt, ' "Beholding in a magic panorama": Television and the Illustration of *Middlemarch*', in *The Classic Novel: From Page to Screen*, ed. by Robert Giddings and Erica Sheen (Manchester: Manchester UP, 2000), pp. 71–92.

—— 'The BBC *Middlemarch*', *George Eliot Review*, 25 (1994), pp. 73–5.

Malay, Jessica L., 'Industrial Heroes: Elizabeth Gaskell and Charlotte Brontë's Constructions of the Masculine', in *Performing Masculinity*, ed. by Rainer Emig and Antony Rowland (Basingstoke: Palgrave Macmillan, 2010), pp. 41–59.

Marchand, Leslie A., *Byron: A Biography*, 3 vols (New York: Alfred A. Knopf, 1957).

—— *Byron's Letters and Journals*, 12 vols (London: John Murray, 1973–82).

Marotti, Arthur F., and Marcelle Freiman, 'The English Sonnet in Manuscript, Print and Mass Media', in *The Cambridge Companion to The Sonnet*, ed. by A. D. Cousins and Peter Howarth (Cambridge: Cambridge UP, 2011), pp. 66–83.

Mason, Philip, *The English Gentleman: The Rise and Fall of an Ideal* (London: André Deutsch, 1982).

McDayter, Ghislaine, *Byromania and the Birth of Celebrity Culture* (Albany, NY: State University of New York Press, 2009).

McGann, Jerome J., *Byron and Romanticism*, ed. by James Soderholm (Cambridge: Cambridge UP, 2002).

—— *Fiery Dust: Byron's Poetic Development* (Chicago: University of Chicago Press, 1968).

—— 'Hero with a Thousand Faces: The Rhetoric of Byronism', *Studies in Romanticism*, 31 (1992), pp. 295–313.

McMaster, Juliet, 'Will Ladislaw and Other Italians with White Mice', *Victorian Review*, 16:2 (1990), pp. 1–7.

Mellor, Anne K., *Romanticism & Gender* (New York and London: Routledge, 1993).

—— ed., *Romanticism and Feminism* (Bloomington, IN: Indiana UP, 1988).

—— 'Why Women Didn't Like Romanticism: The Views of Jane Austen and Mary Shelley', in *The Romantics and Us: Essays on Literature and Culture*, ed. by Gene W. Ruoff (New Brunswick, NJ: Rutgers UP, 1990), pp. 274–87.

Mermin, Dorothy, *Godiva's Ride: Women of Letters in England, 1830–1880* (Bloomington and Indianapolis: Indiana UP, 1993).

Middlemarch, directed by Anthony Page, screenplay by Andrew Davies (BBC, 1994).

'*Middlemarch* on TV – A Symposium', *George Eliot – George Henry Lewes Studies*, 26–7 (September 1994), pp. 36–81.

Miller, Lucasta, *The Brontë Myth* (London: Jonathan Cape, 2001).

Miss Austen Regrets, directed by Jeremy Lovering, screenplay by Gwyneth Hughes (BBC, 2008).

'Modelling the Self: Subjectivity and Identity in Romantic and Post-Romantic Thought and Culture', special issue of *Romanticism and Victorianism on the Net*, 51 (August 2008), guest eds. Mark Sandy and Sarah Wootton, http://www.erudit.org/revue/ravon/2008/v/n51/index.html?lang=en.

Mole, Tom, *Byron's Romantic Celebrity: Industrial Culture and the Hermeneutic of Intimacy* (Basingstoke: Palgrave, 2007).

Moler, Kenneth L., '*Pride and Prejudice*: Jane Austen's "Patrician Hero" ', *Studies in English Literature, 1500–1900*, 7:3 (1967), pp. 491–508.

Monaghan, David, ' "A cheerful confidence in futurity": The Movement Motif in Austen's Novel and Dear/Michell's Film Adaptation of *Persuasion*', in *New Windows on a Woman's World: Essays for Jocelyn Harris*, ed. by Colin Gibson and Lisa Marr, 2 vols (Dunedin, New Zealand: University of Otago, 2005), II, pp. 69–92.

Moore, Doris Langley, *Lord Byron: Accounts Rendered* (London: John Murray, 1974).

Moore, Grace, ed., *Pirates and Mutineers of the Nineteenth Century: Swashbucklers and Swindlers* (Farnham: Ashgate, 2011).

Moore, Thomas, *The Works of Lord Byron: With his Letters and Journals, and his Life*, 14 vols (London: John Murray, 1832).

Morgan, Susan, *In the Meantime: Character and Perception in Jane Austen's Fiction* (Chicago and London: University of Chicago Press, 1980).

—— 'Jane Austen and Romanticism', in *The Jane Austen Companion*, ed. by J. David Grey (New York: Macmillan, 1986), pp. 364–8.

Morrow, Fiona, 'Still Sitting Pretty', *The Independent*, 19 December 2003.

Neill, Natalie, ' "The trash with which the press now groans": *Northanger Abbey* and the Gothic Best Sellers of the 1790s', *Eighteenth-Century Novel*, 4 (2004), pp. 163–92.

Newton, K. M., 'Byronic Egoism and George Eliot's *The Spanish Gypsy*', *Neophilologus*, 57 (1973), pp. 388–400.

—— *George Eliot: Romantic Humanist: A Study of the Philosophical Structure of her Novels* (London: Macmillan, 1981).

Newey, Vincent, 'Rival Cultures: Charles Dickens and the Byronic Legacy', in *Romantic Echoes in the Victorian Era*, ed. by Andrew Radford and Mark Sandy (Aldershot: Ashgate, 2008), pp. 67–83.

Nixon, Cheryl L., 'Balancing the Courtship Hero: Masculine Emotional Display in Film Adaptations of Austen's Novels', in *Jane Austen in Hollywood*, ed. by Linda Troost and Sayre Greenfield, 2nd edn (Lexington, KY: University Press of Kentucky, 2001), pp. 22–43.

Nokes, David, *Jane Austen: A Life* (London: Fourth Estate, 1997).

North and South, directed by Brian Percival, screenplay by Sandy Welch (BBC, 2004).

Northanger Abbey, directed by Giles Foster, screenplay by Maggie Wadey (BBC, 1987).

Northanger Abbey, directed by Jon Jones, screenplay by Andrew Davies (ITV, 2007).

O'Keefe, Bernard, 'The "Soaping" of *Middlemarch'*, *English Review*, 5:2 (1994), pp. 7–12.

Oliphant, Margaret, 'Modern Novelists – Great and Small', *Blackwood's Edinburgh Magazine*, 77 (May 1855), pp. 554–68.

—— et al., *Women Novelists of Queen Victoria's Reign* (London: Hurst & Blackett, 1897).

O'Neill, Michael, ' "In the Sea of Life Enisled": Byron and Arnold', in *Byron and the Isles of Imagination: A Romantic Chart*, ed. by Alistair Heys and Vitana Kostadinova (Plovdiv: Plovdiv UP, 2009), pp. 67–87.

—— guest editor, 'Romanticism and its Legacies', special issue of *Romanticism*, 14:1 (2008).

—— *The All-Sustaining Air: Romantic Legacies and Renewals in British, American, and Irish Poetry since 1900* (Oxford: Oxford UP, 2007).

—— ' "The burden of ourselves": Arnold as a Post-Romantic Poet', *Yearbook of English Studies*, 36:2 (2006), pp. 109–24.

—— 'The Romantic Bequest: Arnold and Others', in *The Oxford Handbook of Victorian Poetry*, ed. by Matthew Bevis (Oxford: Oxford UP, 2013), pp. 217–34.

Oxford English Dictionary Online, http://www.oed.com.

Pace, Timothy, 'Who Killed Gwendolen Harleth? *Daniel Deronda* and Keats's "Lamia" ', *Journal of English and Germanic Philology*, 87:1 (1988), pp. 35–48.

Panek, Jennifer, 'Constructions of Masculinity in *Adam Bede* and *Wives and Daughters'*, *Victorian Review*, 22 (1996), pp. 127–51.

Passero, Kathy, 'Pride, Prejudice and a Little Persuasion', *A&E Monthly*, December 1996.

Persuasion, directed by Adrian Shergold, screenplay by Simon Burke (ITV and WGBH, 2007).

Persuasion, directed by Roger Michell, screenplay by Nick Dear (BBC and WGBH, 1995).

Phelps, Gilbert, ed., *The Byronic Byron: A Selection from the Poems of Lord Byron* (London: Longman, 1971).

Pinion, F. B., *A Jane Austen Companion: A Critical Survey and Reference Book* (London and Basingstoke: Macmillan, 1973).

—— 'Byron and *Wuthering Heights'*, *Brontë Society Transactions*, 21 (1995), pp. 195–201.

Pinney, Thomas, 'Another Note on the Forgotten Past of Will Ladislaw', *Nineteenth-Century Fiction*, 17:1 (1962), pp. 69–73.

Pomarè, Carla, *Byron and the Discourses of History* (Farnham: Ashgate, 2013).

Pope, Rebecca A., 'The Diva Doesn't Die: George Eliot's *Armgart'*, *Criticism*, 32:4 (1990), pp. 469–83.

Praz, Mario, *The Hero in Eclipse in Victorian Fiction*, trans. by Angus Davidson (London, New York, and Toronto: Oxford UP, 1956).

—— *The Romantic Agony*, 2nd edn, trans. by Angus Davidson (Oxford: Oxford UP, 1951).

Pride and Prejudice, directed by Cyril Coke, screenplay by Fay Weldon (BBC, 1980).

Pride and Prejudice, directed by Joe Wright, screenplay by Deborah Moggach (Universal Pictures, 2005).

Pride and Prejudice, directed by Robert Z. Leonard, screenplay by Aldous Huxley and Jane Murfin (MGM, 1940).

Pride and Prejudice, directed by Simon Langton, screenplay by Andrew Davies (BBC, 1995).

Pride and Prejudice Revisited, directed by John Hay, narrated by Emilia Fox (BBC, 2005).

Radcliffe, Ann, *The Mysteries of Udolpho*, ed. by Bonamy Dobrée, intro. by Terry Castle, rpt (Oxford: Oxford UP, 2008).

Reader, I Married Him, presented by Daisy Goodwin (BBC, 2007).

Redinger, Ruby V., *George Eliot: The Emergent Self* (London: Bodley Head, 1975).

Reed, John R., 'Soldier Boy: Forming Masculinity in *Adam Bede*', *Studies in the Novel*, 33:3 (2001), pp. 268–84.

Rees, Jasper, 'Return of the Chameleon', *The Telegraph*, 5 June 2006.

Regan, Stephen, ed., *The Nineteenth-Century Novel: A Critical Reader* (London and New York: Routledge, 2001).

Reiman, Donald H., Neil Fraistat, and Nora Crook, eds., *The Complete Poetry of Percy Bysshe Shelley*, 3 vols (Baltimore, MD: John Hopkins UP, 2000-).

Riga, Frank P., 'Dismantling Traditionalist Gender Roles: An Exotic Counter-World in Byron's *Don Juan*', in *The Foreign Woman in British Literature: Exotics, Aliens, and Outsiders*, ed. by Marilyn Demarest Button and Toni Reed (Westport, CT and London: Greenwood, 1999), pp. 1–15.

Rignall, John, ed., *Oxford Reader's Companion to George Eliot* (Oxford: Oxford UP, 2000).

Roberts, Marilyn, 'Catherine Morland: Gothic Heroine After All?', *Topic*, 48 (1997), pp. 22–30.

Robinson, Peter, 'Captain Benwick's Reading', *Essays in Criticism*, 57:2 (2007), pp. 147–70.

Roe, Nicholas, ed., *Romanticism: An Oxford Guide* (Oxford: Oxford UP).

Ruddick, Bill, 'George Du Maurier: Illustrator and Interpreter of Mrs Gaskell', *Gaskell Society Journal*, 1 (1987), pp. 48–54.

'Rufus Sewell', *Elle*, June 1996.

Russell, Bertrand, *A History of Western Philosophy* (London: Routledge Classics, 2004).

Rutherford, Andrew, *Byron The Best-Seller*, The Byron Foundation Lecture (Nottingham: University of Nottingham, 1964).

—— ed., *Byron: The Critical Heritage* (London: Routledge, 1970).

Rutherford, Jonathan, *Men's Silences: Predicaments in Masculinity* (London and New York: Routledge, 1992).

Rzepka, Charles J., 'Making it in a Brave New World: Marriage, Profession, and Anti-Romantic *Ekstasis* in Austen's *Persuasion*', *Studies in the Novel*, 26:2 (1994), http://lion.chadwyck.co.uk.

Sadoff, Dianne F., 'Marketing Jane Austen at the Megaplex', *Novel*, 43:1 (2010), http://lion.chadwyck.co.uk, accessed 29 August 2012.

Saglia, Diego, 'Touching Byron: Masculinity and the Celebrity Body in the Romantic Period', in *Performing Masculinity*, ed. by Rainer Emig and Antony Rowland (Basingstoke: Palgrave Macmillan, 2010), pp. 13–27.

Sandy, Mark, ed., *Romantic Presences in the Twentieth Century* (Aldershot: Ashgate, 2012).

Sears, Albert C., 'Male Novel Reading of the 1790s, Gothic Literature, and *Northanger Abbey'*, *Persuasions*, 21 (1999), pp. 106–12.

Sedgwick, Eve Kosofsky, *Between Men: English Literature and Male Homosocial Desire* (New York and Chichester: Columbia UP, 1985).

Sense and Sensibility, directed by Ang Lee, screenplay by Emma Thompson (Columbia Pictures, 1995).

Sense and Sensibility, directed by John Alexander, screenplay by Andrew Davies (BBC, 2008).

Shakespeare, William, *The Complete Oxford Shakespeare*, ed. by Stanley Wells and Gary Taylor, 3 vols (London: Guild Publishing, by arrangement with Oxford UP, 1987).

Shannon, Sarah, 'Love in a Cold Climate', *The Independent*, Online Edition, 10 November 2004, 3pp.

Sheen, Erica, ' "Where the garment gapes": Faithfulness and Promiscuity in the 1995 BBC *Pride and Prejudice'*, in *The Classic Novel: From Page to Screen*, ed. by Robert Giddings and Erica Sheen (Manchester: Manchester UP, 2000), pp. 14–30.

Simmonds, Posy, 'Voices from the Other Side', *The Guardian*, 31 May 2003.

Smith, Margaret, ed., *The Letters of Charlotte Brontë: With a Selection of Letters by Family and Friends*, 3 vols (Oxford: Clarendon Press, 1995–2004).

Sokol, Ronnie Jo, 'The Importance of Being Married: Adapting *Pride and Prejudice'*, in *Nineteenth-Century Women at the Movies: Adapting Classic Women's Fiction to Film*, ed. by Barbara Tepa Lupack (Bowling Green, OH: Bowling Green State University Popular Press, 1999), pp. 78–105.

Solinger, Jason D., *Becoming the Gentleman: British Literature and the Invention of Modern Masculinity, 1660–1815* (New York: Palgrave Macmillan, 2012).

——— 'Modern Masculinities', *Novel*, 42:1 (2009), 5pp, http://lion.chadwyck.co.uk, accessed 29 August 2012.

Southam, Brian, 'Was Jane Austen a Bonapartist?', *Collected Reports of the Jane Austen Society*, 5 (2000), pp. 312–20.

Spittles, Brian, '*Middlemarch*: TV Versus Text?', *English Review*, 7:1 (1996), pp. 22–5.

Stabler, Jane, *Burke to Byron, Barbauld to Baillie, 1790–1830* (Basingstoke: Palgrave, 2001).

——— *Byron, Poetics and History* (Cambridge: Cambridge UP, 2002).

——— 'Literary Influences', in *Jane Austen in Context*, ed. by Janet Todd (Cambridge: Cambridge UP, 2005), pp. 41–50.

——— ed., *Palgrave Advances in Byron Studies* (Basingstoke: Palgrave Macmillan, 2007).

——— 'Romantic and Victorian Conversations: Elizabeth Barrett and Robert Browning in Dialogue with Byron and Shelley', in *Fellow Romantics: Male and Female British Writers, 1790–1835*, ed. by Beth Lau (Farnham: Ashgate, 2009), pp. 231–53.

Stauffer, Andrew M., 'Byronic Anger and the Victorians', in *Byron: Heritage and Legacy*, ed. by Cheryl A. Wilson (New York and Basingstoke: Palgrave, 2008), pp. 197–205.

Stein, Atara, ' "I Loved Her and Destroyed Her": Love and Narcissism in Byron's *Manfred'*, *Philological Quarterly*, 69:2 (1990), pp. 189–215.

——— 'Immortals and Vampires and Ghosts, Oh My!: Byronic Heroes in Popular Culture', in *Romanticism and Contemporary Culture*, ed. by Laura Mandell and Michael Eberle-Sinatra. Special issue of *Romantic Circles Praxis Series* (February 2002), http://www.rc.umd.edu/praxis/contemporary/stein/stein. html, accessed 8 April 2002.

—— *The Byronic Hero in Film, Fiction, and Television* (Carbondale, IL: Southern Illinois UP, 2004).

Stone, Donald D., *The Romantic Impulse in Victorian Fiction* (Cambridge, MA and London: Harvard UP, 1980).

Stone, Marjorie, 'Elizabeth Barrett Browning and Victorian Versions of Byron and Wollstonecraft: Romantic Genealogies, Self-Defining Memories and the Genesis of *Aurora Leigh*', in *Romantic Echoes in the Victorian Era*, ed. by Andrew Radford and Mark Sandy (Aldershot: Ashgate, 2008), pp. 123–41.

Stoneman, Patsy, *Brontë Transformations: The Cultural Dissemination of 'Jane Eyre' and 'Wuthering Heights'* (London: Prentice Hall/ Harvester-Wheatsheaf, 1996).

—— 'The Brontë Legacy: *Jane Eyre* and *Wuthering Heights* as Romance Archetypes', *Rivista di Studi Vittoriani*, 3:5 (1998), pp. 5–24.

—— '*Wives and Daughters* on Television', *Gaskell Society Journal*, 14 (2000), pp. 85–100.

Stovel, Bruce, '*Northanger Abbey* at the Movies', *Persuasions*, 20 (1998), pp. 236–47.

Surridge, Lisa, 'Working-Class Masculinities in *Mary Barton*', *Victorian Literature and Culture* (2000), pp. 331–43.

Sussman, Herbert, *Victorian Masculinities: Manhood and Masculine Poetics in Early Victorian Literature and Art* (Cambridge: Cambridge UP, 1995).

Swingle, L. J., 'The Perfect Happiness of the Union: Jane Austen's *Emma* and English Romanticism', *Wordsworth Circle*, 7:4 (1976), pp. 312–19.

—— 'The Poets, the Novelists, and the English Romantic Situation', *Wordsworth Circle*, 10:2 (Spring 1979), pp. 218–27.

Tanner, Tony, *Jane Austen* (Basingstoke: Macmillan, 1986).

Tayler, Irene, *Holy Ghosts: The Male Muses of Emily and Charlotte Brontë* (New York: Columbia UP, 1990).

Tennyson, Alfred Lord, *Tennyson: A Selected Edition*, ed. by Christopher Ricks (Berkeley and Los Angeles: University of California Press, 1989).

The English Dialect Dictionary, ed. by Joseph Wright, 6 vols (Oxford: Henry Frowde, 1898).

Thomas, Keith G., 'Jane Austen and the Romantic Lyric: *Persuasion* and Coleridge's Conversation Poems', *ELH*, 54 (1987), pp. 893–924.

Thompson, Laura, 'Austen's Power', *The Daily Telegraph*, 1 July 2006.

Thomson, Douglass H., Jack G. Voller, and Frederick S. Frank, eds., *Gothic Writers: A Critical and Bibliographical Guide* (London: Greenwood Press, 2002).

Thornell, Kristel, 'Film Adaptations of *Emma* Between Agency and Submission', *Mosaic: A Journal for the Interdisciplinary Study of Literature*, 43:3 (2010), 17pp, http://lion.chadwyck.co.uk.

Thorslev, Peter L., *The Byronic Hero: Types and Prototypes* (Minneapolis, MN: University of Minnesota Press, 1962).

Throsby, Corin, 'Byron, Commonplacing and Early Fan Culture', in *Romanticism and Celebrity Culture, 1750–1850*, ed. by Tom Mole (Cambridge: Cambridge UP, 2009), pp. 227–44.

Tischler Millstein, Denise, 'George Eliot's *Felix Holt, The Radical* and Byronic Secrets', in *Victorian Secrecy: Economies of Knowledge and Concealment*, ed. by

Albert D. Pionke and Denise Tischler Millstein (Farnham and Burlington, VT: Ashgate, 2010), pp. 135–48.

––––– 'Lord Byron and George Eliot: Embracing National Identity in *Daniel Deronda*', *Forum: University of Edinburgh Postgraduate Journal of Culture & the Arts*, 1 (Autumn 2005), http://www.forumjournal.org/site/issue/01/denise-tischler-millstein, accessed 20 July 2012.

Todd, Janet, ed., *Jane Austen in Context* (Cambridge: Cambridge UP, 2005).

––––– ed., *The Cambridge Companion to Pride and Prejudice* (Cambridge: Cambridge UP, 2013).

––––– *The Cambridge Introduction to Jane Austen* (Cambridge: Cambridge UP, 2006).

Tomalin, Claire, *Jane Austen: A Life* (London: Viking, 1997).

Tosh, John, 'The Old Adam and the New Man: Emerging Themes in the History of English Masculinities, 1750–1850', in *English Masculinities 1660–1800*, ed. by Tim Hitchcock and Michèle Cohen (London and New York: Longman, 1999), pp. 217–38.

Tuite, Clara, *Romantic Austen: Sexual Politics and the Literary Canon* (Cambridge: Cambridge UP, 2002).

Ty, Eleanor, 'Catherine's Real and Imagined Fears: What Happens to Female Bodies in Gothic Castles', *Persuasions*, 20 (1998), pp. 248–60.

Uffelman, Larry K., 'Elizabeth Gaskell's *North and South*: The Novel in Progress', *Gaskell Society Journal*, 14 (2000), pp. 73–84.

Uglow, Jenny, *Elizabeth Gaskell: A Habit of Stories* (London: Faber & Faber, 1993).

––––– *George Eliot* (London: Virago, 1987).

Van Dyke, Henry, *Studies in Tennyson* (New York: Charles Scribner's Sons, 1920).

Viera, Carroll, '*The Lifted Veil* and George Eliot's Early Aesthetic', *Studies in English Literature*, 24:4 (1984), pp. 749–67.

Voiret, Martine, 'Books to Movies: Gender and Desire in Jane Austen's Adaptations', in *Jane Austen and Co.: Remaking the Past in Contemporary Culture*, ed. by Suzanne R. Pucci and James Thompson (Albany, NY: State University of New York Press, 2003), pp. 229–45.

Wagner, John, 'In Praise of "Low-Brow" Allusions, or Is the Fonz Really a Byronic Hero?', *English Journal*, 71:2 (1982), pp. 42–3.

Waldron, Mary, *Jane Austen and the Fiction of her Time* (Cambridge: Cambridge UP, 1999).

Wallace, Anne D., '"Vague Capricious Memories": *The Lifted Veil*'s Challenge to Wordsworthian Poetics', *George Eliot – George Henry Lewes Newsletter*, 18–19 (1991), pp. 31–45.

Wandling, Timothy J., 'Early Romantic Theorists and the Fate of Transgressive Eloquence: John Stuart Mill's Response to Byron', in *Nervous Reactions: Victorian Recollections of Romanticism*, ed. by Joel Faflak and Julia M. Wright (Albany, NY: State University of New York Press, 2004), pp. 123–40.

Watson, J. R., 'Elizabeth Gaskell: Heroes and Heroines, and *Sylvia's Lovers*', *Gaskell Society Journal*, 18 (2001), pp. 81–94.

Watson, Shane, 'A New Romantic', *Vogue*, June 1993.

Watts, Alaric A., ed., *The Literary Souvenir; or, Cabinet of Poetry and Romance* (London: Longman et al., 1827).

Williams, Michael, 'Jane Austen and Lord Byron: A View of Regency London', *Unisa English Studies*, 21 (1983), pp. 11–16.

Williams, Wendy S., *George Eliot, Poetess* (Farnham: Ashgate, 2014).

Wilson, Frances, ed., *Byromania: Portraits of the Artist in Nineteenth- and Twentieth-Century Culture* (Basingstoke: Macmillan, 1999).

Wilson, Margaret Madrigal, 'The Hero and the Other Man in Jane Austen's Novels', *Persuasions*, 18 (1996), pp. 182–5.

Wilt, Judith, 'Jane Austen's Men: Inside/Outside "the Mystery"', in *Men by Women*, ed. by Janet Todd (New York and London: Holmes and Meier, 1981), pp. 59–76.

Wiltshire, John, 'Mr. Darcy's Smile', in *The Cinematic Jane Austen: Essays on the Filmic Sensibility of the Novels*, ed. by David Monaghan, Adriane Hudelet, and John Wiltshire (Jefferson, NC: McFarland & Co, 2009), pp. 94–110.

—— *Recreating Jane Austen* (Cambridge: Cambridge UP, 2001).

Winnifrith, Tom, *The Brontës and Their Background: Romance and Reality* (London and Basingstoke: Macmillan, 1973).

Wives and Daughters, directed by Nicholas Renton, screenplay by Andrew Davies (BBC, 1999).

Wolfson, Susan J., ' "A Problem Few Dare Imitate": *Sardanapalus* and "Effeminate Character" ', *ELH*, 58:4 (1991), pp. 867–902.

—— 'Hemans and the Romance of Byron', in *Felicia Hemans: Reimagining Poetry in the Nineteenth Century*, ed. by Nanora Sweet, Julie Melnyk, and Marlon B. Ross (Houndmills: Palgrave, 2001), pp. 155–80.

—— *Romantic Interactions: Social Being & the Turns of Literary Action* (Baltimore, MD: Johns Hopkins UP, 2010).

—— ' "Their She Condition": Cross-Dressing and the Politics of Gender in *Don Juan*', *ELH*, 54:3 (1987), pp. 585–617.

Wootton, Sarah, *Consuming Keats: Nineteenth-Century Representations in Art and Literature* (Basingstoke: Palgrave Macmillan, 2006).

—— ' "Picturing in me a hero of romance": The Legacy of *Jane Eyre*'s Byronic Hero', in *A Breath of Fresh Eyre: Intertextual and Intermedial Reworkings of 'Jane Eyre'*, ed. by Margarete Rubik and Elke Mettinger-Schartmann (Amsterdam and New York: Rodopi, 2007), pp. 229–41.

—— 'The Byronic in Austen's *Persuasion* and *Pride and Prejudice*', *Modern Language Review*, 102:1 (2007), pp. 26–39.

Wordsworth, William, *The Pedlar, Tintern Abbey and the Two-Part Prelude*, ed. by Jonathan Wordsworth (Cambridge: Cambridge UP, 1985).

—— *The Prelude: 1799, 1805, 1850*, ed. by Jonathan Wordsworth, M. H. Abrams, and Stephen Gill (New York and London: W. W. Norton & Company, 1979).

Wright, Julia M., ' "Growing Pains": Representing the Romantic in Gaskell's *Wives and Daughters*', in *Nervous Reactions: Victorian Recollections of Romanticism*, ed. by Joel Faflak and Julia M. Wright (Albany, NY: State University of New York Press, 2004), pp. 163–85.

Index

anti-hero, 2, 12, 19–21, 25–8, 37–8,
  42, 46, 62–3, 76, 84, 90, 98,
  107, 119, 122, 128, 138, 149,
  151, 165, 182, 188, 213, 221
Arnold, Matthew, 10, 14, 22, 28, 57,
  166–7, 177–8, 187, 188–9
Auden, W. H., 35, 192–3
  'Letter to Lord Byron', 35, 192–3
Auerbach, Nina, 64, 69
Austen, Jane, 3, 4, 9, 10, 11, 15, 21,
  23–7, 30–94, 99, 104, 107, 119,
  122, 124, 126, 129, 131, 182–3,
  187–9, 192–3, 193–5, 199,
  201–3
  Works:
  Emma, 24, 25, 33, 34, 38, 39, 41–3,
    81, 82, 86
  'Lines of Lord Byron, in the
    Character of Buonaparté', 36–7
    see also Byron, 'Napoleon's Farewell'
  Northanger Abbey, 4, 23, 25–6, 30,
    35, 37, 38, 45–9, 56, 61, 63–4,
    81, 195, 197–8,
  Persuasion, 10, 12, 21, 24, 26, 34,
    37, 38, 42, 49, 58, 59, 61–77,
    76, 84, 91, 107, 131, 187–9,
    195, 202–3
  'Plan of a Novel', 38, 55
  Pride and Prejudice, 2, 12, 15, 21, 23,
    26, 32, 33, 34, 37–41, 42, 58,
    61–2, 72, 77–91, 81–4, 86–91,
    115, 116, 118, 171, 189, 209,
    213
  Sanditon, 63, 201
  Sense and Sensibility, 23, 25–6, 30,
    34, 37, 42, 46, 49–60, 62, 77,
    82, 104, 162, 197
  Screen adaptations:
  Northanger Abbey (1987), 198
  Northanger Abbey (2007), 23, 47–9,
    56, 198
  Persuasion (1995), 24, 26, 34, 66,
    70, 73–6

Persuasion (2007), 26, 49, 73, 76–7
Pride and Prejudice (1940), 89, 206–7
Pride and Prejudice (1980), 89, 207
Pride and Prejudice (1995), 15, 23,
  25, 26, 34, 40–1, 62, 86–91,
  121–2, 171
  see also Fielding, Helen, *Bridget
    Jones's Diary*; Austen revival,
    'Darcymania'; Firth, Colin
Pride and Prejudice (2005), 26, 90, 209
Sense and Sensibility (1995), 24,
  54–6, 58
Sense and Sensibility (2008), 23, 55–60
Austen revival, 24, 34, 39, 62, 86–92,
  205–6
'Austenmania', 24, 86–7, 88–9
  see also 'Byromania'; 'Darcymania'
biopics, 87
'Darcymania', 15, 24, 40, 87–90, 91
  see also 'Austenmania'; Austen,
    Pride and Prejudice (1995);
    'Byromania'; Firth, Colin
Firth, Colin, 15, 24, 25, 26, 87–91,
  121–2, 171, 189, 201, 206
  see also 'Austenmania'; Austen,
    Pride and Prejudice (1995);
    'Darcymania'; Fielding, Helen,
    Bridget Jones's Diary
Lost in Austen, 88

Bakhtin, Mikhail, 63, 201
Barrett Browning, Elizabeth, 1, 8, 22,
  32, 59, 115, 134, 147, 186, 191,
  193, 200
  Works:
  Aurora Leigh, 8, 32, 147
  'A Vision of Poets', 22, 115, 186
  Stanzas on the Death of Lord Byron,
    1, 8, 134, 191
BBC, the, 14–5, 23–4, 26–7, 29, 34,
  40, 49, 56, 59, 62, 73, 86–91,
  109, 111, 117, 120–2, 152, 171,
  177, 179–81

Blake, William, 142, 171, 177–8
Blessington, Marguerite, Countess of, 13, 188
Bodenheimer, Rosemarie, 96, 117
Bond, James, 1, 183
Brontë, Anne, 8–9, 21, 86, 130, 162, 186–7, 217
   Works:
   The Tenant of Wildfell Hall, 8, 20, 130, 162, 217
Brontë, Charlotte, 2, 8–9, 21, 77, 86, 95, 149, 165, 177, 186–7, 201, 225
   Works:
   Jane Eyre, 8, 9, 11, 20, 21, 77, 87, 118, 177
   Villette, 149, 165
Brontë, Emily, 2, 6, 8–9, 21, 50, 86, 91, 98, 148, 186–7, 208
   Works:
   Wuthering Heights, 2, 8–9, 50, 91, 98, 148, 208, 209
Brownstein, Rachel M., 30–1, 35–6, 77, 192
Brückmann, Patricia C., 63, 71
Bulwer-Lytton, Edward, 6, 19
Burke, Edmund, 43, 80
Burney, Fanny, 43, 45, 61
'Byromania', 14, 15, 24, 86, 89, 91, 154, 183
   see also Austen revival, 'Austenmania'; 'Darcymania'
Byron, BBC biopic, 14, 34, 73, 189, 194
Byron, George Gordon, Lord,
   and celebrity, 1–2, 10, 12–14, 30, 77–88, 86, 175, 181, 183, 184, 189–90, 195, 206
   see also Byronism, cult of
   and the Greek War of Independence, 7, 22, 134, 168
   and incest, 14, 20, 27, 34, 129–30, 160, 175, 198
   see also Leigh, Augusta
   and infamy, 11, 14, 20, 28, 33, 49, 74, 86, 102, 129, 131, 133–4, 154, 178, 181, 183, 191, 194, 217
   see also Stowe, 'Separation' scandal
   and the Luddites, 22, 168
   as a political poet, 7–8, 11, 22, 24, 28–9, 31, 96–7, 112–15, 123,
   134, 149, 153, 175, 178, 180–2, 185–6, 196, 223
   physical appearance of, 15, 30, 40, 55, 88, 105, 110, 119, 121–2, 145, 156, 177–8, 196, 211, 213, 225, 228
   and sexuality, 7, 11, 14–15, 18–20, 23–4, 30, 40–1, 49, 189–91, 223
   Works:
   Cain, 13, 190, 221
   Childe Harold's Pilgrimage, 1–2, 3, 13, 34, 44, 69–70, 77, 79, 80, 86, 88, 102, 130, 133, 154, 178, 188, 210
   Don Juan, 4, 13–14, 18, 30, 35, 38, 68, 94, 97, 111, 127, 130, 166, 187, 190, 197, 218, 222
   'Fare Thee Well', 73–4
   Hebrew Melodies, 168, 225
   'I Would I Were a Careless Child', 23, 109–11
   Lara, 13, 85, 182
   Manfred, 11, 13–14, 16–17, 21, 28, 40, 44, 50, 78, 82, 111, 114, 127, 137, 138–9, 143, 144, 146, 149, 151, 154, 182, 211, 217
   Marino Faliero, 16–17
   'Napoleon's Farewell', 36–7
      see also Austen, 'Lines of Lord Byron, in the Character of Buonaparté'
   'Ode to Napoleon Buonaparté', 105
   Poems 1816, 37
   Sardanapalus, 11, 20, 157–8, 162
   'So, we'll go no more a roving', 23, 57–9
   The Bride of Abydos, 69, 70–1
   The Corsair, 10, 13, 18, 35, 36, 63, 67, 70–2, 78, 79, 81, 84, 98, 113–14, 115, 119, 120, 129, 132, 142, 176, 222, 223
   The Deformed Transformed, 11, 13
   'The Dream', 154–5
   The Giaour, 13, 19, 67, 69, 71, 72, 99, 115, 119, 178, 180, 213
   The Island; or, Christian and his Comrades, 27, 112–14
   The Prisoner of Chillon, 68–9, 102
   The Siege of Corinth, 99, 132

Byronic hero, 1–6, 8–9, 11–13, 15–30,
    37–8, 40–1, 43–4, 55, 58, 60–2,
    68, 72–3, 75–80, 82, 84–7, 91,
    93–6, 98, 111, 115, 119–21,
    123–5, 127, 130, 138, 142–3,
    145–54, 156, 158–60, 162, 168,
    170–1, 177–8, 180–3, 185–6,
    188, 190–2, 213, 221, 227
  and dissent, 2, 4, 22, 44, 86, 93,
    96, 102, 112–14, 123, 128, 131,
    148, 157–8, 180–1, 184, 190
  and exile, 13–14, 28, 36–7, 72, 138,
    143, 151, 183, 193, 203, 210
  hubris of, 28, 125
  and individualism, 1, 5, 10, 17,
    27–8, 38–9, 41, 80, 82, 102,
    119, 125, 132–4, 143, 146–7,
    151, 165–6, 168, 171, 221
  inscrutability of, 3–4, 6, 11–13, 18,
    21, 26, 29, 72, 78–9, 84–6, 94,
    108, 122, 127, 144, 156, 169,
    176–7, 188
  melancholy of, 5–6, 13, 14, 18, 22,
    36, 44, 51–4, 56, 58, 63–4, 69,
    71, 84, 91, 104, 107, 110–11,
    113, 114, 122, 127, 134, 136,
    138, 143, 145, 192, 194, 213, 223
  myth of, 5, 8, 12–14, 23–4, 44, 154,
    174, 192
  profligacy of, 18, 20, 22, 30, 98,
    102, 182
  and social reform, 22, 27–8, 128,
    134, 180–1
  theatricality of, 10–11, 13–16, 22,
    27, 40, 44, 54–5, 57, 91–2,
    104–5, 127–8, 138–9, 151, 165,
    177, 179, 181, 189
Byronic heroine, 28, 147–50,
    165–6, 185
Byronism, 2–3, 8–11, 15–19, 22, 27, 34,
    50, 74, 91, 93–5, 105, 128, 133,
    147, 149, 152, 154, 157, 170,
    177, 178, 184–6, 191, 204, 208
  cult of, 1–3, 8, 11, 14, 19, 77, 91,
    94–5, 105, 128, 133
  see also Byron, celebrity

Campbell, Joseph, 119, 213
Cantor, Paul, 18–19

Carlyle, Thomas, 6, 18, 20, 22, 94–5,
    96, 122, 128, 129, 134, 145,
    146, 147, 148, 156, 177, 180–1,
    214, 216
  Captains of Industry, 122, 214
    see also industrialist hero; self-
    made man
Carroll, Alicia, 131, 157, 158
civility, 39–43, 54, 72, 75, 79,
    83, 196
  see also gentleman, figure of the,
Cohen, Michèle, 43, 82–3
Coleridge, Samuel Taylor, 98–9, 101,
    103, 112, 126, 139, 145, 165–6,
    197, 202, 224
  Works:
    'Love', 165
    'This Lime-Tree Bower my Prison',
    224
    'The Rime of the Ancient Mariner',
    126, 145, 165, 166, 224
Cowper, William, 23, 50, 56–7,
    103, 201

Dandy, figure of the, 19–21, 40, 154,
    177, 191
Davies, Andrew, 15, 23, 24, 27,
    47–8, 55–6, 58–60, 87–8,
    90–1, 109, 111, 171, 179, 191,
    200, 207
  see also screen adaptation
Deresiewicz, William, 35, 37, 59
Dickens, Charles, 6, 185, 191, 210,
    221, 223
Disraeli, Benjamin, 6, 19, 88,
    191, 206
Dramin, Edward, 153, 159, 168, 178

Edgeworth, Maria, 43, 61, 101
Elfenbein, Andrew, 6, 19, 94
Eliot, George, 3–4, 9–12, 20–3, 27–8,
    30, 39, 86, 93–9, 124–82, 187,
    215–21, 223–7, 229
  Works:
    Adam Bede, 124–7
    Armgart, 4, 28, 125, 148–51,
    165, 222
    'Brother Jacob', 132–3, 135, 154,
    172

Daniel Deronda, 22, 28–9, 124, 125, 143, 147, 148, 152–5, 160–70, 171, 181
'Evangelical Teaching: Dr Cumming', 22, 133–4, 191
Felix Holt: The Radical, 20, 22, 28, 124, 125, 152, 153–60, 171, 172, 181, 223
Middlemarch, 11–12, 14–15, 21, 22–4, 28–9, 91, 96, 105, 122, 124, 125, 128–9, 130, 147, 152, 170–81, 217–18, 224, 227, 229
Poetry and Prose from the Notebook of an Eccentric, 137–8, 139
Scenes of Clerical Life, 127, 134, 147
'Janet's Repentance', 129, 134
'The Sad Fortunes of the Reverend Amos Barton', 127
'Tennyson's *Maud*', 140
'The Lifted Veil', 28, 125, 135–7, 138–42, 148, 151, 159, 161, 168, 170, 219
The Mill on the Floss, 131, 132, 148, 215
The Spanish Gypsy, 4, 22, 28, 125, 142–8, 149, 151, 170, 220
'Thomas Carlyle', 128, 216
'Worldliness and Other-Worldliness: The Poet Young', 127, 136
Screen adaptations:
Middlemarch (1994), 14–15, 23, 24, 29, 91, 122, 152, 171, 177, 179–81, 212, 228–9
see also Sewell, Rufus
Engels, Friedrich, 22, 175–6

fandom, 6, 11, 33–4, 37, 64, 87, 121, 183
Fielding, Helen, 15, 189, 206
Bridget Jones's Diary, 15, 87, 189, 206
see also Austen revival
Fischer, Doucet Devin, 34, 77
Franklin, Caroline, 7, 20, 186
Frantz, Sarah, 39–40

Gaskell, Elizabeth, 3–4, 9–12, 20, 22–4, 27, 30, 39, 83, 86, 91, 93–124, 126, 128, 131, 133, 143, 154–6, 159, 165, 181–2

Works:
Cranford, 99–100, 210
Mary Barton, 94, 95, 97, 99, 115
North and South, 12, 15, 21, 22, 24, 27, 83, 91, 93, 95–7, 99, 101, 102, 104, 106, 112–23, 155, 159, 171
Sylvia's Lovers, 94
'The Heart of John Middleton', 94, 97
'The Sexton's Hero', 94, 98
Wives and Daughters, 4, 20–1, 23, 27, 93, 100–1, 102–12, 131, 133, 154, 156, 165, 210, 223
Screen adaptations:
Cranford (2007), 233
North and South (2004), 15, 24, 27, 91, 117–18, 120–3, 171, 209, 214
Wives and Daughters (1999), 23, 27, 109–11
genre, 2, 4, 6, 10, 12, 25, 27, 31, 45–6, 48, 62, 86, 88–9, 103–4, 106, 112, 152, 174, 182, 192, 197
gentleman, figure of the, 9, 13, 21, 25, 38–43, 55, 72–3, 78–84, 90–1, 104, 118–19, 122, 154, 159
see also civility
Gill, Stephen, 126–7, 215
Goethe, Johann Wolfgang von, 94, 99, 128, 130, 182
Gothic villain, 5, 25, 38, 44, 46, 81, 119, 184
Montoni, 45–6
see also Radcliffe, Ann
Gross, Jonathan, 11, 18

Halperin, John, 35, 62
Hardy, Barbara, 154, 172, 175, 178, 180
Harris, Margaret, 117, 121–2
Hazlitt, William, 63
Hemans, Felicia, 7, 20, 23, 99, 101, 103, 109, 112
Henry, Nancy, 150, 174
Homans, Margaret, 127, 174, 215

industrialist hero, 21–2, 83, 95, 118
see also Carlyle, Captains of Industry; self-made man

James, Henry, 89, 128
Jones, Darryl, 37, 49, 67

Keats, John, 47, 50–1, 67, 86, 99, 107–8,
        136–7, 139, 144, 160–1, 163,
        166, 168–70, 172, 176, 226
    Letters:
        'camelion Poet', 137, 169
        Negative Capability, 86, 161, 169
        'The vale of Soul-making', 136
    Works:
        'La Belle Dame sans Merci', 17, 50,
            51, 190
        Lamia, 137, 139, 160–1
        'Ode to a Nightingale', 108–9
        'On Seeing the Elgin Marbles', 166
        'The Eve of St Agnes', 47
        'To Autumn', 107, 108
Kestner, Joseph, 38, 41, 95
Kramp, Michael, 39–41

Labbe, Jacqueline, 18–19
Lamb, Lady Caroline, 7, 33, 35
Landon, Letitia (L.E.L.), 1, 7, 16
    Works:
        'Stanzas, Written beneath the
            Portrait of Lord Byron, painted
            by Mr. West', 7
        *The Portrait of Lord Byron at
            Newstead Abbey*, 1, 16
Lansdown, Richard, 11, 221–2, 223
Lau, Beth, 31, 47, 203
Leigh, Augusta, 20, 35, 129
    see also Byron, incest
Lewes, George Henry, 130–1, 172–3
Lockhart, John Gibson, 33–4, 197
    'Letter to the Right Hon. Lord
        Byron', 33–4, 197

Macaulay, Thomas Babington, 80,
        105, 184, 188
MacKillop, Ian, 14, 177, 179
masculinity, 2, 4–5, 14–15, 18–19,
        21–7, 38–43, 44, 50, 52–3,
        55, 58, 61, 73, 75–7, 81, 83,
        87–90, 93–5, 106, 115–19,
        124, 128, 134, 136, 140, 143,
        156–7, 159–60, 167–8, 179,
        181, 203

McGann, Jerome, 12, 80
Milbanke, Anne Isabella (Annabella),
        Lady Byron, 19, 33, 34, 48,
        73, 129
    see also Stowe, 'Separation' scandal
Mill, John Stuart, 22, 96–7, 173
Mills and Boon, 2, 19
Millstein, Denise Tischler, 154, 168,
        217, 225
misreading, 4, 10, 25–6, 28, 33–5,
        45–6, 50–2, 54, 56, 61, 63, 71,
        73, 103, 126, 137, 141, 151,
        159, 162, 165
Moore, Thomas, 132, 172, 177
Morris, Pam, 102, 103, 108
Murray, John, 34, 68

Newton, K. M., 132, 134, 143–4, 147,
        165, 167, 170
Nixon, Cheryl L., 55, 88

Oliphant, Margaret, 118, 121
O'Neill, Michael, 10, 28

Platt, Alison, 14, 177, 179
Poetry, 1–4, 6–14, 16, 18–19, 21–3,
        26–8, 33–4, 36–8, 40, 44, 47,
        50, 56–9, 61–4, 66–71, 73–4,
        77, 91–2, 94, 96–106, 109–10,
        112–14, 120, 123–6, 129–32,
        134–5, 137–44, 146–7, 149–51,
        153–7, 160–1, 163, 164–5, 167,
        169, 171–8, 182, 184, 186–8,
        190, 195, 211, 215, 218, 226
    in the novel, 3–4, 10, 23, 26–8, 50,
        56, 61–4, 66–71, 74, 77–8, 97,
        99–109, 112, 114, 125–6, 132,
        137, 154, 161, 163, 164–7,
        170–4, 201, 211, 215, 224,
    recited on film, 14, 23, 56–9, 73–4,
        109–11, 212
Praz, Mario, 2, 5, 44, 127

Radcliffe, Ann, 23, 35, 43–8, 119
    The Mysteries of Udolpho, 35, 45–6,
        48–9
    see also Gothic villain; Montoni
Regency rake, 21, 25, 37–8, 55, 126
Richardson, Samuel, 35, 37–8, 43, 63

The History of Sir Charles Grandison, 35, 38, 78
Romantic dialogues and legacies, 3, 6, 24–6, 31–2, 134, 182, 193–4
Ruskin, John, 22

Saglia, Diego, 15, 88
Scott, Sir Walter, 10, 12, 23, 26, 35, 43, 50, 57, 61–4, 73, 87, 101, 104, 131–2, 164, 172
screen adaptation, 2–3, 5–6, 11, 14, 23–7, 29, 34, 40, 47–50, 54–5, 57, 60, 62, 66, 70, 73–7, 86–94, 109–11, 117–18, 120–3, 152, 171, 177, 179–82
Sedgwick, Eve Kosofsky, 18, 145
self-made man, 22, 27, 73, 91, 118–19, 122, 155
see also Carlyle, Captains of Industry; industrialist hero
Sewell, Rufus, 14, 23, 122, 171, 228
see also Eliot, *Middlemarch* (1994); screen adaptation
Shakespeare, William, 36, 56, 57, 94, 100, 130, 139, 151
Shelley, Mary, 7, 13, 135
Shelley, Percy Bysshe, 23, 50, 95, 99, 135, 136, 139, 141–2, 166–7, 172–6, 220, 226
Works:
Alastor, 50, 202
'Lift not the painted veil', 135, 141
'On the Medusa of Leonardo da Vinci in the Florentine Gallery', 139
'Ozymandias', 135
Prometheus Unbound, 167, 176
'The pale, the cold, and the moony smile', 135, 141
silver-fork novels, 6, 19, 156, 172
Southey, Robert, 61, 99, 172, 225
Stabler, Jane, 23, 35
Stein, Atara, 6, 9, 15, 79
Stone, Donald D., 101–2, 108, 109, 119, 125, 134, 142, 172

Stowe, Harriet Beecher, 19, 129–30
'Separation' scandal, 28, 34, 48–9, 73, 129–30, 134, 154, 217
see also Anne Isabella (Annabella) Milbanke; Byron, infamy
Swinburne, Algernon, 72, 204

Tennyson, Alfred, Lord, 6, 99–100, 103, 140–1
Works:
'Locksley Hall', 99
'Mariana', 103–4
Maud, 140, 141
'The Gardener's Daughter', 99–100
Thomas, Keith G., 66, 84, 202
Thorslev, Peter L., 5, 19, 44
Todd, Janet, 61, 68, 202
Trollope, Anthony, 6, 154

Uglow, Jenny, 98, 131, 140, 168–9

vampires, 1, 2, 49
Viera, Carroll, 138, 170

Westminster Review, 22, 140
Wilson, Frances, 5, 175
Wiltshire, John, 64, 81, 89
Wolfson, Susan J., 12, 18, 20, 21
Woolf, Virginia, 4
Wordsworth, William, 58–9, 64, 98–9, 101–2, 108, 125–7, 130–1, 134, 135–7, 140, 159, 163, 166, 171–2, 201–2, 210, 215, 219, 221, 223, 224
Works:
'A Slumber Did My Spirit Seal', 101
'Ode to Duty', 171
'Preface to *Lyrical Ballads*', 125, 126, 135, 136, 181, 223
The Excursion, 125, 215, 223
The Prelude, 101, 126, 135, 215
'The Thorn', 126
'Tintern Abbey', 58–9, 101, 109, 163, 171

18036440R00143

Printed in Great Britain
by Amazon